Roman Satire

Michael Coffey

Roman Satire

LONDON
Methuen and Co Ltd
Barnes & Noble
NEW YORK

First published 1976
by Methuen & Co Ltd
11 New Fetter Lane, London EC4P 4EE
© 1976 Michael Coffey

Photoset by William Clowes & Sons Ltd,
The Benham Press, Colchester, Essex
and printed by William Clowes & Sons Ltd,
The Spottiswoode Ballantyne Press,
Colchester, Essex.

ISBN *hardbound* 0 416 85120 7
ISBN *paperback* 0 416 85130 4
U.S.A.
ISBN *hardbound* 0-06-471 251-6
ISBN *paperback* 0-06-471 252-4

To Brigitte,
Margaret and Monica

Contents

PART THREE
Menippean satire; the alternative convention

Preface

This book is an attempt to provide information about the surviving literature of the Roman satirists from Ennius to Juvenal and to offer some critical judgement on their work. It is in three parts. The first is a discussion of the nature of the genre, its origins, and the first tentative beginnings by Ennius. The second is an exposition of the satires of Lucilius, Horace, Persius and Juvenal. This involves an examination of the main topics most of which they have in common: autobiography, the censure of individuals, political and social comment and parody and criticism of writers and philosophers. The third part contains a similar discussion of satirists in the Menippean tradition, in form a mixture of prose and verse. It was first practised by Varro and then by Seneca and Petronius.

Though this book is primarily a work of literary history it also includes some literary criticism. The examination of the structure of a poem often gives rise to critical evaluation, and the exploration of the satirists' style from time to time occasions detailed analysis and criticism. Furthermore, since satire is connected with the events and opinions of its period, it has been necessary to include some social and political history. In attempting to assess the relevant background material from the immediate aftermath of the final victory over Hannibal to the age of Hadrian, I have ventured into the fields of specialists who may find much to fault. To these experts I offer an apology, especially to any whose works I may have misreported or misrepresented.

Though this book is intended primarily for students of classical literature and civilization, it is hoped that there is something useful for scholars working in later periods of Western literature and also for the general reader who is interested in the Romans. Such readers may be advised to omit the gritty material of the chapters on origins, Ennius and Varro. If the general reader passes from the descriptions and evaluation of the Roman satirists in this book to the excellent English translations available nowadays, and even better to versions in which the Latin and English are side by side, I shall be more than content.

The following colleagues and friends have all given generous assistance in various ways: Professor W. S. Maguinness, Professor Otto Skutsch, Mr J. G. Griffith, Dr P. Considine and Dr J. A. North. I am particularly indebted to Mr E. Courtney, who has read the whole typescript and given me the benefit of his wide learning, and to Mr A. H. Griffiths and Professor Niall Rudd, who performed a similar kindness. I am also grateful to Professor E. W. Handley and Dr. M. Winterbottom for their help in correcting the proofs. I take complete responsibility for all deficiencies and inaccuracies in the book.

I must mention the names of two scholars who are no longer living, M. P. Charlesworth, my director of studies at St John's College, Cambridge and T. B. L. Webster, first an inspiring teacher of Greek for me in Manchester and for many years a colleague and friend in London. And, if I may look back a little further in my career, I wish to express my thanks to Professor W. H. Semple, of the University of Manchester, and to Fr J. H. Crehan S.J., who taught a young sixth-former always to go back to primary sources. To these men, and to the learned companionship of my colleagues at University College for many years, I owe much of what scholarship I have.

My thanks are also due to the librarians and staff of the library of University College London, and of the Institute of Classical Studies, and also to the secretaries who have typed my unkempt manuscript, particularly Mrs Amanda Cheadle, who has been most helpful in preparing the final stages of the typescript.

MICHAEL COFFEY
University College London

Abbreviations

References to Latin and Greek authors are abbreviated according to the conventions of the *Oxford Latin Dictionary* (intro. to first fascicle, 1968) and of Liddell-Scott-Jones, *Greek-English Lexicon* (1940), Preface, xvi–xliii.

A.J.Ph.	*American Journal of Philology.*
Astin	A. E. Astin, *Scipio Aemilianus* (Oxford, 1967).
Buecheler	F. Buecheler, *Kleine Schriften*, 3 vols. (1915–30).
B.I.C.S.	*Bulletin of the Institute of Classical Studies.*
C.A.F. (Kock)	T. Kock (ed.), *Comicorum Atticorum Fragmenta*, 3 vols. (Leipzig, 1880–8).
C.G.F. (Kaibel)	G. Kaibel (ed.), *Comicorum Graecorum Fragmenta* (Berlin, 1899).
C.Gl.L.	*Corpus Glossariorum Latinorum*, K. Sächsische Akademie der Wissenschaften, 1–7 (Leipzig, 1888–1923).
Cichorius	C. Cichorius, *Untersuchungen zu Lucilius* (Berlin, 1908).
Cichorius, *Röm. Stud.*	C. Cichorius, *Römische Studien* (Leipzig–Berlin, 1922).
C.&M.	*Classica et Mediaevalia.*
Collignon	A. Collignon, *Étude sur Pétrone* (Paris, 1892).
C.Ph.	*Classical Philology.*
C.Q.	*Classical Quarterly.*
C.R.	*Classical Review.*
C.W.	*Classical World.*
D'Alton	J. F. D'Alton, *Roman Literary Theory and Criticism* (London, 1931).
Degr.	A. Degrassi, *Inscriptiones Latinae Liberae Rei Publicae*, 2 vols. (Florence, 1957, 1963).
Entr. Fond. Hardt	*Entretiens sur l'antiquité classique Fondation Hardt* (Vandoeuvres, Geneva).
Fraenkel	E. Fraenkel, *Horace* (Oxford, 1957).
G.I.F.	*Giornale Italiano di Filologia.*
G.L.K.	H. Keil (ed.), *Grammatici Latini*, 8 vols. (1855–1923).
G.L.P.	D. L. Page, *Greek Literary Papyri* I (London–Harvard, 1950).
Gött. gel. Anz.	*Göttingischer gelehrte Anzeigen.*
G.&R.	*Greece and Rome.*

Highet	G. Highet, *Juvenal the Satirist* (Oxford, 1954).
Housman, *Class. Papers*	J. Diggle and F. R. D. Goodyear (coll. and ed.), *The Classical Papers of A. E. Housman*, 3 vols. (Cambridge, 1972).
H.S.C.Ph.	*Harvard Studies in Classical Philology.*
I.L.S.	H. Dessau (ed.), *Inscriptiones Latinae Selectae* (1892–1916).
Kiessling-Heinze	A. Kiessling and R. Heinze, *Q. Horatius Flaccus Satiren* (Berlin, 1957⁶).
Knoche	U. Knoche, *Die Römische Satire* (Göttingen, 1971³).
Korzeniewski	D. Korzeniewski (ed.), *Die Römische Satire* Wege d. Forschung 238 (Darmstadt, 1970).
Kroll	W. Kroll, *Studien zum Verstandnis d. Römischen Literatur* (Stuttgart, 1924).
Leo, *Ausgew. kl. Schr.*	E. Fraenkel (ed.), F. Leo, *Ausgewählte kleine Schriften*, 2 vols. (Rome, 1960).
Leo, *Gesch.*	F. Leo, *Geschichte der Römischen Literatur* (Berlin, 1913).
Lesky	A. Lesky, *A History of Greek Literature*, transl. J. Willis and C. de Heer (London, 1966): translation of *Geschichte der Griechischen Literatur* (Bern, 1965²).
McCrum-Woodhead	M. McCrum and A. G. Woodhead, *Select Documents of the Principates of the Flavian Emperors, A.D. 68–96* (Cambridge, 1961).
Marx	F. Marx (ed.), *C. Lucilii Carminum Reliquiae*, 2 vols. (Leipzig, 1904, 1905).
M.R.R.	T. R. S. Broughton (ed.), *The Magistrates of the Roman Republic*, 2 vols. (New York, 1952).
Münzer	F. Münzer, *Römische Adelsparteien und Adelsfamilien* (Stuttgart, 1920).
N.Jbb.	*Neue Jahrbücher für d. klassische Altertum* (1898–1925).
Norden, *Agn. Th.*	E. Norden, *Agnostos Theos* (Leipzig–Berlin, 1913).
Norden, *obs. sel.*	E. Norden, 'In Varronis Saturas Menippeas observationes selectae', *Jahrbücher für classische Philologie*, Supplbd. 18 (1892), 267–358 = *Kleine*

Schriften zum Klassischen Altertum, ed. B.
Kytzler (Berlin, 1966), 1–87. The pagination of
the 1892 printing is so clearly presented in the
Kleine Schriften (1966) that it seems unnecessary
to offer the reader the modern page references
in addition to the old.

O.C.T.	*Oxford Classical Text.*
O.L.D.	*Oxford Latin Dictionary* (1968–).
O.R.F.	H. Malcovati (ed.), *Oratorum Romanorum Fragmenta* (1955²).
Otto	A. Otto, *Die Sprichwörter und sprichwörtlichen Redensarten der Römer* (Leipzig, 1890).
P.C(amb.)Ph.S.	*Proceedings of the Cambridge Philological Society.*
P.d.P.	*La Parola del Passato.*
P.I.R.²	E. Groag and A. Stein (ed.), *Prosopographia Imperii Romani Saeculi* I, II, III (1933²).
R.A.C.	*Reallixicon für Antike und Christentum.*
R.C.C.M.	*Rivista di Cultura classica e medioevale.*
R.E.	Pauly-Wissowa-Kroll, *Real-Encyclopädie der klassischen Altertumswissenschaft.*
R.E.A.	*Revue des Études anciennes.*
R.E.L.	*Revue des Études latines.*
R.F.I.C.	*Rivista di Filologia.*
Rh.M.	*Rheinisches Museum für Philologie.*
Röm. Sat.	W. Krenkel (ed.), *Römische Satire*: Wissenschaftliche Zeitschrift der Universität Rostock, Gesellschafts- und Sprachwissenschaftliche Reihe, 15 (1966) Heft 4/5, pp 407–584.
Rudd	N. Rudd, *The Satires of Horace* (Cambridge, 1966).
Schanz-Hosius I⁴	*Geschichte der römischen Literatur* vol. I (Munich, 1927⁴).
Schanz-Hosius II⁴	*Geschichte der römischen Literatur* vol. II (Munich, 1935⁴).
Scullard	H. H. Scullard, *Roman Politics 220–150 B.C.* (Oxford, 1973²).
S.H.A.	*Scriptores Historiae Augustae.*
S.I.F.C.	*Studi italiani di Filologia classica.*

Strömberg	R. Strömberg, *Greek Proverbs* (Göteberg, 1954).
Stubbe	H. Stubbe, *Die Verseinlagen im Petron,* Philologus Suppld. 25, 2 (1933).
Sullivan	J. P. Sullivan, *The Satyricon of Petronius: A Literary Study* (London, 1966).
Susemihl	F. Susemihl, *Geschichte d. griechischen Literatur in d. Alexandrinerzeit,* 2 vols.(Leipzig, 1891–2).
S.V.F.	J. von Arnim (ed.), *Stoicorum Veterum Fragmenta,* 4 vols. (Leipzig, 1905–24).
Syme	R. Syme, *The Roman Revolution* (Oxford, 1939).
T.A.Ph.A.	*Transactions and Proceedings of the American Philological Association.*
Th.L.L.	*Thesaurus Linguae Latinae.*
Vahlen	J. Vahlen (ed.), *Ennianae Poesis Reliquiae* (Leipzig, 1928³).
Vahlen, *coniect.*	J. Vahlen, *Coniectanea in M. Terentii Varronis Saturarum Menippearum Reliquias*(Leipzig, 1858).
Walsh	P. G. Walsh, *The Roman Novel: The Satyricon of Petronius and the Metamorphoses of Apuleius* (Cambridge, 1970).
Warmington	E. H. Warmington (ed.), *Remains of Old Latin,* vol. I: *Ennius and Caecilius* (Loeb Classical Library, 1956); vol. III: *Lucilius; Laws of the XII Tables* (Loeb Classical Library, 1938).
Weinreich	O. Weinreich, *Römische Satiren* (Zürich and Stuttgart, 1962²).
Williams	G. W. Williams, *Tradition and Originality in Roman Poetry* (Oxford, 1968).
W.St.	*Wiener Studien.*
Y.Cl.S.	*Yale Classical Studies.*

Note: there is a copious list of abbreviations in common use in writings on classical subjects in the *Oxford Classical Dictionary*, 1970², pp. ix–xxii, a volume of the greatest value for quick reference. A complete list of the abbreviations of periodicals is to be found at the beginning of volumes of *L'Année Philologique*.

PART ONE

The Roman genre of satire and its beginnings

I

Satire as a Roman literary genre[1]

When in the later part of the third century B.C. the Romans experienced the overmastering influence of Greek literature, the Greeks had already developed and brought to perfection a wide range of poetic genres from heroic epic and tragedy to scurrilous epigram. The greatest achievements of the Greek city states, notably Athens and the cities of Ionia, were followed in the third century by those of the Hellenistic period of elegance and refinement in Ptolemaic Alexandria. The Romans, although already under Greek influence of many kinds from Sicily and the settlements on the Italian mainland, had developed no indigenous literary culture of their own apart from various rustic measures, and accepted the mature forms of the Greeks of the mainland and of Alexandria with enthusiasm, making them their own. From crude beginnings Latin writers, by a gradually improving process of creative imitation, developed and expanded the main forms, epic, tragedy, comedy and, later, elegy, in such a way that much of Roman literary history may be seen as an attempt to continue and to rival the Greek tradition. But there was one important exception. For the Greeks satire was not an independent literary form. This was a unique Roman invention.

Towards the end of the first century A.D. the professor of rhetoric, Quintilian, in his work on the education of an orator, *Institutio Oratoria,* makes a critical comparison and evaluation of Greek and Roman literature genre by genre. Having asserted parity of success for Greeks and Romans in elegy he continues: *satura quidem tota nostra est* (satire is entirely Roman).[2] At this point he is no longer comparing relative

3

merits. His claim is based not merely on the positive achievement of Roman satire but also on the lack of a body of Greek literature to which it could properly be compared. He hints obliquely at the primitive early satire of Ennius, but regards Lucilius as the first major satirist. After evaluating Horace and Persius very briefly he praises certain contemporaries whom he does not mention by name. He was no doubt referring particularly to Turnus, a satirist of the age of Domitian, whose works are no longer extant. It is very unlikely that Juvenal published any satires until after the death of Quintilian. The rest of Quintilian's syllabus of satire is devoted to Varro, who wrote in the alternative convention of a mixture of prose and verse the kind of satire that was usually known as Menippean.[3] Quintilian offers no value judgement on Varro's satires, perhaps discreetly, but praises the vast range of his scholarly antiquarian output. That he does not mention the two great examples of Menippean satire of the first century A.D. that have come down to modern times is not surprising: Seneca's *Apocolocyntosis* was a slight work by an author for whom he had an unusual antipathy and the *Satyricon* of Petronius, in form a mixture of the Menippean convention and the despised genre of the novel, contained paederastic and other erotic topics such as could not have been prescribed to the youthful aspirant to eloquence.[4]

Quintilian's list makes it clear that we have access to all the Roman satirists except Turnus. Though the remains of the satires of Ennius, Lucilius and Varro are sets of disjointed fragments, the works of Horace, in Quintilian's view the finest satirist of all, Persius and Juvenal, and the *Apocolocyntosis,* have been transmitted complete, and the cruelly mutilated remains of the *Satyricon* are substantial enough to allow the modern reader to appreciate the qualities of this hybrid composition. Juvenal was the last Roman satirist. It is thus possible to study the history of Roman satire as an evolving literary form and to assess with some confidence the individual qualities of most of its pre-eminent exponents.

In discussing literature by genres Quintilian conformed to a method that was fundamental to Greek and Roman thinking about literature. Hellenistic scholars, some of them accomplished poets, proposed a complex system of classification that formed the basis of later literary theory.[5] Associated with criticism by 'kinds' was the notion of propriety. To Aristotle's immediate successor, Theophrastus, decorum was one of the four categories under which style was to be considered; a papyrus fragment which probably belongs to his work on style prescribes that certain words are to be admitted and others rejected.[6] In a versified discussion of plays and principles the tragedian Accius considered the nature of the genres and the difference between one and another.[7] His critic Lucilius, as is clear from the testimony of Horace, concerned himself with propriety of style. Horace himself regarded acceptance of generic distinctions as a necessary condition of writing poetry, and in the nicest matters of expression his practice accorded with his theory.[8] In the first century A.D. Seneca recognized in theory (*Epp.* 8,8), and for the most part in practice, finely distinguished levels of style.[9] Martial, complaining that a fellow poet has copied all his activities, lists the genres in descending order of nobility (and size): epic, tragedy, lyric, satire, elegy and epigram.[10] The point of Martial's poem is a self-depreciating descent to the bathos of his own epigrammatic miniatures. The joke depends in part on the tacit acceptance of a hierarchy of genres. Modern stylistic analysis has confirmed that in practice also Latin poetry preserved such distinctions.[11]

Along with the belief in a series of clearly defined genres went two important corollaries: first the recognition of an archetypal master in each genre to whom his successors looked back with a proud loyalty that was tempered sometimes by overt criticism and almost always by some departures in practice in accordance with changes in circumstances or in the taste of the times, and secondly the acceptance of the notion of a *lex operis*, the rules of stylistic behaviour within the genre that could when necessary be modified by the dictates of inventive genius. For all his criticisms of Lucilius in Book 1, Horace saw him as the inventor of the genre by whose standard his own work was to be asssessed, and in Book 2 claimed explicitly that he was writing satire in the manner of Lucilius. Persius and Juvenal both acknowledged the caustic criticisms of Lucilius as the original precedent for attacks on vice and also mentioned Horace as part of their heritage.[12] How Persius and Juvenal used the tradition of Lucilius and Horace will be shown in later chapters. That satire had its own law of procedure is implicit in Horace's discussion of his work in the fourth and tenth satires of Book 1; the word *lex* is used of satire when in the opening of the first satire of Book 2 Horace reveals that to some critics his satire seemed too harsh and pushed beyond the law; but characteristically he juggles with different uses of *lex*, the criminal and civil law as well as the law of the genre. In his sixth satire Juvenal, after an impassioned description of murderesses in high places, exclaims in an indignant rhetorical question:

> *Fingimus haec altum satura sumente coturnum*
> *scilicet, et finem egressi legemque priorum*
> *grande Sophocleo carmen bacchamur hiatu,*
> *montibus ignotum Rutulis caeloque Latino?*
> *nos utinam vani.*

(6,634–8)

(Do you really think that I am resorting to fiction while my satire usurps the style of tragedy, violating the bounds and law ordained by my predecessors and writing frenzied high poetry in a tragic manner of a kind unknown to the hills of Rome and the sky of Latium? I wish that it was all groundless.)

Having answered his question[13] by the wish that he was inventing his own themes Juvenal gives examples of vicious modern practices that rival and outstrip the infamy of heroines of myth and tragic poetry. He was aware that his tradition imposed a certain level of style on him and that his apparent assumption of an alien style required a disclaimer. The tradition of a law of satire is alluded to in late antiquity by John the Lydian, a Byzantine writer of the age of Justinian, who states that while Horace did not go beyond the traditional manner, Turnus, Juvenal and Petronius in their savagery departed from and violated the law of satire.[14] Whatever the pedigree of this judgement it demonstrates the abiding belief that satire was an independent literary genre with its own laws of procedure.

The style held to be appropriate for the satirist was informal and close to the language of everyday speech, for the most part that of the educated. The high style was deemed inappropriate for satire except as parody; hence Juvenal's disclaimer quoted above. In the same way an excess of vulgarity of expression was avoided. Lucilius seems to have admitted words of the utmost obscenity but some of the more extreme verbal obscenities that are common in Martial do not occur in the later satirists. Horace allowed certain obscenities in some of his early satires and in the language of the slave Davus (*Sat.* 2,7) which do not occur in any of his later works. His abandonment of such words reflects his own maturing judgement and perhaps also contemporaries' views on verbal decorum. The obscenities of language found in satirists later than Horace were used for special shock effect and are not part of the staple of their language.[15] This lexical restriction confirms the hint in Martial that satire was considered to be a somewhat more exalted form of writing than epigram.

Complementary to the overall formal classification of Latin literature by genres is a method of classification by topics which may occur in a number of genres. The poet's refusal to laud the exploits of an important political contemporary is found in the satires of Lucilius and Horace, who chose instead to write satire, and in works by Virgil and elegiac writers. The invitation to a frugal and morally unexceptionable meal is a topic common to satire (Juvenal, *Sat.* 11), lyric and epigram.[16]

It is perhaps all the more necessary nowadays to insist on the importance of the formal classification by genres in ancient literature and the existence of a hierarchy of genres, for in modern times there has been a widespread blurring of distinctions to which writers and critics in former ages would have responded instinctively. Though some great writers and distinguished critics have recognized the importance of differentiated genres and conventional topics, there has been a levelling down of stylistic propriety so that the high style no longer exists in literature except for paratragic buffoonery.[17] The ancient writers of the greatest talent were always able to transcend their formal inheritance, much though they respected it, so as to blend the traditional with their own originality. One satirist of great genius, Petronius, broke through the inherited patterns so as to create in the *Satyricon* a unique blend of the quite separate genres of satire and the novel. He had no successor.

It is necessary to eliminate from the study of the Roman genre of satire various writings that have some topics or attitudes in common with it but have their own separate history. Phaedrus, the author of fables in verse who lived in the time of Augustus and Tiberius, has been included among the Roman satirists in some modern discussions on the grounds that fable was a traditional element in satire and that in offering a mixture of amusement and sage counsel his aim was similar to that of the satirists.[18] But in antiquity writers of fable were not regarded as part of the tradition of satire, and in spite of certain instructive affinities between the technique of the satirists and the personal and political innuendoes that underlie the words of Phaedrus, a collection of short fables is far removed from satire in matter and manner.

Nor is there any justification for including Martial among the Roman satirists. Epigram belonged to a different literary tradition, and Martial himself distinguished between satire and his own epigrams. It is only to be expected that in ridiculing wickedness and inanity Martial shared some topics and even some phrases with his friend Juvenal. We may also eliminate the tradition of *iambi* even though Lucilius was given the epithet *iambicus* in imperial times.[19] By writing epodes at the same time as his satires Horace demonstrates his belief that the tradition of Archilochus, which Lucilius seems to have accepted as a source of inspiration for his own work, was something distinct from satire. Quintilian (10,1,96) discusses the iambic tradition separately as a form apart. Also to be eliminated is the miscellaneous corpus of abusive verse that ranged from archaic curses on tablets, scurrilous inscriptions and extended poems of malediction such as the *Ibis* of Ovid, to the verses described as *Fescennini* that were written by the military dictator Octavianus on a defenceless subject, Asinius Pollio.[20] The gambits of rhetoric influenced satire in diverse ways, but the process of *invectiva,* the discrediting and vilification of an opponent in court, was not in itself to be classed as satire.[21] Thus the tradition of Roman satire excludes much that is labelled satirical in a wider context.

It is also important that the tradition of Roman satire should be seen as something quite distinct from that of didactic poetry. Horace's literary epistles of Book 2 and the *Ars Poetica* are a poetic exposition of a quasi-didactic kind that has nothing in common with the *Lucilianus character* of his satires, written many years earlier, other than the hexameter. The didactic poems of Hesiod, Lucretius and Virgil were compositions inspired by the Muse and akin to high poetry. The satirical mode that is found in Lucretius' condemnatory depiction of supersition and sexual passion may owe something of its fervour to Hellenistic popular philosophy, but his impassioned poetry derives from the Greek tradition of Empedocles.[22]

The line of verse satire ended with Juvenal, and satire in a mixture of prose and verse with Petronius. There was no attempt to revive the genre in the later part of the fourth century A.D. at the time of the final creative outburst of pagan literature. The tradition of Roman satire was lost in the dark ages and remained so throughout mediaeval times. The reading of Juvenal by some scholarly men in twelfth-century France and occasional references to the masters of antiquity by mediaeval Latin satirists are no indication of a line of continuity, nor has Nigel Longchamp's *Speculum Stultorum* the authentic qualities of Roman satire, even though it may have an enjoyable variety of contents.[23] A garbled reference to Juvenal by Walter of Châtillon does not inspire confidence. The case for the continuity of the classical tradition of satire cannot be made good.[24]

The beginning of modern scholarship on Roman satire was Isaac Casaubon's fundamental study *De Satyrica Graecorum poesi et Romanorum Satira Libri Duo* (Paris, 1605) in which he devoted the first book to examining the evidence for Greek satyr plays, which he was able to separate completely from Roman satire. An inability to separate these two distinct genres had caused confusion in the previous century. Casaubon's second book is a thoroughly documented study of the different aspects of Roman *satura*, the primitive stage and the Lucilian and Menippean traditions, to which the efforts of modern scholars have comparatively little to add.[25] The next scholarly work of importance on the nature and history of satire was John Dryden's *A Discourse concerning Satire* (1693),[26] which owes much to Casaubon but disagrees with his preference for Persius to Juvenal or Horace. Dryden seems to have switched from an earlier higher estimation of Horace to preference later in life for the more highly charged vituperation of Juvenal. Though his *Discourse* is a classic of English literary criticism, it should be read with some caution.[27]

It may be of use at this point to refer to two definitions of formal literary satire, one from Roman antiquity and the other modern. The fourth-century grammarian Diomedes, using no doubt the pronouncements of predecessors, defined satire as

carmen apud Romanos, nunc quidem maledicum et ad carpenda hominum vitia archaeae comoediae charactere compositum, quale scripserunt Lucilius et Horatius et Persius; sed olim carmen quod ex variis poematibus constabat satura vocatur, quale scripserunt Pacuvius et Ennius.[28]

(a Roman verse form that has been in recent times abusive and composed to censure the vices of men in the manner of Old Greek Comedy, as was written by Lucilius, Horace and Persius; but formerly satire was the name given to a verse form made up of a variety of smaller pieces of poetry such as was written by Pacuvius and Ennius).

The definition is valid in that it describes the essential quality of the Lucilian tradition (the omission of the name of Juvenal does not affect its basic soundness) and also the primitive stage of Roman satire, but defective in its omission of the Menippean tradition. A modern definition is taken from the *Encyclopaedia Britannica*: 'Satire, in its literary aspect, may be defined as the expression in adequate terms of the sense of amusement or disgust excited by the ridiculous or unseemly, provided that humour is a distinctly recognizable element, and that the utterance is invested with literary form. Without humour, satire is invective; without literary form it is mere clownish jeering.'[29] This definition is acceptable for Roman satire, except that 'wit' should be added to 'humour' and 'variety of contents' added to 'literary form'. There are not good grounds for refusing to accept satire as one of the traditional literary kinds.[30] Ancient critics so viewed Roman satire, which throughout its long history retained a recognizable though pliant form. The blend of traditional elements and novelty of subject matter in a supple literary medium gave the satire of the Romans an enduring strength that would lead to satire of high distinction in European literature after the Renaissance.

Satura: the name and origin
of a literary form

The meaning of the word *satura* and its use as a literary term were already a matter for speculation in late republican times. There has also been much discussion on the part (if any) that was played by drama and ritual in the development of the literary form, Roman *satura*.

1. *SATURA* AND THE ANCIENT GRAMMARIANS' TRADITION

The spelling *satura* represents the original form of the word. The spelling *satyra* seems to have arisen early in the Christian era and is based on a postulated connection between the Roman literary form and Greek satyrs and satyr drama. *Satira* is in origin simply a variant on *satyra*. Had *satura* not been the original form it is difficult to see how it could have arisen from *satyra*, let alone from *satira*.[1]

All three syllables of the feminine noun *satura* have a short vowel. As there is no evidence for a Latin nominal termination in -*ŭra*, *satura* is a loan word from another language, or else, as is more likely, it is an in-flexion of the adjective *satur* that has come to be used as a noun, a feminine singular with a feminine noun to be supplied. The noun in agreement with the adjective *satura* through familiar usage came to be omitted, a procedure which can be paralleled, for example, by the op-tional omission of *cena* with *adventicia* or *adventoria*, a supper to celebrate an arrival.[2]

The primary meaning of the adjective *satur* seems to be 'filled full of food', 'replete'. The first attested occurrence is in a hymn of the Arval brothers, the guardians of the fertility of the fields.[3] There is a degree

of metaphor in some of Plautus' uses of the word: in one passage there
is punning on the senses 'filled with food' and 'satisfied with the play as
a substitute for food' and in another *satura* is applied ambiguously to
Alcmena as having the appearance of one who is both replete with
food and also pregnant.[4] The adjective also carries overtones of
richness when used of a deep colour, a fertile landscape or an opulent
style of oratory.[5] Further, anything that is filled may well be filled
with a variety of contents, and although it is unclear to what extent
such associations were uppermost in the adjective *satur*, the shift in
meaning from full to richly variegated was slight. The semantic range
of *satur* was therefore extensive, and when the feminine *satura* came to
be used alone for noun + *satura*, its meaning will to some extent have
depended upon that of the noun omitted.

An approach to the solution of this question is to be found in a
passage of the grammarian Diomedes that is the most important discussion in antiquity of the meaning of the word *satura*:

> *satura autem dicta sive a Satyris, quod similiter in hoc carmine ridiculae res*
> *pudendaeque dicuntur, quae velut a Satyris proferuntur et fiunt: sive*
> *satura a lance quae referta variis multisque primitiis in sacro apud priscos*
> *dis inferebatur et a copia ac saturitate rei satura vocabatur; cuius generis*
> *lancium et Vergilius in georgicis meminit, cum hoc modo dicit,*
> > *lancibus et pandis fumantia reddimus exta*
> *et*
> > > *lancesque et liba feremus:*
> *sive a quodam genere farciminis, quod multis rebus refertum saturam dicit*
> *Varro vocitatum. est autem hoc positum in secundo libro Plautinarum*
> *quaestionum, 'satura est uva passa et polenta et nuclei pini ex mulso con-*
> *sparsi. ad haec alii addunt et de malo punico grana'. alii autem dictam pu-*
> *tant a lege satura, quae uno rogatu multa simul conprehendat, quod scilicet*
> *et satura carmine multa simul poemata conprehenduntur. cuius saturae*
> *legis Lucilius meminit in primo,*
> > *per saturam aedilem factum qui legibus solvat,*
> *et Sallustius in Iugurtha, 'deinde quasi per saturam sententiis exquisitis*
> *in deditionem accipitur'.*[6]

(*Satura* takes its name either from satyrs, because in this verse form comical and
shameless things are said which are produced and made as if by satyrs; or from a
full dish which was packed with a large number of varied first fruits and offered
among primitive people to the gods in a religious ritual and called *satura* from
the abundance and fullness of the material. Virgil too makes mention of this kind

of dish in the *Georgics* when he says [2,194] 'we offer steaming giblets on curved dishes' and also [2,394] 'we shall bring dishes of sacrificial cakes'. It may also be derived from a certain kind of sausage which was filled with many ingredients and according to Varro called *satura,* and indeed there is the following definition in the second book of his 'Problems in Plautus': '*satura* is raisins, pearl barley, pine kernels covered with mead, to which some people add pomegranate seeds'. Others say it was called *satura* from a compendious law which includes many provisions in a single bill, on the argument that in the verse form *satura* many small poems are combined together. Lucilius mentions this compendious law in his first book [48 M]: 'who might absolve from the law an aedile elected by a compendious measure, and Sallust in *Jugurtha* [29,5]: 'then his surrender is accepted as if by a compendious law with precise provisions'.)

The *testimonia* of other Latin grammarians such as Isidore and Festus derive from either Diomedes or his source; with one exception none offers any independent evidence.[7] The piece of additional information given by a scholiast on Horace that the *lanx satura* was offered in the temple of Ceres is probably no more than a plausible inference.[8] Diomedes refers to Varro and to no other authority, and the usual attribution of the main lines of Diomedes to Varro may be accepted with confidence. The etymologies are characteristic of Varro, and it is more than likely that the learned literary historian, himself a satirist, assembled theories of the origins of satire that became standard doctrine.[9] There is nothing of substance in Diomedes' account that need be later than Varro. Only the quotations from Virgil and Sallust are almost certainly later additions; any grammarian from Verrius Flaccus to Diomedes himself could have inserted them. It is likely that Diomedes' testimony all derives from a single work of Varro. One piece of evidence we are told was found in the *Plautinae Quaestiones*; the rest probably came from the same work. If Varro discussed *satura* elsewhere, the likeliest places are the *de Compositione Saturarum* and the *de Poetis*, which may have included a section on satire in its discussion of Ennius.[10]

As Diomedes' source offers four explanations of the derivation and origin of *satura,* it is clear that by the end of the republic much was already speculation and guesswork. None the less in one or other of these theories there may be some approximation to the truth. The first explanation does not deserve credence. Diomedes offers the ribaldry and obscenity of the satyrs, presumably satyr drama, as parallel to the derision and bawdry of satire, which he concludes took its name from these tipsy and frolicsome creatures of Greek myth and drama.[11] On this view the earliest Roman satirist used a Greek loan word as title.

But there are weighty objections. First, such a background of un-
bridled jocularity and boisterous lechery is unsuited to the quiet satires
of Ennius as preserved, which, as will be seen, are influenced mainly by
non-dramatic Hellenistic poetry. This theory presupposes the
vituperative satire of Lucilius and his republican successors.[12]
Secondly there is a linguistic difficulty. The Greek adjective meaning
'connected with satyrs' is σατυρικός; this becomes *satyricus* in Latin, as
in the phrase *satyrica fabula* used by Diomedes.[13] The Greek for satyr
play is either some expression with σατυρικός such as σατυρικὴ ποίησις
or σάτυροι (plural); the latter form appears in Latin in Horace's phrase
satyrorum scriptor.[14] Ennius could not have derived *satura* (singular) or
saturae (plural) from these words. Had he wished to base his title on
satyrs and plays about them we would expect him to have made some
use of the adjective *satyricus*, which occurs with sophisticated ambiguity
in Petronius' *Satyricon libri*.

In Diomedes' second and third explanations *satura* takes its name from
a cult offering to the gods or from a cook's recipe. For the first of these
Diomedes specifies the exact point of the figurative language: *a copia et
saturitate rei*; the words *variis multisque* suggest that the metaphor included variety as well as abundance, and it may be assumed that the
culinary metaphor carried similar associations.

In deriving *satura* from *lanx satura*, Diomedes quotes no evidence for
this phrase; other late grammarians who used the same authorities mention *lanx satura* but no citation can be adduced from any source.
Diomedes may have intended to mean not a *lanx satura* but a type of
lanx called a *satura* (i.e. a noun); he cites two passages of Virgil that illustrate the use of *lanx* without *satura* as the dish on which sacrificial
offerings were placed,[15] but he does not say which gods received such
offerings. His second citation from Virgil refers to an Italian sacrifice to
Bacchus; the first quotation comes from a general description of
sacrifices at which wine was offered to the gods. Ceres must be ex-
cluded from their number, because in her cult no sacrifice of wine was
made.[16] Here there is an implicit discrepancy between Diomedes and
the Pseudacron Scholia to Horace, where it is said the *lanx satura* was
offered in the temple of Ceres. But it is unlikely that the Horace
scholiast preserves the words of the religious antiquarian Varro, while
Diomedes is vague and incorporates quotations which are incompatible
with the original authority. Whether the filled *lanx* belonged to any
particular cult we cannot tell. Ceres is associated with sacrifice of first
fruits, and the offering of a *lanx* to Bacchus does not preclude its use in

a Ceres cult.[17] But there were many other recipients of first fruits and produce, such as Pales and the Lares, not to mention Carna, whose ritual was obsolete by the end of the republic. It is thus impossible to add the overtones of a particular ritual to a metaphorical title derived from *lanx satura*.[18]

Diomedes' third suggestion is that *satura* takes its name from a kind of stuffing. The word *farcimen* can be used either of the stuffing, the filling of the sausage, or the thing that is stuffed, the sausage itself; perhaps this was true of *satura* also.[19] That *satura* does not occur in Varro's description of fat, short and long sausages does not prove that it was not a species of sausage, for the list need not be regarded as including every kind of a food that must in its nature indeed have had many varieties.[20] Diomedes gives a recipe for a dish that seems to be some kind of stuffing and not the thing stuffed, though this is a distinction that should not be pressed. Assuming *satura* here to be an adjective, it is uncertain what noun is to be supplied. *Lanx* is a possible supplement here too, for it is the ordinary word for a serving dish. Other suggestions include *patina* (pan) and *olla* (pot).[21] As applied to a form of literature the point of the metaphor is once again fullness and variety. It is difficult to plot the full associations of the metaphor with precision. The recipe does not correspond closely to anything in Apicius' collection for gourmets of imperial times. This includes a recipe for sausage stuffing which contains the nuts of edible pines and spelt-grits (*alica*) instead of pearl barley. Many other dishes in Apicius contain some of Varro's ingredients,[22] but what sets Varro's recipe apart from these elaborate contrivances is the inclusion of pearl barley. Barley (*hordeum*) is a rare ingredient in Apicius; *polenta* seems not to occur there at all. Barley is the traditional food of gladiators and barley meal was used to feed farm animals.[23] It seems likely that Varro's recipe is a form of a dish eaten in republican times by country folk. Such a culinary metaphor would be suited to the vigour of satire as well as its variety.

This explanation of the word *satura* seems to be alluded to by one of the satirists. Juvenal describes the variety of subject matter of satire as *nostri farrago libelli* (1,86), 'the mash of my book'. *Farrago* is always used of mixed fodder for cattle, never of food for men.[24] It is not quite certain how the whole phrase is to be construed. Though it is generally assumed that the meaning is 'the mixed meal of which my book consists', it is possible to take the genitive as objective: 'the mixed meal that goes to feed my book'; the book is thus conceived of as an animal to be fed.[25] Juvenal with a jaunty and debunking metaphor thus alludes disrespectfully to what must have been by his time a standard textbook theory of origins.

The theory of *satura* as by origin a food rather than an offering to the gods has found most favour in modern times.[26] In our present state of knowledge one or other of these theories is the likeliest explanation of the metaphorical use of *satura*. It is difficult to choose between the two and perhaps they are not mutually exclusive. Whichever of the two views is accepted, it is probable that *lanx* is the noun to be supplied. The analogy of *patina* suggests that *lanx* too could refer to the contents of the dish as well as the dish itself.[27] That a Roman word for dish was used proverbially of a miscellany is clear from a poem of Meleager which after listing a series of scabrous and variegated paederastic achievements concludes:

εἰ γάρ σοι τάδε τερπνὰ θεὸς ὦ μάκαρ οἵαν
ἀρτύσεις παίδων Ῥωμαϊκὴν λοπάδα.

(*Anth. Pal.* 12,95,9–10 = GP 4406–7)

(If heaven were to provide you with such delights, lucky man, what a Roman dish of boys you will be preparing.)

Λοπάς is an ordinary word for serving dish and is almost certainly a translation of *lanx*. The Roman metaphor was so widely known that it could be used at about the beginning of the first century B.C. as the climax to a Greek epigrammatic poem.[28]

It was such a proverbial usage that Ennius took over in devising the title *Saturae*, 'the miscellaneous dish', for his collection or collections of miscellaneous poems. In so doing he had at hand in the Hellenistic tradition Σωρός, 'the heap' (of winnowed grain), the title that Posidippus gave to a collection of assorted poems composed by himself exclusively or in conjunction with other poets.[29] It seems probable that Posidippus' title or some title like it led Ennius to choose a similar word that had no previous literary associations. The existence of Greek collections entitled σύμμεικτα (miscellanies) may have influenced Ennius' desire to compile a collection of poems, but it was a title such as Σωρός that led him to choose for his title a concrete metaphor rather than an abstract description.[30] The establishment of a relationship on the one side between Demeter and the Σωρός and on the other between *lanx satura* and Ceres would favour a metaphor from a religious offering. But both these connections are highly problematical.[31] It may perhaps be preferable to regard the title *satura* as derived from the language of kitchen and dining-room, a heaped and filling country dish of diverse ingredients to describe and illustrate a rich and variegated but unpretentious literary form.[32]

Thus one or even two of the theories preserved by Diomedes show how *satura* came to be used as a literary term; Ennius seems to have been the first to use it in this way. It is true that *satura* is unique among the major Roman literary forms in having a title that is genuinely Italian and not a Greek loan word, but it was the example of picturesque and fanciful titles in Hellenistic poetry that led Ennius to choose a concrete Latin word. The analogy of $\Sigma\omega\rho\acute{o}\varsigma$ suggests that Ennius referred to a collection of miscellaneous poems or a book as *satura* (sing.) and to the whole corpus of his satires as *saturae* (plural). The use of *satura* to denote a single poem, as in Quintilian's reference to Ennius' dialogue between Life and Death as taking place *in satura* (9,2,36), is probably a later development when technical terminology had hardened. But Ennius may not have been consistent in his use of singular and plural, and so it is unwise to insist on a fine distinction in terminology particularly at an early stage in the history of the genre.[33]

Diomedes' fourth suggestion, that the use of *satura* as a literary title derived from legal terminology, may be dismissed quickly. There is no evidence for the phrase *lex satura* except in the statements of grammarians; *lex per saturam* with the meaning of a law with compendious or mixed provisions is attested in the second half of the second century B.C.,[34] but it may be argued that the phrase *lex per saturam* does not exist and is only found in contexts where the phrase *per saturam* is adverbial ('in a disorderly manner') with some such verb as *ferre*.

By this time *per saturam* was a catch-phrase used of a tacked law, a piece of legal engineering that was formally forbidden in 98 B.C.[35] The phrase *per* (or *in*) *saturam* thus implied an agglomeration of disparate items. The linguistic and social background to the development of this phrase is uncertain, but *lex* (*per saturam*) clearly had nothing to do with the origins of satire.[36]

Some scholars, suspicious of the multiplicity of explanations offered by Diomedes, have looked elsewhere for an etymology and connected *satura* with an Etruscan word *satir* or *satre* that is said to mean 'speak' or 'declare'.[37] This theory is attractive, as the title would describe the conversation and discourse of book satire. But there are difficulties. The meaning of the Etruscan word is not entirely certain, and attempts to postulate an Etruscan substrate to a Latin word are usually not without hazard.[38] It is also unlikely that Ennius would have chosen an Etruscan rather than, as was customary, a Greek loan word for the title of a genre that contained so much Greek material in its subject matter and presentation.

2. LIVY AND THE SO-CALLED 'DRAMATIC *SATURA*'

The foregoing discussion rests on the assumption that there was no literary *satura* in Rome or Italy before Ennius. An important piece of ancient evidence, however, suggests the contrary and must now be examined in detail. Livy narrates that after various attempts to rid Rome of the plague had failed, stage shows were introduced for the first time in 364 B.C. as a means of averting divine anger:

> *Sine carmine ullo, sine imitandorum carminum actu ludiones ex Etruria acciti ad tibicinis modos saltantes haud indecoros motus more Tusco dabant. Imitari deinde eos iuventus, simul inconditis inter se iocularia fundentes versibus, coepere; nec absoni a voce motus erant. Accepta itaque res saepiusque usurpando excitata. Vernaculis artificibus, quia ister Tusco verbo ludio vocabatur, nomen histrionibus inditum; qui non, sicut ante, Fescennino versu similem incompositum temere ac rudem alternis iaciebant sed impletas modis saturas descripto iam ad tibicinem cantu motuque congruenti peragebant. Livius post aliquot annis, qui ab saturis ausus est primus argumento fabulam serere, idem scilicet — id quod omnes tum erant — suorum carminum actor, dicitur, cum saepius revocatus vocem obtudisset, venia petita puerum ad canendum ante tibicinem cum statuisset, canticum egisse aliquanto magis vigente motu quia nihil vocis usus impediebat. Inde ad manum cantari histrionibus coeptum diverbiaque tantum ipsorum voci relicta.*

(Livy 7,2,4–10)

(Players were called in from Etruria who danced to the music of the pipes without any verses or miming that corresponded to verses and produced graceful movements in the Etruscan manner. Later Romans began to imitate them, at the same time exchanging jests in improvised verse, suiting the gestures to the words, and so the practice became a custom and developed through regular use. The name *histrio* was given to Roman professional performers, for in Etruscan a player was called *ister*.[39] These did not, as had been the former practice, engage in an exchange of disorganized and uncouth verse like Fescennines, but enacted fully musical 'revues' with what was by now a set vocal line with pipe accompaniment and appropriate miming.[40] The story goes that after some years Livius, who was the first to depart from the 'revues' and compose a

dramatic plot, and, according to the general custom of the times, was the actor
of his own pieces, cracked his voice as a result of too many encores and gained
permission to place a slave in front of the piper to sing, while he enacted the
lyrics with a greater vigour of movement as he was not hindered by having to
use his voice. As a result the practice was instituted for the actors to have the
lyrics sung near to them as accompaniment of their gestures and to reserve
the dialogue alone for their own voices.)[41]

In the next and final stage of Livy's account the performance of plays
was left to professional actors, while amateurs continued the old practice of banter in verse and were responsible for playing the so-called
'after-pieces', which are usually identified with Atellan comedy, a
vulgar farce of Italian origins.[42]

Livy here offers an account of the development of drama in Rome in
five chronological stages, of which a *satura* that is enacted dramatically
is the third, preceded first by imported wordless dances with music and
then by imitation of the dances accompanied by crude rustic verses in
dialogue; it is succeeded by a drama with a proper plot, dialogue and
cantica, that is finally developed by professionals into an art form while
the amateurs developed the rough exchanges of dialogue into formal
after-pieces.[43] The dramatic *satura* that was part of this development
was described as a musical stage show without an organized plot but
with lyrics written out in full and probably dancing, all being accompanied by the music of the pipes, and its organization and
professionalism were to be contrasted with the earlier improvised work
of the amateurs.

There is no other evidence for such a dramatic *satura* except a passage
of Valerius Maximus which is modelled on Livy or his immediate
source and is even more patriotic than Livy in that it makes the first
stage a Roman activity before actors were imported from Etruria.[44]

Some modern scholars believe that there was some such stage show
in the early history of Roman drama but that it was not called *satura*,
whilst others hold that *satura* was its original name.[45] There is,
however, much in Livy's account that invites disbelief. It is possible
that there was a plague in 365–4 B.C., for such information may have
been taken from the Pontifical Annals.[46] It is also possible that players
were imported from Etruria, though the practice during the Punic
Wars of sending to Etruria on occasions of crisis is not necessarily confirmation of procedure in the earlier part of the fourth century B.C. But
there seems to have been no source that could have provided Livy or
his authority with an authentic tradition about dramatic practices in
Rome in the fourth century. Verses of the Fescennine kind were a very

ancient form of folk poetry, for they were associated to some extent with religious ritual. To seek their development in an imitation of an exotic dance form is not even plausible.[47] Livy's fourth stage likewise is demonstrably erroneous. A reliable ancient tradition held that Livius Andronicus produced his first play in Rome in 240 B.C., and this date has been generally accepted by modern scholars.[48] Livy's unspecific *post aliquot annis* neither confirms nor contradicts this, but his vagueness and the length of the chronological stages of his account raise grave suspicions. It is sometimes urged against Livy's veracity that Livius Andronicus was a schoolmaster and not an actor, but there is strong independent evidence that in addition to grammatical and literary activities he was a performer who took part in his own plays.[49] But one of the fundamental facts of Latin literary history is that Livius Andronicus introduced translations of Greek plays; and that it was from these that Roman drama originated. The omission of this fact makes Livy's account of Livius Andronicus incredible, and the absence of any mention of Greek influence discredits the rest of the story.[50]

An explanation may be suggested for part of Livy's procedure. He sketches the development of both the *diverbia* (dialogue) and *cantica* (lyrics) of comedy. Just as his dubious second stage was necessary to explain the *diverbia* of comedy without referring to Greek plays, so also a Roman dramatic lyric without plot was a necessary hypothesis to explain the *cantica* of Roman plays. It thus seems very likely that Livy's chronological sequence is groundless speculation.[51]

It has long been believed that Livy's chapter owes much to the Peripatetic formulation of the development of Greek drama from its beginnings to its maturity. In this theory an art form developed gradually to a peak of excellence, then underwent a slow degeneration and corruption. Even though some of the verbal correspondences suggested between Livy and Peripatetic treatises are not convincing, the description of the stages of dramatic evolution with Livius Andronicus occupying a position analogous to that of Crates, the fifth-century Athenian comic poet, show plainly the ultimate source of the framework of Livy's hypothesis. Livy's Roman sources found in Peripatetic literary theory a method of work that could be applied to the reconstruction of the early stages of Roman drama.[52] Interest was fostered by Crates of Mallos, who broke a leg as a result of an attempt to explore the *Cloaca Maxima*. His visit, thus notoriously prolonged, was an important influence on the development of literary theory at Rome.[53]

The question still remains: why was the hypothetical plotless stage show given the name *satura* or *saturae*? Nothing in Roman drama corresponds to the Greek satyr play, which had an important place in the theory and also the practice of Hellenistic times.[54] It is possible that a Roman theorist finding no existing Roman dramatic form to correspond to a satyr play was able to postulate a primitive form of boisterous stage show and by a piece of linguistic opportunism give to it a similar sounding literary title.[55] Further plausibility would have been given to the hypothesis by the existence of men in the guise of satyrs on the occasion of the *Ludi Magni* in Rome, a feature of the ritual that was instanced as an example of the similarity of Roman customs to those of Greece.[56]

Livy's motive in including this tendentious account of dramatic origins was in part at least patriotic. This accords with his approach to the writing of history: just as the Etruscan domination in politics was to be minimized so Greek influences on dramatic institutions were to be discounted.[57] Patriotism may also be found in his hint (if such it be) that the literary form *satura,* well established by the time he composed his first decade, had an Italian origin; in the etymology of *satura* implied in *impletas modis* he showed that the name also was Italian. But Livy's account is not merely uncritically patriotic. He is also influenced throughout his work by the notion that Rome's political and social life had degenerated from an early integrity.[58] Livy's account of development of drama belongs to this pattern of thinking, in which his hypothetical dramatic *satura* is part of a pristine dramatic purity uncorrupted by actors' vanity or material extravagance.

There has been much speculation about the identity of Livy's source or sources; Varro is often considered the most likely immediate source.[59] Some general indications support this, for patriotism and a belief in human degeneracy are both marks of Varro's way of thinking. But it seems unlikely that Varro, the conscientious and critical literary historian, wrote an account of the development of Roman drama which could not be reconciled with the fact of Greek influence, so that even if some details in Livy may be deemed to coincide with the views of Varro the account as a whole is probably not to be attributed to him. The poet and grammarian Accius has been suggested as Livy's immediate source; another possible source, though this too is a conjecture, is the grammarian Aelius Stilo, who was the teacher of Varro, but no certain solution of this problem is possible.[60]

The play title *Satura* lends no support to the hypothesis of dramatic *satura.* It occurs as the title of one of Pomponius' Atellans. As shown earlier, *satura* can be used of a pregnant woman. That this is the meaning here is confirmed by another Atellan title, Novius' *Virgo praegnans,* and by other descriptive titles.

As Pomponius is known only as a writer of Atellans, *Satura* is unlikely to have been a generic designation of another literary form.[61] *Satura* is also a title of a work by Naevius. This is more problematical. One fragment is extant:

quianam Saturnium populum pepulisti?

(why have you defeated the people dedicated to Saturn, i.e. the Romans?)

The language is not comic; the metre may be Saturnian, and the subject matter seems to be historical and solemn. If it were assumed that the line was in a context of paratragic burlesque, the title could be taken as similar to those discussed above, but this is a speculation, and it is safer to admit that assuming this title to be correctly given we do not understand it.[62]

Some advocates of the dramatic *satura* have sought to trace its influence in extant literary *satura* in such allegedly dramatic scenes and dialogues as the later part of the third satire of Horace's second book. But this approach is illusory. If there had been a dramatic *satura* we would expect it to have influenced early satire, particularly that of Ennius; the extant remains do not show such an influence. Traces of dramatic *satura* have sometimes been found in scenes of revelry and dancing in Roman comedy, but modern knowledge of New Comedy and of the conditions of Hellenistic performances makes such a view untenable.[63]

3. DRAMA AND RITUAL

Dissatisfaction with the traditional etymologies has also led to a postulated connection with Etruscan more complex than that already discussed (p. 17 above). It has therefore been suggested that *satur-no* was the name of a fertility god brought by the Etruscans from Asia Minor who appeared early in Rome with the name Saturu and that scenes of song and dance at his festival were given the name *satura* with *lanx satura* as a symbol of fruitfulness. Livy thus preserves the truth about dramatic importations from Etruria.[64] To this theory there are two main objections. First, apart from the general flimsiness of the linguistic evidence offered, it is a fact of language that the *a* in *Saturnus* is unequivocally long. Secondly, as the extent of Etruscan influence on the

Roman stage is problematical, it is unwise to base an elaborate theory about *satura* on any such hypothetical dramatic connection.

Two more theories link dramatic *satura* to the cult of a god. According to the first *saturi* are demonic men, the followers of Dionysus and *satura*, an abstract noun meaning 'satiety', is the song of the satisfied men. As dramatic *satura* is based on a cult of Dionysus, it is thus the counterpart in Rome of Old Attic Comedy.[65] This ingenious hypothesis has considerable charm, but it is too speculative to win assent, and so it must be concluded that Dionysus has nothing to do with satire.

The second theory seeks parallels for *satura* in the banter that was part of certain Demeter cults in Greece and Sicily and in the κυκέων or mixed potion that had an important place in the religion of Demeter or Ceres.[66] *Satura*, it is argued, is abstract and means 'fullness'. Dramatic *satura* is thus the dance and song that belonged to a Ceres festival.[67] Once again the speculation is enterprising, but it has serious weaknesses. There is no evidence for rough jesting at any Roman ritual belonging to Ceres and, as stated earlier, the association of the *lanx* with Ceres seems nothing other than the guess of a grammarian who speculated where his predecessors and betters had failed to specify.

In conclusion it seems that all attempts to seek the origin of *satura* in jocularities attendant on the cults of Saturn, Dionysus or Ceres fail to convince and that theories deriving the word *satura* from Etruscan are at best not proven. Unless new literary or epigraphical material appears, it is reasonable to accept, possibly with reservations, Diomedes' explanation that *satura* took its name from a full dish offered in solemn ritual or from a stuffed sausage.

3

The Satires of Ennius[1]

Ennius, the author of Rome's first great national epic, was also the creator of Roman *satura*. He was the first Roman to gather into the same book verses of varied topic and metre, and for this miscellaneous collection he chose the name *Saturae*. In making such a collection he followed precedents from Alexandrian poetry and scholarship; in his choice of title he was original, for the word had never been used before of a species of literature, and was unique among Roman literary titles in that it was not a Greek loan-word.

The late Latin grammarian Diomedes, whose testimony goes back to republican times, states that at first *satura* was poetry compounded of various pieces of verse as with Ennius and his nephew Pacuvius, and that later it developed in the hands of Lucilius and his successors into the poetry of castigation.[2] Quintilian also seems to refer obliquely to a pre-Lucilian stage of *satura*.[3] Ennius is the only exponent of this kind of *satura* of whose works we have any knowledge; no doubt they were earlier than the *Saturae* of his nephew Pacuvius, of which nothing whatsoever is known.[4] It is clear from Diomedes that the tone and contents of the earliest *satura* contrasted fundamentally with the vituperation in the works of Lucilius and later satirists. Thus while there is some element of censoriousness in the extant fragments of Ennius' *satura*, the quality for which satire has been famous is relatively unimportant in the work of its first practitioner.

1. THE LIFE OF ENNIUS

Quintus Ennius was born at the small town of Rudiae (modern Rugge), near Lecce in ancient Calabria, the heel of Italy, in 239 B.C.; this was two years after the end of the first Carthaginian war and at a time when there was an intensification of Roman influence in southern Italy.[5] He was of Messapian stock, descended from invaders from across the Adriatic and no doubt with more plausibility than truthfulness claimed as his ancestor King Messapus, who had settled in Italy.[6] It is likely that he received his education at the nearby Greek city of Tarentum, and presumably this took place before Hannibal arrived in southern Italy after Cannae (216 B.C.). He served as a soldier in Sardinia probably with Rome's Calabrian auxiliaries and during this period came to the notice of M. Porcius Cato, quaestor in Sicily in 204 B.C., who was said to have brought him back to Rome with him.[7] The reason for Cato's action has occasioned much speculation. It is unlikely that it was Ennius' military prowess that attracted the attention of Cato. However hostile Cato's attitude to Greek culture then and later, it seems likely that he brought Ennius to Rome in order to be instructed by him in the Greek language, for the story that he learned Greek late in life is improbable.[8] In Rome Ennius, like Livius Andronicus before him, taught Latin and Greek in addition to his dramatic and other literary activities, and for all his connections with great men of the state lived on the Aventine until the end of his life simply and without the appurtenances of wealth.[9] In 189 B.C. he was taken by the consul Fulvius Nobilior on his campaign in Aetolia as his personal poet[10] and five years later, according to the ancient tradition, received Roman citizenship through the son of Nobilior, the colonial commissioner for Potentia.[11] Ennius stated himself and Horace confirmed that he habitually composed poetry when inspired by strong drink. But this should not be taken too seriously, as the connection between the inspiration of wine and that of poetry was traditional.[12] However he died of gout in 169 B.C. at the age of seventy.[13]

Ennius' first language was probably Illyrian, but when later he speaks of having *tria corda* he means that he was master of three media of thought and expression, Greek, Oscan and Latin. Oscan at that time was a *lingua franca* of southern Italy, and Ennius' sister, as the name of her son Pacuvius shows, was married to an Oscan. Greek was the dominant language of education and culture in southern Italy, and the label *semigraecus* was as true of Ennius' intellectual orientation as of that of Livius Andronicus.[14] Tarentum was no doubt able to supply him with a knowledge of the classics of Greek literature, even though its importance as an intellectual centre seems to have been in decline by the later part of the third century B.C.[15] Though Tarentum was probably the source of Ennius' basic knowledge of Greek culture, it did not infect him with the local hostility to Rome, and from early manhood Ennius must have been an admirer of Roman influence and achievement.

When Ennius arrived in Rome Livius Andronicus, by then a poet held in high esteem and honoured by the commission to write a cult hymn in a time of crisis in 207 B.C., may already have been dead,[16] and Naevius the dramatist and chronicler of the first Punic war, after his imprisonment for attacking the Metelli, had left Rome, bequeathing the lesson that without the support of powerful families no poet dare be outspoken.[17] The comic poet Plautus was already producing plays in Rome; in his *Miles Gloriosus* (211) he seems to refer to the imprisonment of Naevius as a current event.

Soon after his arrival in Rome Ennius came under the patronage of Scipio Africanus, whose African campaign culminating in the decisive battle of Zama (202 B.C.) he lauded in a poem *Scipio* (*Varia* 1–14V) probably written shortly after the events. Ennius was highly esteemed by Africanus, and an anecdote preserved by Cicero shows easy familiarity between Ennius and Scipio Nasica, the cousin of Africanus. The tradition that Ennius' statue and even his remains were placed beside those of the Scipios, though unlikely, suggests at least that he was particularly associated with the family and never completely estranged from them.[18] In later years he seems to have owed both a commission and his citizenship to the Fulvii, political rivals of the Scipionic bloc. Fulvius Nobilior was criticized by Cato for having taken Ennius on his campaign in Aetolia. The apparently changed attitude of Cato towards his former client may be explained in various ways. The former soldier who taught Greek had become a purveyor of pernicious Greek culture, and Fulvius Nobilior was a political enemy, who indulged in the Greek practice of having a poet in his retinue to celebrate his success.[19] Ennius was also a friend of Servius Sulpicius Galba, who seems to have been associated with the political group of Fulvius Nobilior.[20] Ennius from time to time served various of the chief men of the state, but he should not be regarded as a catspaw in the political struggles of rival family groups. Whether or not one accepts the opinion of the grammarian Aelius Stilo that the description in the *Annals* of the discreet political confidant is a self-portrait,[21] the stories of easy familiarity with various members of the aristocratic establishment suggest that Ennius was able to perform commissions without being bought exclusively by a single political interest.

Ennius was well equipped to be a poet both of the great deeds of men and affairs and also of the minutiae of their social intercourse. He had lived among people of widely differing societies and languages, and was expert in the classics of Greek literature. He knew military life both as a serving soldier and as the companion of a general in the field, and as the confidant of some of the most successful politicians of the age he was no doubt privy to important manoeuvres of statesmanship.

2. THE WRITINGS OF ENNIUS

Ennius' main work was the *Annals,* the epic chronicle of the development of Rome from the beginnings to his own times. This was the archetypal creation of early Roman poetry and without it later poetry would have been fundamentally different.[22] He was also famous for his tragedies on Greek themes, many of them tales of the valour and suffering of war.[23] Thus he was primarily an inspired poet in the grand manner, the disciple of the Muses of Greek literature, who in the proem to the *Annals* stated that the shade of Homer had passed into him through a Pythagorean transmigration of soul.[24] But he also wrote in less exalted genres of poetry. His comedies, of which almost nothing is known today, had no great reputation in antiquity. He also composed historical plays or *praetextae,* a variety of occasional poems, and the *saturae.*

In this multifarious output no consistent pattern of poetic activity and development can be traced. The fragments are too few to show any stylistic evolution. Criteria from metrical technique are inconclusive, as Ennius may have permitted certain variations between the procedure of the *Annals* and that of the minor works.[25] External indications for dating his works are few. He completed the tragedy *Thyestes* shortly before his death.[26] The political poems *Scipio* and *Ambracia* were presumably written shortly after the events they celebrated.[27] The dating of the *saturae* is problematical. Reference to Scipio (frg. 10–11) would suggest a relatively early date, probably though not certainly before his patron's death in 184 B.C. If, as seems likely, the reference to the Ligurian town of Luna comes not from the *Annals* but from the *Saturae* this is a slight indication for a late date, as Luna did not become a Roman colony until 177 B.C.[28] But there is no reason to suppose that all the miscellaneous poems that made up Ennius' *saturae* were composed at about the same time. His main work, the *Annals*, occupied him for many years and may well have been interrupted from time to time by occasional poems in a more relaxed manner.

Porphyrio states that Ennius wrote four books of *saturae* and there is no good reason to doubt his explicit statement.[29] A corrupt reference in some manuscripts of Donatus was emended by Stephanus into *e sexto satyrarum Ennii*. Even if this emendation were accepted, it would be reasonable to argue that the numeral had been corrupted at an early stage and that the error is more likely to have arisen in Donatus, who quoted merely in order to identify a source of Terence, than in Porphyrio, who states explicitly how many books of *saturae* Ennius wrote.[30]

Our knowledge of the contents of Ennius' *saturae* is scanty. Some thirty-one lines of verse are extant, most of them isolated lines quoted by writers from the Christian era for some lexical or grammatical oddity. There are in addition a prose paraphrase of one of the *saturae* and a few indirect references. Some fragments of Ennius and references are customarily assigned to the *saturae* not through the explicit attribution of the citing authority but on grounds of literary plausibility.[31] Frequently a Greek parallel provides the only means of showing the possible context of a fragment.

Some of the satires are devoted to or at least included the writer's comments on his own life and descriptions of social situations:

> *Enni poeta salve, qui mortalibus*
> *versus propinas flammeos medullitus.*   (6f.)

(Good health to you, poet Ennius, for passing on to mankind a deep draught of blazing verse.)

These lines from the third book of the *saturae* illustrate one of the greatest difficulties in the interpretation of all fragmentary texts: we do not know whether the words purport to be spoken by Ennius or by some speaker whom the poet reports. If the poet is the speaker here, he either preens himself or justifies himself in the manner of a writer of Old Comedy. But the words may be spoken by an admiring god in a dream or (more likely) an ebullient fellow poet at a symposium or even a gratified patron.[32]

Other fragments mention men's calumny and insensitivity to abuse, possibly in a political situation (8–9, 63). There is also praise of Scipio Africanus in the manner of his separate encomiastic poem entitled *Scipio* (10f.).

It is sometimes impossible to tell the difference between the description of a situation from real life and the retailing of a speech or scene from comedy: *malo hercle magno suo convivat sine modo* (1) (he is stuffing himself to the back teeth; let him damn well suffer for it): the language is that of comedy; the subject may be a greedy contemporary or a stage parasite.[33] The proverbial *dum quidquid, des celere* (2) (what you give, give quickly) may have a similar context. The language of drama is also found in a four-line fragment in which Ennius uses the word *frustra* and its cognate verb *frustrari* nine times (59–62). There is a similar *tour de force* of repetitiveness in a higher genre in the soldiers' chorus in his *Iphigenia*.[34] A complaint about people who get in the way recalls scenes in comedy of the *servus currens* finding his path obstructed.[35]

There are certain elements of philosophy and moralizing in the *saturae*:

> *contemplor*
> *inde loci liquidas pilatasque aetheris oras*   (3f.)

(from there I gaze on the bright and compacted edges of the upper air)

The words in themselves may suggest the language of philosophical speculation, for the closest verbal parallel is part of an exposition of Stoic beliefs in Cicero.[36] It is also possible that in the *satura* the solemn words may be deceptive and need not imply a consistently serious poem. Another fragment comments on the resemblance between man and monkey 'ugliest of beasts' perhaps in order to show the difference between appearance and reality.[37]

Moralizing may be present in a *satura* by Ennius in which *Mors* and *Vita* are introduced in debate, but nothing is known of the substance of this work. Quintilian instances it as an illustration of personified abstracts.[38] There is no known example in Greek of personified Life and Death in conjunction, but antithetical pairs of personified abstracts are found debating in both drama and rhetorical prose. Epicharmus wrote some plays in which such a conflict was one of the most important elements: Land and Sea probably expounded in debate the benefits they give to mankind.[39] There is in Aristophanes' *Clouds* a debate of personified abstracts, the Just and Unjust Arguments. In a work by the

fifth-century Sophist Prodicus the young Herakles is confronted by
two women, Pleasure and Virtue, who propounded rhetorically the
advantages of the ways of life represented by them.[40] In Latin Novius
composed an Atellan play with the title *Mortis et Vitae Iudicium*.[41]
What, if anything, Ennius owed to some such theme we do not know;
as he adapted a work attributed to Epicharmus in one of his miscellaneous poems, there is slight support for the influence of Epicharmus here. If the debating abstracts in Epicharmus' plays are any guide
to the contents of Ennius' *satura*, Life and Death disputed over the
benefits they brought to men. How the debate was resolved we do not
know: some character may have decided between the two, or perhaps
as in the *Agon* of Aristophanes' *Clouds* one of the contestants withdrew
defeated.

The Aesopic fable with its attractive codification of simple folk
wisdom provided writers of many kinds with a framework for
moralizing. A fragment of Ennius begins the fable of the man who
tried to catch fish by piping to them. Herodotus had applied the same
story politically to the Eastern Greeks who refused to dance to Cyrus'
tune, but we have no evidence about Ennius' context.[42] There is also
found in Ennius' *saturae* the fable of the crested lark that moves its
young from the ripe cornfield only when the farmer, having sought
help in vain from those who might have been expected to give it,
decides to do the work himself. Gellius paraphrases Ennius' fable in
prose and quotes verbatim the two verses that point the moral; it is also
possible to reconstruct from his paraphrase some of the phrasing of Ennius' trochaic lines.[43] In the Aesopic verses the story is developed in
two stages; in Ennius there are three, for help is sought in vain from
kin as well as from friends and the tale is expanded like a children's
story with careful description of the trepidation of the nestlings. This
simple manner of narration is in the tradition of the Aesopic verse
fable, but it is very different from the subtle contrivance of
Callimachus' fable of the olive and laurel interrupted in their argument
by the bramble bush. Ennius does not seem to have taken anything
from elaborate Hellenistic poetry or from the sophisticated telling of
fable such as is found in Plato.[44] It is more likely that he is reproducing
an Aesopic fable transmitted orally or from a simple school collection.
The convention of retailing in verse simple folk tales with a moral
application is found as early as Archilochus.

We may have some other traces of Ennius' *saturae*. Style suggests that
the reference to *Lunai portum* (quoted by Persius, *Sat.* 6,9) belongs to
them and subject matter suggests the same for the description of a walk

with Galba.[45]

Ennius also wrote a number of minor poems with individual descriptive titles, which some scholars wish to include among the *saturae*.[46] These works are of two types: occasional pieces and adaptations of Greek originals. *Scipio* and *Ambracia* are composed in a particular political context and are obviously original.[47] The rest, based for the most part on minor Greek works, seem to have been written as they took the poet's fancy or as copies came to hand, e.g. *Sota,* a poem of virulence in keeping with the reputation of Sotades, its scurrilous Alexandrian source; the fragments referring to fornication, excrement and possibly human discontent;[48] and *Hedyphagetica,* an adaption, probably not a close translation, of a didactic work on gourmandizing by Archestratus, a fourth-century Sicilian writer.[49] But there is a weighty objection to including these poems among Ennius' *saturae*. Ancient authorities refer to these miscellaneous works by their proper names, but it is unlikely that this would have happened had they been part of the *saturae*. Where *saturae* have individual descriptive titles as with Varro's Menippeans, grammarians almost always cite by title and not vaguely *in saturis.* Two methods of quotation are never used for the same author. Had Ennius' miscellaneous works been part of the *saturae,* they would have been cited not by individual title but by the designation *saturae* with or without a book number. It may therefore be concluded that the *saturae* and *varia* are different works.

To what extent Ennius knew earlier personal poetry such as that of Archilochus and Hipponax either directly or through Hellenistic intermediaries we cannot tell. As discussed in the previous chapter, Posidippus' *Soros* may well have provided a model for Ennius' metaphorical title, but Callimachus' *Iambi* must have been the most famous precedent for a collection of poems on a wide range of themes in a variety of metres. Ennius owed much to Callimachus, who helped inspire the solemn introduction to the *Annals* and offered weighty precedence for writing in many different genres. But while the example of Callimachus' *Iambi* may have helped to induce Ennius to compile his own collection of miscellaneous poems, there is no evidence and little likelihood that he adapted them in detail, for many of their subjects are recherché and their style so artificial and oblique as to have provided later Greek theorists with textbook examples of allegorical expression and irony.[50] As Greek readers required commentaries for these works, Ennius would not have been able to introduce them to a Roman public.[51] His themes were taken from his own personal experience as well as from a wide range of reading.

3. TRANSMISSION AND SIGNIFICANCE

We have little certain knowledge of the extent of the circulation in antiquity or of the quality of the ancient transmission of Ennius' *saturae*. When the text of Ennius was emended soon after his death by the grammarian Octavius Lampadio it is likely that the *saturae* were not neglected.[52] Horace's friend, the civil servant and satirist Julius Florus, made a selection from them along with pieces from Lucilius and Varro either as a commonplace book for his own easy reference or as an anthology for contemporaries.[53] In the general neglect of archaic poetry in the first century A.D., it is likely that copies of the *saturae* became increasingly scarce. In the following century Fronto made a *de luxe* copy of Ennius' *Sota* for the emperor; this may suggest that good copies of the minor works were by then not numerous. Gellius in his unbounded enthusiasm for the old-fashioned, visited learned libraries and painstakingly verified readings in Ennius; he seems to have had a complete edition of the *saturae* before him.[54] After the literary vogue had waned they became, like other archaic poetry, linguistic source-books for grammarians. Nonius in the early fourth century A.D., though having access, as it seems, to a complete text, sometimes ex-cerpted inaccurately from such writers as Gellius, but after this time references to the *saturae* become still rarer.[55] The magniloquent *Annals* failed to survive the dark ages; it is not surprising that the unspectacular *saturae* fared no better.

The place of Ennius' *saturae* in the history of Roman satire is somewhat uncertain. To Diomedes and also by implication to Quin-tilian the Ennian stage of *satura* was in some ways a false start, and it seems likely that it had a very limited influence on later satirists. Lucilius in his earliest works takes over variety of metre but there is little other demonstrable indebtedness. None the less Ennius was the creator of more than the name of literary *satura*. It is perhaps a paradox that this rough-hewn genius sought a precedent for a collection of mis-cellaneous personal poems in highly sophisticated works from a mature stage of Greek civilization. To what extent the enterprising talent was able to overmaster the deficiencies of a crude literary technique we cannot know.[56] But although his *saturae* were probably worthy of the respect of the historian of literature rather than of its critical reader, it is unlikely that they were untouched by the power of his vigorous personality.

PART TWO

The Lucilian tradition

4

Lucilius[1]

In a formal sense Ennius was the first creator of a literary form *satura* in that this was the name that he gave to some of his minor poems, but Lucilius was the early master who devoted to this one genre the whole of his creative activity and gave to it the predominant characteristics of a censorious temper and outspoken criticism. Some later critics described his *saturae*, in contrast to those of Ennius, as *carmen maledicum* (abusive poetry) and, in applying to him the epithet *iambicus* that belonged to Archilochus, referred to his forceful attacks on named individuals.[2] His influence on the form of *satura* was equally decisive, for, after early experiments with various metres in the manner of Ennius, he chose for all his later poems the dactylic hexameter, which became the medium accepted by subsequent writers of verse *satura*. Thus to Horace he was the *inventor* of the genre and in particular the great Roman precedent for personal and social criticism.[3]

I. THE LIFE OF LUCILIUS

C. Lucilius was born in either 180 or, more probably, 168–7 B.C.[4] The place of his birth was Suessa Aurunca (modern Sessa Aurunca), a hill town in *Latium adiectum* five miles south of the Liris, on the borderland between Latium and Campania.[5] The gentile name Lucilius is Roman and the *praenomen* Caius predominantly, though not exclusively, Roman.[6] His family connections included those of senatorial rank: he was the great uncle of Pompey the Great, whose mother Lucilia was described as descended from a senatorial family,[7] and possibly a brother of M.' Lucilius, a senator mentioned on an inscription of 129 B.C.[8] It is sometimes assumed that because Suessa was a Latin colony Lucilius was not born a Roman citizen and never received the Roman franchise.[9] But he could have been Roman by birth, if his father had been either a Roman resident in Suessa or a local magistrate who through his office attained Roman citizenship, and if not born a Roman citizen he was probably given citizenship through the influence of aristocratic friends in Rome, for by tradition aristocratic patrons secured citizenship for their literary protégés.[10] The satirist who denounced influential senators by name must have enjoyed the benefits of citizenship, for even if the Metelli of the later part of the second century were more thick-skinned than their ancestors, no Latin would have dared to attack them over a long period. Yet Horace never even hints that Lucilius suffered at any time through his outspokenness, though in his discussion of the hazards of the satirist it would have been difficult for him to avoid referring to any such incident. Lucilius also regarded himself as entitled to criticize pronunciation that belonged to Latium not Rome (1322).

Lucilius' only known public service was at Numantia in 134–3 B.C. when he served under Scipio Aemilianus as an *eques* possibly with some officlal position.[11] It is possible that he also served in previous campaigns in Spain, though his references to earlier events such as the achievements of the formidable enemy Viriathus (d. 139) were perhaps no more than the talk of soldiers in camp.[12] Military experience was not a preliminary to a political career, but though Lucilius never became a senator and played no active part in Roman politics, he was sufficiently well-known to the public to be lampooned on the stage. It seems however that to ridicule in a public performance was more grave than to circulate abusive poems, and the satirist sued his detractor, but without success.[13]

Lucilius was a man of property and affluence and the owner of estates, probably in Bruttium and Sicily.[14] In Rome he occupied at some period the house that had been built at public expense for royal hostages. The circumstances of his tenancy or ownership are not known, but it is perhaps significant that the Seleucid hostage Demetrius, once a resident in the house, had been a close friend of the historian Polybius, the associate of Lucilius' patron Scipio.[15] References in the poems to public events suggest that, if not a resident in Rome, he was a regular visitor until at least 107 B.C. He died at Naples in 103–2 B.C. and was given the honour of a public funeral.[16]

Nothing is known about Lucilius' education. It is likely, though there is no positive evidence, that at some period he visited Greece. Some references by Lucilius to philosphers in Athens seem to have been based on personal knowledge, and the dedication to him of a philosophical work by the Carthaginian-born philosopher Clitomachus, who became head of the Academy in 127–6 B.C., suggests that the two men met in Athens.[17]

In Rome an ever-widening intellectual enrichment came from Greece, and as the second century proceeded the Greek tyranny over Latin literature and thought extended further. In his energetic and boisterous adaptations of Greek plays Plautus had attempted in part at least to create something essentially Roman, but with Terence's rendering of urbane Greek drama, particularly Menander, in civilized Latin, the hellenization of comedy, perhaps the most important literary form of the age, was complete. The products of this Greek-dominated culture were aimed at the approbation of an élite: Terence's plays, with the exception of the *Eunuchus*, were of only intermittent interest to the populace, but the tradition, however dubious, that Scipio Aemilianus and Laelius helped him to write them shows that they conformed to the taste of the educated.[18] Greek influence extended beyond creative literature, and Greek philosophers and teachers of rhetoric were installed in the houses of senatorial families. Cornelia, daughter of Scipio Africanus, had Greek writers in her entourage and entrusted the education of her sons Tiberius and Caius Gracchus to Greek rhetoricians.[19]

Notable among philhellenes was Scipio Aemilianus, who was given a Greek education and inherited from his father Aemilius Paullus the library of the Macedonian King Perseus. He was a hero for his exploits as military tribune, became consul twice in his career before the prescribed age and yet failed to achieve notable political success. He combined intellectual sensibility with military brutality, tearfully quoted Homer over the blazing ruins of the Carthage that he had destroyed, and while besieging Numantia greeted approvingly with a Greek quotation the news of the murder of his brother-in-law Tiberius Gracchus by a lawless posse of conservative senators.[20] At Numantia many of his cohort of friends were chosen for political or military reasons, but there was also present Polybius, historian as well as military expert, who had been his companion at the destruction of Carthage; and some years previously his entourage for a tour of the East had included the Stoic philosopher Panaetius.[21] The historical tradition of intellectual companionship together with Cicero's imaginative presentation in the Platonic manner of a philosophical discussion in the house of Scipio has led in modern times to the notion of a closely knit Scipionic circle of literary men and thinkers. Such a romantic picture is largely spurious.[22] Scipio, like other political chiefs in Rome, manipulated patronage and friendship for personal advantage. However throughout his life, though not a creative writer himself, along with Laelius he sought the company of poets and thinkers, some of whom in their turn no doubt enlarged the experience of their companions.

Lucilius was among those who enjoyed the friendship of Scipio, and his writings testify that for the last years of Scipio's life and for many years after his death he retained admiration and affection for his patron.[23] Scipio could offer the knight military adventure and the companionship of the great, though the cultural influence of Scipio and his friends should not be overestimated for they were not the only devotees of literature and philosophy in Roman society; Lucilius himself refers to other judicious critics of his work.[24] Lucilius on his side in addition to his services could perhaps offer much needed money for the Numantian campaign,[25] and the poet who could praise Scipio and vilify his enemies were above all politically useful. But Lucilius was not to be regarded as a retainer. There was a story that one day Laelius found Lucilius chasing Scipio round the dining-room couches with a knotted napkin in his hand; the unexpectedness of the anecdote may betoken its credibility.[26]

Lucilius alone of poets in Rome down to the end of the second century B.C. was not a humble outsider in the society in which he lived.[27] He was a man of property who, at least during the last years of Scipio and Laelius, was on equal terms with some of the most eminent politicians of the time. As landowner, soldier and the companion of policy-makers and intellectuals he learned from wide experience to assess the corruption and pretensions of his society as well as some of its achievements.

2. PROBLEMS OF TRANSMISSION

Some 1,400 lines of Lucilius are extant. Like the fragments of the *saturae* of Ennius and Varro most of them are isolated lines or small groups of lines cited on account of a linguistic quirk. The discursive nature of the material usually makes it impossible to place a fragment in its context with certainty especially where the citing authority gives no book number. Reconstruction of whole *saturae* is difficult for many reasons. Hardly anything is known of Lucilius' principles of construction. Nor do we know to what extent individual *saturae* in a book varied in size nor how far diversity of topic could be accommodated within a single unit of composition. Horace, though much influenced by Lucilius, can never be used safely as a criterion for reconstruction, as he may have applied a borrowed theme to a different situation. Yet in spite of these formidable difficulties the patient work of disciplined reconstruction has done much to elucidate Lucilius.[28]

An unusual problem of reconstruction is raised by Nonius' method of citing Lucilius. In each book of Nonius quotations from Books 1–20 of Lucilius are in rising sequence of book number, and in consequence it may be assumed that the fragments are listed in the order in which they occurred in the text of Lucilius. That Nonius listed the fragments of all his authors in proper order is demonstrably true of extant writers and accords with the inflexible regularity of his procedure. However, in citing from Books 26–30 of Lucilius, Nonius departed from his normal practice. The books are quoted in reverse order, citations from Book 30 preceding those from Book 29 and so on, and here too the procedure is equally inflexible.[29] But the order of fragments within Books 26–30 must be determined, whether they are cited in Books 1–20 in the proper order within the book or whether they too are quoted in reverse order. Marx believed that the fragments too were in reverse sequence, arguing that Nonius' roll had been wound the wrong way round; this also implied that in excerpting from this roll Nonius read each column from bottom to top. But though it is possible that grammarians sometimes made short runs of quotations in reverse order, Nonius' remorseless manner of quoting fragments in proper order suggests that he never adopted such a method within a book. Nor perhaps would it have been easy to reverse a papyrus roll permanently in the way that Marx's theory demanded. It is therefore better to assume that, while Books 26–30 are cited by Nonius in reverse order, the fragments within these books are given in their proper sequence.[30]

The title *saturae* must have been given by Lucilius himself. It is hardly likely that he left it to later editors and grammarians to find a title for the one literary form to which he devoted all his creative activities, especially in an age that made careful generic distinctions.[31] It is no doubt the result of incomplete transmission that the word *satura* in a literary sense does not occur in the extant remains, where the descriptive terms *sermo* (conversation) and *ludus* (plaything) are used of his writing. Such a sub-title as *Concilium Deorum* will belong to a later tradition that sometimes sought a convenient designation for a celebrated piece.[32]

3. THE EARLIER SATIRES (BOOKS 26–30)

By the time of Varro the *saturae* of Lucilius were already divided into two main collections; Books 1–21 and Books 26–30.[33] Stylistic development and datable references show that the collection of Books 26–30 was written first and also that each collection is probably in chronological sequence within itself book by book. At first Lucilius used metres that are mainly dramatic: Books 26 and 27 are written in *septenarii* only; Books 28 and 29 contain in addition trimeters and also the non-dramatic hexameter. Book 30 consists exclusively of hexameters, and this metre is used without any alternative throughout Books 1–20.

This pattern of stylistic evolution is supported by references in the poems to historical events. Lucilius began to publish shortly after his return to Rome from the Numantine war,[34] and there was a tradition that in order to gratify Scipio and Laelius he attacked Metellus Macedonicus, who was censor in 131 B.C. Such attacks must have been made before the death of Scipio in 129 B.C. and that of Laelius soon afterwards. A Mettellus is mentioned in Book 26, and certain lines from the same book may plausibly be interpreted as referring to the policies of the censorship of 131 B.C. It is thus probable that some part at least of Book 26 first appeared in either 131 or 130 B.C. In the same way the reference in Book 28 to Lentulus Lupus, who became *princeps senatus* in 131 or 130 B.C., seems to have been part of a similar attack on a political enemy made while Scipio was still alive.[35] The date of Book 30 is not certain, but a possible reference to the revolt of the Latin town Fregellae would demand a dating no earlier than 125–4 B.C.[36]

In Book 26 Lucilius states his literary intentions. He wishes, so he claims, to write for the reasonably educated, excluding from his reading public both the very learned and the utterly ignorant. C. Persius is his man of formidable erudition and his moderately literary men a certain Laelius Decumus, about whom we know nothing, and Iunius Congus, probably the jurist and at the time a very young man. The same idea occurs again, presumably in the same poem, with the substitution of the names Scipio Aemilianus and Rutilius Rufus as the men whose judgement is to be feared and his desired audience not other Romans but the men of Tarentum and Consentia in southern Italy and the Sicilians.[37] Lucilius' sentiments are not without irony, for while a poet in his first published book may be expected to feel apprehension about the judgement of the most discriminating, the mention of peoples who are not even speakers of Latin suggests a facetious paradox possibly at the end of the poem. Other literary forms are discussed in this book. Tragedy, it seems, is dismissed as pretentious and disreputable (587), and a quotation from Pacuvius is no doubt mischievous (653).[38] Lucilius' chosen way is criticized by an interlocutor, who objects to the revelation of private secrets (651f.). Advice is also offered to reject the writing of the history of former times in favour of contemporary themes including the exploits of Scipio (612, 613-6, 621). It is not known with any certainty how far the themes of literary choice were combined or scattered over different poems in the book. Other fragments of this book contain a discussion of marriage and reflections on commerce and on morality.[39]

No sustained pattern of themes appears clearly from the fragments of Books 27–29. In Book 30 Lucilius defends his vilification of contemporaries by name (1008–1038). A man who may be a patron is addressed in lines that are presumably separate lines of dedication. The identity of the speakers is unknown. It has been conjectured plausibly that the patron was the historian C. Sempronius Tuditanus (*cos.* 129 B.C.), but it is less likely that Afranius, writer of *fabulae togatae*, was a victim.[40] Some lines of argument may be traced. Though Lucilius' short poems are more successful than those of any other writer (1013) and are acclaimed by enthusiastic friends (1009), their wounding attacks on the behaviour of named individuals are resented (1014, 1016). They are said to spring from vindictive malice (1015) and to be an intrusion on personal privacy (1019f., 1035). As an example of the procedure a participant in the dialogue is described as a spendthrift whoremonger (1034) and Muscon as light-fingered (1031). Some of the language of vituperation is drastic:

> hic in stercore humi fabulisque, fimo atque sucerdis   (1018)
> (here on the ground among the dung, the goat turds, shit and pig-muck).

Perhaps a speaker challenged Lucilius' own way of life as being not beyond reproach (1017) or even threatened him with legal action, but there seems to be no dispute about literary craftsmanship. Unfor-

tunately we do not know the grounds on which Lucilius based his
defence, whether he claimed social duty as his justification or whether
he appealed to a literary precedent such as Aristophanes or
Archilochus.

Book 30 also contains an addresss to a military commander, probably
the vainglorious Tuditanus, whose martial deeds are celebrated in verse
(1079–87). Once again the angle of Lucilius' remarks is uncertain, but
while it is not necessary to suppose that the poem contains a formal
recusatio or polite refusal to celebrate Tuditanus' deeds no doubt
Lucilius was glad to leave his praises to others, particularly if the extant
fragments of Hostius are typical of the Homeric pastiche that was expected of laudatory verse.[41] Other topics in this book include a description of a vulgar dinner party (1060–77), amatory conquest (1039–49),
organization of the household (1050–7) and the tale of a woman and
her absent husband (991–1004).

4. THE LATER SATIRES (BOOKS 1–20)

There seems to have been no long lapse of time between the
publication of the first collection and the appearance of Book 1. To ensure its success, *The Council of the Gods* must have been published
shortly after the death of Lupus, which occurred some time before the
end of 125 B.C.[42] Likewise the account in Book 2 of the trial of Mucius
Scaevola in 119 B.C. will have appeared immediately after the event.[43]
Metellus Caprarius who was praetor no later than 117 B.C. seems to be
referred to in Book 5 as praetor designate.[44] One poem at least of Book
20, the last extant book could not have been written before 107 B.C.,
as it refers to the tribunate of Licinius Crassus. It is reasonable to
suppose that all the books of this second collection are arranged in
chronological sequence.[45]

Book 1 contains, it seems, one main poem only, the so-called
Concilium Deorum. After a poem in which the exalted theme of the
world's beginning is rejected (1) and a topic promised that deserves
anger (2) the narrative proceeds: the gods hold a council in which they
deliberate and give their judgement concerning the death of Cornelius
Lentulus Lupus, an aristocrat who had been condemned for extortion
as proconsul and yet later became censor and *princeps senatus*.[46] Lucilius'
political and moral attack is made within the framework of a parody of
the divine council in Book 1 of the *Annals* of Ennius, which concerns
the founding of Rome and the promised deification of Romulus

(27–30); Lucilius treats Rome's impending ruin through sedition and vice (5–8).[47] The parody may have a second dimension, if deliberating gods use the conventions of the Roman senate, appropriately as Lupus was its leader. Jupiter, it may be assumed, presides and speaks first. Neptune talks of some insolubly difficult problem (31); Apollo objects to being called *pulcher* (23), and his prophetic powers are mocked (33–5). It is uncertain whether any god defended Lupus, but literary and rhetorical balance seems to demand some arguments in his favour. Romulus (Quirinus), the builder of Rome, has been suggested as the most appropriate prosecutor of Rome's corruptor. There is particular irony in that attacks on Rome's degenerate extravagance and affectations including modish Greek turns of phrase (10–17) occur in the indictment of a man who had been censor.

Book 2 also consists of a single poem, an account of the trial of Q. Mucius Scaevola Augur, the son-in-law of C. Laelius and a famous jurist and devotee of Stoicism. He was praetor probably in 120 B.C. and returned from Asia in the following year to be accused of extortion by T. Albucius, an Epicurean, and tried before a jury of *equites*.[48] Such charges could be trumped up against men of integrity, especially while the knights were in charge of the courts, but Scaevola was acquitted and became consul in 117 B.C. There is a tradition that Lucilius was hostile to Scaevola,[49] and, whatever his overall intention in the poem, grave charges are made against him and possibly his entourage also. Accusations include physical brutality (57–9), a confidence trick (60f.), thieving (67f.), sexual intemperance (72–4) and gluttony (75,78–80). Albucius, by contrast, at one point at least is depicted by Scaevola as a figure of fun, affected in his language and petty in the vindictiveness that led him to bring the case:

> Graece ergo praetor Athenis,
> id quod maluisti, te, cum ad me accedis, saluto:
> 'chaere', inquam, 'Tite', lictores, turma omnis chorusque:
> 'chaere, Tite'. hinc hostis mi Albucius, hinc inimicus.
>
> (91–4)

(and so when I was praetor in Athens I greeted you in Greek as you preferred, when you came towards me: 'Chaere, Titus', said I. My lictors and the whole entourage in chorus shouted out: 'Chaere, Titus', and that is why Albucius is my enemy and foe).

How Lucilius exploited his subject is largely a matter for guesswork. A respected but perhaps uncongenial Stoic was attacked by a precious and

possibly not quite honest Epicurean.[50] The contrasting philosophical
principles of the antagonists may have given rise to incongruous
charges. Perhaps rhetorical techniques also were made to contrast, for
Epicureans in general and Albucius specifically were of undistinguished
oratorical accomplishment.[51]

In Book 3 Lucilius describes in what is probably a more or less factual account a journey that he made from Rome to Capua and from
there to the Sicilian straits. He presumably travelled in order to visit
his estates, but such a purpose did not prevent him from enjoying the
landscape, towns and temples on the route.[52] The stages of the journey,
part of which was by sea, are listed in detail; sometimes there is a
numerical statement of distance covered (107f.). The traveller is
sometimes preoccupied with accommodation and food (132–5), and
among the incidents on the way is a real or mock fight with physically
grotesque participants (117–22).[53] Personal experience (e.g. 127f.) is
presented objectively with an agreeable diversity of incident. The
framework of the poem may have been epistolary, for a friend is
addressed who did not take part in the journey (97f.); it is less plausible
artistically to postulate that Lucilius included in the same book a
separate poem of instructions and good wishes to a friend for a future
journey.[54]

In Book 4 a contest between a spirited gladiator, Pacideianus, and an
ill-favoured opponent is narrated with partisan colouring (149–59) and
the vices and extravagances of the rich are attacked in a spirit of sumptuary moralizing (165–8). But in Book 5 Lucilius satirizes the opposite
fault in a description of a bumpkin's frugal dinner party with its herbs
and vegetables (193–7); the tale of a military exploit, one of Lucilius'
favourite topics, was perhaps part of a conversation at dinner
(213–21).[55] He also addresses a complaint in epistolary form to a friend
who failed to visit him at a time of illness and mocks at a trite rhetorical
assonance that seems to have arisen out of his own improvisatory
writing (181–8). Book 6 includes a central theme of contemporary
politics, the disaffection of *optimates* and *populares*: L. Licinius Crassus or
Q. Mucius Scaevola may have rebutted charges of aristocratic
wickedness made by a democratic leader (240f., 257–62). Whoring and
paederasty are main themes of Books 7 and 8.[56] Books 9 and 10 contain
a number of disparate topics ranging from matters pertaining to a
brothel (330–5) to principles of literary terminology (338–48) and
recommended rules of orthography (349–82).

Book 11 contains anecdotes about contemporary and near-contemporary public figures, in which an unflattering character portrait is an opening gambit. Two at least of the stories concern the disreputable fathers of notorious sons: Aurelius Cotta (cos. 144 B.C.), an old confidence trickster with a fat and stupid son (413–5), and the effeminate Q. Opimius (cos. 154 B.C.), whose treacherous and venal son crushed with brutality the supporters of C. Gracchus while consul in 121 B.C. and was later exiled for accepting bribes from Jugurtha (418–20).[57] It is not known whether each anecdote was a complete poem or part of a larger composition. The remains of the later books are scanty, so that it is particularly difficult to determine the scope of any poem. Book 20 contains a poem in the symposiac tradition, a description of a dinner party given by the auctioneer Granius in honour of the tribune L. Licinius Crassus; it seems that the fare was lavish to excess and the host a braggart as well as a mordant wit.

In addition to the two main collections there are traces of a third group of books. The exiguous remains of Book 22 consist of an elegiac couplet, a sepulchral epigram on one of Lucilius' faithful and highly esteemed slaves (579f.) and single hexameters and pentameters including an announcement in the Oscan dialect of the death of a respected employee (581). These lines have a simple humanity that contrasts with the atrocious callousness shown to slaves especially in the second century B.C.[58] Nothing is known of the chronology of these books or the circumstances of their publication.

5. THE PERSONAL POET

Literary convention does not obtrude in the works of Lucilius. Writing as C. Lucilius the man and citizen he presented in an informal manner without obliqueness his immediate personal experiences and opinions on behaviour and politics.[59] He may have explicitly rejected allegiance to the Muses and have refused to write in anything other than his chosen form.[60] There was an extreme contrast, perhaps deliberately underlined by Lucilius, between his work and the ornate and pretentious compositions of his contemporary Accius. Some poems were epistles in so far as they had a dedicatee, e.g. Iunius Congus (596), but topical subject matter required an audience wider than the close family circle that had been the recipient of Sp. Mummius' accomplished verse epistles from Corinth,[61] and although a privately circulated attack on an enemy could give pleasure, in general political sentiments demanded a large enough public to influence opinion outside a single group of families.

To Horace Lucilius was as much the poet of personal revelation as of political attack and moral castigation. He describes him as entrusting his intimate secrets to his books as·if to confidants so that his whole way of life was open to the public clearly drawn as if on a votive tablet so as to reveal his true nature.[62] The occurrence of the first person singular in fragments is not enough to ensure that the writer is talking about himself, but some of the *testimonia* on Lucilius are explicit. According to Varro (*LL* 6,69 = 925–7) he related in a bedroom scene that he persuaded Cretaea to strip willingly of her own accord. The frankness has led some scholars to offer a palliative literary parallel or even to expunge the name Lucilius by emendation.[63] But shocked disbelief is unnecessary, as he also dedicated a book to a mistress Collyra.[64] In reporting private intimacies he sometimes compromised others, for he was criticized in antiquity on the grounds that he smirched the reputation of the boys Gentius and Macedo by referring to them by their own names and not under the pseudonyms accorded by custom to the beloved in poetry. Lucilius was thus involved in paederastic affairs; a relevant fragment mentioning Macedo is of a virulence that suggests jealousy (275).[65] Without explicit indications in the *testimonia* caution is necessary. A chaste expression of admiration should not be taken as the language of a sincere and personal love:

> qui te diligat, aetatis facieque tuae se
> fautorem ostendat, fore amicum polliceatur   (269–70)

(who loves you, shows himself an admirer of your youth and beauty and promises his friendship).

But whether or not the speaker is Lucilius himself, the proffering of friendship may have been in its context the artful rhetoric of an unabashed philanderer.[66]

To separate the personal from the literary in Lucilius' treatment of women and sex is often impossible, but in the fragments describing horses it is possible to recognize the appreciative eye of the soldier and landowner (476, 506–8, 511, 1278). A penchant for stories about camp life suggests the old campaigner's happy recollection of days of service (398f., 1069). Some of these apparently personal predilections were perhaps incidental, but in the detailed narration of what he had experienced in his journey to Sicily Lucilius offers a sustained essay in the autobiographical. The presentation of himself throughout his years of writing is an important literary achievement. In depreciating himself and in retailing his own amatory experiences without inhibition he is more like Catullus than Horace, who, except in one passage that is sometimes explained as an imitation of Lucilius, is notably circumspect in his self-revelation.[67]

To ancient writers Lucilius' principal characteristic was the astringency of his comments on contemporaries. In this they saw him both as a personal poet in the Greek iambic tradition and also, as it were, a public poet, like the masters of Old Attic Comedy. Horace describes him as the moral chastizer who denounced sinners by name and unmasked the vice hidden under the sleek exterior, and also as the friend of the highly placed, who gave them pleasure by attacking their enemies, both the masses and the party bosses.[68] Although none of Horace's discussions of Lucilius should be taken as objective literary history, they reflect the variety of his personal attacks.

6. POLITICAL AND PERSONAL ATTACKS

During the second century B.C. material prosperity had been accompanied by a decline in political morality. Polybius, though an exponent of imperial self-interest in political behaviour, contrasts the early integrity of Rome with its deterioration in his own time.[69] Provinces were places for plunder and extortion. Generals were no longer men of unquestionable honesty. The perfidy and greed of L. Licinius Lucullus (cos. 151 B.C.), who after treachery and exploitation in Spain evaded prosecution and dedicated a temple to Fortuna, were not unique.[70] There was also an increase in military brutality: the destruction of Carthage caused international disgust; the liberty of Greece, whose protection had been proclaimed by Flamininus, ended in the grim sack of Corinth.[71]

When Scipio on returning from Spain in 132 B.C. had celebrated the conqueror's triumph, Lucilius did not produce laudatory verses to enhance the hero's *gloria*. He was able to provide something of more immediate utility, the mockery and vituperation of political opponents. Scipio had been much hampered especially in the years immediately before his Spanish command by the senatorial establishment, notably Metellus Macedonicus and Lentulus Lupus.[72] While censor in 131–30 B.C. Metellus made a speech in which he disparaged the companionship of women but advocated general marriage for the sake of procreation. The topic, which will have been galling to Scipio, whose marriage to

Sempronia, sister of the Gracchi, was lacking in both affection and progeny, was the theme of a satire from Lucilius' first published book.[73] The choice during Metellus' censorship of Lentulus Lupus as *princeps senatus* must likewise have been odious to Scipio; Lucilius mentions him in Book 28 (785), and it is tempting to suppose that his great attack in Book 1 was first circulated privately before the death of Lupus, which occurred later than that of Scipio and Laelius. Scipio's return to Rome had been during the troubled period in which the followers of Tiberius Gracchus were hunted down. When Papirius Carbo (*trib. pl.* 131 or 130) maliciously asked Scipio to declare his attitude towards Ti. Gracchus, his angry replies damaged his popularity with the people.[74] It is possible that Lucilius' later attacks on Carbo had predecessors written in Scipio's lifetime. The satire in which Lucilius attacked the tribes of the *comitia tributa* (1259–63) probably belongs to this period; the occasion may have been the defeat of Scipio in the vote for the command against Aristonicus, when only two out of thirty-five tribes voted for him.[75]

The death of Scipio in 129 B.C. and that of Laelius shortly afterwards deprived Lucilius of both his great patrons. For the following decade apart from the great attack on Lentulus Lupus little in the fragments can safely be referred to the politics of the day. As a landowner he is likely to have been opposed to the distribution of the *ager publicus,* and as a native of an Italian town to have been sympathetic to Italian demands for citizenship.[76] Lucilius' failure to mention the political crisis of C. Gracchus' tribunate and the murder of his followers may be explained, accidents of transmission apart, as the result of prudence or simply of his absence from Rome.

Loyalty to the memory of Scipio is the mark of some of Lucilius' later references to politicians. Carbo, who became consul in 120 B.C., committed suicide in the following year on being condemned for either *maiestas* or embezzlement; Lucilius classes him with Lentulus Lupus and with Hostilius Tubulus, who committed suicide in similar circumstances while Scipio was censor, as rival of the Cyclops Polyphemus in perjury and infamy.[77] In Book 11 there is some reminiscence of Scipio, and at least one of the anecdotes refers to an event in his political career, the attempt of Claudius Asellus to impeach him for alleged impiety in his censorship. The story may have ended with an example of the mordant wit for which Scipio was famous.[78] In this book Lucilius combines the politics of the past with those of the present.

Much of the political life of the period is obscure[79] and no clear political alignment for the years after the death of Scipio is discernible from the fragmentary lines of Lucilius. His hostility towards the Metelli continued with an attack on a Caecilius Metellus as praetor designate (1130).[80] That Lucilius never mentions Marius may be an accident of transmission. Both belonged to the same social class and served with Scipio at Numantia; from 119 B.C. Marius too seems to have been in opposition to the Metelli. Nothing further can be affirmed. Lack of exact knowledge of chronology sometimes prevents a proper estimate of Lucilius' courage: we do not know whether his attacks on Carbo and Opimius were made before or after their public disgrace. But it is clear even from the remains that most, if not all, the chief politicians were at some stage the objects of his laudatory or more often censorious comments.[81] There is no trace of one of the grimmest external events, the Cimbrian invasion, but there may be a connection between the lines mocking state-organized superstition (484–9) and the atrocious panic-stricken barbarity of human sacrifice decreed by the state in 114–13 B.C.[82]

Lucilius also comments in a more general way on the dishonesty and futility of the political life of both senate and people:

> *nunc vero a mani ad noctem, festo atque profesto*
> *totus item pariterque die populusque patresque*
> *iactare indu foro se omnes, decedere nusquam,*
> *uni se atque eidem studio omnes dedere et arti,*
> *verba dare ut caute possint, pugnare dolose,*
> *blanditia certare, 'bonum' simulare 'virum' se,*
> *insidias facere, ut si hostes sint omnibus omnes*

(1228–34)

(But nowadays as things are from morning until night working day and holiday alike the whole people and senate likewise all bustle about in the forum and do not go off anywhere else. All devote themselves to one and the same aim and expertise, to be able to deceive with circumspection, to hit slyly, to push by using flattery, to pretend to be 'a good type' and to set traps as if each one was everybody else's enemy.)

This moralizing over political life is simple, and the almost stylized description contrasts with the hilarious, exaggerated but realistic depiction by a contemporary orator of the licentious and incontinent behaviour of jurymen.[83] A few lines may give an unrepresentative impression, but there is no mention in Lucilius of the procedural rackets of Roman politics or any hint of the violence that began to be important during Lucilius' years of writing. The characteristic language of Roman politics is seen in the reference to the pretentions of the reliable candidate, but the picture of scurrying men could apply equally well to a Greek *agora*. Perhaps Lucilius' attitude here may reflect that of Scipio, who was notoriously weak in manipulating the machinery of entourage and canvassing.[84] There is more of the flavour of Roman electoral technique in a fragment proclaiming that money (possibly for bribery) and canvassing reveal the qualities of a man (1119f; cf. 1219). Here the theme of political corruption passes into that of personal morality.

Parallel to the degeneration of public life in the second century there was a decline in private morality. Already in the time of Ennius the Bacchanalian scandal of 186 B.C. had shown the impact of a foreign cult on a populace ripe for orgiastic sensations.[85] In later decades orators and historians condemned the affluence that came from plunder.[86] Sumptuary laws were introduced to control the extent of feasting, but evasion was easy and the laws usually repealed quickly.[87] A more comprehensive control of morality was achieved by the censorship. In a censorship (142 B.C.) that was mentioned many years later by Lucilius (394), Scipio Aemilianus conducted his duties of surveillance with a notable harshness, exhorting the people to the traditional virtue of their ancestors and at the same time attempting to humiliate some members of politically hostile families.[88] The analogy was made in Rome between the rigours of a censor's *lustrum* and a dramatist's attack on a named individual, while Horace frequently uses the official terminology of the censorship to describe his own procedures.[89] The official moralizing of the elder Cato in particular offered precedents to the satirists and rhetoricians: attacks on the perverted values of those who paid more for imported fish and a fancy slave-boy than a farm animal and fields were reproduced by satirists and other moralists long after the speeches of Cato were forgotten.[90]

As already shown, Lucilius attacked the moral integrity of some eminent politicians. The aggrieved interlocutors in Book 30, one of whom is on *praenomen* terms with the poet, must, in order to give the dialogue persuasive plausibility, have been persons of some importance, but not all of his victims were prominent contemporaries. The transmitted example of a criminal type from this poem, Muscon, the footpad or cat-burglar (1031), has a Greek name. Cipius, the husband who snored to allow his wife to commit adultery without fear of discovery, has a name that is probably Campanian, and his nickname Pararhenchon (the alongside snorer) suggests a Greek environment (1223). Gallonius the auctioneer illustrates the vice of extravagant gluttony (1238–40); Naevius is the name given to the typically mean man (1212) and Syrophoenix to the unscrupulous profiteer (497f.).[91] Many of the names used to illustrate vices were borne either by Romans of no social consequence or by complete outsiders.

Sometimes an individual is attacked on grounds of social unacceptability. Troginus, probably an auxiliary of Celtic origin in the army at Numantia, who had the nickname *calix* (the tankard), held a dinner party and is sneered at for the rickety furniture (1060, 1062), the bad food (1076f.) and the deplorable female company:

> *Lamia et Bitto oxyodontes*
> *quod veniunt, illae gumiae vetulae improbae ineptae*
>
> (1065f.)

(because those lousy old bags with teeth like razors, Lamia and Bitto are coming, the greedy stupid bitches).

The outsider is thus abused for the crude boorishness of his convivial hospitality.[92] Lucilius is accused of malice by an interlocutor in Book 30 (1015). Unfortunately, often the evidence does not even include the name or status of the victim, as for example in the description of a man as 'a big brute just like a fierce monster of a butcher's dog' (1221).[93]

Sex is a common topic in the poems of Lucilius. In the first published book, against the background of the censor's recent speech, there is a discussion on adultery and the qualities of an old-fashioned wife. The theme of adultery occurs again in Books 29 and 30 along with thoughts on various feminine characteristics including glamour (859f.) and greed (861).[94] Elsewhere Lucilius presents the unchaste (238f.), the bawd (271), the lowest whores (334f.; 1271) and the sexually ambivalent (1058); he also describes in gross language perversion and various stages of coition.[95] But love is sometimes presented delicately, as in the poem with echoes of Anacreon describing the wooing of a young girl (1041–4), and yet even here in the context there seem to be hints of squalor (1047) and moral degradation (1048). Prostitution is once referred to, whether seriously or not, as a sin that might incur divine anger (206f.), but elsewhere it seems that a casual liaison is recommended in preference to the hazards of adultery.[96] Some fragments show a persuasive sensual appraisal (e.g. 859f.), others austere moralizing; it is perhaps wrong to seek a consistency of attitude throughout Lucilius' works. There is a similar ambiguity in fragments concerning food. The moralizing topic of extravagance conforms to the pattern of sumptuary legislation and censorial edict. Elaborate feasting is contrasted with honest food (1288, 1205), but excessively rural fare is also an object of derision (193). To judge from the very imperfect transmission the poems of Lucilius contained in abundance the sensualist's rollicking description of pleasures and passions and also the moralizing satirist's condemnation of those of others. The two existed side by side in the corpus of his poetry. No one in antiquity, so far as we know, accused him of inconsistency, let alone hypocrisy.

7. PHILOSOPHY, LITERARY AND GRAMMATICAL CRITICISM

As counterpart to the destructive criticism of behaviour Lucilius offers much exhortatory moralizing, but it is doubtful whether it was based substantially on the ethical principles of the great schools of Greek philosophy, for such commonplace as choice of activity and discontent with one's lot in life are too obvious to need prompting from Greek sources.[97] The tendency to moralize is fundamental both to the Roman institution of the censorship and also to such literature as Cato's *Carmen de Moribus* which is not dependent on Greek predecessors. Similarly neither Lucilius' mention of Aristippus and Carneades by name nor references based on Plato to the impartial affection of Socrates for handsome striplings need imply deep knowledge of these philosophers' teachings.[98] None the less Lucilius had some contact with the most eminent philosophers of his times. That he was a personal friend of Clitomachus, the successor of Carneades at the Academy, may suggest but does not prove an enthusiasm for philosophy, but it is likely that he was to some extent influenced either immediately or indirectly by Panaetius the future head of the Stoa, who lived in Rome for long periods between 140–30 B.C.,[99] and was the teacher of his friends Laelius and Rutilius Rufus. However, consistent devotion to philosophy is not to be expected from Lucilius, the rich landowner who admired horses and women. Sometimes he mocked: a fragment proclaiming the uselessness of philosophy need carry no weight without a context (515f.), but certain lines are known to have been a parody of the ethical ideals of the Stoa (1225f.) and Stoic terminology is used in a context of dalliance and a rough-house (784–90).[100]

In his concern for literary criticism and theory Lucilius came into conflict with Accius, the most famous tragedian and theorist of the times. With an eye for the pretentious he scoffed at the contrast between Accius' notoriously small physical stature and the large effigy of him placed in the temple of the Muses (794). His dislike may have had a political angle, for Accius' celebration of the Spanish triumph of his patron Iunius Brutus Callaicus at a time when Scipio aspired to *gloria* in Spain may have been displeasing to the Scipionic faction. There may also have been mutual malevolence on literary grounds, for it is likely that the pioneer of an informal literary genre was belittled by Accius and the *collegium poetarum*.[101] In attacking Accius in at least three books Lucilius went beyond the exposure, common to the satirist and the comic poet, of bathos in the high style and attained a serious literary evaluation, for which he won fame in antiquity.[102] Details of Lucilius' attacks are not known, but it is possible that, repelled by Accius' ornate diction and abandonment of the simple metres of his Greek originals, he desired a close approximation to the re-creation of Greek plays such as his friends had admired in the comedies of Terence. In criticizing Ennius and Pacuvius also it is likely that he was hostile to a diction that was sometimes unequal to the magnitude of its subject.[103]

In Book 9 he defends with a reasoned statement of principle criticisms he had made of some part of Homer, arguing that, as there is a fundamental distinction between a long, complete work (*poesis*) and a small piece of verse which may be part of a greater whole (*poema*), in faulting a line, word or passage of Homer he is not disparaging the whole (338–47). The terms *poesis* and *poema* in the sense of the whole work and a smaller unit of verse are first found in Neoptolemus of Parium, a third-century writer of Aristotelian leanings, and occur in some later critics with various changes of nuance of meaning. In Lucilius the terminology is primarily quantitative, but the use of *opus totum* referring to the complete epic hints at the qualitative notion of an organized composition.[104] Other examples in Lucilius of positive literary principles include a discussion of discrimination in choice of phrase or topic.[105] He uses Greek critical language in the course of a jibe at a device of flamboyant rhetoric, the jingling homoioteleuton *nolueris debueris*, which he dismisses as inane, jejune and something to be associated with Isocrates.[106] The over-elaborate in oratory evokes his ridicule, as when Mucius Scaevola is made to praise with destructive irony the intricate mosaics of his opponent's rhetorical composition (84f.). Lucilius' rhetorical judgements may have accorded with the restrained Atticizing practice of Scipio and Laelius and, like them, his ideal orator was to be a man of wide intellectual attainment.[107]

On problems of orthography Lucilius went beyond a mere well-informed repartee and censure and, at a time when there was anarchic inconsistency in spelling, expounded his recommendations systematically.[108] In opposition to the view of Accius who represented long *a* by *aa*, he appeals to Greek usage, advocating the use of a single *a*, whether the vowel is short or long (351–5); he also adapted a Greek theory of vowel modification in suggesting that the plural of *pilum* (javelin) should be spelt *peila* in order that the word's increased size may represent its plurality (358–61).[109] He also included a catalogue of solecisms that won the admiration of a late grammarian.[110] The didactic exposition of literary and grammatical material is an important aspect of Lucilius' work that was not imitated in the formal satires of any later poet but is found in a modified way in the literary epistles of Horace.

8. LITERARY PRECEDENTS

i. Comedy

In an expansive generalization Horace asserts that Lucilius was completely dependent on the poets of Old Attic Comedy and imitated them with a mere change of metre (*Sat.* 1,4,1–7). At this point Horace is thinking primarily of the denunciation of individuals by name and he exaggerates because he wishes to give, by implication at least, a respectable ancestry to his own criticized practice.[111] Lucilius himself in the extant remains never connects his work with Old Comedy, though it is possible that he did so in the course of an apologia for his personal invective.[112] Accius discusses invective on the stage, and contemporary judgements on this element of Old Comedy may have been influenced by Naevius' practice, which later literary theorists considered to have belonged to the same pattern.[113] Whatever Horace's authority for the connection between satire and comedy, his description of the invective in Old Comedy depends ultimately on formulations in Hellenistic literary theory of a kind with which Lucilius will no doubt have been familiar.[114]

Though Lucilius' extant remains show little or no sign of verbal correspondence to what we know of Old Comedy,[115] he is likely, to some extent at least, to have been familiar with it. Common themes in themselves are no proof of literary continuity but it is useful to note the extent of the similarity between the subjects of the two genres.

Aristophanes and his fellow poets of the Old Comedy attacked reprobates by name and combined ridicule of the persons of public figures such as Pericles and Hyperbolus with serious criticism of their policies. They offered advice on public morality such as the dangers of imported religious cults, like other moralists sometimes longed for old-fashioned standards of behaviour, laughed at philosophers, criticizing their opinions as well as ridiculing their quirks, and showed an awareness of literary criticism and linguistic theory while gibing at poets and grammarians.[116] All such approaches were common to fifth-century comedy and Lucilian satire, and just as the comic poets in the parabasis of their plays offered serious counsel to their audience, Lucilius addressed himself personally to his public.[117] But there were important differences between the two apart from the restrictions of the undramatic form of satire. Though Horace recognized the variations in the level of style of Old Comedy as a mark of excellence such as satire should achieve, Roman *satura* never attempted a comparable range from lyrical splendour to unmitigated bawdry nor could it attain such subtle shifts or complexities of tone.[118] Nevertheless the style of all Roman satirists sometimes embraced the rhetorically fervent as well as the informally frivolous.

Moralizing and the assessment of a human situation in ethical terms were among the chief characteristics of New Comedy, and these were an important influence on Lucilius and his successors. The reflection that it is better to be born even the meanest of animals rather than a man occurs in Menander's *Theophoroumene* and in Lucilius. Menander based his comment on the success among the human species of the crawler and the malevolent rather than the noble; Lucilius presumably applied the generalization to a similar example of undeserved success.[119] It was a common gambit of ancient moralizing and rhetoric to take a character from New Comedy as a specimen of a trait or a quality of behaviour, e.g. Thrasonides, the unsuccessful lover from Menander's *Misoumenos,* was made to illustrate uncontrolled lamentation and Cnemon from his *Dyskolos* irascibility;[120] and in the same way Lucilius presents the fatuously anxious lover from Greek comedy to illustrate either a general principle of behaviour or a particular example from contemporary Rome.[121] Lucilius' comic scene, in which a loud-mouthed but timid soldier accompanied by the parasite Gnatho attempts to lay siege to a house (836–45), would no doubt have reminded his readers of a similar scene in Terence's popular *Eunuchus* or its Greek original.[122] It may have been part of a general moralizing, but it may have referred to some real scandal well known to Lucilius' contemporaries, for there were examples to hand of unwarlike generals and demoralized troops.[123]

Not all the comic motifs in Lucilius can easily be explained as moral paradigms. In another narration of the siege of a house (771–91) the setting is Rome, there is an unfaithful wife and a threat of legal proceedings. Objective moralizing would seem to be precluded by the presence of Lucilius himself, if not as a participant in the brawling at least as a man with amatory interests (774).[124] The fragments suggest a strange blend of Greek literary theme and Roman reality. There may be a similar mixture of comic convention and of experience in the poems concerning Hymnis, whose name is that of a courtesan from comedy. In Lucilius she appears in situations found in comedy such as an auction by a pimp; but some of the Hymnis fragments are non-dramatic.[125] While it would be rash to regard the Hymnis poems as wholly autobiographical, some of them at least perhaps referred to the kind of female musical performer who had been introduced into Roman dinner parties.[126] No doubt there was an interaction here between literature and life: comedy sometimes provided examples of cultured immorality that were imitated by young Romans, whose escapades in turn gave relevance to the introduction of comedy motifs into satire.[127]

ii. Greek 'iambi'

Lucilius was also much indebted to the Greek tradition of iambic poetry. He read and imitated Archilochus, the seventh-century master of the genre, whose works were probably a formative influence on his approach to satire. It is perhaps significant that he is explicitly mentioned and adapted in Book 27, one of the earliest books. A speaker in dialogue, possibly Lucilius himself, argues that contrary to what Archilochus had said some things are impossible. The reference seems to be to the speech of the indignant father (not Lycambes), who when faced with the prospect of his daughter's marriage to an ill-favoured son-in-law asserted that any law of nature could be reversed.[128] Lucilius' context is unfortunately unknown. He also reproduces Archilochus' address to his soul (thymos).[129] Archilochus had much to offer Lucilius. He was the first personal poet, and described his own experiences and emotions without inhibition; according to ancient tradition he even portrayed himself as lecher, adulterer and man of violence.[130] But it was the drastic vehemence of his reviling of personal enemies and malefactors that gave him his traditional reputation in antiquity and made him the archetypal master of the iambic genre.[131] His descriptions of sexual experience are akin to those of Lucilius; he also reflected on moral values and on politics and the instability of human affairs. He shared with Aristophanes a wider range of stylistic levels than Lucilius, and sometimes wrote with a radiance that was alien to *satura*, but like Lucilius he was criticized in antiquity for untidy construction.[132]

Lucilius alludes also to Anacreon's lines addressed to the Thracian filly that grazes untamed by the bridle. In Lucilius the horse replies, asking if she is to be subjugated as an unwilling animal for the plough. Anacreon's fragment is a masterpiece of passionate wit; Lucilius' context also is amatory.[133] Lucilius chose as model a poet who as well as lyricist of wine and love was a writer of wittily abusive *iambi* in the tradition of Archilochus.[134] It is impossible to judge how far the later iambic tradition and kindred verse forms helped to develop Lucilius' literary method. Already in the late sixth-century choliambics of Hipponax there were precedents for the extremes of abusive scurrility and scatological obscenity, and sharp descriptions of undesirable social types such as the hypocritical Stoic and the *nouveau riche* were to be found in the later choliambic poets Hermeias and Phoenix, but in general Lucilius' poetry had little in common with the choliambs devoted to the complaints of indigent and underprivileged scroungers.[135] The *iambi* of Callimachus, for all his importance as a literary figure, were too indirect and contrived to have provided exemplars for the blunt Lucilius. More directly relevant is the third-century Sceptic Timon of Phlius, who satirized the Mouseion in Alexandria founded by Ptolemy Philadelphus, and used Homeric hexameters in a dislocated manner to mock philosophers; an irreverent assessment of Homeric heroines by Lucilius (540–6) is clearly derived from the tradition of his *silloi*.[136] But attempts to demonstrate a close connection between Lucilius and miscellaneous Greek writers of mockery in the third century apart from the sillographers are unconvincing, and it is perhaps unprofitable to speculate extensively on Lucilius' indebtedness to poets some of whom may have been known to him, if at all, only by name.[137]

iii. Prose literature

The Socratic dialogue and the symposium influenced the structure and the contents of Lucilius' *saturae*. He refers to *Socratici charti*, quotes from

certain dialogues of Plato, and in two poems uses the form of the
symposium at which there is a discussion about philosophy and
philosophers.[138] Scipio Aemilianus was particularly devoted to
Xenophon's Socratic writings and assumed a Socratic irony himself; his
favourite book was Xenophon's *Cyropaedia*.[139] It is likely that Lucilius
too was impressed by his patron's love of the romantic tale of hunting
and may even have used it to colour his military reminiscences, but of
greater importance for the moralizing satirist were the *Memorabilia* with
their shrewd commonsense wisdom and the *Symposium*, which, though
lacking Plato's subtlety in depicting personality and sustained pattern
of thought, presented the scene with notable skill of narrative. The
formulation of the behaviour of ethical types by Theophrastus in his
Characters could be of value both for moralizing and for describing
people. Early in the first century the rhetorical treatise *ad Herennium*
contains a formulation of the *gloriosus* in Theophrastus' manner, and it
is likely that such sketches were read and enjoyed one generation
earlier by educated men.[140]

9. STYLE

Lucilius' language was not based on the stylized conversational idiom
of Callimachus, still less on theoretical doctrines of a plain style
associated with Panaetius, but on the everyday speech of Rome.[141] It
was an attempt to reproduce not a refined Attic idiom in Latin but
the vigorous emotive language of Roman conversation. In this it
resembles the image-laden idiom of Plautus rather than the stylized
colloquialism of Terence. None the less Lucilius, like Plautus, did not
aim to reproduce spoken language in a consistently naturalistic way, a
notoriously wasteful procedure, but in order to add persuasive force to
his language intensified it with figures.[142] As with Plautus the long
dramatic metres required some expansiveness of phrase removed from
natural speech idiom.

The longer fragments give some insight into the relationship
between content and manner of presentation. The lines on *virtus* express traditional aristocratic Roman concepts combined perhaps with
Stoic ideas of human excellence,[143] but their style is more
problematical:

> *virtus, Albine, est pretium persolvere verum*
> *quis in versamur, quis vivimus rebus potesse,*

virtus est, homini scire id quod quaeque habeat res,
virtus, scire, homini rectum, utile quid sit, honestum,
quae bona, quae mala item, quid inutile, turpe, inhonestum,
virtus quaerendae finem re scire modumque,
virtus divitiis pretium persolvere posse,
virtus id dare quod re ipsa debetur honori,
hostem esse atque inimicum hominum morumque malorum,
contra defensorem hominum morumque bonorum,
hos magni facere, his bene velle, his vivere amicum,
commoda praeterea patriai prima putare,
deinde parentum, tertia iam postremaque nostra.

(1326–38)

(Virtue, Albinus, is being able to pay in full the real price in one's dealings and in the affairs of life. Virtue is knowing what each affair has for a man. Virtue is knowing what is right, useful and honourable for a man, what is good, likewise what is bad, what useless, degrading and dishonourable. Virtue is knowing the boundary and limit of acquisitiveness. Virtue is being able to pay in full the price that is the due of wealth. Virtue is giving what is in truth owed to honour, being an enemy and hostile to bad men and behaviour and on the other hand a champion of good men and behaviour, valuing them highly, wishing them well and being their friend, and in addition to think that the interests of our country come first, then those of our parents and thirdly and last our own.)

There is a degree of stylistic elaboration that is removed from the organization of spoken sentence structure. The piece begins with a careful enjambement, and the last three lines consist of two sets of *tricola*, the first with triple anaphora and the second with two groups of words commencing with *p* in alliteration. But the occurrence of *virtus* at the beginning of six lines and the repetition, rhyme and assonance at 1334f. have led scholars to criticize the lines as the kind of garrulous doggerel that Horace censured in his predecessor.[144] Yet in a demonstrably contrived passage by a poet with a reputation for a sense of stylistic criticism even these devices are unlikely to have been improvisatory stop-gaps. They may be explained either as the deliberate reproduction of the idiom of an archaic gnomic poetry or, perhaps more likely, as an ironical excess of asseveration in lines probably addressed to an exponent of moral backsliding.[145]

In Book 3 Lucilius describes with comic exaggeration the journey across undulating country and some low hills:

verum haec ludus ibi, susque omnia deque, fuerunt
susque haec deque fuere, inquam, omnia, ludus iocusque:

> *illud opus durum, ut Setinum accessimus finem,*
> *aigilipes montes, Aetnae omnes, asperi Athones*
>
> (110–3)

> (but really at this stage all this was a game and no trouble at all; no trouble at all,
> I say, and everything a game and good fun: but when we got to the edge of
> Setia, that was hard work, mountains abandoned by goats, everything an Aetna
> and a craggy Athos).

Once again the first two lines suggest immediately an un-Horatian
doggerel, but the repetition and the movement of the verse represent a
jogging and bumpy progress. Then by contrast movement passes into
imagery with the description of low hills as severe climbs like the most
famous summits of the Mediterranean world. The identifying
metaphors, stronger than similes, belong incongruously to the grand
manner. The style is not intended to be subtle, but is carefully
calculated.

It is clear that Lucilius' works were rich in imagery. He knew the
debunking power of the unheroic animal comparison and metaphor
that contrasts with the formal simile in epic that uses a noble or impressive animal to illustrate actions of heroic grandeur. A predatory
woman is compared with the octopus that gnaws its own tentacles
(861f.) and moths (1358) may illustrate the wastrel or spiv.[146] Soft tar is
used as a descriptive term for a catamite (732), and it has been pointed
out that Lucilius has, perhaps not unexpectedly, a penchant for imagery
from mud and kindred substances.[147] He compares Roman superstitions
with the fears of children who imagine that bronze statues are alive
(486–8). This formal simile is akin to the illustrative and explanatory
simile of the tradition of didactic poetry as used by Empedocles and
later to be an important element in the *de Rerum Natura* of Lucretius.[148]
Perhaps the most remarkable piece of imagery in Lucilius is the conceit
of the comparison of his ailing body and ill-health to the two pirates
Rhondes and Icadion, who were as hostile to the safety of travellers as
his physical disabilities to himself (1292). The animal fable was a conventional ready-made illustrative device, which Lucilius used frequently, the best preserved being that of the lion whose feigned illness
is unmasked by the canny fox (980–9). A similar moral paradigm is
found already in the *saturae* of Ennius, and later satirists were to continue the use of this attractive inherited corpus of folk wisdom.

Lucilius' range of vocabulary was bounded by conversational usage.
He used the epithets of high poetry only for waggishness or as pointed
mockery of attempts to create a grandiose tragic language in Rome.[149]

At the other extreme he was not restrained by any code of convention from including obscene words of the utmost physiological grossness (1186).

There is a remarkably high proportion of Greek words in the poems of Lucilius. The many Greek words in the plays of Plautus belong to certain technical spheres such as sea-faring and banking and provide much of the terminology of pleasure; as befits the themes of the plays, they are particularly associated with slaves and plebian characters.[150] This rich source of vocabulary, which Terence with his desire for consistency of language had eliminated from his comedies, was extended by Lucilius to include words for all aspects of his wide subject matter. Within the range of everyday human experience he used, like Plautus, Greek for imported luxuries, abuse, and things to do with sex,[151] but Greek words were equally part of his way of expressing his thoughts on sophisticated and intellectual subjects. Some examples occur with deliberate frivolity in order to underline an affectation, e.g. *rhetoricoterus* (86), but many others are the serious terminology of philosophy, grammar and literary criticism. Greek words in Plautus are largely loan words accommodated to Latin terminations; by contrast many of Lucilius' Greek words retain their original formation unchanged. In reproducing such forms in his poems Lucilius gives the impression of drawing without reflection on the spoken language of the educated, who regarded Greek as the natural medium of thought on serious topics. To have overcome the notorious intractability of the Latin language by transmuting Greek terms into genuine Latin would have withdrawn the language of his poems from that of spontaneous conversation.[152] Horace's specific criticism of Lucilius' practice shows a new standard of taste (*Sat. 1, 10, 20–30*).[153]

10. SURVIVAL AND EVALUATION

Lucilius was much read and studied throughout the rest of the republican period. His grammarian friends Laelius Archelaus and Vettius Philocomus conducted readings from his works, and a tradition of interpretation was handed on to their pupils, Pompeius Lenaeus, pupil of Laelius, and Valerius Cato, pupil of Vettius, who made an edition. There was exegesis of subject and lexical matter that was sometimes accompanied by a tampering with the text. Both Pompeius Lenaeus and Curtius Nicias, who wrote interpretative studies, were dependants of Pompeius Magnus, so that in late republican times the Lucilian tradition would have seemed to have a political bias, especially as Lenaeus wrote a violent attack on Sallust the historian in reply to vilification of his master and patron.[154] Lucilius was highly esteemed by Cicero, who quoted him frequently and regarded him as erudite and civilized (*doctus et perurbanus*).[155] Horace's judgements, partly critical and partly admiring, are to be explained by his search for standards of writing for his own satires and by the changing political and literary attitudes of his times. In the second half of the first century A.D. Lucilius was an immediate source of inspiration to Persius and Juvenal and, as part of the vogue of the archaic, was valued by some more highly than Horace or any other poet.[156] In late antiquity his works were used only for moralizing anthologies and grammatical studies, and no copy seems to have survived the Dark Ages.

To offer a comprehensive evaluation of the literary worth of Lucilius is obviously impossible. Splintered groups of words are no firm basis for value judgements, and so we must depend largely on the opinions of a wide range of Roman writers of different periods, all of whom testify to the powerful force of his inventive genius; but unless the lava of Herculaneum yields more Latin texts we are unlikely to know whether he had talent enough to support his genius.

5

The Satires of Horace[1]

In the political turbulence of the later part of the republic Lucilius had
no successor of consequence. At a time when many poets were striving
for elegance and refinement his brashness was open to stylistic censure.
But the Lucilian stamp became a byword for uninhibited invective in
verse. Sevius Nicanor, a teacher of grammar, continued the tradition of
satire as autobiography by publishing a hexameter poem in the
Lucilian manner in which he proclaimed that he was a freedman.[2]
Terentius Varro from Atax in Narbonese Gaul was mentioned by
Horace as one of the inept imitators of Lucilius. He attempted many
genres and was no doubt an experimenter rather than a dedicated
satirist.[3] M. Terentius Varro, the famous antiquarian scholar from
Reate who developed satire in a mixture of prose and verse (see ch. 8),
also wrote four books of satires in verse. Nothing is known about their
contents or when they were written.[4] Varro mentions in Book 3 of *de
Re Rustica*, of which the dramatic date is 54 B.C., that an erudite
landowner L. Abuccius wrote in a Lucilian style.[5] Less than three
months after the murder of Julius Caesar C. Trebonius, a member of
the conspiracy, while proconsul of Asia, informed Cicero in a letter
that he had composed verses reviling his political enemy, i.e. M. Antonius, with a coarse fury worthy of Lucilius. Their tone seems to have
been that of a Philippic in verse. In March of the following year
Trebonius was executed in his province by Dolabella, an agent of Antonius.[6] The last republican practitioner of verse in the Lucilian manner
came to a bad end.

In the last decades of the republic there had been much political scurrility in verse. Caesar bore with good humour iambics directed against him by Catullus and also the vitriolic poems of Otacilius Pitholaus which may have been in the tradition of Lucilius.[7] Some years after his death obscene verses were composed by Octavianus as part of the attack on Antonius' wife Fulvia in the Perusine War and formal satire was used to besmirch and also vindicate political reputations. Lenaeus, a learned freedman of Pompey, after the death of his patron and his sons wrote an abusive satire on the politically discredited historian Sallust, whom he dubbed rake and plagiarist.[8] Lucilian satire was a weapon in the hands of the enemies of Caesar and was perhaps associated with the republican cause.[9]

The murder of Julius Caesar was followed by a period comparable in its brutality to the worst days of Marius and Sulla.[10] In November 43 B.C. Octavianus, Caesar's grand-nephew and heir, M. Antonius, the consul for 44 B.C., and M. Aemilius Lepidus, *magister equitum*, joined together in a triumvirate, which though sanctioned as an office of state was a dictatorship based on military power. Immediately there was a proscription in which 300 senators including Cicero and 2,000 knights from both Rome and Italian towns were massacred. Some were political opponents; many were the innocent possessors of wealth and land to be expropriated. The defeat of Brutus and Cassius at Philippi in late 42 B.C., in which most of what remained of Rome's traditional governing class was destroyed, was followed by the eviction of small farmers in Italy in order to find land for 100,000 faithful veterans. After 40 B.C. war between Antonius and Octavianus was averted by a series of uneasy pacts and Antonius became increasingly involved with Eastern affairs and Cleopatra. The alienation of the West from Antonius was intensified by Octavianus, who organized an oath of allegiance to himself sworn by cities throughout Italy (32 B.C.). After the final defeat of Antonius in the following year the military dictatorship of Octavianus was complete everywhere and unchallenged.

During the years that followed the breakdown of republican government there was a transformation in the structure of Roman society. The new society consisted largely of men ennobled by Caesar and those who were enriched by the proceeds of proscription and elevated to high office as supporters of the triumvirs. According to Sallust (*Bell.Iug.* 4,7) the new men of the revolution in contrast to those of republican times made their way to power by deception and plunder. The judgement, though biased and exaggerated, is not without foundation. Military command and political office went to men with no family tradition of service to the state but with an interest in the continuance of the new society. From the beginning of his career Octavianus collected around him henchmen, notably the knights Agrippa, a redoubtable soldier without finesse, and Maecenas, effete aesthete and skilful diplomat, men loyal to their leader whatever crisis might develop within the triumvirate. In his struggle for an absolute supremacy Octavianus encouraged appropriate propaganda in order to ensure personal support for himself and his régime. In literature as in government there had been an almost complete break with the republican past. No poet of consequence survived from former times. It was the task of Maecenas to gather new poets of talent who would celebrate the glories of Octavianus' martial deeds and rally public opinion to his policies. The most promising of Maecenas' discoveries were Virgil and Horace.

I. THE EARLIER LIFE OF HORACE

Quintus Horatius Flaccus was born on the eighth of December 65 B.C. and was thus a near-contemporary of Virgil (born 70 B.C.) and Octavian (born 63 B.C.).[11] The place of his birth was Venusia (modern Venosa) on the borderland between Apulia and Lucania.[12] He was the son of an ex-slave, who had acquired some wealth as a *coactor argentarius*, an auctioneer's agent.[13] His father, ambitious for the future of his talented son, was unwilling to send him to the local school, at which, Horace says, the sons of centurions were notable for their brawn and arrogance. Instead he took him to Rome. While supervising personally his moral upbringing he organized for him the formal education that was normally available only for the sons of the upper classes. Horace received the early stages of a literary training under the exacting and cantankerous Orbilius.[14] From there he went to Athens, where he studied philosophy and particularly ethics. He refers specifically to the Academy, but pre-eminent in Athens at the time was the Peripatetic Cratippus, the friend and tutor of Cicero's son, a congenial companion and the maker of disciples.[15] Philosophical aspirations were caught up in political reality. On his way from Italy in 43 B.C. Brutus stayed in the city traditionally associated with tyrannicide. By attending philosophical discussions he was able to exploit the idealism of the young in order to recruit promising men to the anti-Caesarian cause. Horace, like the younger Cicero, joined Brutus and probably accompanied him to Asia Minor.[16] Before the campaigns of Philippi, though

without any military experience, he was appointed military tribune
with duties controlling a legion. Thus at a time of crisis Horace
through his outstanding personal qualities held an office that would
normally have been far above the reach of the son of a freedman.
Nobles in Brutus' party showed their resentment.[17] At the second
battle of Philippi, in which Brutus was defeated, Horace made his escape. In referring to the occasion years later he uses the Greek poet's
motif of throwing away his shield in battle, but this need not be taken
literally to imply an ignominious dereliction of duty.[18]

Horace obtained a pardon from the victorious party but had lost his
family property in the settlement of veterans after Philippi. He was
given employment as a member of the permanent civil service, a *scriba
quaestorius* concerned with public documents. His later claim that
poverty drove him to writing verse may be another piece of dissembl-
ing irony not to be taken literally.[19] Some time during the years
after Philippi he was introduced to Maecenas by Virgil. Within a
year he was accepted as a member of his coterie and accompanied
him on at least one embassy.[20] Shortly before 31 B.C. Maecenas gave
him a farm in Sabine country.[21] He was now financially independent
and able to withdraw, perhaps gradually, from administrative duties.
His later career, outwardly uneventful, goes beyond the years of the
satires.

By the time Horace reached manhood he had had the best possible
literary and philosophical education that Rome and Greece could
provide, deepened perhaps by acquaintance while in Athens with texts
of Greek writers not readily available in Rome. He also had the advantage, so far as we know, of no advanced rhetorical training. A man of
outstanding personal qualities, he was selected at an early age for a
senior military post by Brutus and later as a companion by Maecenas. It
will not have been sentimentality that induced Augustus to attempt to
steal him from Maecenas in order to make him his own private
secretary.[22] On the evidence of Horace himself and of Suetonius'
biography he was short and sturdy. Horace adds that he was quick-
tempered but easily pacified.[23]

2. THE DATE OF THE SATIRES

Horace's satires belong to the earliest period of his writing. Book 1 was
first made available in complete form about 35 B.C. and Book 2 shortly
after Actium in 31 B.C.[24] As there is no mention of Maecenas in Satire
1,2 and as its matter and language are coarse it is regarded as one of the

earliest poems in Book 1, if not the earliest. Nor does Satire 1,4, which is later than Satire 1,2, to which it alludes, make any mention of Maecenas, to whom an appeal might be expected, if it had been possible, in this discussion of a satirist's social responsibilities.[25] Horace refers to friends to whom he reads his poems but does not name them (73f.). It may be concluded that he either had not yet become part of Maecenas' entourage or felt that it was not yet proper for him to make use of his new social position. On the other hand the absence of Maecenas' name and a dramatic date of 43–2 B.C. does not prove an early date for the short anecdotal Satire 1,7. The crude comedy of the incident during Brutus' praetorship in Asia may have been written as a lightweight later addition to the book of satires. Likewise there are no grounds for dating the tale of the witch (Sat. 1,8), except that it alludes indirectly to Maecenas. All other poems in the book mention Maecenas. In Satire 1,5 the Journey to Brundisium, based on an historical event which may with confidence be placed in the spring of 37 B.C., Horace is already one of the entourage.[26] In Satire 1,3 he shows himself to be on familiar terms with Maecenas (63–5); this suggests a date no earlier and probably later than 37 B.C. Satire 1,6, which includes Horace's description of his introduction to Maecenas and his acceptance, will have been written some time after the winter of 38–7 B.C. The attempts of the social climber (Sat. 1,9) to insinuate himself into the company of Maecenas are in some ways a comic counterpart to Horace's own decorous introduction to his patron (1,6), which will have been written earlier. The first line of Satire 1,1 mentions Maecenas. This introduction to the book is presumably relatively late but nothing further can be said. References to various friends in the tenth and last satire of the book suggest that c. 35 B.C. is the likeliest date for the composition of this poem and so for the release of the book as a whole.[27]

The second book of satires followed quickly. Datable references are few. In the satire in which he thanks Maecenas for the Sabine farm the talk of the day in Rome includes fears of an incursion of Dacian tribes (31 B.C.) and speculation about Octavian's plans for settling veterans after Actium (Sat. 2,6,51ff.). Maecenas' only other appearance in this book is in the story of the dinner party of Nasidienus (Sat. 2,8), at which he is present but does not speak. Agrippa's aedileship (33 B.C.) is an example of what wins public applause (Sat. 2,3,185).[28] Any mention of the Parthians in this book is imprecise. They were a particular concern to Rome from the time of Antonius' abortive campaign (36 B.C.) to Octavianus' adroit diplomacy in 30 B.C.[29] The description of

Octavianus in Satire 2,5 as the terror of the Parthians is a vague and pious hope, but by the time this poem was written he was already conqueror at Actium.[30] Horace's satires belong to the end of an era in the history of Rome.

During the years in which Horace was writing his satires he was also composing a book of epodes, poems of couplets in which a long verse and a short verse alternate. Many of the topics treated in these poems would seem, judging by the precedent of Lucilius, to belong to the Roman genre of satire, but Horace regarded his epodes as following the tradition of Archilochus. Much of the virulence that is associated with Lucilian satire was absorbed by Horace's epodes.

3. THE TITLE OF HORACE'S SATIRES

In the first book of satires Horace does not use the word *satura*, though it might be expected in the two poems in which he discusses his own contribution to the Lucilian tradition. In the fourth satire he refers to 'what I write today and what Lucilius wrote in former times' (56f.) and to 'this genre of writing' (*genus hoc scribendi*, 65). Personal diffidence rather than a search for elegance of expression in a poem that is sometimes brash may have forced Horace to avoid the technical term. He may also have wished to dissociate himself from some late republican and contemporary exponents of the genre and also from the more violent aspects of the *Lucilianus character*.[31] In the tenth satire, a poem of greater precision and elegance, he preferred for stylistic reasons to represent the poetic activities of friends and contemporaries by periphrasis rather than by a bald technical label. Just as he refers to the comedies of Fundanius by their contents and to the eclogues of Virgil by their qualities he merely describes the tradition to which his own works belong.[32] Here too a certain shyness may have prevented him from referring to his satires in impressive literary company by anything more than a disarming understatement. By contrast the statement at the beginning of the first satire of the second book is all the more striking:

> sunt quibus in satura videar nimis acer et ultra
> legem tendere opus
>
> (2,1,1f.)

(some people think I am too virulent in my satire and push my work beyond the relevant law).

He had to show clearly that he was referring to Book 1 of his satires and not to the epodes.[33] Furthermore, as he discusses poetry in this satire with an eminent jurisconsult, it is appropriate that Horace in his irony should use the exact technical term.[34] In the same book he uses the word in the plural as the obvious and natural way to denote examples of his writing in this genre (*Sat.* 2,6,17); here the tone is relaxed and unbelligerent.

One of Horace's favourite expressions for his satires is *sermones* (conversation pieces) and this is their title in the ancient commentators and the manuscript tradition. Lucilius too had used this word of his satires (see p. 40 above). The basic sense of this word of wide meaning is the activity of talking, or a piece of talk, or conversation; akin to this is the sense of the language of ordinary conversation and the level of style appropriate to it. It came also to be used of an elaborate piece of reported formal conversation, a literary dialogue, e.g. Cicero's dialogue between Laelius and his two sons-in-law *de Amicitia*, on friendship. In his *de Officiis*, written in 43 B.C. for his son, he deems that the Socratic philosophers were the supreme conversationalists and considers wit and a tone that is relaxed but appropriate to the subject to be the marks of good talk, with no single speaker monopolizing the conversation and a tactfully organized return to the main topic if there has been a digression.[35] Within a few years Horace was composing works that he was to refer to as *sermones*. In the Epistle to Florus written many years later he lists one branch of his writing as *Bioneis sermonibus et sale nigro* (malicious conversation pieces in the manner of Bion). These words must include his satires, as the epodes are mentioned separately. As usual in talking of himself and his work Horace uses self-depreciating irony. Black malice, as applied to his satires as distinct from the epodes, is a deliberately misleading description.[36] The reference to Bion the Borysthenite also should be taken at less than face value (see p. 92 below). Elsewhere he prefers the wide descriptive term *sermo* to the exact generic technical term even where there is ambiguity.[37]

Dialogue is the essential framework of the literary *sermo* but fundamental also to many forms of linguistic expression. Even where, as in some of Horace's earlier satires, the *sermo* is in the form of a monologue, the discourse gives the impression of being addressed to a listener who is thought of as immediately present. As the style of his satires matures true dialogue becomes an increasingly important element in their structure.

4. THE SATIRES OF BOOK 1

The theme of Satire 1 is *sit finis quaerendi* (92), 'let acquisitiveness be
kept within bounds'. The poem starts informally with a question
addressed to Maecenas asking why men praise other callings as more
comfortable and satisfying than their own; if offered a change by some
god they would be equally dissatisfied (1–22). Ambition to provide
adequately for old age and time of need is given as their reason for enduring burdensome occupations (23–38), but they cannot remain content with a reasonable sufficiency. The talk now moves to the main
argument: the folly and futility of uncontrolled greed (38–51). The
recipient of the discourse, no longer Maecenas but an imaginary
listener, makes objections, the most important of which is that there
can be no limit to acquisitiveness because a man is valued according to
his wealth (51–62). This objection is answered not by argument but by
an evasive expression of commiseration, which leads to the depiction of
the compulsive miser as a man obsessed by a neurotic terror of robbery
and fire and hated by his relations (63–93). The portrait culminates in
the cautionary tale of the rich miser who had a morbid fear of death
through destitution but was murdered by the axe of a freedwoman
(94–100). The doctrine of the ethical mean is stated as a positive moral
position (101–7), and then the opening theme of discontent is suddenly
recalled with a jolt so unconcealed as to suggest parody of an oratorical
preacher: I return to the point from which I departed (108).[38] In the
concluding lines discontent is discussed from a slightly different angle.
Jealous of the success and wealth of others, in the fever of competition
men are heedless of those who fall behind and so they rarely depart
from life with the contentment of the well-filled guest.

It is sometimes stated that the two themes of discontent with one's lot
in life and avarice are distinct and do not coalesce into a unified whole.
But the central topic of avarice is developed discursively as the underlying cause of discontent.[39] In any case the rules of the conversation,
the *sermo*, and the dialogue do not demand the relentless pursuit of a
single argument.

Blaming one's lot in life (μεμψιμοιρία) and manifestations of avarice
were commonplaces of Hellenistic moralizing and would have been so
recognized by Horace's audience.[40] But his satire is more than an
elegant variation on traditional topics. He formulates with neat un-
obtrusiveness his method of work as a moralizing satirist, to speak the
truth with a laugh (23–7), in what is a civilized rendering of τὸ

σπουδογέλοιον, a Greek term for the combination of instruction with entertainment. He preaches tactfully on the search for happiness and on avarice to men, some of whom remembered the career of the un-scrupulous plutocrat Crassus and the less culpable but sometimes un-edifying acquisitiveness of men like Cicero. All will have witnessed dispossession from the land and the sudden rise of upstarts to riches through proscription.

But Horace is discreet. No contentious modern issues are mentioned explicitly.[41] Though Horace's treatment is remote and lacking in modern allusions, his readers will have applied the moral to their own times. In a conversation piece addressed to Maecenas Horace cannot pontificate like an itinerant preacher, and so he tempers moral earnestness with sly parody of the gambits of the sermon. He also uses the concrete illustrations and the comic anecdotes that belong traditionally to Lucilian satire.

Satire 2 starts with a flourish:

> *Ambubaiarum collegia, pharmacopolae,*
> *mendici, mimae, balatrones, hoc genus omne*
> *maestum ac sollicitum est cantoris morte Tigelli.*
> *quippe benignus erat.*
>
> (1–4)

(The corporation of cabaret girls, the pedlars of drugs, the beggars, the tarts from revues, the buffoons, the whole of that crew are sad and upset at the death of the vocalist Tigellius, for he was, they say, so open-handed.)

But the example of the opposite trait, the man who is so afraid of being labelled 'spendthrift' that he refuses to help a destitute friend, is by con-trast a pallid generalization. Other examples follow to illustrate the principle that in avoiding one vice (or the reputation for it) men run into its opposite (4–24). Horace's theme in this satire is sex. The main argument would appear to be the need to keep to a mean, avoiding both the perils of adultery and the degradation of the whore-house (28–32). As the man engaged in adultery with a married woman rarely obtains pleasure for fear of the punishments that follow detection (33–46), the use of a freedwoman is the recommended alternative (47f.). Though the poet turns aside to condemn the folly of those who lavish money on these women of lower status (47–62), they are the mean in his ethical scheme. But he does not however explore the ex-treme of the prostitute in the brothel, but continues with objections on aesthetic grounds to pursuing the married woman. She is surrounded by a retinue and over-dressed, so that it is impossible to inspect her beforehand, whereas the freedwoman is immediately available for viewing (63–103). No complications caused by love with its elusive passion or playful verse[42] should arise over what is no more than the satisfaction of a physical appetite; for an immediate physical need a household slave will suffice (103–18). The final description of the discovery of the adulterous lovers has the rumbustious verve of a bedroom farce (127–34).

The satire is memorable for vigorous details of incidents and of phrase but its argument is somewhat muddled and the structure in consequence lopsided. Its ethics are base, but it is at least free from hypocrisy.

Satire 3, like the previous poem, begins with Tigellius, who typifies the man inconsistent to the point of eccentricity: he would either run like one pursued or walk as if in solemn procession; keep ten slaves or a hundred; at one moment his talk would be kings and tetrarchs, at the next the joys of the humble life; thrifty and prodigal by turns, he would sleep through the day and stay awake all night (1–19). These details are an informal preamble to a discussion of the propriety of judging the actions of friends. The man who disparages others cannot risk the charge of being complacent about himself (19–28). The satirist is not mentioned explicitly, but his vulnerability will not have been overlooked. Stringent condemnation of another's faults, it is argued, must be balanced by forbearance towards the habits of a friend (29–54). With neat disingenuousness Horace uses himself as an example of the somewhat unsophisticated character (*simplicior*) who might, when interrupting Maecenas' reading or solitude with an untimely remark, be dismissed as tiresome and lacking in tactful good behaviour (63–6).[43] If a man is lenient towards a friend's shortcomings, he in turn will be judged tolerantly (67–75). Friendship apart, trivial offences merit a light penalty, for not all sins are of equal gravity (76–98). This leads into a quasi-didactic section that would have been immediately recognized as a condensed summary of aspects of Lucretius' account of human evolution and the social contract in Book 5 of *de Rerum Natura*. Man abandoned primitive violence, developed language, built towns and made laws against brigandage and adultery. Right was developed through fear of wrong (111), not through nature, which is indifferent to morality, or through pure logical argumentation, which cannot distinguish between breaking off cabbage leaves and purloining sacred images (99–117).[44] The slighting of nature and reason as fundamental guides to right and wrong is an attack on the uncompromising ethics of the Stoa, and the rest of the satire is directed against Stoics, for whom all sins were equally heinous.

This conversation piece has two main topics: tolerant forbearance of the faults of friends, and more generally the need to distinguish between degrees of moral culpability. The viewpoint is Epicurean and the influence of Lucretius predominant.[45] The tone of the poem is raised in the adaptation of Lucretius' anthropology, but the satirist lowers the didactic level abruptly by inserting an obscene anatomical term in order to designate female immorality.[46] The introductory sketch of Tigellius may be no more than a colourful prelude, but a contrast may have been intended between the opening portrait of the inconsistent man and the concluding description of the intolerably inflexible Stoic.

Satire 4 is the first of three satires in which Horace discusses literary problems, particularly his attitude towards Lucilius and the status of his own *sermones*. He asserts that the masters of Old Comedy denounced wrongdoers with great outspokenness and that Lucilius, apart from differences of metre, was completely dependent on them. At this stage he neither defends Lucilius' freedom of speech nor admits his own connection with him, but immediately turns aside to criticize the hasty and uncouth prolixity of his verse (1–13). Horace now describes himself as a small scale writer with no flair for the prolific[47] who declines public recitation; his genre (*genus*) is unpopular with the guilty (13–38). In the first stage of his defence he takes up the topic of literary status and as one who writes things rather close to spoken language (*sermoni propiora*, 42) excludes himself from the category of 'poet'. Some have doubted, he adds, whether comedy is poetry (*poema*) at all, as it differs from conversation only in its metrical form,[48] even though it can become impassioned enough to express the righteous indignation of an angry father. Horace has thus shifted his ground to the New Comedy of Terence. But unlike the epic diction of Ennius, the language of comedy like that of Lucilius and of Horace does not show the essential style of the true poet. Having used comedy as a stylistic criterion Horace is now at last able to admit that he writes in the tradition of Lucilius and shelves further discussion of comedy in this satire (38–63).

In the second part of his apologia Horace turns to the consorious aspect of his satire. As he is a poet for a coterie who recites reluctantly, he should not be feared as a public informer. His defence against the charge of malice is that he is a restrained and trustworthy friend and quite unlike the loudmouthed dinner party buffoon who bespatters all present with his scurrility. Horace offers as an excuse for naming wrongdoers the procedure of his father, who pointed to conspicuous sinners and the opprobrium associated with them. Horace's readers were no doubt intended to recall the parallel of the father in Terence who moralized by citing examples, but are not thereby debarred from taking the autobiographical reminiscences as factual.[49] Once again the satirist ends with the unrepentant frivolity that writing poetry is one of the moderate vices still left to him.

Satire 4 is a closely argued and yet overtly discursive conversation piece. Though much of its exploratory discussion will be amplified and elucidated in the tenth satire it should be read and assessed as a poem in its own right.[50]

Satire 5 is an account of a journey from Rome to Brindisi in the spring of 37 B.C., in which Horace accompanied Maecenas and other diplomats who were on their way south for critical negotiations with Marcus Antonius. Also in the company were Virgil and other literary men.

Horace set off from Rome together with a Greek rhetorician, travelling at a leisurely pace along the Appian Way to Forum Appii, a town on the Pomptine marshes, where he suffered from dysentery caused by the notoriously impure water. The next stage was a voyage by night along a canal. The account begins with a deceptively poetical description of the night sky:

>   *iam nox inducere terris*
> *umbras et caelo diffundere signa parabat:*
> *tum pueri nautis, pueris convicia nautae*
> *ingerere: 'huc adpelle'; 'trecentos inseris'; 'ohe,*
> *iam satis est.' dum aes exigitur, dum mula ligatur,*
> *tota abit hora. mali culices ranaeque palustres*
> *avertunt somnos; absentem cantat amicam*
> *multa prolutus vappa nauta atque viator*
> *certatim; tandem fessus dormire viator*
> *incipit ac missae pastum retinacula mulae*
> *nauta piger saxo religat stertitque supinus.*
> *iamque dies aderat, nil cum procedere lintrem*
> *sentimus, donec cerebrosus prosilit unus*
> *ac mulae nautaeque caput lumbosque saligno*
> *fuste dolat: quarta vix demum exponimur hora.*

ora manusque tua lavimus, Feronia, lympha.
milia tum pransi tria repimus atque subimus
inpositum saxis late candentibus Anxur.

(*Sat.* 1,5,9–26)

(And now night was about to draw darkness about the earth and spread the con-
stellations over the sky. Then slaves and boatmen start a slanging match: 'Bring
her in here.' 'You're squashing hundreds in.' 'Whoa! No more!' While the fare
is being demanded and the mule harnessed a whole hour goes by. Vicious
mosquitoes and the frogs of the marshes keep sleep away. A boatman drunk on a
bucketful of bad wine serenades his girl who is far away and the traveller starts
up in rivalry. In the end the tired traveller drops off to sleep and the boatman
puts the mule to graze tethering it to a stone and snores flat on his back. It is
already daybreak when we realize that the boat is not making any progress. In
the end a fiery-tempered passenger leaps out and belabours the head and back of
both mule and boatman with a cudgel of willow. It is as late as ten when we
land and wash hands and face in the sacred water of Feronia. After breakfast
we crawl for three miles and make our way uphill to Anxur that stands on cliffs
that are brilliant white from afar.)

Here they were to join Maecenas and his entourage, and two days later
the highest point of excited anticipation for Horace came with the
arrival of Virgil and his two closest literary associates. Shortly after, in
order to vary the pace of the narrative, he invokes the Muse in a proem
of parody as introduction to a verbal contest between two clowns, one
an Oscan and the other a man freed from slavery by Maecenas. Their
clod-hopping raillery, though primitive and not very clever, gave un-
qualified mirth to the company at dinner (51–70).[51] Their journey continued through Beneventum across towards the Adriatic, all places of
call being mentioned by name except one that could not be accommodated to the hexameter.[52] They then travelled south by Bari and
Egnatia. Here a local miraculous happening occasioned Epicurean sentiments on the gods' failure to intervene in human affairs. An effect of
burlesque is suggested by the use of the weighty language of Lucretius
to crack the nut of a minor superstition. Poem and journey end
abruptly in the next line.

The satire is in the first place a factual report of a real journey of
approximately fifteen days as it actually happened.[53] As a traveller
Horace is amused by people met incidentally on the way, the pretentious local official at Fundi (33) and the host at Beneventum whose excess of zeal in preparing supper nearly set both the meal and the house
on fire (71). He also records minor discomforts and mishaps, bad water,
a smoking fire, muddy roads and the frustration that followed the
failure of a girl to keep her assignation.[54] The satire is also to some

extent an imitation of Lucilius' journey to Sicily. Horace's general outline is similar, and some points of resemblance are immediately obvious, such as a reference to muddy roads and to some sort of contest.
But how far Horace blended literary model with his account of real
events must remain an open question.[55] His poem is not a romantic tale
of the joys of wandering nor is it a eulogy of the landscape of central
and southern Italy. Nostalgia at the sight of the hills of his birthplace is
present only in the use of the local name for the Sirocco (77ff.). Even
the celebrated description of Anxur on top of its brilliant limestone
cliffs may contain a hint of discomfort for the traveller with badly
irritated eyes.[56] Horace let himself appear as an accepted member of the
circle of Maecenas but tacitly mocked those who hoped for important
political revelations.[57] Maecenas goes to play a ball game and Virgil
goes for a siesta (48). As reported by the satirist the top men in politics
and literature gathered not as participants in edifying dialogue on
serious topics but as spectators at the sport of buffoons.

In Satire 6 Horace defends himself not as a writer but as a man in
Roman society, the son of a freedman, who though a friend of
Maecenas was content to lead a self-contained unpolitical life.
Maecenas for all his noble Etruscan lineage holds that a man's parentage does not matter provided he is free-born. Rightly so, Horace
argues, for in the past many lacked distinguished ancestors yet rose to
high office, while some aristocrats were despised even by the people
(1–18). The initial position in this poem could have been argued by a
humbly-born aspirant to public office. The disclaimer is made when
Horace states that a strict censor would have demoted him justifiably as
one not content with his own skin (19–22).[58] He then ridicules with
calculated malice the ambitious ventures of those on the fringe of
eligibility, and reproduces some of the vicious revilings with which he
as the son of an ex-slave is familiar (23–44). He then reverts to his own
career as the son of a freedman.[59] The jangling repetition of the words
libertino patre natum at the end of two successive lines (45f.) expresses the
hurtful force of the gibe.[60] After distinguishing between the jealousy
that may once have been justified towards the tribune in command of a
legion and the envy unfairly felt for the friend of Maecenas chosen
solely for his merits, he relates with some disingenuousness his bashful
first meeting when interviewed by a terse Maecenas and the invitation
some months later to join the circle (45–62). Horace's discreet self-
congratulation on a character marred only by minor faults leads to a
grateful eulogy of his father, who gave him the best education that

Rome could provide, knowing, so Horace says, that his son would, if necessary, return to a humble occupation. He is happy to have been born of unexalted parentage so that he can avoid the quest for high office for which he has neither desire nor aptitude. The public figure is the captive of convention. Horace may journey far by mule, but the praetor who travels to Tibur with five slaves carrying a commode and wine basket is dubbed mean.[61] The poet describes with a naturalistic detail unusual in Roman poetry his daily routine. He visits the market to inquire about the price of vegetables or to the forum in the evening when it is taken over by crooks and charlatans. A simple evening meal of vegetables is served by three slaves on homely ware. Rising late he reads or writes just as he pleases, wanders out for a walk or to bathe, returning idly to a light lunch. Thus he is more contented than those with political ambition (62–131).

The poem is primarily an explicit statement of the poet's present social position and his denial of public ambition. There is a tone of bitterness in his allusions to the sneers at his humble origin. His resentment occasioned his vengeful swipes at untalented careerists. While expressing due gratitude to his patron he tactfully discourages any encroachment on his tranquillity. Horace's description of his daily routine is plausible but a little too innocent to be accepted with any reservation.[62] He probably exaggerates the trivial simplicity of his life out of a wish to make a telling contrast with the harassed lives of those who cultivate the powerful and flaunt an uncomfortable grandeur. Perhaps also the description of his meagre service and cheap ware was intended to tease the sensibilities of ambitious snobs, particularly those recently advanced. Horace's view of the forum as a place for entertainers in the evening is a mockingly distorted image of the forum as a daytime centre of public business. The total intention of a poem that combines the intensely personal with the traditional moralizing topic of vain ambition is difficult to assess. The moral theme justifies Horace's past career and his present social inactivity and is also intended to have some general application wider than his own self-justification.

In Satire 7, a poem of a mere thirty-five lines, Horace narrates with flourishes of epic burlesque a single and trivial anecdote. While Brutus was praetor in charge of the province of Asia there was a legal dispute between an Italian, Rutilius Rex of Praeneste, a member of his retinue and a half-Greek called Persius, a rich trader from Clazomenae. Persius after fulsome oriental praise of Brutus attacks his opponent with torrents of Asianic oratory to which Rutilius replies with the acid abuse that belongs to the Italian countryside, whereupon, in a punning climax, Persius appeals to Brutus as a man with a family tradition of tyrant-slaying to murder this King (*Rex*).

This poem is somewhat puzzling. The parody of the epic situation of the individual combat of such heroes as Hector and Achilles seems cumbersome and banal. It is perhaps presumptuous to pass judgement on qualities of taste in the humour of an ancient poem. Though puns on the names of persons were rife at the time,[63] an anecdote of which the climax was a flippant reference to the assassination of Julius Caesar would seem, whatever its date of publication, to be lacking in civilized decorum.[64] The Lucilian tradition as we know it has been discerned not in the form of the poem but in incidental references to named individuals.[65] It is unnecessary to postulate subtle references to conflicting Greek and Roman literary attitudes. To consider this satire an inept make-weight to fill up the book would not be uncharitable.[66]

Satire 8 is a Priapean poem of fifty lines in which a witches' nocturnal orgy ends in farcical disarray. Priapus, who narrates the happenings, explains that he was once a useless piece of fig-wood but is now a god of formidable phallic equipment, at present a scarecrow to frighten thieves and birds away from a pleasure garden newly laid out on the Esquiline. Formerly the site had been a wretched paupers' cemetery, visited by criminals, beasts of prey and, worst of all, necromancers, whom Priapus, god though he was, could not prevent from gathering bones and noxious plants by moonlight. One night the witch Canidia and her companion Sagana started to perform hideous rites, calling on Hecate and other spirits. Serpents and dogs of the underworld roamed and the dead spoke. But the god, though compelled to watch these horrors, gained his revenge. For the wood of his buttocks split with an explosion, as he broke wind.[67] The witches fled in terror. Canidia's teeth fell out, Sagana dropped her wig and all the magical kit was scattered, a merry sight to behold.

This short piece of entertainment without uplift is very successful and is also truly Augustan in its skilful use of Hellenistic material in a new way. The opening of the poem suggests a dedicatory epigram, in which an object contrasts its former self with its present consecrated state, and in particular the kind of Priapean epigram in which Priapus as a protector of the garden admonishes and threatens would-be thieves, but Horace plays with the motif. Priapus for all his godhead is unable to ward off the horrors of the night except by a physical mishap. There is also a quasi-aetiological element. According to Porphyrio (on 7) the gloomy old cemetery had recently been transformed into a spacious park through the initiative of Maecenas. The poem thus explains Priapus' continuing presence and also pays implicit tribute to the poet's patron.[68] It may be argued that the poem belongs to the Lucilian tradition through the vilification of the hags. Canidia however was also the subject of two epodes and the Priapic theme was associated with elegiacs. The reason for the choice of a particular verse-form by an Augustan poet is sometimes difficult to determine. But the contents of the seventh, eighth and also the ninth satires of this book illustrate the tradition of satire as a miscellany.

Satire 9 is a narrative of Horace's encounter in the street with a man who appears at first to be no more than a tiresome pest but is later revealed as a scheming social climber.[69]

Apart from a few incidental items of narrative such as the mention of places in Rome and brief comments on the poet's rising exasperation and anger the action of the piece takes place through dialogue.[70] A contrast is implied between civilized conduct and the impudent behaviour of one who thrusts where unwelcome and understands social advancement only in terms of opportunism and corruption. The character is not described but develops itself in the course of the dialogue. There are subtle details. Horace's pest suffers from an inability to appreciate a shaft of irony (26–8). He is humourless also in his use of the evangelical commonplace (59f.). It is likely that he was a historical person, but to identify him, even if possible, would not be of consequence for the interpretation of the poem, for in the lines of Horace he exists as a masterly literary portrait. The narrative contains an important element of epic parody in the prophecy, some of the imagery, the poet as military aggressor (42f.) and the final escape in which the poet is rescued as a Homeric warrior saved by the intervention of a god.[71] But the imagery of epic warfare is not all-pervasive. Horace sees himself also as a sulky overladen donkey (20) and a sacrificial victim (73f.). The poem also has a personal relevance. Possibly to disarm envy Horace wishes to display his own modest but secure position in the urbane circle of Maecenas.

In Satire 10 Horace reverts to the subject of Satire 4. He discusses further his attitude to Lucilius and the appropriate style for a satirist. In the opening lines he repeats his earlier judgement of Lucilius (1–5). To make the audience guffaw by itself is not enough. Economy of style also is necessary and a variation of tone that moves from the severe to the gay, sometimes enhancing the stylistic level so as to approach that

of oratory or poetry and sometimes using the calculated restraint that is
a characteristic of the man of civilized humour.[72] Serious matter is
often resolved by mockery rather than by vituperation, as is shown by
the example of Old Comedy, a species of literature unread by the
queer types who represent some fashionable trends (5–19). When
Lucilius' mixture of Greek and Latin words is praised as a great
achievement, Horace replies with a scornful vocative, *o seri studiorum*
(you late learners, 21), itself a demonstration of correct Latin procedure
in rendering a Greek term,[73] and reduces his opponent's notion to the
absurd hypothesis that bilingual diction is even to be permitted in foren-
sic oratory (20–30). He now discusses his own modest writing which,
he says, is not aimed at public acclaim. Each of the main kinds of
poetry has a pre-eminent contemporary exponent, e.g. Varius as epic
poet and Virgil as master of the pastoral.[74] As Lucilius' genre has been
attempted ineffectually in recent times it is fitting that Horace should
try to do better (36–49). Nevertheless he reiterates and defends his
criticism of the undisciplined prolixity of Lucilius. As a writer in a
genre without Greek precedent[75] his achievement was remarkable by
the standards of early republican poetry, but had he lived in Horace's
times he would have made many excisions and corrections (50–71). A
writer must calculate his words with punctilious care if his aim is to
produce work of enduring quality and to win the plaudits of a discriminating minority. Such is Horace's ambition. The list of those
whom he wishes to please is long and impressive; it includes Maecenas,
Messalla, an aristocratic patron, and also Octavius, a man of letters. If
he has their approbation he can disregard the scorn of nonentities, one
of whom is referred to as a bed-bug and others condemned to wail
among their female pupils (76–91).

It is clear from the truculent opening of the poem that Horace's
criticisms of Lucilius had been resented. His opponents almost certainly
included the redoubtable Valerius Cato, editor of Lucilius and arbiter of
literary fashion.[76] But there were also minor figures, some mentioned
by name, who may have combined dislike of Horace's views and
writings with jealousy of his social success and perhaps even contempt
for his turncoat politics. Two poets of the preceding generation,
Catullus and Calvus, both men of republican sentiments, were deeply
committed to Alexandrian elegance. But Horace refers to their
advocates with disdain.[77] Indeed much of the rivalries and jealousies of
the literary cliques in the years after Philippi must remain a matter for
conjecture.

The problem of the satirist's attack on named individuals is alluded to very briefly in this poem (3–4). Old Comedy is praised not as a precedent for vituperation but for its exemplary use of wide stylistic resources. Such a view stems from convenient Alexandrian theory about Attic comedy; it does not necessarily presuppose a reading public for it in Rome at the end of the republic.[78] Horace is concerned with the appropriate style for a satirist in his own times. The interlocutor's defence of Lucilius' mixture of Greek and Roman words is easily rebutted. Lucilius' use of Greek words and of raw Greek forms unaccommodated to Latin terminations was perhaps his most vulnerable practice. Yet Horace had to declare his allegiance to the Lucilian tradition in order to be accepted as his successor. He lists as the minority audience he desires fourteen of the top names in Rome, poets and impressarios. Horace presents the list with disarming modesty (84) and also with great shrewdness. Offence at what might have been construed as hunting after the great is dispelled by a comparison between the poet, who is content with a small audience, and Arbuscula, the actress, who accepted with equanimity being whistled off the stage, as she was the kept woman of a Roman knight. There are other felicitous details such as the account of his dream, which is a telling parody of the bard's dream as related by Callimachus and Ennius.[79] Unlike the pugnacious fourth satire the poem is relaxed and makes a fitting conclusion to the book.

In publishing a book of ten poems Horace followed the example of Virgil's eclogues, but it would have been inappropriate for the writer of an informal *libellus* to assemble his conversation pieces with the contrived artifice that was a mark of some of the major books of Augustan poetry.[80] Nevertheless the arrangement is not haphazard. The book seems to divide into two parts, Satires 1–5 and 6–10. Both begin with an apparently casual address to Maecenas and both end with a poem in which Maecenas is important as personal friend or patron. But there is no detailed symmetry. Moralizing and argument predominate in the first half and entertainment in the second.[81]

5. THE SATIRES OF BOOK 2

Satire 2,1 is a dialogue between Horace and the famous jurist Trebatius Testa on some of the problems of the satirist.[82] As some have criticized his satire as too harsh and exceeding the prescribed law (*nimis acer et ultra legem*) while others regard it as anaemic and lacking in substance,

Horace seeks the advice of his learned friend (1–5). To the reply 'Don't write' Horace insists that his urge to write is compulsive, and so his counsellor suggests that rather than slander wastrels or clowns he should celebrate the martial deeds of Octavianus. But Horace is wary of attempting to eulogize Octavianus prematurely; in the meantime he will write in the manner of Lucilius, who entrusted the secrets of his life to his books as if to confidants. As a man from Venusia, a warlike town in the south, he follows the tradition of Lucilius but will use his *stilus* (writing implement or dagger) merely as a means of self-defence. Every creature uses its own weapon to frighten what it fears, so Horace will continue to write; and in answer to Trebatius' warning against the displeasure of the powerful he appeals to the example of Lucilius, who won the approval of Scipio and Laelius by unmasking the hidden vices of such contemporaries as Metellus and Lupus. Though inferior in rank and talent to Lucilius he too has powerful protectors. While agreeing, Trebatius none the less warns of the danger of legal proceedings against *mala carmina* (the language of the Twelve Tables, condemning evil incantations and defamatory words).[83] But Horace assumes that the expression refers to bad verse. He asks about the judgement on good verses commended by Octavianus or on verses hurled at a miscreant by a writer of integrity. Trebatius concedes that Horace will escape free.

The first satire resumes topics of the literary satires of Book 1, but its approach is fundamentally different. In place of the poet's reasoned exposition of arguments there is a swift dialogue in which issues are evaded by clever shifts of position and ambiguities of language. Defamation is unlikely to have been a serious problem for Horace. To go through the imaginary process of taking the best possible legal advice is the joke of a man who knows that he is unassailable. Horace was a friend of the political establishment not least because he was prudent in refraining from causing dissension in society by an excessive display of literary malice. The first satire of the book was probably the last to be completed. For all his evasiveness on satirizing by name Horace knows that, as he was about to forsake the *Lucilianus character*, there were to be no more assaults even on unimportant targets. Nor should Horace's judgements on Lucilius in this poem be taken out of context. His portrait of Lucilius as the poet of self-revelation was probably based on a wider-ranging and more balanced assessment than he was able to allow himself in Book 1. The great predecessor is used as a convenient many-sided example, the poet of reflection, the poet who praised great contemporaries or the poet who lampooned with the approval of his friends. Horace's attitude to Lucilius is more relaxed in this poem, not so much because he has learned more about him but because he discusses favourable aspects such as are appropriate for his argument. Stylistic matters receive a passing mention in the opening lines. The poem is consistently distinguished in its expression down to the personification of the last line in which the legal tablets are convulsed with laughter, but the reader should not be deluded by the brilliance of the artistry into regarding a fundamentally frivolous piece as a major contribution to Horace's poetics.[84]

Satire 2,2 is a homily on frugality said to have been spoken by Ofellus, a smallholder known to the poet since childhood, who now works as a tenant on the farm that was once his own. Much of the homily, though put into the mouth of a south Italian peasant, is devoted to the stock sumptuary prescriptions of urban Rome. Some foolish fashions are capably ridiculed, but Ofellus' dogged exhortation to austerity is protracted and some sentiments such as the dragging down of the soul to earthy dross and the proper use of money would have been better suited to a Greek moralist.[85] It would have been inappropriate for Horace in his own person or through the medium of Ofellus to denounce Umbrenus the landlord directly. The negative portrayal of a man who does not appear is telling. Ofellus reflects that one day Umbrenus will lose the farm through his villainy, his ignorance of the law, or the intervention of an heir who will outlive him. The landlord is meant to be seen as a boorish scoundrel. Horace himself knew the grim fact of dispossession. Literary expertise communicates indirectly something of the experience that found moving expression in Virgil's eclogues.

Satire 2,3 is a dialogue between Horace and the bankrupt dealer Damasippus, who reports a homily by the Stoic Stertinius on the topic of universal madness. After the failure of his business Damasippus was saved from suicide by the arguments of Stertinius, who convinced him that he was no madder than anyone else. This is the immediate homily for Damasippus' crisis. Stertinius now makes a formal harangue on madness in general. Avarice, the cardinal vice, receives attention first. The parsimonious Staberius ordered his heirs to engrave on his tomb the amount of his estate; Aristippus threw away gold in the desert to speed the journey. To hoard is madness; but the miser is not commonly accounted a lunatic, because the majority suffer from the same disease. Men who protest they can live on little commit crime in order to get more. The rich miser Opimius on the point of starvation is prescribed rice pudding as emergency nourishment, but is dismayed at the cost of the medicine (82–157). Next, ambition: Servius Oppidius on his deathbed urged his sons not to squander the family resources in the quest for political office. The vice is exemplified at length in a dialogue between Agamemnon and a critic who accuses him of madness on the grounds that he had sacrificed his daughter Iphigenia for the sake of his grandiose ambitions (158–223). Next the comprehensive vice of extravagance: one wastrel dissipated his inheritance in frivolous luxury and irresponsible largesse; another dissolved a pearl in vinegar just in order to make the drink expensive. Then love: the grown man who plays such childish games as harnessing mice to a truck is no more insane than the frustrated lover, whose absurd antics are displayed by a moral paradigm that is a close adaptation of a scene from Terence's *Eunuchus* (224–80).[86] Lastly the vice of superstition, i.e. fear of the gods, and the insane ritual and promises which it involves (281–95). In the final exchanges, as Horace with complacent irony challenges Damasippus to find in him any marks of insanity, Damasippus applies the homily to Horace, accusing him of various kinds of madness: he extends his buildings, writes bits of peotry (*poemata*), has a bad temper, lives beyond his resources and has innumerable love affairs. As a smaller to a greater madman Horace pleads for mercy (296–326).

The poem is for the most part well-constructed. The humorous exchanges between Damasippus and Horace at the beginning and the end balance each other. The sermon of Stertinius is carefully arranged except that superstition, as it gives less scope for righteous indignation, is treated with disproportionate brevity. But the poem is inordinately long, being more than twice the length of any other of Horace's satires. The sermon of Stertinius is something of a puzzle; in itself it is substantially longer than any poem in either book. Its main thesis that all except the Stoic wise men are mad is in Horace's view elsewhere absurd. But there is no overt parody in the sermon. Some of the examples which are expanded into anecdotal form would be effective outside the framework of a Stoic's popular moralizing. It is possible to see mocking persiflage in the technique of the preacher's harangue, the mythological dialogue and the processed moralizing of the comedy scene, both devices associated with the popular sermon, and the heartfelt *tandem* (at last) in the final line suggests mockery as well as relief.

While the role of Stertinius is problematical that of Catius in the next poem, Satire 2,4, is disreputable. The satire starts with the rapid introductory gambits of a Platonic dialogue, in which the narrator encounters an acquaintance in the street who relates the interesting teaching or discussion that he has heard. Catius is in haste to write down a discourse that will surpass the teaching of Socrates or Plato (1–10). Though he cannot reveal the name of this great master, he repeats his precepts on the topic of what makes a good dinner party. He begins with the introductory egg that should be oval not round, discusses varieties of shell-fish, wines, sauces and kinds of dessert, and ends with injunctions to ensure that lavish fare is accompanied by appropriate cleanliness of service (11–87). With Socratic irony Horace beseeches Catius to lead him into the company of the great man in order to experience not merely his teaching but also his charisma so that he too may drink deep of the precepts of the life of bliss (88–95).

To assess the tone and intention of this work is unusually difficult. The lecture on good food is directed not only at the seeker after the recherché. Cheap shell-fish are recommended as a remedy for constipation (27ff.). Some of the precepts are no more than common sense, e.g. do not lavish all the care on a single item (48ff.); but the suggestion that the stomach heated by wine is best satisfied by any dish brought from a dirty cook-shop (59–62) hardly belongs to a guide on the dinner party *comme il faut*. The overall impression of the lecture is of a rag-bag of miscellaneous and not particularly consistent precepts, ranging from the commonplace to the grotesquely comic. It is not uniformly absurd and belongs to a tradition of writing on food and dinner parties that includes Ennius' *Hedyphagetica* and Varro's Menippean *nescis quid vesper serus vehat*. But Horace places it in the setting used in philosophical dialogue and aspirations to the good life of philosophy.[87] Catius according to an ancient scholiast was an Epicurean.[88] If so, perhaps Horace derided the art of the dinner party as a debased version of Epicureanism.

Satire 2,5 is a dialogue in the underworld between Odysseus/Ulixes and Teiresias. The Homeric Odysseus had inquired of the seer what he would find on returning home to Ithaca. The modern Odysseus asks how he is to repair his plundered fortunes in a Rome in which birth and merit are worthless unless accompanied by wealth (1–8). Teiresias advises him to hunt for legacies. The advice on strategy and tactics is detailed. Offer yourself obsequiously as advocate to whichever party is childless (the justice of the case is irrelevant) or, in order to avoid a dangerously obvious approach, pay court to a family where the heir is delicate. Ally yourself with the dishonest woman or freedman who looks after an aged imbecile and so win their commendation. Above all ingratiate yourself with your quarry directly:

> 'scribet mala carmina vecors:
> laudato. scortator erit: cave te roget; ultro
> Penelopam facilis potiori trade.' 'putasne
> perduci poterit tam frugi tamque pudica,
> quam nequiere proci recto depellere cursu?'
> 'venit enim magnum donandi parca iuventus
> nec tantum veneris quantum studiosa culinae.
> sic tibi Penelope frugi est; quae si semel uno
> de sene gustarit tecum partita lucellum,
> ut canis a corio numquam absterrebitur uncto.'

[*Sat.* 2,5,74–83)

('If in his folly he writes bad verses, praise them. If he is a womanizer, don't wait for him to put a proposition. Take the initiative and readily offer Penelope to a man with more power.' 'Do you think a woman of such self-control and so chaste can be seduced, for the suitors could not turn her aside from her right course?' 'Yes, because young men came who were stingy about big presents and less interested in sex than the cooking. On those terms your Penelope is virtuous. But if she has once tasted the profits of one old man and shared it with you, she will never be scared off again any more than a dog from a greasy hide.')[89]

Measure with care the urgency of your attentions. A woman of Thebes in her will once compelled her heir to carry her greasy corpse on his bare shoulders on the chance that after her death she might slip from his grasp. Be reticent or like the garrulous slave of comedy, whichever is appropriate (84–98). Even when you are in possession of a quarter share, win praise for your magnanimity, particularly if an elderly co-heir has a promising cough. Teiresias then returns to the shades (99–110).

Horace adapts the literary convention of Hellenistic sillographers, who in order to mock and moralize parodied Homeric scenes and dislocated Homeric verses. Timon of Phlius made somewhat unimaginative attacks on other philosophers in a dialogue set in the underworld.[90] Horace uses the Hellenistic form of Homeric parody to expose the corrupting Roman practice of hunting for legacies particularly from the childless. The time is specifically portrayed as contemporary and the milieu is that of Roman institutions and cults. There is another possible aspect of parody. Part of Horace's intention may be that in a social crisis even Odysseus, to Stoics and Cynics the acme of resolute self-restraint, has his price. The poem explores with a ruthless and obsessive intensity the vice of legacy hunting, which it accepts with ironical approbation. It rests on the postulated axiom that human nature is immeasurably base. The tone is unvaried; it is pungent and cynical but detached and unrhetorical with a colloquial level of language. The poem has found disfavour with some scholars of the nineteenth and twentieth centuries, who have wrongly dismissed it as Juvenalian in spirit.[91] Read as a *tour de force* based on an extreme thesis it may be assessed as a unique and masterly satire; it should not be discounted because it appears unrepresentative of Horace's temperament and works.

In Satire 2,6 Horace contrasts the peaceful life on his newly acquired farm, for which he offers fitting thanks, with that of his daily official round in Rome and illustrates the two by the fable of the town and the country mouse. The poem begins with a description of the farm that was just what he had prayed for, compact, with spring water nearby and a piece of woodland. Horace then describes a day in Rome with its numerous demands and worries. This is followed by a contrasting picture of country life, in which food is simpler, the tempo of living slower and friendships more relaxed. The poem ends with a fable of two mice. A frugal country mouse in his woodland hole entertained a friend from the town. Reclining on straw he offered him what delicacies he could find. But the town mouse after a few disdainful nibbles persuaded his companion to forsake his primitive life for the glamour of the city. Entering a sumptuous house at night, they settled themselves on purple couches and were feasting on the remnants of a banquet, when suddenly there was an alarm. Doors banged and great hounds bayed. The country mouse hurriedly departed, saying that for the future he would be content in his hole with simple food; he would at least be free from danger (79–117).

The structure of this *sermo* is complex and the tone varied. The farm is described factually at the beginning and later idealistically as seen from Rome as a safe haven of escape from city frivolity and a place where problems in ethics are discussed by countrymen. The opening prayer to Mercury, though not an act of religious devotion, uses the accepted literary framework of Greek and Roman prayer formulae as a serious means of expressing thanks. By contrast the address to Janus is an ornate stylistic flourish with a measure of parody to lower the tone as a prelude to the not too serious description of the poet's harassing stay in Rome, where the feverish bustle is depicted realistically by snatches of requests and questions.[92] The mention of a possible audience with Maecenas leads to an explanation of the limitations of Horace's relationship with the real donor of the farm (a fact not stated explicitly in the poem). This autobiographical statement was intended to be read as a supplement to what was stated in poems 6 and 9 of the first book. Maecenas in the second book is a more remote figure. The concluding fable of the mice is introduced skilfully as an example of the moral wisdom that belongs to the world of Horace's country retreat. The parable to some extent refers to Horace's own life. Like the country mouse, Horace wishes to return to his safe citadel though lured by a city life which is none the less tense and possibly even hazardous. Perhaps there is a suave hint to Maecenas of Horace's desire to withdraw from official commitments. Outside any personal framework the fable is of general application. The country mouse has some of the characteristics of Ofellus in the second satire, frugal yet hospitable; the town mouse is debonair but pretentious. The fable as a whole rejects the values of luxurious excitement in favour of modest security. Many regard this satire as Horace's finest; at all events it is a civilized poem of great distinction.[93]

In Satire 2,7 Horace's slave Davus makes use of the traditional freedom of the Saturnalia to give a homily on the paradox that as only the sage is free the master is morally as much in thrall as his own slave. Davus declaims in general terms on human inconsistency and also on constancy in vice (1–20). He then attacks Horace directly. Though eulogizing pristine simplicity, the poet would be unwilling to live under the primitive conditions of early Rome; though extolling plain living he avidly accepts an invitation from Maecenas. A parasite confesses his gluttony, but Horace cloaks his own by righteous denunciation of others (21–45). Davus then retails a sermon repeated to him by the doorkeeper of the philosopher Crispinus. A Davus who enjoys a hired whore is no more a slave than the free citizen who hazards the dangers of an adulterous affair (46–82). The *sapiens* is a free man: he has self-control and is unmoved by fear, ambition or onslaughts of fortune (83–8), whereas the man who is obsessed by sex cannot call himself free. The admirer of the fourth-century painter Pausias is labelled a connoisseur of classical masterpieces, while the slave who is excited by an equally naturalistic rough drawing of gladiators is dubbed an idler.[94] The slave who is greedy for a tit-bit is no worse than the gourmet: both suffer for their gluttony (89–111). Davus then accuses his master of uncontrollable restlessness, but is finally silenced by threats (111–18).

The dialogue form of this satire, though no more than a framework for the homily, helps to give a convincing impression of an encounter between real people. The central thesis of a Stoic paradox has already been used in the third satire of this book. The relevance of Davus' criticisms to the real Horace varies. The mock modesty in reference to Maecenas' invitation is plausible, but there is probably little connection between the historical Horace and the adulterous knight (53–69). There is recurrent imagery from the attributes of the slave: the erring freeman is bound to the real slavery, which is moral.[95]

Satire 2,8 is an account, narrated to Horace by his friend the comic poet Fundanius, of a hilariously disastrous dinner party given by the upstart Nasidienus Rufus. The company consisted of Maecenas and two minor figures from his entourage, Fundanius and two other literary men and Nasidienus with two parasites, one of whom had the duty of explaining to Maecenas the hidden delicacies of the fare. After the first course slaves entered as if in solemn religious procession bearing choice wines from Latium and Chios. As the meal proceeded Nasidienus explained in detail the recipe for the special course of *muraena* (lamprey) which he had devised himself; as he did so an awning fell on the table with a cloud of thick dust. In his tearful despair he was consoled with cruel irony by one of Maecenas' companions, whom with complete lack of critical humour he thanked for his generous humanity. After an intermission during which he reorganized the menu, Nasidienus returned; but he then discoursed at such length on the natural history of each item that the guests departed, leaving the food untasted.

Nasidienus was probably a real person, though his name, unlike those of the famous guests, is fictitious. Although Satire 2,8 had a precedent in Lucilius (see p. 45 above) it is likely that such a banquet occurred at which the *parvenu*, having invited literary celebrities, dominated the conversation with importunate chatter. Some of his talk about the food belongs to the Hellenistic tradition of deipnosophistic literature, itself a fitting target for satire.[96] Nasidienus, like the nameless social climber in Satire 1,9, has a pretentious and misguided opportunism but he lacks the other's self-confident effrontery. The behaviour of the guests, though culpable by modern standards, may be read as a just condemnation of Nasidienus; others may regard the poem as an offensive piece in which Horace shows an unexpected insecurity in social judgement. The tale itself is neatly and economically narrated: note the ease and humour with which the seating plan is expounded (20–6); but this satire is less important as a poem in its own right than as a document in the history of symposiac literature.

As with Book 1 there are indications that Horace arranged the poems of the second book carefully. The book may be divided into two parts: Satires 1–4 and 5–8. 1 and 5 balance each other formally as true dialogues in which a senior person gives advice, but their subjects have little in common; 2 and 6 vindicate the parsimonious values of life in the country; 3 and 7 are both based on a Stoic paradox and contain a reported sermon. Four and 8 demonstrate the follies of extravagant feeding. But too much should not be made of any such connections. The enormous bulk of 3 is an argument against any tidy scheme. More important is the principle that the reader is aware of the variety with which a single topic is handled in more than one poem: for example, sumptuary excess is a matter for the countryman's austere moralizing in 2; it becomes in 4 a quasi-philosophical way of life with a bogus mystique and in 8 an unhappy status symbol for a pretentious upstart.

6. AUTOBIOGRAPHY, INVECTIVE AND MORALIZING

Horace had learned from Lucilius the power of the satirist's hexameter as a means of self-revelation. But what had been for Lucilius an unabashed exposé of the deeds and misdeeds of a man of property was for Horace a calculated defence of his career and way of life.

Horace used satire as a means of expressing his gratitude in the first place to the memory of his dead father for his devotion to his son's education and also, though with tactful obliqueness, to Maecenas for his patronage and the gift of the Sabine farm. But the rest of Horace's references to himself should not be taken uncritically at face value.[98] The disarming description of the unsophisticated man who interrupted Maecenas' thoughts (1,3, 63–6) has an echo of a Theophrastus character that suggests that fiction is combined with fact. Even the naturalistic account of the poet's all too simple daily life in Rome must be read as part of the apologia of a man proclaiming his lack of interest in riches and political power. Horace's portrait of a life of unambitious contentment at his farm (Sat. 2,6) is also a hint to would-be employers and a general comment on human values. The mocking guffaws of the slave in the next poem qualify the picture of unambitious contentment.

Horace understood the power of Lucilius' political and personal attacks on individuals who were denounced or ridiculed by name. But in the 30s it would have been dangerous, especially for a freedman's son, to write political lampoons and in any case Horace probably would not have wished to do so. Even when he wished to mock the pretensions of an upstart, either he mentioned no name or, as with Nasidienus, used a pseudonym. Horace reserved the force of Lucilian invective for the inept ambitions of those who were just eligible for political office (*Sat.* 1,6,23–44). Here Horace's satire was an instrument for revenge. But in general no living person of note was pointed out as an example of immorality. A reference to the womanizing of the politically discredited Sallust was an exception that Horace would not have allowed himself in his later satires. Early gibes, especially in Satire 1,2, and the use of the names of living persons as illustrations of moral theses had clearly caused resentment. Horace laughs off one such sally but became increasingly restrained in his use of living examples of vice.[99] But he had an eye for the absurd as well as the vicious, notably the inconsistencies of the flamboyant Tigellius (*Sat.* 1,2 and 1,3). There is no reason to suppose that outspokenness ever brought Horace in danger of legal action. A reference to the warnings of the Law of the Twelve Tables (2,1,81ff.) is no more than a quip in a poem of adroit evasion.

Horace's irony and urbanity should not mislead the reader into underestimating the gravity of some of the vices he examines, notably avarice at its most corrupting, adultery and gluttony. To regard Horatian satire as a gentle mockery of 'foibles' is to misrepresent its matter and manner.[100] Such a view accords ill with the mercilessly thorough exposure of legacy hunting in the Teiresias dialogue (*Sat.* 2,5). Nevertheless for Horace positive affirmation is more important than censure. As a student in Athens he had attended lectures by philosophers of the major persuasions, but in his satires he discusses moral situations without adhering to the doctrinaire viewpoint of a philosophical system. In Satire 1,1 avarice is discussed with reference to a commonsense ethical mean. The poem consists of the well-wrought use of the stock themes of Hellenistic popular moralizing rather than the tenets of a major philosophical school. In Satire 1,3 he expounds the Epicurean view of the development of civilization in order to discredit Stoic ethical intransigence, and uses Stoic paradoxes as a disreputable extreme to contrast with his moderate and ironical method of moral assessment. In the second book he seems to regard these paradoxes with a greater measure of detachment. *Socraticae chartae* were important to Horace both as an exemplar of an ironical manner and as a source of ethical doctrine.[101]

7. SOME HELLENISTIC INFLUENCES

In a late epistle (2,2,60) Horace refers to his satires as 'venomous discourses in the manner of Bion' (*Bioneis sermonibus et sale nigro*).
Although the aggressive description is only half serious it raises the
question of Horace's relation to Hellenistic popular moralizing.

Diatribe, a combination of philosophical dialogue and epideictic
oratory, was employed by many moral teachers.[102] The word was
defined narrowly by Hermogenes, a Greek theorist of the second century A.D. as 'the development of a short ethical notion', but it also
comprised a wide range of moralizing discourse, reports of the
teachings of various sages, anecdotes, and ready-made ethical
judgements.[103] While books referred to as diatribes by previous
philosophers are attested, Bion of Borysthenes was the first main
exponent of diatribe as a form of rhetorical philosophy.[104] Born of low
origin at Olbia on the Black Sea he arrived in Athens after many
vicissitudes. For a time he was a pupil of Theophrastus but was more
influenced by the teachings of Crates the Cynic. Even allowing for
novelistic elements in the hostile biography of Diogenes Laertius, Bion
may be regarded not so much as an original philosopher as an itinerant
sophist hawking from city to city an eclectic ethic chosen from the
teachings of Academics, Cyrenaics, Stoics and Cynics in a highly
coloured language spiced by parody.[105] Many of Bion's sayings were
reported in the diatribes of Teles, a Cynic of the late third century B.C.,
whose drab works such as the περὶ αὐταρκείας (on self-sufficiency) are
extant in reported excerpts.[106] The themes of the diatribe remained
stereotyped and uniform from the third century B.C. to the second A.D.
and many of the conventions constant. The Epistles of Seneca and
Arrian's reporting of the Discourses of Epictetus reflect the more exalted aspects of this sub-genre, and features of its style have been
detected in the Epistles of St. Paul.[107] But some of its exponents were
disreputable. Dio Chrysostom describes Cynics at the street corner who
gather a crowd of sailors and youngsters and trick them with their
gibes, word-spinning and vulgarity. Even less flattering is Lucian's
satirical portrait of the Cynic preacher who bawled his exhortation to
virtue, became frenzied in a peroration, and was led away sobbing.
The worst of these excesses may have belonged to the Cynic revival of
the first century A.D., but a certain tawdriness of presentation was a
danger implicit in a form which from the beginning was associated
with the Asianic oratory of Demetrius of Phaleron.[108] Marks of

diatribe style include the introduction of an imaginary interlocutor, anecdotes, fables, parody, the personification of an abstract idea such as poverty, proverbial illustrations, and a wide range of imagery from everyday life.[109]

Discontent which has a root cause in avarice is the theme of Horace's Satire 1,1 and also of a Greek diatribe on discontent of unknown authorship which was included in a corpus of letters attributed to Hippocrates. It is probably of later date than that of Horace's satire but their striking similarities of argument and illustration indicate a common origin in Hellenistic times. The 'Hippocratic' diatribe reveals its Cynic basis in the argument that animals having satisfied their appetite are immediately content, whereas man's passion for luxury is insatiable.[110] Horace's first satire shows many of the other aspects of diatribe mentioned above, e.g. the imaginary opponent, the moralizing fable, *exempla* from everyday life and informality of structure.[111] But Horace views the ways of popular moralizing with detached irony. He does not accept uncritically the doctrines or the methods of the long-winded Crispinus (*Sat.* 1,1,120f.). His detachment is more obvious in the second book, where topics associated with diatribe are put into the mouths of other persons. The lengthy tirade by Stertinius on human madness is to some extent Horace's amused pastiche of the ranting of a sophist, though it has a central core of good sense. Horace's satires are primarily compositions written in the Callimachean tradition for a discriminating minority audience. To label any of them diatribe satires may not do sufficient justice to Horace's many-sided irony.[112] His use of the fables extends far beyond that of the preacher's example; it reflects also the work of his predecessors Lucilius and Ennius. In the first satire Horace alludes to the Hellenistic preacher's slogan of serious matter in flippant guise, but his own urbane blend, primarily a personal achievement, is based on a wide range of civilized literature, particularly the traditions of philosophical dialogue and of comedy.[113]

8. THE STYLE OF THE MORALIST

In the fourth satire of Book 1, as part of a tentative exploratory discussion of the style of the writer of satire, Horace had declared that it was only metrical form that distinguished his *sermones* from mere prose (40ff.), a claim that is immediately disproved by his careful structural arrangement of the words; but in the tenth satire (9ff.) he concedes that the satirist should aim at a flexible style with elements, as appropriate, of oratory and poetry.[114] The following passage may be taken as a characteristic specimen of Horace's language of informal persuasion:

> vel dic quid referat intra
> naturae finis viventi, iugera centum an
> mille aret? 'at suave est ex magno tollere acervo.'
> dum ex parvo nobis tantundem haurire relinquas,
> cur tua plus laudes cumeris granaria nostris?
> ut tibi si sit opus liquidi non amplius urna
> vel cyatho et dicas 'magno de flumine mallem
> quam ex hoc fonticulo tantundem sumere.' eo fit,
> plenior ut siquos delectet copia iusto,
> cum ripa simul avolsos ferat Aufidus acer.
> at qui tantuli eget quanto est opus, is neque limo
> turbatam haurit aquam neque vitam amittit in undis.
> at bona pars hominum decepta cupidine falso
> 'nil satis est', inquit, 'quia tanti quantum habeas sis':
> quid facias illi? iubeas miserum esse, libenter
> quatenus id facit: ut quidam memoratur Athenis
> sordidus ac dives, populi contemnere voces
> sic solitus: 'populus me sibilat, at mihi plaudo
> ipse domi, simul ac nummos contemplor in arca.'

(*Sat.* 1,1,49–67)

(Tell me what difference it makes to the man who lives within the bounds of nature whether he ploughs a thousand acres or a hundred. 'But it is a pleasure to take from a large heap.' As long as you let me take the same amount out of a small store, why should you praise your granary more than my bin? It is as if you needed no more than a pitcher or ladle full of water and were to say: 'I'd rather draw the same amount from a great river than from this little stream.' And so it comes about that men who are delighted by a greater quantity than is right are carried off by the pitiless Aufidus along with the river bank, whereas the person who takes no more than the little he needs neither drinks water polluted by dirt nor loses his life in the surge. Even so a large proportion of men duped by misleading greed says: 'No amount is sufficient, because you are valued at whatever you possess.' What can you do for such a one? Tell him to be wretched, seeing that he chooses to be so, like the rich miser at Athens in the story who was accustomed to disregard the abuse of the people in this way: 'The people hiss at me, but I give myself an ovation at home the moment I gaze upon the money in my strong-box.')

The topic of large possessions as against proper sufficiency resumes a similar idea mentioned a few lines earlier (44f.). The word *acervus* (heap) occurs in both places (44, 51). The metaphor continues with a contrast between the granary of acquisitiveness and the corn bin for immediate need (52f.). The imagery then changes and the broad river becomes the symbol of the great source of supply, but now there is added the notion that excess is dangerous: flood waters are both polluted and violent. Most of the argument up to this point has been conducted through metaphor and simile.[115] The objection that society is timocratic is answered by an evasive rhetorical question that leads to the anecdote of the Athenian miser. This is followed by the mythological example of Tantalus, whose modern analogue treats his untouched money bags as sacral objects. All such anecdotes, like the example of the provident ant (32f.), are devices of Hellenistic moralizing, but Horace incorporates them in his own kind of civilized discourse. The granary seems to have been a stock example, for Horace does not mention that the owner of the large granary in Italy has the problem of ensuring that his grain remains good, though this would have strengthened his argument. But in referring to the dangerously turbulent Aufidus (Ofanto) of his native Apulia he drew on experience that was to find weighty expression in a late ode (C. 4,14,25ff.), in which he compared the spearhead of a military attack to the onset of the river's floods.[116] In Horace literary motif and personal experience are closely intertwined.

The colloquial level of language in Horace's satires is apparent from his frequent use of everyday imagery, his presentation of ideas in pictorial terms, e.g. puffed out cheeks as an expression of annoyance (Sat. 1,20f.), and from the frequent diminutives (e.g. fonticulus, 1,56).[117] Lexical vulgarity and obscenity are rare and mostly confined to the early satires of Book 1. But Horace's artificial word order sometimes shows a degree of complexity that is removed from mere colloquialism.[118] The skill of the satirist is particularly noteworthy in parody. Ennius as the sacred cow of Latin literature was the occasion for some of Horace's best. The parody of the poet's dream has already been mentioned (p. 81 above); the harangue on adultery is introduced by an impudent parody of a noble line of Ennius' Annals.[119] Horace's tone ranges from the vulgar farce in Satire 1,2 through the cynicism of Satire 2,5 to the mellowness of Satire 2,6. A diversity of resources in versification matches the variations of verbal style within the conversational idiom; e.g. the satire in which Horace asserts the unpoetical nature of the genre is notably rich in monosyllabic endings, which are avoided in the high style except for special expressiveness.[120] The easy conversational manner of his verse allows him to quote a long septenarius from Terence

with only minimum change.[121] The truculence of Davus is expressed
with an appropriate metrical informality, and the grand manner in
verse composition can be used to portray pretentiousness, as of the
town mouse's panache or for a comically enhanced stylization.
Sometimes, as in Satire 1,1, a section that is structurally more formal
shows a greater metrical strictness.[122] Such variety is a mark of the controlled skill of a poet who was to show himself one of the greatest
masters of verse forms.

9. THE AFTERMATH OF THE SATIRES

After the publication of Books 1–3 of the odes Horace composed the
first book of epistles, in which the conversational *sermo* turned from
monologue and dialogue to epistle, something almost unprecedented in
ancient literature;[123] it also attained a degree of earnestness and moral
involvement that was inappropriate for the methods of the Lucilian
satirist. It is at first sight difficult to make a formal distinction between
the satires and the epistles. Horace sometimes referred to his epistles as
well as to the satires by the non-technical term *sermo*. His commentator
Porphyrio states that the two are identical in subject matter and style,
differing only in title, but elsewhere makes the qualification that the
satires are addressed as it were to someone actually present and the
epistles to those absent.[124] But though there is some continuity of topic,
the lack of the *Lucilianus character* in the epistles, its invective and miscellany of contents, makes a distinction between satires and epistles
valid.[125] This becomes obvious in the two epistles of the second book,
extended compositions which, while consistently subtle in their poetic
craft, expound literary history systematically, and still more so in the
Epistula ad Pisones, the so-called *Ars Poetica,* in which the exposition of
Hellenistic literary doctrine, though characteristically Horatian in its
calculated structure and poetic felicity, is more akin to didactic
writing.[126] But in the last analysis the products of Horace's ripest
literary skills should not be pressed into too rigid a generic
classification.

As Horace's satires are only a part of his poetical works, it is not
necessary to discuss their transmission, but a few observations may be
offered. Horace's poems were widely read as a standard classic
throughout the early and later empire and corruptions in the text were
rife at an early stage. In Neronian times Seneca gives a dubious reading
in a citation, and the work of the scholarly metrician Caesius Bassus has

preserved one that is quite impossible.[127] There is a contemporary or near-contemporary interpolation at the beginning of *Sat.* 1,10; a plausible but insidious tampering with the text at 1,6,126, that is earlier than the ancient commentators, has been revealed through the witness of a single manuscript source.[128] Horace soon received the attention of scholars. Works appeared on the personal names in Horace, perhaps in the first century A.D. At about the same time the learned grammarian Valerius Probus scrutinized various passages of Horace, but there are not adequate grounds for supposing that he produced an edition.[129] Of the extant ancient commentaries that of Porphyrio is probably of the fourth century; it is erratic and often misleading, but contains much that is reliable. The so-called Pseudacron Scholia have little to do with the second century scholar Helenius Acro but are a compilation of a time no earlier than the fifth century. Much of their commentary is elementary; many of the judgements offered are silly, but there are also some pieces of genuine information that derive from earlier sources.[130] There was much editing of the text of Horace in late antiquity and many variants in the paradosis are of ancient provenance. The subscription of Mavortius (cos. 527) preserved in some manuscripts, claiming that he did editorial work on Horace, should not be regarded as significant for the history of the text.[131] No manuscript of Horace is earlier than the middle of the ninth century. A few early Carolingian manuscripts are of key importance for the constitution of the text, notably Ambrosianus O 136 sup. (ninth/tenth century), Bernensis 363 (ninth/tenth century), Vaticanus Reginae 1703 (mid-ninth century). Though it has been found administratively convenient to divide the readings of the manuscripts of Horace into two main classes that seem to go back to ancient editions, the text of an author who was read widely, copied and corrected in Carolingian times became so contaminated that it is impossible to construct a convincing scheme of the affiliations of the manuscripts.[132]

Horace the satirical moralist was much read and quoted in mediaeval times, but it was not until the late sixteenth century that the form of Horatian satire began to be used again as a model for adapters and imitators. The richest development of the Horatian tradition in post-Renaissance times is found in the satires of John Dryden and in Alexander Pope's *Imitations of Horace*. Pope used not merely the satires of Horace but the full range of the ancient tradition to write the maturest political, social and literary satire in an age in which men of education could appreciate the quality of great artistry.[133]

6

Persius[1]

Horace the satirist had no known successor until the time of Nero, the better part of a century later. The consolidation of imperial dictatorship by Augustus and his successors ended political liberty and also freedom of speech. Augustus ignored lampoons against himself but had vituperative attacks on other contemporaries burned in public.[2] Cassius Severus, a scabrous pamphleteer, was sent into exile.[3] In the reign of Tiberius the aged and venerable Cremutius Cordus, a man of blameless life, who in his histories described the horrors of the proscriptions, was accused at the instigation of Sejanus, the emperor's ambitious favourite. Cremutius' speech in his own defence vindicated the traditional right to assess the dead without censorship; but in order to forestall condemnation he committed suicide and his books were burned.[4] According to Tacitus, Tiberius at about the same time (A.D. 24) spared a Roman knight who had composed scurrilous verses against him (*Ann.* 4,31); on the other hand after the downfall of Sejanus a lampooner was executed in A.D. 36 (*Ann.* 6,39). The historian who passed judgement on the recent dead and the verse writer who mocked the reigning monarch endangered themselves at a time of civil tension.

Men were also imperilled by what was construed by enemies as innuendo against the great. A reference to Tiberius was detected in a tragedy on the theme of Atreus by a Roman aristocrat, Aemilius Scaurus,[5] and the Greek-born freedman Phaedrus was prosecuted for alleged allusions to Sejanus in some of his fables.[6] Though the fables of the low-born Phaedrus do not seem to have been widely read his experience as a writer who claimed to castigate vice without referring to individuals will have been of significance for any intending satirist.[7]

In addition to the repression of liberty by the imperial system further reasons may be suggested for a lack of satire. There was probably a shortage of talent for any literary activity. The long period of murder and proscription had deprived Rome of a substantial part of its educated men, and the political and social upheavals may have caused a failure of nerve in the remainder.[8] It will not have been overlooked that Horace the satirist enjoyed the friendship and protection of the masters of the Roman world; furthermore his many-sided achievement must have seemed to offer an almost unattainable standard of excellence.

I. THE LIFE OF PERSIUS

Aules Persius Flaccus was born on 4 December A.D. 34 at Volaterrae (modern Volterra), an attractive Etruscan hill town some fifteen miles from the Tyrrhenian coast.[9] In an apparently autobiographical context he mentions pride in Etruscan birth; he also shows affection for the Riviera di Levante.[10] He was a well-to-do equestrian with aristocratic connections, but had neither public career nor administrative experience. His personal life was blameless and ascetic, and he was devoted to his mother, sister (or sisters) and aunt; his father died when he was about six. Persius himself died of a stomach disease at the age of twenty-seven on 24 November A.D. 62.[11]

After his early years of education at Volaterrae Persius studied in Rome with the grammarian Remmius Palaemon, the author of an influential systematic Latin grammar and probably a teacher of Quintilian. Remmius Palaemon was a man of peerless arrogance, a notorious womanizer and ostentatious spendthrift, who also composed poetry in a variety of metres.[12] Persius' other literary teacher was the rhetorician Verginius Flavus, a famous instructor and rhetorical theorist, who was to be exiled along with the philosopher Musonius Rufus three years after the death of Persius. After the detection of the Pisonian conspiracy against Nero Verginius Flavus was according to Tacitus harmed by his illustrious teaching of eloquence to the young.[13] Of great importance to Persius was his continuous friendship from the age of sixteen with the freedman scholar and Stoic Annaeus Cornutus. In Satire 5 he praises in a lavish, almost fulsome way the protreptic zeal of his moral preceptor. Cornutus was a versatile writer on philosophical and rhetorical topics.[14] He too was to be condemned to exile, probably in

A.D. 65. Forthright remarks to the dilettante Nero on the merits of his poetry were said to have been the occasion, but at the time any philosophical teacher was open to attack.[15]

Persius' friends included the lyric poet and metrician Caesius Bassus, the addressee of Satire 6, and Servilius Nonianus, consul in A.D. 35, a historian of merit and a man of civilized refinement whom Persius is said to have regarded as a father.[16] The story that Lucan declared with enthusiasm that Persius wrote true poetry while he himself was a trifler is perhaps no more than a happy invention, and may in any case belong to a time before the composition of the first book of Lucan's de Bello Civili.[17] Persius' lack of enthusiasm for Seneca, the dominant literary figure of the age, indicates critical independence.[18] He had a particular admiration for two older men who were also disciples of Cornutus, but of wider import was a deep friendship of ten years with Thrasea Paetus, whom he accompanied on journeys. Thrasea, suffect consul in A.D. 56, an aristocrat of uncompromising moral integrity and biographer of the younger Cato, became the centre of republican sympathies and refusal to co-operate with Nero.[19] By the time of Persius' death Thrasea was already a marked man: in A.D. 59 he walked out of the senate while the memory of Agrippina was being condemned and in A.D. 62 spoke against the death penalty for a praetor who had composed and recited defamatory verses against Nero. He was not concerned in Piso's conspiracy against Nero but in the following year was forced to commit suicide. He was accused of attracting disciples who, it was alleged, despised the licentiousness of the emperor.[20]

The evidence suggests that Persius lacked personal independence. Unmarried and inexperienced he was no doubt much admired by his mother and sister and seems to have spent much of his life leaning on a succession of philosophical father-figures.[21] His own direct experience of public affairs was negligible, but his friends included some of the most eminent men of the time, for whom political responsibility and action became a grievous ethical problem. The premature death of Persius was a tragic waste of talent, but he did not experience the grim events of the next four years, in which most of his friends and associates including Lucan perished. The other outstanding literary figures, Seneca and Petronius, were also destroyed. It is improbable that Persius, who was related to Thrasea's wife Arria, would have survived the purge.[22]

After his formal education was concluded Persius, under the influence of the tenth book of Lucilius, turned with enthusiasm to the writing of satire; as a schoolboy he had written a *fabula praetexta* and other verses.[23] It is also stated that he composed infrequently and slowly (the judgement is true by the standard of the achievement of the prolific Lucan, whose life span was a little shorter), and that his single book of satires was left unfinished at his death and edited for publication by Cornutus and Caesius Bassus.[24]

Only one possible reference to a historical event may give any hint of the date of composition or relative chronology of Persius' satires.[25] It is obviously futile to trace a spiritual or even stylistic evolution in the works of a youthful poet who left unrevised six satires, of which the total bulk is no more than some 650 lines. The published order of the poems is unlikely to be that of composition. The fourteen choliambs are obviously prefatory in intent and are rightly placed before the six satires. The transmitted order of the six satires, whether decided by Persius or his executors, was perhaps suggested by criteria of quality as well as of appropriateness. The subject matter of Satire 1, which includes the satirist's apologia in its criticism of literature, and its impressive quality make it an appropriate beginning for the book; its excellence suggests but does not prove late composition. The weak and relatively short Satire 2 and Satire 4 are surrounded by the longer and superior Satire 1, Satire 3 and Satire 5.[26] Satire 6 has many characteristics of a Horatian epistle and is therefore fittingly placed after the collection of satires proper.

2. A PRELIMINARY CRITICAL PROBLEM

Persius' unusually concentrated manner of expression gives rise to a fundamental critical problem that deserves immediate mention. It is necessary to decide which words in a satire are to be assigned to the poet himself and which to an imaginary interlocutor, whose intervention is not usually accompanied by any words of introduction. The objector in Persius is not a firmly delineated person as in some of Horace's satires or in a Platonic dialogue; he is a rhetorical mouthpiece for a postulated line of objection or a passing thought. The quick exchange between speaker and imaginary objector is characteristic of the kind of philosophical discourse often referred to as diatribe; this method of exposition, which is best exemplified by Epictetus, a pupil of Musonius, will have been familiar to Persius from his teacher Cornutus.[27] Sudden and unprepared changes of speaker do not however seem to have troubled ancient readers, who encountered them particularly in comedy.[28]

3. THE PROLOGUE AND THE SATIRES

In a prologue of fourteen lines Persius declares scornfully that he has had no access to a hallowed source of inspiration and divine guidance; he contrasts himself with poets of a higher style, particularly Ennius.[29] As one only half-initiated he brings his own verse to the traditions of Roman poetry (1–7).[30] As for men's real motives in writing poetry:

> quis expedivit psittaco suum 'chaere'
> picamque docuit verba nostra conari?
> magister artis ingenique largitor
> venter, negatas artifex sequi voces
>
>   (8–11)

(Who helped the parrot to his own 'hallo' and taught the magpie to try human speech? It was the belly, master of art and bestower of talent, virtuoso for imitating unnatural ways of expression.)[31]

Hope of patronage and remuneration turns a strident and obsequious imitator into a poet (or poetess) of the grand manner (12–14).

The theme of the pretentious and contemptible verse-making of Persius' contemporaries in contrast to his own modest satire is a foretaste of a main theme of Satire 1;[32] much of what is expressed with brevity and allusiveness in the prologue is expanded in the poem that follows. The prologue is written in choliambic, the limping iambic metre, a verse form associated with sneering and also with scrounging; it occurs nowhere else in verse satire.[33] The terse prologue in an unexpected metre makes an arresting introduction to the satires.

The theme of Satire 1 is the pretentious and disreputable literature of the day, which is contrasted with satire. The poem may properly be regarded as a dialogue and not a monologue with asides, for though the interlocutor is not a person like Horace's Teiresias who participates on equal terms, he is a constantly present entity.[34] After initial sparring between the two[35] the poet asserts that as Rome's standards are corrupt he must use his own criteria and so mock with impudent wit.[36] Poetry in the grand manner that is recited in a seductive crooning voice panders to a degenerate audience with low taste (13–43).[37] Although desire for popular esteem is a natural impulse the fashionable modern poetry is no more than an after-dinner entertainment (44–62).

The interlocutor as advocate of the modern style extols its virtuosity and suggests that a contemporary grand manner can even be used to denounce luxury including the banquets of the wealthy, a deft twist of Horatian irony (63–8).[38] Persius then points out that poets accustomed to writing light verse in Greek are nowadays encouraged to undertake heroic themes, though they are even unable to describe the countryside and the traditional festivals of Rome (69–75). Here the old and Roman contrasts with the modern and degenerate, which is derived from Greece. When the interlocutor asks in lines of mocking parody whether anyone pays any attention to the archaic language of Accius and Pacuvius (76–8),[39] Persius retorts that this attitude leads to a debasement of letters, so that a speech in a criminal case is aimed primarily at applause for the ingenuity of its style (79–91). Further examples are given in parody form of Silver Age extravagance, preciosity and slickness; on his side the interlocutor quotes the opening of the *Aeneid* as an example of the bloated and passé.[40] In several places Persius uses the language of sexual excess and perversion to describe the degeneracy of the modern style.[41]

At this point the theme changes: The interlocutor warns against the writing of satire and the satirist makes his defence:

> 'sed quid opus teneras mordaci radere vero
> auriculas? vide sis ne maiorum tibi forte
> limina frigescant: sonat hic de nare canina
> littera'. per me equidem sint omnia protinus alba;
> nil moror. euge omnes, omnes bene, mirae eritis res.
> hoc iuvat? 'hic', inquis, 'veto quisquam faxit oletum'.
> pinge duos anguis: 'pueri, sacer est locus, extra
> meiite'. discedo. secuit Lucilius urbem,
> te Lupe, te Muci, et genuinum fregit in illis.
>
> (1,107–15)

('But what is the point of lacerating sensitive ears with the biting truth? Please take care that the thresholds of the establishment don't grow cold for you, for there is the nasal snarl of the dog here.'[42] As far as I am concerned then let everything from now on be whiteness itself; I don't care. Bravo! You all do marvellously; you will be fabulous. Is that all right? 'On this spot', you say, 'I forbid anyone to commit a nuisance.' Draw the emblem of the two snakes. 'Boys, the place is taboo; have a piss outside.'[43] Off I go. But Lucilius slashed at Rome, at Lupus and Mucius and broke a molar on men like them.)

Persius quotes the precedent of Horace also, but promises to bury his own poems and share with his book his comic secret that everyone is a target for satire (116–23). His work, he claims, is for those who respect the tradition of Old Comedy[44] and not for the connoisseurs of cheap jokes. The point of the facetiousness of the last line is not certain; it is probably: 'to philistines like that I offer a morning of legal business and a low pantomime show after lunch'.[45]

The satire is well constructed. The traditional theme of the rejection of uncongenial genres and topics becomes a detailed denunciation of contemporary bad taste and the moral corruption that underlies it; this is followed by the satirist's defence of his chosen genre. The concluding part reveals the secret of the poet's laughter that was mentioned at the beginning, namely that everyone has the ears of an ass.[46]

Satire 2, addressed to Macrinus,[47] is a slight homily on improper and futile prayers. Most men make honourable requests when praying aloud in a temple, but they dare not repeat the prayers which they whisper to the gods in secret. Such hypocrisy is an insult to Jupiter and the ritual that accompanies it is absurd and sometimes repulsive. The underlying cause is greed. It is because men prize silver and gold above all else that they have made effigies of the gods out of precious metals (52–60).[48] Mockery gives way to angry denunciation: through our sinful flesh (*ex hac scelerata ... pulpa*, 63) we attribute our material values to the gods and indulge in violent and unnatural luxury. Persius concludes with earnest moral injunction: it is goodness and purity of soul, not expensive sacrifice, that we must offer to the gods.

Persius' second satire is often compared with Juvenal's tenth, an extended masterpiece on a similar topic,[49] but apart from the obvious difference in scale there is an important difference in angle of presentation. Juvenal shows the wretched consequences of the fulfilment of men's prayers, Persius the disposition of the person at the time of making the prayer and also the unseemly mechanism of sacrificial rites. His satire has signs of technical immaturity[50] and is marred by unevenness of tone, but it is not to be discounted. The succinct presentation of wicked prayers, the ironical contrast between the scrawny infant and the extravagant prayers made for him and the repellent descriptions of public sacrifice and private superstition are in the tradition of Lucilius and Horace but do not blend with the impassioned moral fervour of the concluding part.[51]

In Satire 3 the poet is found sleeping late in the morning. It is uncertain whether the opening section is an inner dialogue of self-reproach or the words of a companion who expostulates with him for his laziness and weakness of will.[52] The comic scene leads into a sermon on the need to practise the teachings of philosophy with the specific injunction to cease from envying another's wealth. The call to apply oneself to metaphysical and ethical problems is interrupted by a hairy centurion who ridicules the obscure beliefs of philosophy (63–87). Then follows abruptly a parable about a man who died after neglecting medical advice (88–106). The point is misunderstood by a speaker who protests that he is physically healthy but is unaware that he is a moral invalid.

The unity of the poem is to be found in its single theme of exhortation to live a strict life controlled by moral philosophy. Sections of intense moralizing contrast sharply with passages which are predominantly comic, e.g. the poet's tantrum, the schoolboy's malingering trick, and the uncouth jokes of the loudmouthed muscleman. The combination of grave and gay is achieved not by a consistent urbanity of discourse but by abrupt transitions from the one to the other. However, some austere sections are rounded off by satirical irony, e.g. the picture of the man without philosophical wisdom hurling random missiles at crows or the description of the funeral procession of the dead man stiff with *rigor mortis* smeared with greasy unguents and escorted by his newly manumitted slaves now bearing the cap of citizenship. In a poem intended to proceed by abrupt contrasts it is wrong to alter the ordering of the text.[53] After the centurion's scoffing, in which the satirist seems to laugh at the moralizing of satire, the remaining thirty lines seem an appendage, but the final Stoic paradox is an appropriate conclusion.

Satire 4 is a short discourse on the theme that it is easy to give good advice to others and yet be blind to one's own sins and limitations. The first section incorporates parts of the Socratic dialogue *Alcibiades I* ascribed to Plato in a way similar to that in which Lucilius, Horace and Persius himself use passages of comedy as a basis for moralizing.[54] Socrates explains to the vain and precocious Alcibiades that although he can give measured political advice to an assembly, he shows in his personal life no greater knowledge of ethical values than a hag who peddles aphrodisiacs to a debauched slave (1–22). Two lengthy examples follow. Awareness of another's faults is illustrated by the gossip's information about a very rich but sordid miser (25–32), and complacency over one's own vices by a physically brutal and obscene description of an effeminate's public display of his private parts for the purpose of depilation (33–41).[55] In a final piece of moralizing the poet urges that a man should face his moral condition honestly and refuse praise for virtues that he does not possess.

The opening Platonic passage is urbane, but the mixing of Greek and

Roman elements is discordant (Alcibiades is made to address an assembly of Roman citizens); it is uncertain to what extent the later part of the poem still refers to Alcibiades. As the two *exempla* in the middle take up a third of the whole, the structure is ill-balanced. The second example is prurient and sadistic in an adolescent way and its application to the moral argument forced. The obvious faults of the poem outweigh any merits; it is as a whole a failure.

The first part of Satire 5 is a eulogy of Cornutus, and the second a sermon on true and false liberty. In the opening lines Persius invokes a hundred voices in order to celebrate his lofty theme. For this epic cliché he is rebuked by an interrupter, who protests that such a style is alien to his satires.[56] Persius replies that although he wishes to use an unambitious style (*Camena*, 21) to display his moral progress, he would need the full resources of poetic magniloquence to express his indebtedness and affection (1–29).[57] For at a time when an adolescent has a roving eye Persius was protected by Cornutus, a friend to whom he was joined by a common astrological geniture (30–51).[58] Persius then contrasts various kinds of folly with the Stoic education offered by Cornutus, and appeals to young and old not to delay their moral regeneration:

> sed cum lapidosa cheragra
> fregerit articulos veteris ramalia fagi,
> tunc crassos transisse dies lucemque palustrem
> et sibi iam seri vitam ingemuere relictam.
> at te nocturnis iuvat impallescere chartis;
> cultor enim iuvenum purgatas inseris aures
> fruge Cleanthea. petite hinc, puerique senesque,
> finem animo certum miserisque viatica canis.
> 'cras hoc fiet'. idem cras fiat. 'quid, quasi magnum
> nempe diem donas!' sed cum lux altera venit,
> iam cras hesternum consumpsimus; ecce aliud cras
> egerit hos annos et semper paulum erit ultra.
> nam quamvis prope te, quamvis temone sub uno
> vertentem sese frustra sectabere canthum,
> cum rota posterior curras et in axe secundo.

$$(5,58-72)$$

(But when the stiffness of arthritis breaks joints like the branches of an old beech, then too late they lament that their days have passed by in grossness and their sunshine in the mists of the marsh and what they have neglected in their life. But your pleasure is to study your books deeply far into the night; for as a husbandman of the young you clear the ground and plant in their ears corn that comes from Cleanthes. Young and old, seek from this source a fixed aim for your mind and sustenance for your hapless old age. 'This will happen tomorrow.' Let it happen tomorrow. 'What! Anyone would think that with one day you were giving a great present.' But when another day has dawned we have already wasted the tomorrow of yesterday. You see that another tomorrow carries off the years and is always a little further ahead. Although the revolving rim is near you and under the same waggon you pursue it in vain, for you are the rear wheel and on the second axle.)[59]

The pupil then delivers a sermon of a kind that he will have heard from Cornutus; its theme, the need for liberty, is stated in the first words: *libertate opus est* (73). True liberty is not the mere acquisition of citizenship, nor is it the right to do anything that is not illegal (73–90). A man does not deserve to be called free until he has ethical knowledge and control (91–114). Unless his control is complete and permanent he is to the Stoic a fool (115–23) and unless he has mastery over his desires he is no more free than the man with the legal status of slave (124–31).

The personified abstracts *Avaritia* and *Luxuria* endeavour to enslave the man who heeds them (132–60) and a moral paradigm taken from the *Eunuchus* of Menander demonstrates that real freedom includes the ability to escape the slavery of sex (161–75).[60] Superstition is the final illustration of man's moral enslavement. The first example seems at first to be an attack on political ambition but turns into a satirical presentation of Jewish practices (176–84). Further examples of superstition, fear of native Roman *Lemures* and the exotic customs that belong to Cybele and Isis (185–8) lead abruptly into a facetious Horatian conclusion: a centurion with varicose veins guffaws at the moralizing and offers a low price for the wisdom of Greece.

The bipartite structure of the work is akin to that of some other Roman satires in which a main section narrating or expounding a principal topic is preceded by introductory material which has only a tangential connection with what follows. Attempts to find an overall unity of theme seem forced, particularly as some structural informality was characteristic of the genre.[61]

The fifth satire is often praised for its sustained uplift, but the quality of Persius' moralizing may be assessed by a comparison with a discourse on a similar theme delivered one generation later by Epictetus, a pupil of Musonius Rufus, a contemporary and associate of Cornutus. The emancipated slave Epictetus was able to illustrate his theme of the true nature of freedom by examples from the career structure of contemporary Rome, from near-contemporary political scandals and also from the moral slavery of Caesar's advisers (*amici Caesaris*). Like Persius Epictetus uses the gambit from comedy but he likens Thrasonides explicitly to a Roman campaigner. His discourse is that of a perceptive, courageous and humane man, free from spiritual arrogance.[62] Persius may have been particularly careful to avoid political references,[63] but by comparison with Epictetus his somewhat self-righteous exposition of a Stoic theme, though no doubt pleasing to Cornutus, is somewhat pallid and immature.[64] The strength of the poem is in the many striking details of expression.

Satire 6 is in the form of a Horatian epistle. It is addressed to Persius' friend, the poet Caesius Bassus. Like Horace (*Epp.* 1,4) Persius refers first of all to his friend's place of retreat and speculates on what he is writing.[65] He then describes his own winter resort: he is staying at Luna (La Spezia) on the Ligurian coast where there are great cliffs and a deep inlet of the sea. After praising Luna in lines that make fun of Ennius Persius talks of his own contentment. He is unconcerned whether or not comparisons are made between his resources and those of his neighbours. As a man of moderate means he advocates the use and enjoyment of what he has. This amiably selfish doctrine is qualified by a willingness to bestow part on a friend in need, but the poet is unmoved by the prospect of his heir's disapproval.

The hypothetical heir is now given a provocative lecture on his prospects.[66] The poet will mount a lavish celebration in honour of an imperial victory and give largesse to the proletariat; the heir would be well advised not to object. Nor will the poet stint himself in order that his heir's grandson may live a life of debauchery (41–74). Persius' final reflection is that it is impossible to set a limit to man's acquisitiveness, but an interrupter has the last word: he claims to be able to stop at any point that is prescribed for him and therefore to have solved the logical problem of Chrysippus' heap. Persius' ironical silence proclaims that the boast is futile.[67]

The structure of the poem is that of a Horatian epistle. The address to the avaricious imaginary heir expands the topic of the corresponding vice, greed: the unreality of such teasing arguments as the celebration of the triumph of Caligula and the hunt for a beggar as the remotest kin is meant to add ironically to the discomfiture of the rapacious heir. The satire contains many vigorous expressions and some unusually obscure phrases;[68] the conclusion is one of the neatest in Roman satire.

4. ASPECTS OF SUBJECT MATTER

The immediate presentation of real human experience was of little interest to Persius. His autobiographical reticence contrasts with the unashamed disclosures of Lucilius and the calculated self-portraiture of Horace. For Persius satire had little to do with personal poetry. It is unlikely that he ever stopped like Horace to inquire into the price of vegetables in the market; it is inconceivable that he could have considered such apparent trivialities as worthy of the reader's attention. His only statement of the immediately factual is the description of Luna at the beginning of Satire 6, and even this leads to thoughts on human conduct. His story in Satire 3 of a schoolboy's malingering ruse purports to tell what the young Persius actually did, but it is highly suspect as autobiographical fact. Persius' father died when he was six, and the attack on the attempts of parents and teachers to force an unhealthy precocity from the young is a commonplace of contemporary criticism.[69] But at least there is a noteworthy contrast between Persius' evocation of his father sweating with parental anxiety as a sort of comic rhetorical cipher to illustrate an argument and Horace's expression of loving gratitude to a real person. There are probably some hints of Persius' own life and circumstances in the references in Satire 3 to the knight who belongs to an Etruscan family; these accord with the information given in the ancient Life.[70] So much may safely be assumed from the poem but no more. His one certain autobiographical statement is the description in Satire 5 of his relationship with Cornutus. But even that merely contains a mention of earnest labour and prim relaxation without any particulars. There is no personal portrait of the moral director. Rather than any details about life with Cornutus Persius gives an elaborate description of their astrological lot. In describing his close personal associates Persius subordinates individual personality to moral generalizations.

The same is true of his presentation of vice and of all his references to persons. By tradition satire proclaimed that it had the right and duty to attack erring contemporaries by name. Persius pays lip-service to his predecessors' boast when he states that he has the talent to scratch at the morals of men afraid of detection and to transfix sin in civilized jesting (5,15f.). The language resembles that of the passage in Satire 1 on the dangers of following Lucilius and Horace.[71] But Persius had no intention of assailing contemporaries by name; he merely implies that he writes as a satirist who owes much to Lucilius and Horace.

Persius is not noteworthy for his depiction of vice. There is no exposure of a single vice comparable with Horace's treatment of legacy-
hunting and few examples of the quick and vivid presentation of a
vicious scene as in Juvenal. Only in the activities of the indeterminate
exhibitionist in Satire 4 and in the gluttony and lechery of the heir's
grandson in Satire 6 is vice described in the physically repulsive
language used by Lucilius and in later times by Juvenal.

The majority of proper names in Persius are labels for stock types
with no discernible contemporary overtones. Many derive from
Horace. Davus and Dama are Horatian names: Davus suggests a comedy figure; Dama, whose name suggests a slave of low origin, becomes
in Persius Marcus Dama, who has suddenly attained the respectability
of citizenship. Persius' use of the name Pedius for his rhetorically
elegant crook on trial (1,85) seems at first sight no more than a borrowing of Horace's Pedius Poplicola, who was likewise busy in court and
subject to stylistic scrutiny. But in A.D. 59 Pedius Blaesus, as Tacitus
relates, was publicly disgraced for fraud and corruption. If Persius' first
satire was written later it would have been difficult for a reader not to
think of the recent public scandal. Such a blend of the literary and the
real seems to be unique among Persius' names.[73]

Of the names which have no Horatian background some, such as
Bathyllus (5,123) the dancer of Augustan times, and Masurius (5,90),
the jurist of the age of Tiberius, seem to be chosen as historical names
almost proverbial for a professional activity.[74] Vettidius purports to be
an example for all to see of the mean man of wealth (4,25) but is almost
certainly imaginary. The poet Attius Labeo (1,50) may have been a real
person but was certainly of no consequence.[75] Persius' use of proper
names that are for the most part typical and insignificant illustrates
further his lack of interest in the individual person.

Searching references to contemporary politics and administration are
not to be expected from an inexperienced writer living in times of increasing tyranny. There was a tradition that in preparing Persius'
works for publication Cornutus altered the words *auriculas asini Mida
rex habet* (King Midas has the ears of an ass) into *auriculas asini quis non
habet?* (1,121), the reading of the manuscripts, on the grounds that such
a reference might be seen by Nero as an attack on himself. The story is
unlikely, even though Satire 1 refers more than once to a secret
mockery; it is in any case doubtful whether Persius himself would have
intended a reference to Midas to be anything other than a general gibe
at patrons without judgement.[76] The only reference to an event from

imperial history is the poet's celebration in Satire 6 of an imperial triumph, Caligula's alleged victory over German tribes in A.D. 39, when Persius was a child. The triumph, according to Suetonius, was a masquerade, in which Gauls were given false hair and dressed up as Germans; Caligula directed that to save public expense the resources of private citizens should be used.[77] The poet's effusive enthusiasm for the triumph, his eagerness to spend his own money and his reference to a counterfeit triumph suggest undertones of mockery. The possibility cannot be discounted that Persius' allusion to a public scandal during the reign of the irresponsible Caligula could be directed also at the contemporary playboy on the throne. If so, it escaped Cornutus' vigilance. In general Persius' themes and examples are remote from contemporary Roman society and politics.

For Persius the satirist's traditional interest in vice was the negative side of moral exhortation. His protreptic zeal has an intensity alien to Horace's restrained urbanity. To Persius, as to other moralists, self-criticism and knowledge is the beginning of ethical improvement: 'reject violently what you are not', he exhorts (4,51); the enlightened part of the self recognizes the backsliding Doppelgänger (3,30). Vice may lurk as a secret or undetected ulcer (3,113, 4,44). Persius is well aware of the inherent sinfulness of human nature (2,63). He describes the enroachment of sin and its overthrow of the moral self:

> *sed stupet hic vitio et fibris increvit opimum*
> *pingue, caret culpa, nescit quid perdat, et alto*
> *demersus summa rursus non bullit in unda*
>
> (3,32–4)

(This man is stupefied by sin. A thick layer of fat grows around his heart. He has no sense of guilt. He is unaware of what he is losing. Submerged in deep water he no longer sends up bubbles to the surface.)

As a Stoic he frequently associates wrongdoing with madness; the paradox that none but the Stoic sage is sane, which is mocked by Horace, is accepted without irony by Persius.[78]

In Satires 3 and 5 Persius is an impassioned advocate of Stoicism. Satire 6 by contrast emphasizes a lack of commitment and may mark a break with a Stoic youthfulness and the refusal of a Roman to concern himself too deeply with philosophy. But it is more likely that it assumes the detached tone as well as the outward convention of a Horatian epistle.[79]

As critic of literature Persius is both moralist and satirist. In the

Prologue and Satire 1 he rejects forms of writing other than satire, not on the grounds that he is unable to aspire to their demands (indeed his witty mimicry of both ancient and modern writing suggests a proved stylistic virtuosity) but because fashionable contemporary literature is a product of a corrupt and degenerate society. Through effeminate delivery and debased style it titillates unhealthy desires and aims at immediate unreflecting acclamation. By contrast he describes his own work as something more concentrated (decoctius – lit. 'more boiled down').[80] The figurative language is more effective than an exposition of literary principles. The descriptions of Lucilius and Horace that precede it (1,114–8) and also that of Ennius in Satire 6 (10f.) are masterly examples of friendly caricature.

In Sature 5 also he contrasts the mythological subjects of tragedy and its pretentious manner with his own modest writing. Even though he wishes to write a panegyric of Cornutus he spurns the clichés of the high priest of poetry. His own procedure is different:

> verba togae sequeris iunctura callidus acri,
> ore teres modico

> (5,14f.)

(You follow the language of ordinary life, skilled at the pungent connection of words, rounded off smoothly in an unpretentious style.)

Horace had recommended that a poet should make a common expression seem new by an ingenious collocation of words. Persius follows Horace's advice even to the extent of attaching to Horace's iunctura the epithet acer, used by Horace both of good critical judgement and of censoriousness. Persius' diction is that of ordinary Roman dress. The level of style is unexalted, but the work has a well carpentered finish.[81]

Persius abhors the smooth style of the Neronian age. He upholds traditions in a decadent period of innovation, as is shown by his great indebtedness to the Augustan Horace and by his implied respect for Virgil. His critical credo was probably not unlike that of Petronius, who extols Horace and Virgil, disparages by pastiche and pointed criticism the modern historical epic of Lucan and despises contemporary rhetoric. Persius too disliked the modern style of oratory and was not captivated by the talent of Seneca.[82] Whether Persius' criticisms, like some of those of Petronius, were intended to besmirch the poetry written by Nero's court flatterers must remain uncertain, but sharp comments on writers incapable of describing the Roman

countryside and its customs may cast more than a sidelong glance at the
pretentious ineptitude of some of the bucolic poetry of the age of
Nero.[83] But it is unlikely that Cornutus, who was consulted by Nero
as literary adviser, would have allowed the publication of any lines of
Persius that could be construed as mocking Nero himself, who was
notoriously sensitive about his artistry.

5. IMAGERY AND STYLE

In studying Persius' imagery some modern critics prefer to seek the underlying unity of a satire in a dominant metaphor rather than view
recurring images as subordinate to the argument of the poem. But it is
also possible to demonstrate that certain kinds of imagery are associated
with the same or a similar theme in different poems. There are also images whose impact is all the greater because they do not recur.[84]

In the opening section of Satire 5 the recurring imagery is based on
oral impulses, the mouth that utters poetry and the mouth that eats and
blows. The hundred mouths invoked for epic utterance and the gaping
mask of the tragedian are transformed into the mouth into which there
are stuffed the large lumps of food that are made up of heavy poetry
(1–6). Ugly realism is thus added to a poetic cliché and the metaphor
of food is sustained in the contents of the pot of Thyestes that are a meal
for an actor (8f.). Misguided attempts to compose in the grand manner
evoke a quick succession of images, blowing a bellows (10f.), a
metaphor perhaps suggested by a similar expression in Horace (*Sat.*
1,4,19ff.) and also by catching the mists on Helicon (7), making a deep
noise like a crow (*cornicaris*, 12) and puffing out the cheeks to let them
collapse with a plop (*scloppo*, 13): the infantile onomatopoeic *scloppo*
may also have been a neologism.[85] In the lines of positive precept on
writing the mouth is used as the organ that utters the kind of poetry
that is appropriate for Persius (*ore modico*, 15) in contrast to the poetry
suited to the banquet of Mycenae. At this second mention of the
gruesome tale of the house of Atreus cannibalistic details give a bizarre
and revolting dimension to the mythological theme (17f.). Such fare
contrasts with the *plebeia prandia* of the satirist (18). Poetic activity is thus
discussed in verse that has a quick changing but well organized pattern
of imagery. The metaphors of food and the mouth are discarded at this
point and do not occur again in any significant form for the rest of the
poem.

A wider range of physiological imagery arises naturally out of the discussion in Satire 1. The physical organ that hears the recitation suggests the metaphorical ear of critical judgement.[86] The mouth that in reality uses a provocative manner of delivery suggests the inner process of creating depraved verse.[87] Erotic material gives rise to imagery connected with the sexual response of the audience, for whom a physical reaction is the outward manifestation of the twisted judgement of depraved critics.[88] Less than justice is done to Persius' variety of expression by attributing to Satire 1 a dominant metaphor of hearing or of sex,[89] for bodily functions used in the imagery combine and interact to express the participation of the modern writer and his audience in something unworthy and despicable.

Self-knowledge and right judgement in matters of morals and poetry are expressed in a series of metaphors from measurement and the testing of materials. Such imagery is not confined to a single satire but recurs throughout Persius' work. The process of distinguishing between the true and false in morals is illustrated by the metaphor of the cracked sound that is heard when a badly fired pot is struck; this is developed into an extended metaphor of the potter's wheel to describe moral education (3,21-4). Persius, unlike Horace, rarely uses the leisurely device of the simile in order to place image and argument side by side; by his metaphorical technique the two are closely identified. In Satire 1 the advocate of modern smooth versification is made to describe the calculation of composition as running the finger over a smooth polished surface.[90] This is succeeded by the description of the versifier as a builder who closes one eye to ensure that a line is straight (1,64-6). The metaphor of a balance is used of false literary judgement (1,6), and of correct moral judgement in politics (4,10f.). The use of a steelyard to measure the dose of a drug (5,100f.) is a moral analogy for a calculation that is based on expert knowledge.[91] Persius was much concerned throughout his work with the mechanism of judgement.

For Persius, as for his predecessors, unpleasant imagery is part of the technique of moral dissuasion. The depraved man with the fat of iniquity growing deep within him is deeply submerged and no longer causes bubbles on the surface of the water (3,32-4, quoted p. 111 above). Trees, that for the epic poet are a living whole, are for Persius examples of the decayed and withered. Fingers twisted by arthritis are identified with the gnarled branches of an old beech (5,58ff., quoted p. 106 above). An overblown style of poetry is compared to the swollen bark of the cork-oak (1,97).[92] An irresistible urge to write is identified with the ability of the fig tree to break through a hard surface (1,24f.). Persius' unidyllic tree imagery has a moral purpose.

Sometimes Persius' words suggest an arresting coinage, as in his promise to drag the old grannies out of the lungs of his listener (5,92), a comically violent and brief metaphor for discouraging old-fashioned prejudices.[93] Perhaps the most remarkable piece of gnomic imagery in Persius is the extended metaphor that expresses man's moral nature in relation to the operation of time: you cannot, he says, catch up with the rim of the front wheel because you are a wheel on the rear axle (5,70–2, quoted p. 106). By avoiding simile and thus identifying the man with the rear wheel, Persius gives a sinister impression of a determinism from which the individual, whirled by something outside his control, has no longer any way of escape. This metaphor seems to be without parallel in ancient literature.[94] It is memorable also in its placing. For Persius here ends a main section with a gnomic metaphor that has an organic func- tion in its context and also a moral relevance as an independent saying. By his concrete and unexpected use of imagery Persius transmutes con- ceptual notions into the essential stuff of poetry.

An additional dimension is given to the richness of Persius' poetry by his constant allusion to the poems of Horace. Persius' relationship to Horace is closer than the normal allegiance of a Roman poet to a major predecessor in his genre. This unusual dependence was not the product of the poet's unconscious reminiscence. Persius seems to have expected the reader to be immediately aware of the lines of Horace that he uses as an ingredient in his total verbal intention. At the beginning of the seventeenth century Casaubon drew up a list of Persius' imitations of Horace, which are taken from the epistles and satires and also to a lesser extent from the odes.[95] The opening of Satire 5 will provide some representative examples. Horace (*Sat.* 1,2,86) has used the phrase *regibus hic mos est* (it is the custom of 'big men') of the wealthy who choose a mistress looking for hidden faults as they would in a horse for sale. Per- sius begins his exposé of the pretentious ways of poets with *vatibus hic mos est* (5,1). Thus by a deft allusion he adds sordid associations to the mock solemnity of his description of the man of letters. Horace prescribes that Thyestes' banquet (*cena Thyestae*) should not be narrated in undignified language (*A.P.* 90f.); Persius' metaphor of Thyestes' pot (*olla Thyestae*) on the boil (5,8f.) uses just such undignified language as a reminder of Horace's precept. In adapting Horace's use of a moraliz- ing *exemplum* from Terence's *Eunuchus* in, as it seems, a spirit of mis- chievous rivalry Persius changes a proper name into that used by Terence's source, Menander, thus displaying his more accurate use of literary history.[96]

Persius' descriptions of his writing as concentrated and colloquial with arresting turns of phrase apply to all aspects of his style, but his concentrated idiom is far removed from the contemporary spoken language even of the educated. Concentration is found in his penchant for using the inifinitive of the verb as a substantive: one occurrence, *nostrum istud vivere triste* (that sombre way of living of ours, 1,9), is quoted by Quintilian as his example of the figure.[97] Persius' conformity to the colloquial language of his predecessors appears notably in his extensive use of diminutives; this characteristic mark of the spoken language is frequently made to bring a jab of derision, e.g. *aqualiculus* (pot-belly, 1,57) or *elegidia* (miserable little elegies, 1,51).

The subtle juxtaposition of words gives Persius' style its unique distinction and also a reputation in modern times for obscurity. The following is a typical example. Persius refers to the nearby field as *non adeo . . . exossatus* (lit. 'not sufficiently cleared of bones', i.e. of stones, 6,51f.). The context is the threat that an angry crowd might hurl stones at the heir, who would in his meanness deprive them of a gladiatorial show. The description of stones as the bones of the earth was traditional, but its use in a situation of frivolous menace turns a poetic kenning into a noteworthy comic riddle.[98] Persius' descriptions of his poetic art show a high degree of self-awareness. His whole style is introverted and aimed at an audience of a judicious few.

6. TRANSMISSION

The single book of Persius prepared for publication by Cornutus and Caesius Bassus found immediate favour, and by the time Quintilian and Martial wrote, his reputation was secure as a writer of small output but high quality.[99] The ancient Life of Persius according to its title was taken from a commentary on him by Valerius Probus. This suggests at least that from a very early stage Persius' difficulties were thought worth the trouble of careful elucidation. Writers are said to have seized upon the book with enthusiasm;[100] the remark does not apply to Juvenal, whose adaptations though obvious were limited. As an unrhetorical poet Persius escaped the uncritical derision with which his contemporary Lucan was attacked in the second century A.D. by Fronto.

Persius was widely read throughout later antiquity even during periods when Lucan and Juvenal seem to have been out of favour. It is recorded that Alexander Severus, who was emperor from A.D. 222–35, quoted Persius on the futility of gold offerings in order to justify his own parsimonious donations to temples,[101] and even before the main revival of classical literature in the fourth century Lactantius quotes with approval lines that ridicule superstitition.[102] Ausonius echoes phrases of Persius; Claudian also seems to show some signs of having read him.[103] But it was for St Jerome and St Augustine that Persius was pre-eminent as both moral teacher and poet.

St Jerome spices malicious attacks on opponents with quotations and allusions. In his preoccupation with virginity he bombards the unfortunate Iovinianus with abusive quotations and adaptations.[104] Even when Jerome is anxious to renounce his dependence on the great pagan poets, his writing is imbued with adaptations of them; borrowing from Persius may be detected in the letter in which he narrates his warning dream (A.D. 384) and also in a letter written many years later in which he reproduces a neologism and some characteristic imagery.[105] St Augustine, who thought highly of Lucan's literary qualities, shows himself much impressed by Persius as moral teacher and writer. In de Civitate Dei he quotes solemn lines from the third satire (66–72) as an example of exalted precepts of a kind which pagans did not hear in their own temples.[106] He has also absorbed something of the power of Persius' imagery, as when in order to illustrate the solidity of Holy Scripture he alludes to Persius' metaphor of the firm wall that contrasts with painted plaster.[107]

Persius is quoted frequently by most of the important grammarians and commentators of the later empire. Porphyrio's commentary on Horace, compiled before the renewal of interest in some of the major Silver Age writers in the fourth century, shows a sharp eye for Persius' adaptations of his predecessor. Aelius Donatus, who never mentions Juvenal, refers twice to Persius. The Pseudacron Scholia to Horace, though belonging to a tradition in which Silver Age literature is esteemed, make a much less intelligent use of citations from Persius than is found in the earlier commentary of Porphyrio.[108] In the final stages of the ancient classical tradition he is cited probably not at first hand by Priscian, the sixth-century grammarian who taught at Constantinople, and at the beginning of the seventh century by Isidore, bishop of Seville, in his encyclopaedic Etymologiae.[109]

In A.D. 402 Flavius Iulius Sabinus, a man of senatorial rank on imperial service, read Persius at Barcelona and Toulouse and corrected his one manuscript as best he could. This manuscript was the ancestor of one written probably in the early part of the sixth century, from which are descended two manuscripts of the late ninth century and

tenth century, whose readings are one of the two main sources of
reliable witness for what Persius wrote.[110] The other principal source
of value is P(ithoeanus), the famous ninth-century Lorsch manuscript,
now in Montpellier, which also contains a text of Juvenal. There is
also a recently discovered Vatican manuscript of the tenth century
(X) that shows some traces of an independent ancient tradition.[111]

The ancient Scholia, the so-called *Commentum Cornuti,* are more
perceptive and informative than most ancient Latin commentaries but
also contain much that is false. They belong not to the first century A.D.
but to late antiquity.[112]

Persius was much read and quoted in mediaeval times. It will be sufficient to instance from England William of Malmesbury and John of
Salisbury and, from scholars active in Italy, the Flemish Ratherius,
Bishop of Verona, and the Lombard historian Liutprand of Cremona,
both of the tenth century.[113] The first printed edition was made in
Rome in 1469 or 1470, but it was with the great edition of Casaubon
(1605) that Persius entered the modern world.

7

Juvenal[1]

The era of the Flavian dynasty (A.D. 70–96) was unpropitious for the
forthright criticism of contemporary behaviour,[2] but there were some
practitioners of formal satire. Manilius Vopiscus, a wealthy Epicurean
from Spain, and owner of a villa of remarkable expense and
elaboration, turned to *saturae* along with other dilettante pursuits as a
harmless recipe for the untroubled life.[3] A certain Silius also, sometimes
identified tentatively with an addressee of Pliny, is said to have written
satires.[4] More important was Turnus, a man of humble birth who
found favour with the emperors Titus and Domitian. The two lines of
his work that survive refer to the palace politics of the previous
dynasty, the employment by Nero of Lucusta, a notorious female
poisoner, to murder Britannicus, the son of Claudius. No doubt Turnus was one of the unnamed contemporary satirists alluded to by Quintilian. His name at least was known to some writers in late antiquity.[5]
After the assassination of Domitian, halls in Rome were filled with
poets of all kinds; their recitations are described by Pliny with
approbation and by Juvenal with contempt.[6] But of all this activity
only one example remains, the satires of Decimus Iunius Iuvenalis.
Time perhaps has not been unjust.

I. THE LIFE OF JUVENAL AND LITERARY CHRONOLOGY

The exact dates of Juvenal's birth and death cannot be ascertained. In
13,16f. he describes Calvinus, a real or imaginary addressee, as born
during the consulship of Fonteius, rightly identified with Fonteius

Capito, the unmemorable consul of A.D. 67. Perhaps that was also the year of his own birth.[7] The argument is slender, but the date accords with what is known of Juvenal's literary career. A somewhat earlier birth date is possible, but the date A.D. 55 based on the testimony of a single and unreliable 'ancient' Life is too early.[8] In a late satire (15,27) Juvenal mentions a consulship of A.D. 127 as something of recent occurrence; but the reference is vague, and so it is possible that he survived Hadrian (d. A.D. 138) and lived on into the reign of Antoninus Pius.

Juvenal perhaps was not of Italian origin, for his *gens*, the Iunii, included many who came from Spain, and the *cognomen* Iuvenalis, though held by C. Iulius Iuvenalis, one of the consuls of A.D. 81, may have been by origin foreign and in general indicates humble birth. This *cognomen* was borne by two freedmen who live near Aquinum, a town in the neighbourhood of Monte Cassino, which is mentioned by the poet in an apparently personal context (3,319) and may have been the place of his birth.[9] Also belonging to Aquinum is an inscription, now lost, that records an offering dedicated to Ceres by a Iunius Iuvenalis, tribune of a cohort of Dalmatian auxiliaries, who was a local magistrate (*duumvir quinquennalis*) and priest (*flamen*) of the cult of the deified Vespasian.[10] As military tribune he had equestrian status and as *duumvir quinquennalis* censorial authority; he was probably a man of affluence. The military tribunate may sometimes have preceded an equestrian career of imperial service, but there is no evidence that a Iunius Iuvenalis attained such a position.[11] Whether the officer and wealthy grandee from Aquinum was the poet or a kinsman (possibly from a later period) cannot be known with certainty. Ceres is held in particular respect by Juvenal (3,320), but it is unlikely that the complaints in the sixteenth satire against the petty advantages of the soldier over the civilian were written by a man who had been an officer in the army. Juvenal had personal experience of Egypt in circumstances about which we know nothing (15,45), but his references to Britain do not imply immediate knowledge, for at the time many officers were able to relate their experiences, and the recent appearance of Tacitus' *Agricola* would have occasioned further interest in the distant province.[12]

The three poems of Martial addressed to Juvenal proclaim some degrees of personal friendship. In one, published in A.D. 92, Juvenal is called *facunde,* an epithet used indiscriminately by Martial of any rhetorical or literary activity and, in a poem written about A.D. 102 in Spain, Martial compares his own retirement with Juvenal's exhausting daily routine in Rome.[13] Martial may exaggerate the discomfort of Juvenal's life, for the cynical indictment of provincial narrowness in the prose preface to Book 12 shows that he overstates his own contentment. However, the description of Juvenal paying court to the influential is similar to that of the daily round of the *cliens* as depicted in his first, third and fifth satires. It corresponds less well to the recorded career of the magistrate of Aquinum, even if allowance is made for differences between personal status in municipal and in metropolitan life. In a satire written some years later Juvenal invites a friend to a simple meal at Tibur (Tivoli). Juvenal's property at Tibur no doubt existed, but as such invitations were in part a literary commonplace, the profession of frugality may have had only a limited autobiographical relevance.[14]

The one ancient Life of Juvenal, from which all the others derive, is unreliable, for it is ill-written, and deficient in factual information.[15] In the first sentence Juvenal is described as the son or ward of a rich freedman, who practised declamation for its own sake until middle age. This information, which is intrinsically plausible, may have been based on a genuine tradition, but it is possible that Horace's mention of his parentage and Juvenal's remarks about his own declamatory experience gave rise to this tradition.[16] The rest of the Life alleges that Juvenal inserted into a later satire verses about the sale of offices practised by the pantomime actor Paris (once a favourite of Domitian but executed in A.D. 83),[17] and that this reference to an old imperial scandal was construed as having a contemporary application, so that at the age of eighty the poet was sent, under the pretext of a military posting, to the farthest part of Egypt, where he died shortly afterwards. But it is highly unlikely that a Roman emperor should have given an aged man an auxiliary command on the boundaries of the empire. The story is suspect on general grounds. Helvidius Priscus the younger was executed by Domitian in A.D. 93 for having written an *exodium*, a minor dramatic piece, about the mythological Paris, which, it was alleged, alluded to the scandal of Domitian's divorce. In such a political atmosphere it is inconceivable that Juvenal would have suffered nothing worse than exile for writing about the real Paris; for in the black years of totalitarian terror described by Pliny and Tacitus, not merely Helvidius Priscus, who bore a famous and suspect name, but also outsiders of no political importance like the historian Hermogenes of Tarsus, were done to death on the most flimsy suspicion of having slighted the imperial majesty.[18] Trajan and Hadrian, who spent many years away from Rome, are unlikely to have found hidden innuendo in a poet's sneer at the court favourite of a discredited predecessor; nor would Juvenal have run the risk of offending the emperor, least of all in a satire that begins with a vague hope for imperial patronage (almost certainly that of Hadrian).[19] If Juvenal was sent into exile, we have no knowledge of the date or circumstances.

The story of an exile was probably invented in the fourth century A.D. at a time of revived interest in Juvenal, in order to provide the curious reader with one colourful event in the life of a poet concerning whom no genuine biographical tradition remained; it ought not to be used in a reconstruction of Juvenal's personal development, according to which the poverty and humiliation that followed his return from exile drove him to angry satire until his later years were mellowed by success or patronage.[20] Perhaps Juvenal experienced disappointments in his career, but impassioned denunciation may also have been a product of temperament as well as of social grievance and belonged particularly to the rhetorical convention of the age. If Juvenal benefited from patronage, we do not know the circumstances. Hadrian as a patron was less than generous.[21] Pliny, who befriended Juvenal's friend Martial and prided himself on his comprehensive personal acquaintance with contemporary writers, maintained a silence about Juvenal that has been taken to be a sign of strong dislike, a plausible but not necessary assumption. As Juvenal is very reticent about his own career and way of life, since late antiquity it has been tempting to speculate; but we have fewer facts about his life than about that of any other Roman satirist.[22]

In accordance with the practice of the times Juvenal before publishing will have given recitations from his work. Scattered references to external events suggest that Juvenal published his satires book by book in the order in which they have been transmitted. Book I consists of Satires 1–5. The fourth satire, Domitian's council, has a dramatic date of A.D. 82,[23] but as it refers to his assassination cannot have appeared until after 96. In the first satire Juvenal mentions Marius Priscus, who was condemned in A.D. 100 for extortion (1,47–50). This reference to a notorious case merely provides a *terminus post quem*.[24] The effeminate behaviour of Otho is, according to Juvenal, (2,102–3) a matter that deserves to be related in the latest annals and a newly published history. He may have had Tacitus' *Histories* in mind, first known of in A.D. 105 and possibly completed by the end of A.D. 109. If there is also an imprecise allusion to Tacitus' *Annals*, then Juvenal's first book cannot have been published much before A.D. 115.[25] But a reference to Tacitus, though plausible, is far from certain. The second book consists of the sixth satire only, the great attack on women. The officious female busybody is the first to have seen the comet of A.D. 115 and to have heard the news story of a great earthquake in December of the same year (6,407–12).[26] The impact of the references would perhaps have been greater if the events had taken place recently. Book 3 (Satires 7–9) expresses in its opening lines (7,1–3) a hope for imperial patronage; it is thus likely to have appeared not long after the accession of the dilettante Hadrian and before his departure in A.D. 121 on a tour of provinces.[27] Book 4 (Satires 10–12) contains a description of Trajan's inner harbour at Ostia (12,75–81), which was probably completed about A.D. 113.[28] The remaining satires (13–16) are gathered into the fifth book. The fifteenth satire, which narrates events that took place in A.D. 127 as something of recent times (*nuper*) in contrast to something from the mythological past (15,27), will have been written within approximately five years of that date. More precise evidence for the dating of the satires cannot be offered.[29]

2. RHETORICAL POETRY

That Juvenal's satires were fundamentally rhetorical was inevitable in an age in which the conventions of rhetoric had permeated social attitudes as well as prose and verse literature. There had been some measure of rhetorical organization in previous Roman poetry: much of the *Aeneid* was imbued with an impassioned rhetoric. But in the work of Ovid, who was a virtuoso declaimer, and still more in that of the post-Augustan poets, there was a much intensified reliance on the procedures of a formal rhetoric. Exercises for declamation included imaginary speeches of exhortation, legal debates frequently on absurd, sordid and gruesome topics, sensational descriptive speeches on natural phenomena or unusual places and objects, and denunciations of the morals of the age.[30] Of particular importance was the *color*, the angle of the presentation or quality of emotion that could be given to the set topic.[31] Such exercises had become a literary end in themselves.[32] The effect on creative literature was the unrelenting search for the impressive or shocking. The subordination of parts to a carefully constructed whole was of less importance. The effects of rhetoric went further than literature. In their own lives men acted the rhetoric that they declaimed and historical events were reported in rhetorical language. The hideous sensationalism of Iocasta's speech in Seneca's *Oedipus* before she drives the sword *coram populo* into the offending part of her body had its counterpart in real life, as narrated by Tacitus, in the comparable gesture and final command made by Agrippina to the assassins sent by her son, the Emperor Nero.[33]

Perhaps the most influential representative of the rhetoric of the first century A.D. was the epic poet Lucan. Among his early works was a debating exercise based on a recent and sordid *crime passionel*.[34] His poem *de Bello Civili* exemplifies many of the basic approaches of the schools, e.g. the speech of exhortation in scenes of grim military heroism, the formal debate on whether Pompey should be murdered, accounts of proscription and carnage, and memorable epigrammatic sayings.[35] He also denounced with fervour corruption and sensuality, for like all major writers in the century after Ovid he was driven by an insistent rhetorical indignation as well as by personal anger.[36]

Juvenal too was impelled by *indignatio*, a clamorous anger (1,79f.).[37] He had practised declamation (1,15ff.) and wrote, particularly in his earlier books, not so much for the pleasure of friends as for the applause of a public audience that expected the extrovert declamatory manner.[38] While he was conscious of following the tradition of Lucilius and Horace[39] Juvenal alone of extant satirists derived an urgency and vehemence from the idiom of rhetoric, which left its mark on his methods of composition and structure as much as on the staple of his language.[40]

3. THE SATIRES

i. Book 1 (Satires 1–5)

Juvenal's first satire begins with an impassioned statement of intentions, without any preliminary verses or the prose preface that had become fashionable.[41] Surrounded by the din of declaiming poets Juvenal will retaliate, not with another mythological work of high poetry, but with satire; subject matter is close at hand in the sins of the age. A rising sequence of examples of viciousness culminates with a rapidly enriched freedman of Near Eastern origin (26–9); in a series of rhetorical questions and of insistent expressions of anger Juvenal incites the audience to share his indignation. He sees a sedan chair bulging with the obese bulk of a rich barrister, followed by a treacherous and venal public informer; he is then pushed aside by gigolos who vie with each other in the extent of their services to a wealthy old woman (32–44). Later (63–72) when he talks of standing at the street corner and filling his tablets with the misdeeds of passers-by, like the effete forger and the successful female poisoner, Juvenal's listeners are appealed to as if actually present at the scene.[42]

The stated theme of his book is real life, past and present, in all its aspects, but he makes it plain that he means the plenitude of vice, avarice in particular.[43] Then follows a more expanded description of the daily round of life in Rome as experienced by the poor client: this includes queueing for the daily dole handed out by the rich and influential. In the final section (147–171) the satirist is warned that he may be destroyed if he attacks the powerful. He therefore promises to attack the dead alone; by this he means that he will use the dead as *exempla* of wickedness. The single theme of Satire 1 is the rejection of the innocuous unrealities of mythological epic for the hazards of writing satire in a world dominated by avarice, where sinners are men of power. The treatment of the theme is varied: vivacious and rapidly changing presentation is followed by more leisurely narrative and argumentation.[44]

The theme of Satire 2 is the hypocrisy that accompanies homosexual behaviour, and the betrayal of the traditions of the Roman governing class. Sodomites of grim aspect strike attitudes of moral superiority. Their hypocrisy is as crass as that of a Verres condemning theft or of the emperor who upheld stern moral legislation and begat incestuous offspring.[45] Laronia, representative of the class of prostitutes,[46] contrasts the uncomplicated failings of her sex with the system of mutual protection, complicated activities and devious pretences of the male hypocrites. Her speech leads into the next topic: the stern barrister who, though denouncing loose women, wears a diaphanous gown himself. A further example of perversion may be found in the 'marriage' of a homosexual couple, a horn player and the aristocratic Gracchus.[47] Republican heroes and the dead of Cannae, who are conjured up from the underworld in a final rhetorical *Nekyia*, turn in revulsion from modern degenerates (149–58). It is vain to achieve the domination of Britain and the East if the innocent and subjugated are to be corrupted by the debauchery of their conquerors.[48] Throughout this grim and impressive satire the honourable Roman warriors of early times are contrasted with their degenerate successors, including an emperor who is a hypocritical moralist, another who is effeminate even on the eve of battle, and an aristocratic priest who is a pathic exhibitionist.

In Satire 3 also the simple decency of old republican life contrasts with the corruption and danger of the modern capital. Umbricius, a native Roman of small means, is retiring in disgust to Cumae on the Bay of Naples. His complaint makes up the bulk of the poem. Its angle of vision is that of the honest (but querulous) Roman who is without wealth, but believes that a simple innocent way of life is still to be found in provincial Italy.[49] The long speech is framed by a description of the place and circumstances like a formal dialogue. At the beginning Umbricius and the poet walk while the removal cart is being loaded under the arches of the Capuan gate; at the end, as the sun sinks, Umbricius departs. The poem's balanced structure, its orderly succession of topics and its naturalistic humanity have won it a high esteem that has been extended by Samuel Johnson's magisterial adaptation, 'London'.[50]

Satire 4 purports to describe a single historical event, a special meeting of Domitian's council of advisers (*consilium principis*); its characters were in real life members of the emperor's council, and in spite of exaggerations its account of the procedure of an imperial council is probably accurate.[51] A fisherman at Ancona had caught a huge turbot and, realizing that any extraordinary fish would be seized upon by sea-shore informers and officials as imperial property, decided to present it to the emperor at his Alban villa. The emperor called his council to deliberate on the fate of a fish too large for any pan. Among the eleven *amici* mentioned were the adroit trimmers Vibius Crispus and Rubrius Gallus, the honourable imperial servants, Acilius Glabrio, father and son, the military commander Cornelius Fuscus, the sinister Catullus, a lecherous blind informer and adulator of things he could not see and also the odious Veiento.[52] A sequence of increasing flattery ends in a decision to have a special pan made for a fish so rare.

The poem is political satire in that it shows a farcical misuse of a responsible body of imperial advisers, and contrasts such frivolity with the cruelties of Domitian's oppressive tyranny.[53] But it is also a study in moral degradation, in which at the court of a suspicious tyrant men of integrity and ability were forced to grovel in base adulation along with the time-servers and the sinister. Another kind of ironical comment is conveyed through a parody of Statius' laudatory poem on Domitian's Northern wars. The main narrative is preceded by a virulent tirade against Juvenal's *bête noire*, Crispinus, an Egyptian immigrant, who in spite of lacing seduction with sacrilege rose from hawking fish to a place on Domitian's council. As Crispinus receives only a passing mention in what follows, the relation of the introduction to the account of the Council is problematic. It may be regarded as an inconsequential prelude in the Horatian manner; there is possibly deliberate correspondence between the extravagance and wickedness of Crispinus and the large scale folly and crimes of the monstrous emperor.[55]

Satire 5 uses the traditional theme of the dinner party to describe the humiliations endured by the client at a meal given by his patron. There is a series of contrasts between what is offered to the host and to his guests: Virro is served with wine of illustrious vintage, his clients with wine that drives men to crazed brawling; Virro's wine-waiter is a handsome youth, but the clients are served by a dark-skinned ruffian who looks like a highway robber. They are even abused by the waiter for taking bread reserved for the patron. Humiliation continues until the dessert: Virro has so acted not out of meanness (though it had been suggested in passing that a wealthy guest without issue would have been treated with an effusive solicitude) but because he takes cruel pleasure at the spectacle of the humiliated retainer. The viewpoint in the poem is not that of the client himself but of a sympathetic but critical onlooker, who at the beginning and the end chides him for accepting invitations that lead inevitably to insult. Balancing these reproaches there is in the middle of the description an appeal to the patron to treat his retainers not lavishly but with urbanity. The humiliating dinner party is not a theme from a bygone age but is a contemporary malpractice condemned both by Pliny the patron and by Martial the client.[56]

ii. Book 2 (Satire 6)

The sixth satire is an enormous indictment of women in married life that unfolds item by item to fill the whole of a roll of nearly 700 lines. Its thesis is the loss of female integrity in a society in which marriage inflicts intolerable humiliations on the husband. It is impossible to separate marriage and the vices of women, for the poem's subject is the misdeeds of married women, at which a husband is usually no more than a helpless onlooker.[57] The proem (1–20) treats ironically the theme of degeneration from an age of primaeval bliss: chastity existed only in a Golden Age in which the women, dressed in hides, were as hirsute as their acorn-belching husbands. The departure point of the poem's argument is an attempt to dissuade Postumus from his intention to marry and raise a family. In Rome women in the theatre are beside themselves at the sight of a mime actor, and their children are likely to have the features of a performer (60–81). There follow two garish examples of adultery (82–132): Eppia abandoned her senatorial husband and her children to elope to Egypt with a repulsive gladiator, and Messalina, the wife of the Emperor Claudius, slipped from the palace at night to act as a common prostitute. A woman's money, beauty or aristocratic lustre gives her an independence and arrogance that ruin marital happiness (133–83).

The topic of infidelity is interrupted by a brief reference to the litigious female and by a portrait of the unsexed woman who practised gladiatorial exercises with gusto (242–67). Near the halfway point there is a set piece on the corruption of old Roman integrity by the advent of Greek luxury after the Hannibalic war (286–300); the catalogue of depravity is then resumed. Female cults are the occasion for nocturnal orgies, and lust is sought after by women of all social classes (300–65). Married women learn the ways of debauchery from obscene family retainers whose alleged epicene nature is a counterfeit.[58] Many too enjoy the pleasures of a real eunuch. Other character types are presented as equally deplorable and humiliating to the husband: the musical enthusiast, usually with a passion for a virtuoso (379–97), the busybody with a knowledge of world affairs, talking on equal terms to a military commander (398–412), the aggressive athlete who vomits before dinner (413–33), the blue-stocking with a voice like percussion who is expert on grammatical nicety (434–56),[59] the seeker after beauty through cosmetics and elaborate coiffure who flogs a slave for miscalculating a curl (487–507). A final intensification of the argument begins with a description of a procession of Ma-Bellona led by an enormous eunuch (511–21); the married woman, cowed by such superstition, performs outlandish expiation.[60] Anubis is followed by a Jewish beggar woman and eastern fortune-tellers and astrologers. While the lower-class women who consult them bear the children they conceive, the sophisticated turn to abortion (582–97). For a hated husband or stepson there is death by poison or even, where that fails, a sword blade. In Rome the horrors of reality surpass the worst deeds of mythology.

The degree of rhetorical intensity in the poem is varied. It contains irony and a certain grim humour, but there is no whimsical facetiousness in the presentation of the literary woman, for it is fundamental to the slant of the argument that conjugal happiness is broken as thoroughly by eccentricity as by depravity.[61] It seems impossible to impose an orderly plan of structure on material that is presented in a long succession of scenes and descriptions. Catalogue form was a traditional basis of ancient attacks on women,[62] and it is misguided to fault the structure of Juvenal's sixth satire by standards that seem to be based on pedimental balance or on Peripatetic advice about writing tragedy.[63]

iii. Book 3 (Satires 7–9)

Satire 7 begins with a statement that the emperor alone encourages intellectual activity (1ff.). In a stilted and unenthusiastic call to a younger generation of poets (*iuvenes*) Juvenal proclaims that Caesar looks for deserving talent in serious poetry (17–21). The emperor is referred to in the third person; he is not even named, and there is no hint that Juvenal expects success for himself.[64] This tone contrasts with that of the previous period, as found in the prayers of Martial to Domitian and also in the dedications offered to the earlier Flavians by poets and prose writers.[65]

The poem then exposes the meanness of private patrons and deplores the condition of even successful writers and of practitioners of rhetoric in contrast to that of traders and entertainers. The poet suffers many privations, but the careers of Virgil and Horace show that a writer of inspired originality needs material security (53–71). Statius, who could charm a full house with his *Thebaid,* was compelled to write scenarios commissioned by a pantomime actor (82–92). The historian too receives no reward for his voluminous labours (98–104). Even the barrister, no matter how eloquent, receives meagre fees unless he has an aristocratic name and can impress prospective clients by a flamboyant display of affluence. The teacher of rhetoric is poorly compensated for his tedious work (150–88). It was only good fortune that made Quintilian a landowner. Even the highest positions are precarious. Some professional appointments have led to personal disaster, and a well-known Gallic instructor in declamation was beaten up by his pupils (203–14). The schoolmaster fares even worse, for though he is expected to show high standards of knowledge and probity he must bargain ignominiously to obtain his miserable fee (215–43).

Satire 8 develops the thesis that exalted birth must be justified by personal integrity and achievement (20); often the behaviour of aristocrats is contemptible. The poem is appropriately addressed to Ponticus, a

high-born aspirant to a provincial governorship. No details of his
background or personality are given, and he is perhaps no more than a
plausible literary fiction.[66] After an introductory section (1–38) there is
an address to the aristocratic but inept snob Rubellius Blandus,[67]
pointing out that efficiency often depends on the man of plebeian birth
(39–55). A series of moralizing commonplaces (74–86) precedes the
particular advice to avoid rapacity in a province. Examples of
degraded nobility follow, drawn from the behaviour of Lateranus,
Gracchus and Nero.[68] A final section reverts to the outstanding public
services done by new men (231–75). Rome, threatened by the
aristocratic Catiline, was saved by Cicero the *novus homo* from Ar-
pinum, just as another man from the same town, Marius, rose from the
ranks to take precedence over his noble colleague in the consulship
after destroying the invading Cimbrians. The poem concludes with
reflections arising out of similar *exempla*.[69]

Satire 9 is the only poem of Juvenal that makes consistent use of the
dialogue form as it is found in Horace; and like Horace's Teiresias
satire (2,5), it sustains a tone of ironical approbation. The dialogue is
between the author and a discarded male prostitute called Naevolus,
who complains of his poor earnings and his occupational hazards.
Eventually the satirist assures Naevolus that his future will be secure,
for there will be pathics as long as the Seven Hills of Rome remain. In
his final speech Naevolus rejects consolation, and in a catalogue of increasing lavishness states his requirements for a peaceful retirement and
a steady pension.

At several points Homeric parody, including a twisted quotation of
the Greek, underlines the contrast between an heroic world and one of
the ultimate turpitude, and a reference to the stylized homosexuality of
the pastoral milieu of one of Virgil's eclogues emphasizes the grossness
of the social reality.[70] Naevolus' acquisitive impudence as well as his
self-pity is illustrated ironically by his allusion to the fleeting values of
the normal sensuous world: the garlands, perfumes and girls of
amatory poetry that contrast with his commercial perversion.[71] This
satire explores the ultimate degradation of a relationship that had
already been treated in Satire 5: in the earlier work the patron (also
Virro) is mean and takes pleasure in humiliating others; in Satire 9 he is
completely corrupt and violently malevolent; so too the honest but imprudent client of Satire 5 contrasts with the immoral and greedy
Naevolus.[72] The repulsive subject matter of Satire 9 is offset by the deft
irony and parody of its treatment; it is a distinguished piece of stylistic
virtuosity.

Some changes of theme and technique may be noted between Book 3 and Juvenal's previous work. Satire 7 contains less vehement denunciation, not because of a new-found optimism, but because such treatment was less appropriate for the theme of the hardships experienced by poets and rhetoricians. Satire 8 is Juvenal's first attempt to offer in quasi-epistolary form, not merely a condemnation of vice but also exhortation to the corresponding virtue; in this poem there is also a more extended exposition of historical *exempla*. As Satire 9 is unique in its method, it is difficult to fit it into a consistent pattern of development, but it is of notable technical maturity.

iv. Book 4 (Satires 10–12)

In Satire 10 Juvenal expatiates on the futility of most prayers, a theme akin to that of Persius' second satire. Suffering and destruction come to men through the fulfilment of their wishes. The gruesome catastrophe that befell Sejanus illustrates the danger of the fulfilment of the prayer for supreme political power; it is better to be a petty official in a depopulated town. Cicero and Demosthenes are examples of the power of the highest eloquence to destroy its creator: Cicero would have been safe had his oratory been of the same quality as his doggerel verses (122ff.). Hannibal illustrates the futility of prayer for supreme military power: having at last reached Italy the one-eyed commander on top of an elephant is a sight fit for a grotesque caricature (157f.). As a defenceless refugee at an Eastern tyrant's court he committed suicide and became after his death a topic for schoolboys' rhetorical exercises. Alexander and Xerxes are further illustrations of the same theme. The consequences of the prayer for long life (188) are demonstrated first by a catalogue of the ills that accompany old age; and then by a description of the fate of aged heroes of mythology, notably Priam, who mourned the death of their children and the destruction of all they valued:

> Longa dies igitur quid contulit? omnia vidit
> eversa et flammis Asiam ferroque cadentem.
> tunc miles tremulus posita tulit arma tiara
> et ruit ante aram summi Iovis ut vetulus bos,
> qui domini cultris tenue et miserabile collum
> praebet ab ingrato iam fastiditus aratro.
>
> (10,265–70)

(What then did length of days bring him? He saw his whole world destroyed and Trojan power engulfed by flames and military force. At this point he laid aside his crown and bore arms as a quivering foot-soldier and fell before the altar of Jupiter the greatest like an aged ox that yields its skinny and pitiable neck to the sacrificial knife of its master now that it has been turned off from the pitiless plough.)

Marius and Pompey are corresponding examples from Roman history of a fall from earlier greatness to a wretched old age. The last futile prayer, a wish for beautiful children, is discussed in a similar way. A catalogue of the hazards that threaten a handsome son precedes examples from Greek mythology and Roman history of innocent men destroyed by immoral women (289–345).

Juvenal then argues briefly that the fulfilment of each man's prayer is best left to the gods themselves, who see into the future (346–53). His final formulation of correct prayer is an epigrammatic codification of the conventional Roman wish for well-being of mind and body, *mens sana in corpore sano* (356), which is expanded into a robust statement of a self-sufficient *virtus*.[73] The poem is uncomplicated in structure.[74] It combines grave nobility and cynical wit. The former quality is reproduced in Johnson's adaptation, 'The Vanity of Human Wishes'.

In Satire 11, which is in the form of an epistle, Juvenal invites a friend to a meal that is gastronomically modest and morally blameless. It is in three parts. The first (1–55) is a homily about living within one's means. In diet as in other matters the Delphic maxim 'know thyself' is a fundamental rule. The second section (56–183) describes the meal that matches the precepts. Juvenal offers Persicus the fresh simple produce from his farm at Tibur, a kid, eggs and poultry, and prime quality fruit (65–76). Juvenal's cups, bone-handled cutlery, the inexpert service of his country-born slaves, and a reading from epic poetry are made to contrast with the resplendent ware, the exotic and debauched waiters, and indecent floor-shows by Spanish dancers at the banquets of the wealthy and immoral. In the final section (183–208) Juvenal reiterates the invitation and describes the chariot racing of the Megalesian games in Rome, when if the popular team is defeated the whole city has a sad expression like that of the vanquished at Cannae. This parody use of a grim *exemplum* of national disaster is part of the depiction of a mood of relaxed contentment in the last part of Satire 11, in which the poet looks forward to enjoying the spring sunshine in peace as one of the restrained pleasures of a man who is no longer young.[75]

The invitation to a simple dinner is a literary topic with many variants. Horace in a famous ode (3,29) invites Maecenas to an unpretentious banquet before reflecting on the vicissitudes of fortune; Martial in language similar to Juvenal's mentions the absence of Spanish dancers from his simple dinner (5,78, 26ff.). Juvenal's contrast between simplicity and luxury may be seen as a satirical variant of the invitation from a poet of modest means to a wealthy and important guest.[76] The reader is told little about Persicus. We do not even know whether or not he was a real person. The question is not important, for Juvenal by a blend of traditional elements and a realistic presentation of the here and now creates an impression of verisimilitude.

In Satire 12, nominally an epistle to Corvinus, about whom we are told nothing, Juvenal describes the sacrifice that he is about to offer in thanksgiving to the gods for the escape of Catullus from a storm at sea. There is a mock-solemn narrative of Catullus' ordeal, which avowedly contains the ingredients of a poetical storm (23f.). Catullus' willingness to jettison the treasures of the cargo is compared to the stratagem of the beaver that escapes destruction by biting off the testicles for which it is hunted (34–6). The comparison suggests a certain irony in the poet's attitude.[77] In a passage of Virgilian colouring the ship comes at last into the safety of the land (62–82). As Catullus has children, the poet is able to rebut any charge that his concern is that of the legacy hunter (93ff.). A consistent frivolity of tone expresses his fundamental lack of sympathy for Catullus whose losses it is implied, were exaggerated and made an occasion for self-pity.[78]

The three poems of the fourth book show the extreme points of Juvenal's range. Satire 10 has in places an almost tragic intensity of expression; its long examples are taken for the most part from the distant past. Satire 11 moralizes in a more relaxed manner; it also contains some personal comment and a naturalistic description of a public holiday in contemporary Rome. Satire 12, though not a poem of high distinction, manipulates a rhetorical persiflage with skill and offers a vivid description of the sacrificial animals and of the poet's private ritual of thanksgiving.

v. Book 5 (Satires 13–16)

In Satire 13 Juvenal offers to Calvinus, who has been defrauded of a sum of money, a consolation that uses gambits of the formal literary *consolatio* addressed to one who had suffered bereavement.[79] He counsels moderation in anger and grief, for in a world in which virtue is a freak of nature (64f.) Calvinus' loss is not great, least of all when compared with the damage done by hired thuggery, arson and sacrilege (144–56). Such crimes are common in a Rome that has degenerated even lower than the iron age (26–30). The conventional appeal to the consolation of philosophy is set aside both early in the poem and at a later point, when the poet offers advice as one who is philosophically uncommitted.[80] Juvenal's attitude towards his addressee is remote and detached; for Calvinus himself there is no hint of solicitous concern. While the poem is not a parody of the *consolatio*, there is irony in the application of some of its gambits to an unimportant loss; the reflection that the dishonest culprit is likely to be haunted by the nocturnal vision of a larger-than-life Calvinus, as in an epic dream, adds an element of the grotesque that precludes a uniformly serious interpretation.[81]

The main theme of Satire 14 is that parents by their bad example teach their children vices, particularly that of greed, which is encouraged like a virtue. Juvenal first gives examples of sins that can obviously be imitated: gambling, gluttony, sadism and sexual promiscuity (4–30). He then states the principle that a child must be respected and shielded from all scandal and occasion of sin (44–9). The purpose of such protection is to rear a good farmer who is useful in both peace and war (70–2).[82] The first section concludes with two further examples of activities that were prone to be imitated, the building of extravagant villas and Jewish practices (86–106). The rest of the poem discusses aspects of avarice. Juvenal castigates first the affluent miser (109–40), and then the land-grabber, whose deeds are described ironically (156ff.) as a refuge from disease, bereavement and other human ills (140–66). The virtuous republican peasant (179–88) is contrasted with the modern parent who urges the young to study as a preparation for an ambitous career in the army or commerce (189–205). The child taught to desire wealth will turn to perjury and homicide, even parricide (205–55). The trader's acquisitiveness is then shown to be absurd (256–302). The poet enjoins that, though the ideal limit of possession is a mere sufficiency to avoid hunger and cold, the maximum permissible holding is the property qualification for the equestrian rank.

The theme of bad parental example gives a unity of structure until the sensational description of the merchant's risks at sea (265–302). From this point the topic of education is abandoned. The poet becomes preoccupied with the immediate impact of rhetorical horror,[83] and the final moral exhortation is a conclusion appropriate to a denunciation of avarice. The poem is vitiated by its use of some of the most unreal commonplaces of Roman rhetoric.[84]

In Satire 15 Juvenal, who knew Egypt from personal experience and hated it, narrates an incident of recent times (29ff.): a battle between two villages arose as the result of a vendetta; a man was captured, torn apart and eaten raw by the crazed victors.[85] The narrative (33–92) is followed by condemnatory arguments: some centuries previously a beleaguered town in Spain turned to cannibalism, but the modern Egyptian villagers had no such excuse at a time when a veneer of Greek and Roman culture was spread throughout the world (93–115). Not even the most ferocious northern barbarians have acted with comparable savagery (124f.); such a crime is an utter violation of natural law (131–58). The poem ends with an appeal to the example of Pythagoras who abstained from all flesh as if it were human. Some of the arguments have a restrained irony characteristic of Juvenal's later work (e.g. 110ff.), but the introduction and narrative revert to the explosive violence of his earlier manner.

The fragmentary Satire 16 expresses from the viewpoint of a civilian underdog a sense of grievance at the privileges of military life: the civilian has no satisfactory redress against assault by a soldier and is compelled to endure long delays in litigation; the soldier also has some testamentary privileges (51–60).[86] All manuscripts of Juvenal break off at this point in the middle of a sentence, and the Scholia show no further knowledge. In spite of doubts expressed in the Scholia the poem is certainly genuine: the ironical description of military luck as better than a letter of recommendation from Venus to Mars (4ff.) and the reference to delays in court (35–50) are characteristic of Juvenal's manner. It is uncertain whether the author left Satire 16 unfinished or whether it was mutilated by an accident of transmission. It is possible that a scrupulous literary executor, unlike Persius' editors, allowed the fragment to be published untrimmed, but it is perhaps more likely that at a time when the source of the text of Juvenal was a codex (which was more liable than a papyrus roll to be damaged at its end) the last pages of Book 5 were lost.[87] It is impossible to reconstruct what Juvenal wrote or would have written after the break, but the total number of lines in the earlier books suggest that the last poem of the fifth book was not of unusual length.

Every poem in Book 5 has a nominal addressee about whom nothing is known. Calvinus (*Sat.* 13) alone, through his loss, is connected with the matter of the poem; the rest, unlike Horace's epistolary addressees, have no more place in the poem than a colourless vocative in the first line; some of them may be imaginary. There is a greater use of irony and argument in these poems, but Juvenal's literary conventions demanded that such topics as the storm at sea in Satire 14 and the monstrous tale in Satire 15 should be treated with a taut ferocity.[88]

4. PERSONAL AND SOCIAL TOPICS

i. The impersonal poet

Juvenal tells little about his origin, career and daily life. In this he contrasts with his predecessors Lucilius and Horace, particularly the latter, for whom discreet autobiography and descriptions of his daily round were an essential part of his work as a satirist. He contrasts also with two of his most important contemporaries, Martial and Pliny. The outsider Martial was proud of his Spanish origin (4,55); in addition to retailing personal hardships so as to win a patron's support he describes travels from Rome (3,1) and the pleasures of his Nomentan farm (6,43). Pliny, who is anxious to present himself to posterity as assiduous administrator and virtuous benefactor, describes his villas in great detail (2,17) and also his daily life in Tuscany from morning until night (9,36). Both relate with pride anecdotes concerning the recognition of their fame as writers.[89] Juvenal's notable reticence may be attributed to an aloof and proud disposition or to a lack of appreciation by contemporaries. His declamatory satire, delivered to what may have been a public audience, was an unsuitable medium for autobiographical revelations particularly at a time when some of the traditional subject matter of satire, the writer's day-to-day opinions and feelings, had been appropriated by other informal genres of poetry.[90]

ii. The danger of attacks on contemporaries

In imperial times new dangers threatened the satirist. First, he would have been anxious to avoid the reputation of being himself an informer.[91] Although by the time Juvenal published his first book the odious delators of Domitian's reign had disappeared, there was still a fear that even a liberal emperor might one day turn tyrant and encourage once more these hated instruments of oppression.[92] More serious was the risk of being informed against.[93] Pliny, when about to attack in the senate a man with an infamous past, was warned that his victim had the support of powerful friends and that any attacker would be a marked man in the eyes of future emperors.[94] Various kinds of pressure could be used to suppress embarrassing truths. Early in the second century A.D. a writer, possibly Tacitus, was persuaded not to continue the recitation of a history that brought shame and discredit to some of his hearers.[95] At the highest level of all, even during a relatively liberal period, emperors could not be expected to tolerate outspoken criticisms of their own behaviour and policies.[96] It is therefore not a matter for surprise that Juvenal makes no direct attacks by name on important contemporaries nor, except in the fourth satire, does he vilify the recently deceased, for the guilty dead had associates who were still in a position to retaliate.[97] Most of the proper names linked with vice are either fictitious or belong to a past remote enough to have no dangerous overtones.[98]

It was however possible that a near-contemporary example may have suggested an even more modern application. Juvenal uses the trial of Marius Priscus in A.D. 100 to illustrate provincial maladministration. His readers may also have remembered the disgrace of Vibius Maximus, prefect of Egypt, some seven years later.[99] Also, where less serious defects were involved, Juvenal may have been willing to glance at living contemporaries. There is, for example, an unflattering reference to Isaeus, Pliny's teacher (3,74) and some scholars have detected allusions to Pliny himself and his family.[100] Juvenal's general caution in making personal attacks may be due not solely to considerations of safety and prudence. It seems that in an age of recitations, civilized convention discouraged the naming of victims, as this was a practice associated with uncouth philosophical sects.[101]

iii. Social attitudes

Just as some of Juvenal's attacks on individuals have no firm basis in contemporary reality, so some of his social themes seem to belong to the past. An angry rhetorician is not a reliable critic of the society of his time. Nobility that fell short of its obligations was a standard theme of ancient declamation.[102] By the time of Juvenal the aristocracy that he attacks in Satire 8 was largely extinct. Weakened by proscriptions and the upheavals at the end of the republican period it turned to frivolity and extravagance, gradually lost its importance under the Julio-Claudians and displayed a final political impotence in the short reign of the patrician Galba.[103] But an old reference may from time to time suggest a new application. The satirist may have seen a parallel between the behaviour of the aristocratic but inept Galba and that of the highly born but ineffectual Nerva.[104] Juvenal's attacks on degenerate nobility could also be relevant for contemporaries in so far as they might be construed as referring to the immorality and unseemly behaviour of high officials of state and senators as a class. Juvenal's noble Gracchus cavorting in the arena is matched by the senator and former consul of a later date who sported in a public show with a prostitute dressed as a female leopard.[105]

The new governing class of Flavian and later times is often, and no doubt rightly, praised for its high standards of rectitude.[106] But there were occasional lapses: Pliny reports with disgust that on one occasion senators defaced their ballot papers with scurrilities.[107] Juvenal's analysis of the virtuous *novus homo* (8,245ff.) is a suspect sentimentality that gives little insight into the transformed structure of Roman society during the early empire.[108] In any case for Tiberius Julius Alexander, a renegade Jew and Flavian supporter, whose equestrian career culminated in the prefecture of Egypt (A.D. 67–70) and probably of the praetorians also, he expresses uninhibited loathing.[109] As he is a rhetorician, his social attitudes are not consistent. He regards the moral standards of some distant provincials as superior to those of the Roman officials who introduce them to corrupt practices, but he also expresses contempt for their aspirations to the Roman way of life.[110]

Juvenal's hatred of Julius Alexander is characteristic of one of his social attitudes, prejudice against the successful careerist of Greek or oriental origin.[111] He often combines racial hatred with class prejudice, elements not easily to be separated. By the end of the first century A.D. some Greeks and Levantines had permeated Roman society; some were in positions of power and influence.[112] In attacking their corrupt versatility Juvenal shares an attitude with many Romans of his own and earlier times.[113] Like other Romans he despised the way of life of Jews, but tempered his denunciation, as few of them were of social importance.[114] It was for the wealthy freedmen, many of whom were of Levantine or oriental origin, that Juvenal reserved his fiercest anger. His attitude is that of the freeborn but idle parasite who felt contempt and loathing for the upstart who amassed a fortune by his own labours.[115] No doubt many freedmen were pretentious and ridiculous, but Juvenal's view needs correction from the letters on Pliny and, more reliably, from inscriptional evidence.[116]

Juvenal's description of his own slaves at his farm at Tibur

(11,145–60) has a kindly tolerance that matches the relaxed economy of the whole scene. In general his attitude towards slaves, particularly the cruelly treated, is one of compassion; but for the sleek flunkey of the rich and for the slave informer his scorn is tersely expressed.[117] His views on the treatment of slaves accord with enlightened opinions of the early empire and the imperial policy of the times.[118] In his descriptions of the downtrodden and the humiliated among the free citizens there are hints of a humane attitude unusual in Latin literature.[119]

On all matters of vice it is difficult to decide how far Juvenal reproduces the standard commonplace of rhetoric and the tradition of satire and how far he reflects the morals of his own times, for there are no completely reliable sources for contemporary social history. Many of Martial's epigrams are expanded by Juvenal with declamatory force.[120] While it would obviously be a mistake to take a pornographic epigrammatist as a guide to contemporary Roman sexual ethics (though he reveals what made his public snigger), it is equally unwise to take the women described by Pliny as typical of the virtue of his times, for his background is municipal rather than urban and he is anxious to appear as a man with exemplary connections.[121] Perhaps the enterprising but decadent old lady mentioned by Pliny, who owned her own dancing troupe much to her grandson's disapproval (*Epp.* 7,24), reflected the tests of the Neronian rather than a later age, but it need not be supposed that adultery and sodomy became any less fashionable in the Flavian or later eras.[122] The intellectual aspirations of some of the women in Pliny would have fallen within the brief of Juvenal's sixth satire.[123]

It is likewise impossible to disentangle the personal and immediate from the traditional in Juvenal's tirades on luxury and greed. Rhetorical practice had at its disposal ready-made commonplaces which could be applied to any given situation.[124] Nevertheless the class structure of Roman society with its assessment of status based on wealth necessitated, as a preliminary to advancement, acquisitiveness or subservience to the wealthy.[125] Legacy hunting was still widely practised in Roman society in the early second century A.D.; this custom was linked with the Roman concept of *amicitia,* whereby it was expected that a man's friends would be remembered in his will. Hence the frustrated legacy hunter's discomfiture was a matter for mirth in real life as well as in literature.[126] Juvenal, like his predecessors, took the role of satirist seriously, and he is well aware of the moral qualities that were expected of a teacher [127] How far he could have expected his own denunciations and precepts to have any influence is open to question. But he was accepted with enthusiasm in later ages as a moralist.[128]

iv. Rhetorical philosophers

Juvenal appeals to the precepts of Stoicism in Satire 15 but he is not a doctrinaire moral reformer.[129] Following the precedent of Horace, he asserts that he is not commited to any sect.[130] He means what he says, for what references there are to organized philosophy in his work reveal no more than the general intellectual equipment of the educated rhetorician.[131] To Juvenal, in contrast to Persius, philosophers are eccentrics or hypocrites; his view accords with the traditional Roman prejudice against philosophy,[132] an attitude that was confirmed by the deportment of many sophists. Rhetorical publicity was combined with philosophy to produce what Quintilian described as 'self-seeking commercial travellers in wisdom'.[133] There were arrogant sophists of foreign origin, men of power who ingratiated themselves with the imperial government. Favorinus of Arles, a wealthy sophist of philhellenic pretensions and dubious morals, who enjoyed the friendship of both Hadrian and Plutarch, behaved with such crass irresponsibility that even the dilettante emperor may have been compelled to send him into exile.[134] Euphrates, a man of Syrian origin, was praised by Pliny for his distinguised appearance and bland precepts, but was also regarded as a social climber and a man of commercial adroitness.[135] Others had been perfidious betrayers of former associates: the infamous conduct of Egnatius Celer, the Stoic confessor, is mentioned by Juvenal.[136] Demetrius the Cynic lived on a bed of straw and proclaimed that a life without suffering was like a dead sea, but his later public conduct called his integrity into question.[137] While many philosophers were influential counsellors and worthy of the greatest respect, the ostentatious sycophants and mountebanks will have caught the public eye.[138] Juvenal's moralizing seems uninfluenced by the homilies of contemporary philosophers and sophists, most of whom were of Greek and oriental origin. Philosophy as a guide to man's inner spiritual life seems to have been of little consequence to Juvenal.

5. ASPECTS OF JUVENAL'S STYLE

i. Example and imagery

The use of the traditional analogy is an essential part of Juvenal's style.

The example or appeal to a precedent was a recognized part of the rhetorician's equipment and is found in all Roman literature with a moralizing flavour.[139] For Juvenal, the *exemplum* from history as a pattern of moral behaviour is of fundamental importance (14,322ff.). He also uses analogies from mythology and geographical learning; these have affinities with high poetry, particularly that of Lucan.[140] To the moralist the stock examples from Greek and Roman history were used to point to a standard of behaviour often of an ideal uprightness and integrity compared with that of the writer's own times. There were also in the rhetorical textbooks examples of over-reaching or futile behaviour such as Alexander and Xerxes; these too challenged the rhetorician's inventiveness.

Juvenal shows inventiveness not in his examples from heroes of Greek history or even for the most part from worthies of early Rome, but in his handling of examples from imperial history, in which he combines historical reality with rhetorical commonplace. In satire to before citing standard illustrations of ambition (Hannibal, Alexander and Xerxes) Juvenal gives an extended description of the sudden and hideous downfall of Sejanus, which may derive some of its power from the narrative of Tacitus.[141] As part of the irrational frenzy of the fickle mob Juvenal describes the destruction of equestrian statutes of Sejanus to make domestic utensils. The melting down of the statute of a fallen tyrant to make humble domestic equipment, including chamber pots, is a commonplace of Greek and Roman rhetoric.[142] The pulling down of the statue of a hated tyrant is also a recurring fact of history; Juvenal himself may have witnessed the destruction of statues of Domitian after his assassination.[143] Juvenal uses the behaviour of Messalina to illustrate the degradation caused by the lechery of a princess. The wife of the emperor served in a brothel, exposing a body that had borne a prince, and returned bringing to her royal bed the odours of the whorehouse.[144] The picture, which may have had some basis in historical fact, is combined with prurient details taken from an unreal rhetorical exercise concerning a kidnapped priestess sold into prostitution: the name of the girl over the entrance to her cubicle, the kiss of the arriving customer, his cash payment and the persistent smells.[145] Historical and rhetorical plausibility coalesce.

The inherited mass of rhetorical examples sometimes occasions the satirist's sneer. The trite theme of Hannibal ends with an appeal to him to cross the Alps and become a theme for declamation (10,166f.). The standard example of Marius is enlivened by gruesome detail in the manner of Lucan: after the defeat of the Cimbri the carrion crows had larger corpses to feed on than ever before.[146] The ironical use of a traditional parallel is also found in Juvenal. Cornelia, mother of the Gracchi, a model of maternal virtue in the books of rhetorical examples, is to Juvenal a type of female arrogance to be compared directly to Niobe, who is in turn compared to the fecund white sow of Alba.[147]

Example is not easily separated from simile. Juvenal's imagery is wide in range and tone. As moralist in the tradition of satire he uses analogies taken from the animal kingdom. The provident ant of Horace (*Sat.* 1,1,32–8) is given a twist. Nominally an illustration of male foresight, by implied contrast it is made to emphasize the heedless extravagance of women (6,359–62). The unnatural behaviour of human beings evokes the moralists' example that animals live in peace with their own species (15,159–68); the parallel seems to have been accepted as an ethical analogy since the time of Aeschylus.[148] Sometimes a grotesque simile illustrates unseemly behaviour: the athletic woman who drinks immoderately and vomits is compared to a snake that falls into a vat (6,431f.) In the description of the client's dinner the mythological references to an apple of ideal quality combined with the image of an apple eaten by the performing monkey presents through the constrasting sources of analogy and their multifarious associations a situation of intense arrogance and degradation.[149] The pallor of the gigolo, enervated by his demanding duties, is compared with that of the man who steps barefoot on a snake (an allusion to an incident in the *Aeneid*) and of the orator who has to speak at the humiliating and hazardous competition instituted by Caligula at Lyons. Here epic and historical associations are combined in a collocation of complex irony.[150]

In many of these similes an epic element is used with jocular incongruity. But in other places the tone is more complex. Juvenal compares the helpless paralytic with mouth wide open and fed by others, to a baby swallow (10,228–32). Here there is an uneasy mixture of disgust and pathos.[151] A few lines later the fall of the aged Priam is compared to that of an old ox sacrificed at the altar. By drawing on the associations of Virgil's narrative of the last night of Troy in Book 2 of the *Aeneid,* Juvenal raises the level of his style to a tragic dignity in order to express pity for the man whose prayers for longevity have been answered.[152]

ii. Rhetorical language and level of style

The rhetorical manner, which dominates the structure of Juvenal's poems, their use of ethical commonplaces and examples, and the presentation of arguments is found also in the shaping of sentences and phrases. The *sententia,* the epigrammatic reflection, either a general maxim or a comment invented for a particular situation, is characteristic both of the declamatory schools and of prose writers and poets in the first century A.D. Lucan and Tacitus are expert in using the epigrammatic phrase. Juvenal too is master of the *sententia,* the generalization with a gnomic tone or the paradoxical and cutting phrase on moral obloquy.[153] Juvenal is conscious that too smooth a maxim may be dismissed as a rhetorician's device and so fail to persuade, as when he asserts that his warning about the danger of the mutiny of exploited provincials is not a processed phrase but the truth (8,125).[154] For the most part he uses the rhetorical convention with critical control. There are other marks of the rhetorician's organization of sentences. Rhetorical questions are part of the evocation of indignation in Satire 1; along with them will be found numerous repetitions (*anaphorae*) to reinforce the questions with an inescapable insistence.[155]

Juvenal's language like his *exempla* and imagery shows a wide range from the colloquial to something that approaches the high style in oratory and the epic manner. In variation of stylistic level his work is markedly different from that of all previous satirists. He follows their practice in assuming the grandiose in order to provide ironical force or to parody. The epic manner underlines the monstrous deed of cannibalism in Satire 15 (esp. 65–70). The tale of the turbot is introduced and narrated with many comic twists of the epic manner as befits the account of an inane imperial council.[156]

The convention of periphrasis can be used to add a sneer in order to accommodate an intractable word to the hexameter. The kind of cheap ware given to the client at dinner known as *calices Vatinii* becomes *Beneventani sutoris nomen habentem . . . calicem* (the cup bearing the name of a cobbler from Beneventum).[157] Other periphrases are serious. Cumae, to which Umbricius intends to return, is referred to as the place where Daedalus cast off his wearied wings (3,24f.); the circumlocution is appropriate for the desires of the man exhausted by life in the city. In referring to fire as the husband of Venus (i.e. Vulcan) and also in his use of the vocative of the proper noun in apostrophe that is part of the fabric of Lucan's verse, Juvenal accepts in a routine way the conventions of contemporary high poetry.[158] Sometimes, as in his description of the more immediate presence of the gods in early Rome, with its undertones of awe and tranquillity, he attains a poetic solemnity that transcends the rhetorician's theme of pristine innocence and virtue (11,111–6). Towards the end of Satire 6 Juvenal himself seems conscious of an intensification of manner that may appear to violate the traditional law of the genre of satire. The context is an impassioned denunciation of unnatural murderesses, and he is able to evade a charge of stylistic pretentiousness and impropriety by asserting that the wicked deeds of the heroines of tragic poetry belong to everyday experience in contemporary Rome.[159]

His choice of words also shows a greater range than that of his predecessors. As befits a satirist he uses many colloquialisms, and Greek words help to mock Greek influence and to express either a serious or a parodic *sententia*.[160] A poetic form necessitated by the demands of the hexameter may be made to carry a sneer, as the ironical approbation implicit in the archaism *induperator* used of the disreputable Domitian in a context containing many expressions of parody.[161] Hyperbole in choice of word may contain ridicule or may intensify the horror as in the use of *mons* (3,258) to describe a mass of masonry that crushes a pedestrian in Rome.[162] A poetic expression, e.g. *Maronis/altisoni* (magniloquent Virgil, 11,180f.) is intended without irony as a device to enhance the tone of a passage. In such places Juvenal raises the level of his hexameters from the Horatian ideal of urbane colloquialism to that of the impassioned language of the epic poets of the first century A.D.[163]

6. SURVIVAL AND TRANSMISSION

Even in his own lifetime Juvenal's declamatory satires may have seemed old-fashioned. Their manner was far removed from the anaemic preciosities of Hadrian's own verse-making and is unlikely to have appealed later in the second century to the uncompromising archaism of the literary taste of Marcus Aurelius' correspondent Fronto, for whom the rhetorical style of Lucan was a matter for a superior snigger.[164] Juvenal was not read by Lucian, the Phoenician-born writer of satirical dialogues in Atticizing Greek; such common topics as are apparent belong to a shared stock of traditional themes or to similar experiences of Roman society.[165] Juvenal's style would have been utterly repugnant to Lucian.

Marcus Aurelius' successor Commodus appeared as a gladiator; in such times Juvenal's works may have appeared politically tendentious as well as stylistically uncongenial.[166] While Juvenal seems to have become an unpopular author, it need not be supposed that copies disappeared altogether. Tertullian in his impassioned attacks on pagan immorality seems to have absorbed something of Juvenal's forcefulness and shows a few verbal reminiscences, but he is cited by hardly any grammarian before Servius late in the fourth century A.D., not even by Servius learned teacher Donatus.[167]

In the later part of the fourth century A.D. there was a renewal of interest in Juvenal. Servius quotes him frequently and Ausonius of Bordeaux cites him and imitates some of his sayings.[168] Towards the end of the century he became highly fashionable. The historian Ammianus Marcellinus mentions him along with Marius Maximus, the author of a scurrilous anecdotal history of the Antonine period, as a writer much in vogue with contemporary aristocrats who, he alleges, disdained all other reading. It seems that Juvenal's denunciation of spectacular vice in high places had avid readers, but Ammianus, himself a capable portrayer of vice, disclaims knowledge of the reasons for the cult.[169] Traces of Juvenal have been found in the compilation known as Scriptores Historiae Augustae.[170] He is also used to good effect by Claudian in poems which combine satirical invective with the grand epic manner.[171]

The circumstances and the scope of this revival are unknown. St Jerome, for all his malicious wit, reveals a minimal and almost certainly second-hand knowledge of Juvenal,[172] and St Augustine shows slight acquaintance and perhaps little interest.[173] But almost all poets and grammarians of late antiquity throughout the Roman empire show some knowledge of Juvenal and his work. Sidonius Apollinaris, the fifth-century Gallic bishop, seems to refer to the unauthentic biographical tradition concerning the poet's exile (*Carm.* 9,271–3). He is cited frequently by the grammarian Priscian in Constantinople (*c.* A.D. 500) and John Malalas, a sixth-century chronicler of Antioch, alludes in garbled form to the story of an exile.[174] For creative writers and for scholars Juvenal was a major source of inspiration and interest.

Juvenal may have altered the original version of some passages of his poems but there is no firm indication of a complete revision.[175] Some of the worst corruptions probably belong to the period of relative neglect before the revival of interest in the later part of the fourth century.[176] To this period belongs the ancestor of P(ithoeanus) or Montepessulanus (also a principal manuscript of Persius), and of its associates.[177] Though it contains some corruptions not found in the rest of the tradition, it is relatively free from the kind of arbitrary alteration that disfigures another version of the text made at about the same time, in which, in order to make Juvenal more acceptable to an unlettered reading public of the kind referred to by Ammianus, many unintelligent changes were made that turned original genius into normalized mediocrity. This so-called interpolated recension was the origin of the majority of extant manuscripts. The text was emended, though not necessarily fully edited, by Nicaeus in the house of Servius.[178] The two sets of short notes that make up the ancient Scholia of Juvenal belong to this age of industrious but erratic scholarship.[179]

The text of an author who survived the Dark Ages in more than one manuscript was subjected to an increasing process of contamination, so that we are unable to trace with any confidence the stages by which it was transmitted into Carolingian times. Heiric of Auxerre (b. 841) was the first mediaeval scholar to devote detailed attention to Juvenal, both by exegesis and by adaptations in his own poems.[180] The famous manuscript P was written at Lorsch in the ninth century.[181] Juvenal's influence began to spread throughout western Europe particularly after the eleventh century. As satirist and moral teacher he had a secure and important place in the development of renaissance culture.[182] But the mediaeval and humanist manuscript tradition was subject to a further process of contamination and falsification. The first printed edition was made at Rome in 1467–9.[183] All early printed texts were based on the so-called interpolated tradition. The first edition to make use of the Montpellier manuscript was that of Pierre Pithou in 1585. This manuscript was then neglected until it was rediscovered in the nineteenth century and used by Jahn as the basis of his edition of 1851.[184] Modern editors while recognizing the unique excellence of the tradition represented by P, have achieved a more balanced assessment of a manuscript tradition of unusual complexity.[185]

Juvenal and Tacitus both displayed the vices and pretensions of imperial Rome. They were the last great writers of Latin from classical antiquity. After them pagan literature lacked energy, so that a writer in the second century A.D. could refer to *mundus senescens,* a world that was growing old.[186] Infamy was now attacked with fervour by men who were committed to the Christian view of the world. At the time of the pagan literary revival of the later fourth century A.D. the best writers of the period, Ammianus and Claudian, were experts at corrosive denigration, but, so far as we know, there was no formal satire of consequence.[187] Juvenal had no ancient successors.[188]

PART THREE

Menippean satire;
the alternative convention

8

The Menippean satires of Varro[1]

The alternative convention of satire in which prose discourse or narrative was interspersed with a variety of verse forms to enhance a moment of the story or to illustrate the argument was, compared with other genres of Roman literature, an instrument of unique flexibility. It began in the first century B.C. as a creative by-product of the philosophical zeal of the antiquarian Varro, who described his *saturae* as adaptations of the writings of Menippus, a Phoenician cynic of the third century B.C. A miscellany of form and content in Menippean satire was later exploited in the first century A.D. by Seneca and Petronius.

I. THE LIFE OF VARRO

M. Terentius Varro was born in 116 B.C. at Reate (modern Rieti), a Sabine city situated in the fertile valley of the Velinus (Velino) which was famous in antiquity for its natural beauty.[2] He was probably a descendant of Terentius Varro, the consul of 216 B.C. (the year of the disaster at Cannae), who was said to have been the first to bear this *cognomen*.[3] Varro was a wealthy land- and property-owner and devoted much energy to stock-breeding and raising crops.[4] Widely experienced in agricultural life and the values of country folk, he retained deep respect for the traditional morals and customs of Rome and Italy. At the time of Lucilius' death he was fifteen years old. His early manhood was spent in a period of political turbulence with callous murder and savage revenge on a scale unknown even at the time of the Gracchi.

When the Social War began he was twenty-five and had held the minor magistracy of *triumvir capitalis,* a prison administrator.[5] He was quaestor, possibly in 85 B.C., during the time of the consulships of the Marian supporter, Cinna, while Sulla was in the East.[6] Varro's public and political career is known in outline but the exact chronology is for the most part uncertain.[7] He was a legate in Dalmatia 78–7 B.C. and served for a lengthy period under Pompey in the war against Sertorius in Spain. He held the tribunate and the praetorship and acted as propraetor in 67 B.C., once again under Pompey in his campaign against the pirates in the eastern Mediterranean.[8] Having attacked the First Triumvirate of Pompey, Caesar and Crassus in a prose pamphlet entitled *Trikaranos* (The Three-headed Monster) he served none the less, presumably out of loyalty to Pompey, as one of twenty officials who in 59 B.C. redistributed land in order to settle Pompey's veterans.[9] During the next decade he took no part in public life and did not aspire to office above the praetorship. During the civil war, once again as a supporter of Pompey, he commanded two legions in 49 B.C. but after Caesar's success at Ilerda was compelled to surrender.[10] His life was spared, and in 45 B.C. he was appointed director of the newly founded public library in Rome.[11] After the assassination of Caesar he was proscribed by the Second Triumvirate on account of his great wealth rather than his Pompeian politics,[12] and spent the remaining years of his life in literary studies until his death in 27 B.C.[13] Few men who had had a public career in the late republic died a natural death at the age of ninety.

Varro's account of the austerity of his early upbringing may well be true; it accords with his views on parsimonious virtue expressed both in the satires and in the treatise *de Re Rustica*.[14] In Rome he was the pupil of the learned grammarian and literary scholar Aelius Stilo.[15] While in Athens, probably 84–2 B.C., he attended the lectures of the Academic philosopher Antiochus of Askalon, who was also an important influence on the philosophical writings of Cicero.[16] Under the influence of Stilo Varro became a wide-ranging grammarian and literary scholar; he was also an encyclopaedist and codifier of the customs and antiquities of Rome, and wrote at length on almost every aspect of ancient knowledge including law, geography and agriculture.[17] In philosophy he seems to have been eclectic, adding Pythagorean elements to the broadly-based doctrines of Antiochus of Askalon.[18] He was married, but nothing is known of his personal life.[19]

Some impressions of Varro's personality are obtained from the letters

of Cicero, to whom he appeared formidable, cantankerous and not entirely reliable. In 59 B.C. Cicero, when threatened by Clodius, found
him difficult as a person but for the most part politically useful. In exile
the following year he was less satisfied.[20] But in the years of civil war
there was some degree of friendship between the two men. During the
feverish days before the announcement of Caesar's victory in Africa (46
B.C.), when many Romans engaged in a frenetic pursuit of pleasure,
Varro suggested that he and Cicero should retire to the fashionable
seaside resort of Baiae, which he had described years previously as a
place where old men become boys again.[21] Cicero was shocked by the
unexpected proposal. He feared that their ascetic habits and
philosophical integrity might be damaged by a visit to a place of such
notoriety.[22] In the following year, he decided to introduce Varro as a
speaker who would expound the philosophical position of Antiochus
the Academician in a revised version of his dialogue *Academica*. He discussed with Atticus the reasons for his choice with a punctilious care
for Varro's views and feelings. It is clear from a discreet remark of Atticus, a close friend of Varro, that Varro's social prestige may have
been higher than that of Cicero.[23] In the covering letter to Varro (*Fam.*
9,8) he forestalls any possible displeasure by explaining that through
the accepted convention of dialogue it was permitted to compose a
conversation that had never taken place. With what favour Varro
received the work and its dedication we do not know. Late in the next
year Cicero derived great amusement from what seems to have been
some minor literary contretemps that befell Varro.[24]

2. *TESTIMONIA* AND CHRONOLOGY OF THE MENIPPEANS

In the proem to the *Academica* Varro, the first main speaker in the
dialogue, discusses his lifelong eagerness to expound the doctrines of
Greek philosophy, particularly the technically difficult views of the
Academy, so as to make them intelligible and acceptable to the Roman
reader. He continues:

> *et tamen in illis veteribus nostris, quae Menippum imitati non in-*
> *terpretati quadam hilaritate conspersimus, multa admixta ex in-*
> *tima philosophia, multa dicta dialectice, quae quo facilius minus*
> *docti intellegerent, iucunditate quadam ad legendum invitati.*
>
> (Cicero, *Ac.* 1,8)[25]

(Yet in those works I wrote years ago as adaptations, not translations, of

Menippus, which I diversified with merriment of a sort, many items of technical philosophy were included and many were expressed in the manner of a logician. In order that men of no great education might understand them more easily they were induced to read by a certain attractiveness of presentation.)

These adaptations are then contrasted with Varro's works of technical philosophy. Cicero had been anxious to avoid anything that might cause Varro displeasure, and so this account of Varro's intentions in writing his Menippean satires may be assumed to be in substance accurate, though it is possible that in the context of a philosophical dialogue there was undue stress on their protreptic aim. For Quintilian, Varro was the pioneer and developer of a kind of satire older than that of Lucilius, in which variety was given not merely by change of metres but also by a mixture of prose and verse.[26] He says nothing about the contents or merits of Varro's Menippeans but, being obliged to mention them as a stage in the history of Roman satire, comments on the range of Varro's scholarly works. The omission may imply a value judgement.

Cicero writing in 45 B.C. makes Varro, then aged seventy, describe his Menippeans as old works. Applied to a voluminous writer such a designation need not in itself carry much weight, but it accords with datable references to historical events which fall between 81 B.C. and 67 B.C. The satire Κοσμοτορύνη (World-Stirrer) refers to the African phase of the civil war (225).[27] In 81 B.C. Pompey was sent by Sulla to destroy Marian supporters in Africa. In fighting near Utica 17,000 out of an army of 20,000 were slaughtered and their commander, the proscribed Cn. Domitius perished. The same satire may allude to Varro's assumption of the post of legate in Illyria in 78 B.C.[28] It is possible that Varro did not circulate any satires with contemporary political references until after the death of the dictator Sulla in the same year. His knowledge of the works of Menippus, a writer unlikely to have been widely known, if at all, in Italy, may be attributed to his stay in Athens. In Γεροντοδιδάσκαλος (The Instructor of the Aged) there is righteous indignation concerning slaves who take up arms against their masters (193). Varro probably refers here to the slave revolt led by Spartacus in 73 B.C. On returning from service in Spain with Pompey he may have taken part in Pompey's final liquidation of Spartacus' followers.[29] Varro's satire Sesculixes (Ulysses and a Half) the tale of a man who wandered for thirty years (alternatively for fifteen years), may be to some extent autobiographical, culminating in his return from Spain.[30] A speaker, probably Varro, boasts of handing over his horse to the censor as a formal mark of his return to civil life (478). Pompey went through the same procedure with a panache that emphasized his illegal demand for the consulship of 70 B.C. Pompey was probably briefed on the details of the ceremony by Varro, who wrote a book of instructions for the guidance of his chief in his rapid transition from army commander to the highest civil office of the state.[31] In ὄνος λύρας (364) there is a description of a visit to the cave of Zeus in Crete, which Varro visited while serving under Pompey in his campaign against the pirates of the eastern Mediterranean in 67 B.C.[32] This is the latest datable reference in a Menippean satire. *Trikaranos*, a work concerning the triumvirate of Caesar, Pompey and Crassus of 60 B.C., was in all probability a pamphlet in prose. Even though the title suggests fanciful caricature, Menippean satire would not have seen the appropriate medium for an urgent political document. It is described by the Greek historian Appian as a little book written by a historian and should not be included in the corpus of the Menippean satires.[33]

3. TRANSMISSION AND TITLES

The ancient catalogue of Varro's writings preserved by St. Jerome lists 150 books of Menippean satires.[34] No satire is preserved complete. What remains is some 600 fragments, usually of about a dozen words, cited on a point of linguistic interest by Nonius Marcellus or by some other late grammarian.[35] The problems of Varro's Menippeans are even more baffling than the problems of Lucilius. The fragments are short and difficult to interpret. Many of the quotations are not even complete sentences. The high proportion of verse fragments in the citations by the grammarian Nonius should not be taken as an indication of the relative importance of prose and verse in these works.[36] The traditions about the works of Menippus are very vague (see pp. 162–3 below) and of little help for the elucidation of Roman Menippeans. The medium is flexible and discursive. Varro's material was sometimes bizarre and fantastic. It is thus impossible to reconstruct a single satire, even where, as with *Eumenides*, we have almost fifty quotations. Seneca alone in *Apocolocyntosis* provides a likely exemplar for the scale and shape of the works of his Roman predecessor.[37]

Varro called his satires in a mixture of prose and verse Menippeans (*Menippeae*). They were also called Cynic satires (*cynicae*).[38] Each satire seems to have had a distinctive imaginative title. According to the elder Pliny (*N.H. Praef.* 24), unlike some Greek writers who gave resplendent titles to drab and vacuous works, Varro gave an enterprising title to interesting contents, such as *Sesculixes* (Ulysses and a Half). Many of the ninety or so titles attested are double titles, the second part of which is not a true alternative title as in comedy, but a Greek title with περί and an abstract noun or general expression stating, as in philosophical dialogues, the subject of the satire. One part for eye-catching entertainment, the other for information, the titles epitomize the dual purpose of the works. Often the double titles are a better guide to the contents than the fragments themselves.[39] Posterity has been unkind to seekers for the sensational. For the work entitled *Caprinum Proelium, περὶ ἡδονῆς* (The Battle of the Goats, concerning pleasure), three small colourless fragments of moralizing are attested; for the next title, *Catamitus,* one word only, *scabere* (to scratch). The contrast between the earlier Menippean satires and the later *Logistorici* (Books of History and Philosophy) is instructive.[40] Some of the topics are similar but Varro had now shed the guise of offering something for pleasure, and in accordance with late republican taste abandoned the lavish interspersion of Greek vocabulary and with it Greek titles.

Some of Varro's titles were chosen just for fun. *Papia Papae* is the Latin equivalent of a Greek expression of surprise or disapproval, something similar to what used to be conventionally represented in English by 'Tut tut!' The second title is explicit: περὶ ἐγκωμίων (Concerning Speeches of Eulogy). The fragments show that, as may be expected, the *encomia* were either praise of the undeserving, e.g. in funeral orations (376) and laudations of beauty (370–5), or speeches of abuse in the law-courts (377) and in politics (378). There also appears to be some literary brawling (378, 381): people are mentioned whose Greek slogan is 'Blame rather than emulate'. We have no idea of the purport of Varro's satire.

Akin to the frivolous titles are those with a background in comedy. The seemingly boastful title Τρίφαλλος (Triple Phallus) is found in Naevius and also, with a minor modification, in Aristophanes.[42] According to the second title the subject of Varro's satire, part at least of which is dialogue with the author as participant, is masculinity. Varro's portmanteau proper name *Oedipothyestes* has its counterpart in Timocles' notorious *Orestautocleides*.[43] In such titles it is possible to see that the powerful influence of Old and New Comedy on Roman satire continued after Lucilius either directly or indirectly through Menippus and other mediators. There are also mythological titles which may have had some dramatic framework, e.g. *Aiax Stramenticius* (The Ajax

of Straw)[44] and *Eumenides*. There is also *Pseudaeneas* and various Hercules titles such as *Hercules Socraticus*.[45] These titles may owe something
to the Roman Atellans, but probably more to Hellenistic mockery and
particularly to Cynic reinterpretations of myths. Some titles are Cynic:
Cynicus, Cynodidascalica (The Dog's Handbook of Instruction) and
Κυνορήτωρ (Dog the Orator).The name of Menippus occurs in one
attested title only, Ταφὴ Μενίππου (Menippus' Tomb, or Funeral).

Drollery and moralizing are linked in proverbial titles. Some of the
first titles are Greek: Εὖρεν ἡ λοπὰς τὸ πῶμα (Every Dish Finds its Lid).
The area of contact is defined by the second title περὶ γεγαμηκότων
(concerning the married). Τὸ ἐπὶ τῇ φακῇ μύρον (Sweet Oil in the Lentil Soup), i.e. something precious wasted or the inclusion of something
incongruous, is glossed by a second title that is philosophically esoteric,
περὶ εὐκαιρίας (On the proper occasion for virtue), a technical term of
Stoicism. The Greek proverb seems to have had no Latin equivalent.
Cicero's discussion of εὐκαιρία, which he renders by *opportunitas,*
suggests austere moralizing[46]. Proverbial titles are found in Old Attic
Comedy, another link between Varro's Menippeans and drama.[47] A
Latin proverb with a metrical shape that may suggest a mime title,
Mutuum muli scabunt (Mule Scratches Mule), is accompanied by an un-
expected Greek gloss περὶ χωρισμοῦ (concerning separation). The
proverb was usually applied to mutual flattery, but the subject of
Varro's work was probably the separation of body and soul in death.[48]

4. THE FRAMEWORK OF THE MENIPPEANS

Dialogue in various forms is an important element in the Menippeans.
Someone is told: 'And you, I think, can shut up, seeing that up to now
you too have been behaving like a teenager' (550). Neither speaker nor
listener can be identified. Like Lucilius, Varro is addressed by name in
his own works either intimately by the *praenomen* Marcus (505, 175) or
more formally as Varro. In the satire concerning masculinity, the complaint is expressed: 'I can't see a thing, Varro. This great tall chap in
front of me, whoever he is, is in my light' (562). Unfortunately we do
not know what the three men were trying to do. Many different conventions of dialogue were available to Varro from a complicated Greek
literary tradition, dramatic dialogue from comedy, philosophical
dialogue either of the Platonic kind with conversation between
speakers of more or less equal status or of the Aristotelian kind with
one speaker expounding from a position of authority to an audience of
subordinates, and also works in which a single speaker was interrupted

from time to time in the manner of the diatribe. Varro may have used all these approaches either through direct borrowing or through the medium of Menippus. Varro used a Greek model outside the tradition of Menippus for his satire *Tithonus*, περὶ γήρως (on old age). A dialogue with the same title was written by the third-century Peripatetic Ariston of Ceos. Cicero, however, some three decades later was to consider *Tithonus* an unsuitable title for a dialogue on old age (*Sen.* 3).

Varro adapted other items from Greek descriptions of banqueting and symposia. A Menippean satire entitled *Agatho*, the host in Plato's *Symposium*, may contain criticism or parody of the sexual *mores* of the Platonic original: a speaker, possibly Agathon, says 'I have become a bat, something that is neither mouse nor bird' (13), a reference presumably to sexual ambivalence or deficiency.[49] There is also disapproval of modern Roman banquets, at which unmarried girls were in danger of hearing the vocabulary of sex (11). Plato's Agathon could have had further relevance, as he describes his speech on love as consisting of elements of jest and of moderate seriousness (*Symp.* 197e), an appropriate motto for the Menippean satirist. The satire *Nescis quid vesper serus vehat* (You don't know what late evening may bring) was described as a most elegant work (*lepidissimus liber*) by Aulus Gellius, whose zeal as a collector of literary antiques often surpassed his critical acumen. The excerpts he gives do not support his judgement, for they are a series of commonplace precepts for a correct dinner party, not too little, not too much, guests to be not fewer than three, not more than nine. They should be neither too talkative nor too contemplative; banquets should be improving as well as enjoyable.[50] If Varro used these precepts as a preliminary to a not entirely serious discourse on the transience of human fortune, it is possible that Gellius may have overlooked any irony in the treatment of the subject.

Another kind of framework is provided by the semblance of a dramatic plot based on a well-known play. In the *Eumenides* of Aeschylus Orestes, driven insane by the Furies, finds sanity and absolution from a jury of Athenians presided over by Athena. The theme of Varro's *Eumenides* (A Ship of Fools) is the insanity of contemporary life.[51] Either Varro himself or some dramatic character encounters various aspects of madness. He is taken for a madman by others until he believes it himself (146), but is in the end declared sane by a tribunal of advocates (*forenses*) who recommend that *Existimatio* (Good Reputation) should register him among the sane (147).[52] Men seen by the observer on a high watch-tower are driven to frenzy by three Furies (117), who are interpreted allegorically as the cardinal vices of the times accompanied by the appropriate penalties. Superstition seems to have been the chief Fury that goads men to madness and is abetted by avarice and overreaching ambition. Manifestations of insanity are devious and include physical degeneration through drink (137), sexual infatuation (136) and the belief that all men are mad (148). In his attempts to shake off his apparent madness the central character has recourse to the temple of Cybele, whose eunuch priests and shrieking ritual are presented with garish elaboration,[53] to the equally futile cult of Serapis, and to some of the conflicting sects of philosophy including those of Epicurus and Zeno. Philosophy too may appear as a quack remedy, as in the reflection that there is no delirious dream-vision of the fevered that cannot be explained away by a philosopher.[54] It is tempting to assume that the man's essential sanity was established with the help of Truth (*Veritas,* 141), embodied in the commonsense judgement of Roman citizens as well as in the beliefs of the Academy.[55]

Varro also made use of epic narrative. *Sesculixes* describes the wanderings of a modern Roman who may be identified with Varro himself. To the wanderer's experience of real places, Asia Minor, Athens and Rome, are added intellectual wanderings in different philosophical persuasions. The modern Ulysses like Homer's Odysseus is a real traveller; there is also mention of the idealized Hellenistic Odysseus/Ulysses of the Cynics, compared to Diogenes in the simplicity of his dress (469). The Roman wanderer returns to find that by the standards of former generations morals are debased: the foppish rider compares ill with the tough soldier, who did not hesitate to ride a mount that bit and kicked (479f.); illicit sex contrasts with a true man's joy in the charm of a wife (481f.), an obvious adaptation of the Ulysses theme.

Varro adapts various narrative forms such as a sea journey and a voyage through the night sky, in order to expound his favourite themes, notably the values of philosophy and the contrast between the morals of previous decades and those of his own. *Periplous* (journey of circumnavigation), a title used properly of pilots' guides for navigation and of descriptions of long and adventurous voyages, mentions Rome (415) and Syracuse (416) as if items in a traveller's guide book, but the second part is devoted to philosophy. The Menippeans glide from the world of real experience to that of abstract thought. *Sexagesis* (The Man Aged Sixty) tells of a man who fell asleep as a child and woke up fifty years later (491) when everything in Rome had changed for the worse; lack of loyalty, treachery and indecency in place of former virtues (495) and in place of strict legality the universal law of mutual back-scratching (498).[56] But an interlocutor breaks in: *'erras' inquit 'Marce: accusare nos ruminans antiquitates'* ('You're wrong, Marcus,' he said, 'to accuse us as you chew over tales of antiquity') (505). In this way the satirist defuses his own righteous indignation. In *Endymiones* (The Long Sleepers) the narrator sends his *animus* all over the city to spy out what men were doing when they were awake (105), an enterprising way of presenting a kind of peep-show on human misbehaviour.[57]

The name of Menippus occurs in one title, Ταφὴ Μενίππου (The Burial Place, or possibly Funeral, of Menippus). The funeral games devised by Varro provide a contest in intellectual athletics between philosophers, among them Stoics and Cynics.[58] But the bulk of the fragments contains an indictment of the material values of modern Rome, rich dwellings with tesselated floors (533), elaborate plumbing (532), ostentatious clothes (538) and love of good food and wine (529f.). In *Andabatae* (Blindfold Gladiators) a quaint form of spectacle makes the basis for entertainment and instruction. The antics of the groping performers symbolize man's intellectual blindness and moral waywardness. Many human beings wander to and fro (28); 'no wonder your vision is dim, seeing that gold blinds your eyes as much as a skinful of neat booze' (30). The moral proposition is illuminated by a dominant symbol. Here again Varro has a blueprint for a work of enterprising invention, but we have scant means of appreciating the quality of his craftsmanship.

5. LEADING TOPICS OF THE SATIRIST

Like other satirists Varro recounts what purports to be personal experience and uses the first person as a mouthpiece for intellectual attitudes. But it is not easy to disentangle general ethical propositions from what is truly autobiographical. Reminiscence is often a peg for exhortation, and historical accuracy is subordinated to a moral thesis. *Sesculixes*, as already suggested (p. 157), contains some reporting of Varro's own career. *Bimarcus* (Varro Split) seems to be a dialogue between his two selves, a clash between his different activities, presumably literature and scholarship against philosophy. When writing on human behaviour (περὶ τρόπων, 60), he seems to have started to recite from the *Odyssey*, the tale of the man of many resources (πολύτροπος). His interrupter, the other Marcus, does not understand why, as he assumes that the work will be a study of rhetorical tropes, and therefore maintains that his other self does not know the *Odyssey* (45). Probably the two Marci were continually stumbling over each other's arguments through deliberate misunderstanding of ambiguous terms. But *Bimarcus* is a flippant satire, not to be interpreted as a significant personal document of divided loyalties.[59] Other titles based on Varro's name are more problematical. *Marcipor* (The Boy of Marcus) might suggest a dialogue in which Varro's slave, like Horace's Davus, chastises his master's faults, but the fragments suggest a treatment of moral immaturity. Perhaps the two are not incompatible. *Marcopolis* (Varro's City) is even more baffling. The second title, περὶ ἀρχῆς is ambiguous, as it can refer both to political power and office and also, though this is less likely, to a philosophical first principle. Perhaps Varro's ideal city was of the intellect rather than of real politics. There is nothing in Varro's presentation of himself, in so far as he intended to describe a real individual, to suggest anything of Lucilius' intensely personal assertiveness; it would be inconsistent with what we know of Varro's character.

Attacks on politicians by name may have seemed alien to a Hellenistic medium aimed at philosophical instruction. Crassus, the possessor of wealth on a proverbial scale (36), is the only notable contemporary mentioned by name,. But the eye of the respecter of old Roman integrity looked askance at improper behaviour at *comitia* and elections (450–5), dishonesty in the courts (377f.) and the manipulation of the state religion (278).[60] Provincial affairs also caught his attention. The administration of Macedonia in 77 B.C. was a bad example of extortion and rapacity, and the satire *Flaxtabula*, περὶ ἐπαρχιῶν (on provinces), may have attacked such abuses.[61]

The antithesis of good old times and the bad and new is constantly present in Varro's treatment of human behaviour. The stereotyped example of the woman who carded wool but did not let the cooking spoil (190) is contrasted with the modern woman who, though raped by an unidentified waggon driver, nevertheless overtaxes his resources (192). In former times the new bridegroom gently undid his wife's girdle (187); the words describing the modern contrast are not preserved but his actions (and hers) may easily be guessed. Roman readers may have been patient in accepting the reiteration of the same moralizing attitude. But Varro's topics, though predictable, had real life counterparts. Sempronia, wife of Iunius Brutus, consul of 77 B.C. was, as described by Sallust (*Cat.* 25), a cultured and profligate intriguer. Some years later Clodia, wife of the consul Metellus, behaved in the manner of Varro's bad women.[62] Similarly Varro's indictment of lavish banquets (e.g. 403f.) calls to mind Sulla's sumptuary law of 81 B.C. and other regulations.[63]

Throughout his long life Varro professed the moral values of the countryman who affected to despise city ways. Hunting, originally a respectable pursuit in Italy, had become a farce for the *poseur*.[64] Its modern misuse is the object of Varro's satire *Meleagri* (Great Hunters like Meleager). Men hunt animals insatiably (297f.), stalking deer (293) not for profit, as there could be no market for so many carcasses (295), nor for pleasure, as it is more comfortable to watch a hunt in the theatre than to have one's legs scratched to pieces in woodland (296). Women hunters too (as it seems) strut along with bare legs and their buttocks almost sticking out, whereas Menander's courtesan Thais wore her tunic down to the ankles (300–2).[65]

In his comments on religious matters Varro in his satires shows the reverence for traditional Roman belief and observance that may be expected of Rome's greatest antiquarian. He is not influenced by Menippus' mockery of the gods. He enjoins the good citizen to carry out the customs of Roman cults as duly ordained (265, cf. 94) and he portrays with revulsion the orgiastic religions imported from the Orient.[66]

In Varro's mockery of philosophers it is possible to see a later and more relaxed Cynicism. He portrays the futile battle of words between Stoics and Epicureans (243) in Λογομαχία (The War of the Arguments), and in the kindred Σκιαμαχία (Shadow-Boxing), which has as second title περὶ τύφου, a word used by Cynics and other writers of delusion and more generally of humbug. Like Horace and many other Romans Varro ridicules the claim of the Stoic sage, exemplified for him by Cleanthes, that he alone attained perfection (245). Varro also includes favourable anecdotes concerning Socrates (99,490) and Diogenes (281); In Γνῶθι σεαυτόν (Know Yourself – the Delphic motto) Socrates is important as the man who brought philosophy down from natural speculation to ethics. Varro's attitude to Democritus, a favourite of the Cynics is less certain.[67] In the satire *Cycnus, περὶ ταφῆς* (The Swan, on the funeral) it is reported that the Academic Heraclides Ponticus advocated burning the dead, Democritus pickling them in honey. Burning is preferred as the other method would be intolerably expensive (81). But whether the light-hearted frivolity at the expense of

Democritus is Varro's own opinion or that of another we do not know. The Cynics' principal mythological hero, Heracles, is important in the Menippean satires, and Prometheus, who taught men the cunning ways of civilization, is the subject of *Prometheus,* a satire of uncertain tenor.[68]

The negative outlook of the Cynics had much in common with the scepticism of the Academy during the period of Carneades, who was at war with the dogmatic assertions of the rival sects.[69] But for Varro this attitude was unsatisfactory. He was a pupil of Antiochus, who combined a return to the approach of the original Academy with a measure of eclecticism. More important he was a Roman with experience of public affairs and a reverence for traditional Italian values. While it is impossible to establish a consistent philosophical method and position from fragments, many of which may not express Varro's own view, moral exhortation seems to have been at least as important as dialectical subtlety. It was more appropriate for a Roman and a satirist.

Principles of literary criticism are the main subject of the satire *Parmeno.*[70] The title alludes to the Greek proverb: εὖ μὲν ἀλλ' οὐδὲν πρὸς τὴν Παρμένοντος ὗν (Good, but nothing compared to Parmeno's pig). This is probably based on the story of the actor Parmeno, who reproduced the squeaking of a pig so convincingly that the audience was persuaded only by inspecting his cloak that he had not hidden an animal underneath. His virtuosity was challenged by a rustic, who on the following day produced similar squeaks. The audience preferred Parmeno's noises. Whereupon the rustic produced a pig from under his cloak and guffawed at their critical standards.[71] For the satirist this was an appropriate label for a discussion of the principles of poetry, not least the Aristotelian doctrine of imitation. Varro's framework seems to have been a poetic competition between Greek and Roman (396); the verse insertions may have been extended compositions.[72] The satire also contains an *ars poetica* in prose, with a Hellenistic formulation on the organization of subject matter and style in poetry similar to that given by Lucilius (398), some metrical injunctions (397) and an assessment of the merits of the comic poets in the manner of the canon of Volcacius Sedigitus (399).[73] Ideas which Varro incorporates here in the entertaining medium of a satire were to be developed later in one of his literary treatises, *de Poematis.*[74]

The satire ὄνος λύρας (The Donkey hears the Lyre) is concerned with the power of music.[75] In contrast to the ethos of the greedy philistine, who among other things engages in blood sports for pleasure

(350, 361), Pythagorean harmony and music provide a way to ennoble human life and assuage violent emotions. The harmony of the spheres is described in ornate metaphor as the lyre of the gods ruled by the sun (351). Amphion, perhaps in contrast to his uncultured cattle-drover brother Zethus, may have been introduced to illustrate the force of music as an instrument of ordered civilization (367). Even the wild Phrygian eunuch priests were able with the sound of their timbrels to make a fierce lion gentle (364).[76] Music also helps men in their everyday life. Artless ditties are sung by the labourer in the vineyard and by the seamstress at her frame (363). But there is another aspect of the power of music. It can arouse the passions of the audience in the theatre (365) or stimulate sexual desire. There is a constant play on music and sex by means of ambiguous terms. Briseis was accustomed to play on Achilles' strings; the word *nervia* can refer either to the strings of a lyre or to private parts (368, cf. 366). The satire is baffling in shape as well as in subject matter and argument. There is a comic prologue in iambic trimeters spoken by the personified abstract Φωνασκία Voice Production (348, 355), which introduces itself as 'a stimulant to the voice and the singers' dunghill cock'. There is also the cut and thrust of controversy in dialogue (359–61). An opponent mentions the fourth-century musical theorist Aristoxenus as Varro's principal authority (360). As Aristoxenus combined the Peripatetic approach with elements of Pythagoreanism, he would have been congenial to Varro, who advocated a renewed interest in the beliefs of Pythagoras. Varro's musical satire belongs rather to the world of Greek mathematics and philosophy than to the raucous music-making of the Roman republic, perhaps one of the least distinguished periods in the history of music.[77]

6. THE TRADITION OF MENIPPUS

Direct evidence for the life and work of Menippus is scanty and indirect evidence often difficult to assess.[78] Menippus, who lived about the middle of the third century B.C., was a Phoenician of servile origin, from Gadara who combined Cynicism with profitable usury but in the end committed suicide. Lucian's portrait of him as a jester in a Cynic's cloak who mocked at the pretensions of philosophers may be a dramatic fabrication but the invention is plausible.[79] He is described by various sources as a barking Cynic who bit and jested at the same time, and as a philosopher who combined the serious and the frivolous. Marcus Aurelius saw him as an acrimonious and villainous scoffer at men.[80]

The biography in Diogenes Laertius associates him with mocking laughter without positive moral content and lists among his works: *Nekyia* and 'Wills'. He also wrote a *Symposium* and a work entitled 'The Sale of Diogenes'.[81] The Homeric evocation of the dead in order to ask them questions had comic possibilities. Menippus may have used it as a framework for ridiculing philosophers and other worthies. Horace drew on it for social satire in the dialogue with Teiresias (*Sat.* 2,5). The work entitled 'Wills' was presumably a parody of the wills of philosophers such as Epicurus; a similar title is found in Varro (540–3).[82] The *Symposium* probably used the dialogue form of Plato and Xenophon; in it a dance is called 'The Conflagration of the World'. On the strength of this evidence Menippus sometimes wrote the kind of fantasy found in Varro's satires. Symposiac in contents, if not an alternative title for Menippus' *Symposium,* was the work entitled *Arcesilaus*, from which comes the single extant example of Menippus' prose: 'Some revellers had a drinking party and someone ordered a Spartan ragout; immediately a few pieces of partridge were carried round, roast goose and a fine assortment of cakes'. This gastronomic excerpt will have been part of a satirical philosophers' banquet. Arcesilaus was an Academic philosopher of the third century B.C., an influential sceptic, much concerned with the theory of knowledge. He was said to have been generous by nature and to have died in a fit of drunkenness at the age of seventy-six.[83]

Menippus is said by the grammarian Probus to have embellished his satires with verses of all kinds. One tiny fragment, a piece of a hexameter line, has been preserved: 'Myndos that drinks the brine'.[84] The epic-style epithet for the place, a town on the coast of Caria near Halicarnassus, is not attested elsewhere. The verse may well be original and not a quotation. Lucian's dramatic character Menippus, a dubious guide to the historical person, is accused of making a kind of literature that was neither prose nor verse but an outlandish mixture like a hippocentaur.[85] It would seem that the real Menippus was the inventor of a mode of writing in which prose was combined with original verses and, as occasion arose, with quotations.

7. PROSE AND VERSE

While it is possible to indicate in broad terms the framework of Varro's Menippeans, to assess the texture of his mixture of prose and verse is difficult. The preponderance of verse citations by grammarians is un-

likely to correspond to the relative importance of prose and verse in the
original works. We may assume that such verses as the galliambics in
Eumenides were introduced as an organic part of the narrative. Likewise
the iambic prologue in ὄνος λύρας was a quasi-dramatic introduction
to the work. The range of the metres is large. By far the commonest is
the iambic trimeter, but there are also many examples of the longer
dramatic metres, *septenarii* and *octonarii*. Varro's hexameters, far fewer
in number than the dramatic metres, show some technical advance on
those of earlier exponents. Varro also included verse forms not found in
Lucilius, for example the choliambic and hendecasyllabic metres that
were attempted by Laevius, an experimenting dilettante of the generation after Lucilius. In addition to the simpler lyric systems, such as
bacchiacs and glyconics, he also introduced the Aristophanic and Sotadean metres.[86] We have too small a sample to assess Varro's verses
fairly, but it would appear that they are the work of an industrious
grammarian and scholar rather than an inspired writer.

The prose parts of Varro's Menippean satires as preserved show dis-
concerting extremes from the stylistically well-ordered to the apparently careless, but the brevity of the fragments makes any general
judgement on his use of prose for satirical discourse and dialogue
hazardous.[87] It has been suggested that the prose of Cynics was in an
Asianic tradition, but, even though in later years Cicero reports that
Varro recommended an Asianic orator,[88] any such flamboyance except
for persiflage would be alien to satirical literature. His style contains
the proverbs of everyday discourse, diminutives and other colloquialisms and also characteristic etymological word-plays. The free admixture of Greek words sometimes suggests the easy informality of the
usage in Cicero's letters to Atticus. The Menippeans were written
when the stylistic standards of the age of Lucilius still prevailed.
Varro's Greek springs from his Hellenistic subject matter, but also from
his acceptance of Greek words even where Latin equivalents were
readily available. The tradition of satire was still lexically permissive.[89]

Varro's mixture of prose and verse had descendants in the masterpieces of Seneca and Petronius. After the first century Menippean satire
disappeared as a vehicle of importance for the creative imagination, but
its form was used in the learned extravaganza of Martianus Capella *The
Marriage of Mercury and Philology*, and in Boethius' *Philosophiae Consolatio*
as the legacy of 'the most learned of the Romans'.[90]

9

The *Apocolocyntosis* of Seneca[1]

The Emperor Claudius died suddenly on 13 October A.D. 54, poisoned at the behest of Agrippina, his wife and niece, in order to ensure the succession of her son Nero. He was, however, accorded splendid obsequies. The senate decreed his apotheosis; the worship of the deified Claudius was associated with that of Augustus, and Agrippina became priestess of his cult.[2] On the day of the funeral an oration was delivered by the new emperor. The praises of Claudius' public career and literary achievement were received with serious attentiveness; but at the mention of his foresight and good sense neither audience nor speaker could restrain their mirth. This ambiguous eulogy was written by Seneca and commended by Tacitus (*Ann.* 13,3) for an urbanity suited to the taste of its age.

But that was not all. There has come down under the name of Seneca a satire in a mixture of prose and verse on Claudius' death and deification. This work purports to narrate the events that took place in heaven and in the underworld on 13 October. Released by the Fates from his mortal agony, Claudius follows the route to heaven previously taken by Augustus and Tiberius. He arrives outside the assembly of the gods, and at first his mis-shapen appearance and uncouth voice terrify Hercules, who fears the coming of a thirteenth labour. His true origin is, much to his anger, revealed by the goddess Febris (Fever), who alone has accompanied her palsied protégé on his journey. Hercules, thus reassured, threatens Claudius, who turns from bluster to flattery. There is a lacuna in the transmitted text; the missing piece must have described the manner of Claudius' entry into the council of

165

the gods. When the text resumes, a god (we do not know who) is deriding Claudius' claim to divinity. After being called to order by Jupiter for not adhering to proper senatorial procedure, the gods give their judgement. Though Janus speaks against accepting Claudius into heaven, Diespiter argues in his favour, and this view seems to prevail; but the deified Augustus, speaking for the first time in the divine assembly, indicts his conduct with such fervour that Claudius is expelled and despatched to the underworld under the escort of Mercury. On the way down he admires the sights and sounds of his own funeral procession. In the underworld he is surrounded by the men and women he had killed and is brought to trial before the tribunal of Aeacus. After a one-sided trial of a kind that he had sometimes presided over while Emperor, he is at first condemned to play his favourite game of dice with a bottomless box. The Emperor Caligula appears suddenly and successfully demands the enslavement of Claudius; and so, having been the dupe of freedmen in his lifetime, he becomes the slave of a freedman in the underworld and is compelled to work as a lawyer's clerk. His degradation is thus complete.

The title *Apocolocyntosis* is not found in the manuscript tradition. The epitome of Cassius Dio (60,35) mentions, among the jokes and frivolities that followed the death of Claudius, a work written by Seneca with the title *Apocolocyntosis*, and it glosses this unparalleled word with the comment 'as a sort of deification'.[3] Of the three oldest manuscripts S(angallensis) has an inscription at the beginning: *Divi Claudii incipit ἀποθέωσις Annaei Senecae per satiram* and a similar subscript at the end. V(alentianensis) and L(ondiniensis) along with most of the later manuscripts have *Ludus de morte Claudii (Caesaris)*.[4] There is a clear connection between the title in S and the title and comment given by Dio. The word *ludus* is used regularly in classical Latin, e.g. Lucilius 1039M, of the activity of literary composition, but not known as a specific work or title. This usage is first found in such post-classical dramatic or quasi-dramatic titles as Ausonius' *Ludus septem sapientum* and the twelfth-century *Ludus de Antichristo*, but it may belong to classical times also, for it is not improbable linguistically and may also be regarded as a rendering of the Greek παίγνιον.[5] The strange title *Apocolocyntosis* could hardly have been invented by anyone other than the author. Dio's comment shows that even for Greek readers the bizarre coinage needed a gloss, and in the title given by S there has been substituted for the incomprehensible original an explanatory title which, though Greek, could be found in the text of a Latin author

(Cic. *Att.* 1,16,13). *Ludus de morte Claudii* may have been added by Seneca himself or by contemporaries, not as a double title in combination with *Apocolocyntosis* in the manner of Varro,[6] but merely as a convenient alternative title which described the contents; it is, however, more likely to have been added in late antiquity or in Carolingian times.

The word ἀποκολοκύντωσις is clearly a parody of ἀποθέωσις (apotheosis), but the meaning of the word and the implications of the parody have caused much speculation. It cannot mean 'transformation into a pumpkin', for in the work as transmitted Claudius is not turned into a pumpkin, nor is it likely that such a metamorphosis took place at the end of the work in a section no longer extant, for the subscript in the oldest manuscript suggests that the text is complete, and the pungent conclusion as we have it could hardly be bettered.

The basis of the word ἀποκολοκύντωσις is the Greek κολοκύντη, Latin *cucurbita*, the gourd or pumpkin. Various vegetables of the order *cucurbitaceae* were used in antiquity as food and as storage vessels.[7] It is not certain whether Seneca had in mind the large round *cucurbita maxima* or the *lagenaria,* the so-called bottle gourd. It is often assumed that the gourd was associated unequivocally with stupidity. In Latin it is only in Apuleius that *cucurbita* is used indisputably of a silly empty head: *nos cucurbitae caput non habemus ut pro te moriamur* (*Met.* 1,15,2). The meaning at Petronius 39,12 may be similar, but the context does not settle the matter. In proverbial usage the Greek κολοκύντη is associated not with stupidity but with health, e.g. Epicharmus 154 (*CGF* (Kaibel)); nor is there any necessary connection between κολοκύντη and stupidity in the passages adduced by commentators.[8] While the Latin *cucurbita* bore some associations of stupidity, the Greek κολοκύντη, which is the basis of Seneca's title, seems to have had none. Nor can the formation of ἀποκολοκύντωσις be used to determine the meaning, for as a parody it may have been permitted to violate any canons concerning the relationship between the form and meaning of an abstract noun.[9]

It has been suggested that as Claudius was a fool both in life and in death, the word is to be interpreted as 'deification of a pumpkin'.[10] But this assumes as certain the problematical association of κολοκύντη with stupidity. A very different view has been accepted by a number of modern critics, that in form and meaning ἀποκολοκύντωσις is based on ἀποραφανίδωσις, the Greek punishment for adultery in which a horseradish was thrust into the adulterer's body *per anum* and that, as the gourd is the largest of vegetables and the shape of some species particularly suited to the action, the title is an indecent joke depending on comic exaggeration. In favour of this view is the parallel in formation between the two words, for both are based on a vegetable. But no stories from antiquity depend on such a jocular exaggeration; nor is it likely that a work which is for the most part free from obscenity should have been given a coarse title. Finally the reference is perhaps too recherché, for the old Greek practice, itself a comedian's joke, is rarely referred to by Latin writers.[11]

It is clear from Dio's gloss that *Apocolocyntosis* represented a parodied deification and was intended by the author to imply that this apotheosis was a ludicrous sham. The form of the word but not its meaning may have been suggested by ἀποραφανίδωσις, and any such morphological association would in itself carry a sneer. Perhaps Seneca chose the pumpkin as the means of ridiculing Claudius' divinity, on the grounds that it would be difficult to think of anything more lacking in positive characteristics than a pumpkin.[12] It seems also that, just as in England children often find the word 'sausage' grounds for a giggle or a guffaw, there was something intrinsically comical about a pumpkin, for why otherwise did the comic poet Epicrates (frg 11K) ridicule the philosophers who attempted to classify it?

It cannot seriously be doubted that Seneca is the author. Dio attributes an *Apocolocyntosis* to Seneca; the oldest manuscript, which bears a title related to Dio's, attributes the work to Seneca. It is ingenuous to argue that Seneca the philosopher, in writing a satire, could not have made light-hearted jests about philosophy, or that Seneca the politician, who was in close association with Agrippina and Nero, could not have attacked the government and apotheosis of Claudius.[13] As for the date of the work, it was composed during the early months of the reign of Nero, some time after the death of Narcissus, and possibly it was at first circulated anonymously.[14] We need not suppose that its publication was delayed until about A.D. 60; for Seneca is unlikely to have had any hesitation in attacking immediately the man whom he hated; and at the beginning of his reign Nero promised the senate that the malpractices of his predecessor's régime would cease (Tac. *Ann.* 13,4). Further, Dio mentions *Apocolocyntosis* along with jokes that belong to the beginning of Nero's reign.[15] It has been argued that *Apocolocyntosis* was written in A.D. 60 for Nero's newly instituted festival, the *Neroneia,* as part of the propaganda for a new golden age. But the terminology of a golden age is found not merely in the fourth chapter of *Apocolocyntosis*

but also in Seneca's *de Clementia* (A.D. 55–6) and in the first eclogue of
Calpurnius Siculus (late in A.D. 54).[16] Moreover, a Menippean satire
would not have been a suitable vehicle for a recitation at a public
festival.

Unlike many writers of satire, Seneca was no outsider hungry for
recognition or recompense at the time of the composition of
Apocolocyntosis. Born a few years before the beginning of the Christian
era he was a son of L. Annaeus Seneca, the eminent teacher of rhetoric
whose compilations of *Suasoriae* and *Controversiae* are still extant; he
was also an uncle of the poet Lucan. Famous at an early age as an orator,
he obtained a quaestorship and was saved from being executed by the
jealous Caligula through the pleadings of one of the Emperor's mis-
tresses. As protégé of Claudius' wife Agrippina, he had been Nero's tutor
for five years and had held the office of praetor. On the death of
Claudius he became Nero's chief political adviser, and his collabora-
tion with Afranius Burrus, the praetorian prefect, ensured imperial
stability for some years.[17] In addition, Seneca was already famous as a
Stoic writer of uncompromising morality.[18] When a man who is pre-
eminent in the state and in letters writes a satire that is directed not at a
class or a movement but at an individual, it is legitimate to inquire
into his motives.

The language of *Apocolocyntosis* is venomous in its vilification of
Claudius, as in the description of the trembling hand that was only firm
in making the gesture that condemned men to death (6,2). Seneca was
moved by a desire for revenge. At the beginning of Claudius' reign he
had been banished to Corsica on the charge of having slept with Julia
Livilla, the Emperor's niece.[19] During his years of exile, in spite of his
adulation of Claudius in the *Consolatio* dedicated to the influential imperial freedman Polybius, he is unlikely to have felt affection for the
Emperor who had condemned him on a charge that was no more than
plausible. The tone of embitterment and vindictiveness in *Apocolocyntosis* should not be attributed to Seneca's Spanish origin, for though
born in Spain he was of Italian or near-Italian stock.[20] He wished to
take posthumous revenge on the man who deprived him for eight years
of his prime from sharing in the political, social and intellectual life of
Rome. Both the restrained pessimism of the *Consolatio*, addressed to his
mother Helvia, and the frenzied adulation of *ad Polybium* show that
Corsica was as loathsome to Seneca as Tomis to Ovid.[21] In later years
he was, according to Dio (61,10,2), anxious to disclaim earlier excesses
of adulation forced on him by necessity, and so the contrast between

the flattery in *ad Polybium* and the denigration in *Apocolocyntosis* is less violent than would appear from the strictures of some of his moralizing critics.[22] That Seneca ridiculed Claudius' bodily infirmities and handicaps is not surprising, for the ancient tradition of invective allowed malicious representation of an enemy's physical characteristics.[23] More important, his portrait of Claudius as a slobbering and infirm dolt is supported by Suetonius' Life. It seems that to both writers the physical disabilities were part of a contemptible warped personality.

It is difficult to separate the personal invective of the aggrieved subject from the statesman's political criticisms. Seneca attacks Claudius for executing thirty-five senators and 221 knights (14,1), for extending the franchise to untamed provincials (3,3), for travesties of law-court procedure (12,3,19–23) and for failing to control arrogant freedmen (6,2). These attacks are confirmed in detail by Suetonius, by the incomplete account of Tacitus, and also by Cassius Dio. Part of Seneca's indictment is concentrated in the speech of Augustus who, as the founder of the dynasty, was an effective mouthpiece for complaints against the executions during Claudius' reign;[24] but attacks are made throughout the work, especially in the funeral lament and the scene in the underworld. Such criticisms by the statesman who was close to palace affairs should be taken seriously, and in fact they correspond to aspects of Claudius' policy which are of fundamental importance in modern scholarly interpretations. Whether or not Claudius was harassed by the plots of a senatorial opposition,[25] the indictment of his destruction of the traditional ruling class stands; it is instructive to note the relief expressed by Calpurnius Siculus at the beginning of the next reign (1,60ff.). While Claudius' extension of the franchise seems far sighted to some modern scholars, to contemporaries it must have seemed imprudent; it was also one of the causes of corruption at court among freedmen whom Claudius could not or would not restrain. Nero's promise to the senate to do better (Tac. *Ann.* 13,4) shows clearly that Claudius' abuses of justice were hated and feared. Some modern scholars with the aid of documentary evidence have argued that there was some effective control by the Emperor himself and not merely the capricious rule of self-seeking freedmen. But the rehabilitation of Claudius, in some measure justified, can be taken too far, and Seneca's criticism, for all its vindictiveness, has some value as a historical document.[26]

It is more difficult to assess the relationship between *Apocolocyntosis* and events early in the reign of Nero. The hexameters of chapter 4 contain fulsome adulation of Nero's imperial *numen* and his literary and musical virtuosity, but apart from a promise of a rule of law (4,1,24) there is no mention of statecraft. Sentiments on the arrival of a new golden age, both here and in the contemporary first eclogue of Calpurnius Siculus (1,42ff.), suggest common hopes or agreed views.[27] So much of Seneca's political aims and attitudes may be discovered from *Apocolocyntosis*. But the work should not be interpreted as a defence of Agrippina against the suspicion of having had Claudius poisoned; for though the narration seems to support the official version of Claudius' death, it also contains little that could specifically contradict rumours of poisoning. Nor should it be taken as an indictment of Agrippina's conduct during the reign of Claudius, for such political implications, though possible, are too remote to have been an important part of Seneca's intentions.[28] It is, however, absurd to maintain that he conceived of the work as a manual of political behaviour like *de Clementia*.[29] A satire may have political implications without being either a practical manifesto or a theoretical treatise.

Apocolocyntosis is sometimes interpreted as an attack on Claudius in particular as the unworthy recipient of divinity, or in general on the convention of imperial apotheosis. It is unlikely, however, that the work was part of a campaign to have Claudius' apotheosis rescinded; at all events Claudius, who as Emperor had been a god to the Britons, even at the end of the reign of Nero retained the title *divus*, as is shown by inscriptions from both Italy and Egypt.[30] The deification of Claudius, though a matter for levity, was accepted for official purposes; the atmosphere was thus completely different from that associated with a *damnatio memoriae*. In such a situation *Apocolocyntosis* was not to be construed as a protest against an unsuitable deification but to be enjoyed as part of the frivolity. The success of the equivocal *laudatio* which Seneca wrote for Nero may even have suggested the opportunity for the satire: both the official panegyric and the funeral lament in *Apocolocyntosis* damn by fulsome praise.[31]

Nor should the work be considered as a philosopher's revulsion from the official apotheosis of a dead human being.[32] For just as Seneca had looked forward in *ad Polybium* to Claudius' future apotheosis (12,5) in *Apocolocyntosis* and also in *de Clementia* he describes Nero in language that goes beyond what belongs to a mortal man. Where he deems it appropriate he uses the persuasive language of courtly flattery; parallels were to hand from Cicero as well as from the Augustan poets Virgil and Horace.[33] Furthermore, Seneca was probably too astute a politi-

cian to underestimate the value of apotheosis as an instrument of imperial rule in oriental and backward provinces. However, from the
time of Alexander the deification of a ruler living or dead was to the
sophisticated a matter for amusement as well as disbelief; it evoked a
rhetorical sneer from Lucan and provided the occasion for Vespasian's
last joke on earth: *vae! puto deus fio* (Oh dear! I think I'm turning into a
god, Suet. *Vesp.* 23,4).[34] *Apocolocyntosis*, the title itself a parody of
apotheosis, mocked the imperial convention, but that was not its principal function.

To assign a single function to *Apocolocyntosis* as an exclusive explanation of its contents and form is to miss the many-sided subtleties of a
work in which personal invective passes imperceptibly into the
criticisms of a statesman, and in which a fine literary craftsman,
without going beyond what is appropriate for a satire, exhibits a wide
range of stylistic virtuosity.

The narrative is notably terse and economical. No words are wasted
on tempting but unnecessary descriptions of Claudius' route to and
from heaven. The prose is brisk, sometimes playfully jerky with
calculated nonchalance of expression; vocabulary and construction
belong to the language of educated speech.[35] The colloquial is intensified in incongruous places, and many homely proverbs are uttered by
the gods in council.[36]

Literary burlesque is discernible at various points. A jaunty parody
of the historian's preface declares theme and sources and vouchsafes ob-
jectivity.[37] But as events in the sky and the underworld belong rather
to the writer of fabulous narrative from whom an oath of veracity was
to be expected, Seneca offers such a pledge.[38] Later in the work he
gibes at historiography, when in reporting the speech of Janus, he
refuses to rewrite the original words with the historian's customary
stylization.[39] The speech of Augustus parodies his *Res Gestae* and
possibly some quirks of his way of speaking.[40]

The essential characteristic of the work as a Menippean satire is the
insertion of original verse into the prose narrative. Many pieces of imaginative literature such as Plato's *Phaedrus* and Theocritus' *Thalysia*
begin with an elaborate statement of time and place as part of an artistic
mise-en-scène. Seneca begins his narrative with overblown epic hexameters to describe the season and the time of day, and so parodies both
this respected convention and also the style of contemporary poets.[41]

After the promise of the Fate Clotho to kill Claudius, there follow
thirty-two hexameters in an elevated style, in which Apollo praises

Nero and predicts a new golden age.[42] Here a traditional literary language is combined with the language of Hellenistic ruler-cult. Nero is compared with the evening and morning stars in accordance with literary precedents, but a comparison with the sun suggests rather the formal language for the worship of a monarch.[43] The flattery is gross but relevant, for Seneca implies a contrast with Claudius and then intensifies the exaltation of Nero by plunging to the vulgar phrasing of Claudius' last words. A great man's last words were considered characteristic of his life. Claudius' final *vae! me concacavi* was interpreted by Seneca as particularly suited to the quality of his government.[44]

To make himself more formidable before Claudius, Hercules utters a tragic speech of fourteen iambic lines using the language of high poetry. It has been plausibly suggested that Seneca here parodies his own *Hercules Furens*, just as in the anapaests of lamentation for Claudius he travesties a convention which he himself used in tragic *naenia*.[45] The situation in which Claudius meets his own funeral procession is intrinsically comic, and the mock solemnity of the dirge discredits him through ironical praise:[46]

> *deflete virum, quo non alius*
> *potuit citius discere causas,*
> *una tantum parte audita,*
> *saepe ne utra. quis nunc iudex*
> *toto lites audiet anno?*
> *tibi iam cedet sede relicta,*
> *qui dat populo iura silenti,*
> *Cretaea tenens oppida centum.*
> *caedite, maestis pectora palmis,*
> *o causidici, venale genus.*
> *vosque poetae lugete novi,*
> *vosque in primis qui concusso*
> *magna parastis lucra fritillo.*

delectabatur laudibus suis Claudius et cupiebat diutius spectare. inicit illi manum Talthybius deorum et trahit capite obvoluto, ne quis eum possit agnoscere, per campum Martium et inter Tiberim et Viam Tectam descendit ad inferos.

(12,3,19–31 – 13,1)

(Weep for the hero who could take cognizance of cases quicker than anyone else, hearing one side only and often not even that. What judge today will hear through the whole of the year? For thee that giver of judgements to a mute throng, the ruler of a hundred townships of Crete, will give place and vacate his seat. Beat your breasts with blows of lamentation, you barristers, a bribeable brigade. Mourn too, you modern poets, but especially you who have made a pile at the shake of the dice-box.

Claudius was delighted at his laudation and wanted to watch the procession longer, but Mercury, the Talthybius of the gods, laid hands on him and dragged him away with his head covered so that no-one could recognize him, and crossing the Campus Martius went down to the underworld between the Tiber and the Covered Way.)

Hellenistic writers, the sillographers in particular, quoted lines from Homer in incongruous contexts and with a dislocation of meaning.[47] For Seneca such quotations are an instrument of ridicule and vituperation. In questioning Claudius, Hercules uses the Homeric line:

$$\tau i \varsigma \, \pi \acute{o} \theta \epsilon \nu \, \epsilon i \varsigma \, \acute{a} \nu \delta \rho \hat{\omega} \nu, \, \pi \acute{o} \theta \iota \, \tau o \iota \, \pi \acute{o} \lambda \iota \varsigma \, \acute{\eta} \delta \grave{\epsilon} \, \tau o \kappa \hat{\eta} \epsilon \varsigma;$$

(*Od.* 1,170)

(Who are you? Where are your city and parents?)

Claudius is delighted by the hint of culture among the gods, and replies in an appropriate and innocent Homeric line. But once again a traditional motif is applied in a new way, for Claudius in his lifetime was an antiquarian dilettante who had quoted Homer both in the courts and before the men of the watch.[48] In an additional jab of malice Seneca comments that Claudius' reply ought rather to have been the next line of Homer:

$$\H{\epsilon} \nu \theta a \, \delta' \, \dot{\epsilon} \gamma \grave{\omega} \, \pi \acute{o} \lambda \iota \nu \, \H{\epsilon} \pi \rho a \theta o \nu, \, \H{\omega} \lambda \epsilon \sigma a \, \delta' \, a \acute{v} \tau o \acute{v} \varsigma.$$

(*Od.* 9,40)

(and there I sacked a city and put the men to death.)

Quotations for ironical use are taken from the established classics and from a variety of sources. The phrase *non passibus aequis* in the *Aeneid* describes the short steps of the little boy Iulus in contrast to the long strides of his father Aeneas. In *Apocolocyntosis* the same phrase is used of Claudius' shuffling limp.[49] The tag πάντα φίλων πλήρη 13,6), a parody of the saying attributed to Thales, πάντα θεῶν πλήρη (DKV A22), is found in Hellenistic Cynic literature.[50] Seneca puts it into the mouth of Claudius when surrounded by the kinsfolk and administrators whom he had executed; for, as Suetonius comments (*Claud.* 39), he was notoriously absent-minded about the fate of his victims. The good taste of *Apocolocyntosis* has been questioned by some; its literary resourcefulness is beyond reproach.

While Seneca's originality is guaranteed by his topical theme and his expert criticism of Claudius' policies, his indebtedness to two traditional motifs, the journey to the underworld and the council of the gods, is less easy to assess. Varro's Menippeans were obviously Seneca's immediate forerunners in form: a quotation in *Apocolocyntosis* (8,1 from *Men.* 583) shows that he was familiar with them. But no model can be found for Seneca's theme in the extant fragments of Varro. The influence of Varro's source, Menippus, is problematical, and could be dismissed were it not for certain resemblances between *Apocolocyntosis* and various works of Lucian, who wrote in the second century A.D. independent of the Latin literary tradition. In *Icaromenippus*, Menippus visits the court of heaven and on entering is asked for his identity by Zeus, who quotes the same Homeric line that is used for a similar question in *Apocolocyntosis* (*Icaromen.* 22f.). In Lucian's *Council of the Gods* the gods complain that undesirable *parvenus* are deified, and a bill is passed which allows impostors to be thrown into Tartarus (*Deorum Conc.* 1 and 15). The similarity with Seneca's satire is obvious.[51] But while it is at least plausible to suppose that there was in Hellenistic times a number of comic works by Menippus or other writers which contained a journey to heaven, a divine assembly and a condemnation in the underworld, we cannot estimate the extent of the influence of such works on Seneca, not least because gods in comic dispute were to be found outside Hellenistic Cynic literature, notably in Old Comedy and in the *Battle of the Frogs and Mice.*[52] In the same way, a visit to the underworld and an ascent to heaven could be paralleled from Aristophanes.

Whatever the influence of Greek forerunners on the framework of Seneca's satire,[53] there was a Latin precedent for the use of the divine assembly to attack the life and career of an individual mentioned by name. In Lucilius' *Concilium Deorum* the gods deliberate about the death of L. Cornelius Lentulus Lupus, and then pronounce sentence. But we can judge only imperfectly how Lucilius developed his attack, and so firm conclusions about Seneca's debt to him are impossible. Nor do we know what Seneca owed to the literature of political pamphleteering.[54] There is nothing in the transmitted evidence to contradict the view that by ancient standards *Apocolocyntosis* is a work of unusual originality.

That Seneca's satire was an immediate success we cannot doubt. But shortly afterwards the political disgrace of Seneca, a change in literary tastes, and the topical subject of the work may all have contributed to its eclipse, for it is not referred to again until Cassius Dio mentions it in the early part of the third century A.D. But Suetonius probably used it as a source, and Juvenal may have it in mind at the end of his sixth satire.[55] Quintilian's silence may have betokened either personal dislike or political discretion, and a pasquinade on a recently deified Caesar was perhaps deemed unsuitable reading for the embryonic orator of imperial Rome.[56] That Tacitus does not refer to it has been explained satisfactorily on the grounds that to have mentioned it would have been alien to the dignity of history.[57] Seneca was much read by Christian writers at the time of the revival of letters at the end of the fourth century A.D. but did not enjoy a vogue among pagan writers.[58] It is unlikely that there was widespread renewal of interest in *Apocolocyntosis*. Commentators and grammarians never cite it, nor are any ancient Scholia preserved, but perhaps the respected name of its author ensured its preservation at the time when the roll was being superseded by the codex. The earliest evidence that it had passed into Carolingian times is an imitation by Radbert, the distinguished theologian of Corbie, who died about A.D. 860.[59]

Our text is based primarily on three manuscripts, the most important of which is a codex of ninth- or tenth-century date in St Gall, Sangallensis 569 (S), probably of German origin, and possibly from Fulda; the other two are Valentianensis 411 (V), a manuscript from the Rheims area to be assigned to the end of the ninth century, and Londiniensis add. 11983 (L), a manuscript of French origin now in the British Library, probably of the second half of the eleventh century. They derive from a common archetype, for all three have the same lacuna at the end of chapter 7. None of the later manuscripts, some forty in number, seems to offer witness of an independent transmission.[60] The mediaeval glosses to be found in an Oxford manuscript (Bodl. 292 [2446]), which are somewhat similar to the commentary on Seneca's Tragedies by Trevet, preserve nothing of textual value, nor do the comments include anything based on ancient tradition.[61] The first edition was produced in Rome in 1513.[62] The second edition, printed in Basle in 1515, was made under the supervision of Rhenanus, who recommended the work in his preface as an example of the castigation of a bad ruler. This same volume also contains *Moriae Encomium*, written in England in 1509 by Erasmus, who in his preface mentioned *Apocolocyntosis* as a precedent for a piece of sharp frivolity.[63] *Apocolocyntosis* has now become part of the living tradition of European literature.[64]

That Seneca the philosopher and statesman also wrote satire has sometimes caused surprise and disapproval. None the less, *Apocolocyntosis* has its proper place in his creative work. Through his wide knowledge of political policy and close connection with Claudius' successor, and because of the temporary optimism of the times, he was able to write something almost unique in the imperial age, an informed political satire. This was only possible because the theme was congenial to his imperial master.[65] But *Apocolocyntosis* is more than a political satire. It contains adroit parody of many forms and conventions, some of which Seneca had practised himself, and its sharp satire is akin to the caustic comments on human behaviour that occur in many of his serious prose works.[66] An element of playful inconsequentiality in the narrative may suggest that the work was intended primarily as an accomplished *jeu d'esprit* for the immediate entertainment of knowledgeable readers rather than as a possession for posterity. But it is to be esteemed as a classic of Menippean satire and a masterpiece of savage jocularity.

The *Satyricon* of Petronius[1]

I. THE AUTHOR AND DATE OF THE *SATYRICON*

Petronius, the author of the *Satyricon*, may safely be identified with Petronius the consular whose career and last days are described by Tacitus in the *Annals* (16,18–19). As governor of Bithynia and as consul he had shown energy and administrative ability, but his natural bent was idleness and a mastery of civilized dissipation so discriminating that Nero became completely dependent on his judgement as consultant on refined luxury (*elegantiae arbiter*). As one of the close intimates of Nero he incurred the jealousy of the praetorian prefect Tigellinus. In A.D. 66 false accusations were brought and the death of Petronius demanded. He ended his own life at Cumae near the bay of Naples, spending his last hours in a spirit of elegant nonchalance.

The leading characteristics of Petronius as portrayed by Tacitus are in many ways an inversion of established Roman values. Though of proved capability in imperial service he gained fame not through ambitious devotion to duty but from a studied indolence reversing the role of night and day. In vice also he was an eccentric, no commonplace debauchee and spendthrift but a connoisseur of the lavish and the recherché. In an age of the grand manner and artificial posturing he was informal and blasé, his words and actions all the more acceptable because they gave the appearance of unrhetorical candour. His death scene contrasts with the enforced suicides recorded in the previous chapters of the *Annals*. Seneca's death, in many ways an imitation of that of Socrates, was a model of philosophical correctness and fortitude.

Lucan died reciting his own heroic poetry and his father Mela, in a hasty final will, left wealth to Tigellinus.[2] The style of Petronius' death was different. There were no exhortations to unflinching self-possession, no improving precepts from philosophers or reflections on the immortality of the soul; instead, the recitation of frivolous verses. In place of a will flattering and enriching Nero and his favourite Tigellinus, Petronius prepared a detailed catalogue of the Emperor's debaucheries with the names of partners attached and despatched it to the palace. Nero's surprise that his nocturnal enterprises should be known to Petronius indicated that the 'arbiter' was not a party to them. Although Tacitus seems to have had a covert admiration for Petronius, he does not mention the *Satyricon*. His silence is not surprising. The senatorial historian who ignored the *Apocolocyntosis*, even though it was of political interest, could not acknowledge acquaintance with disreputable novelistic writings.[3]

The full name of the author of the *Satyricon* was in all probability T. Petronius Niger, suffect consul in *c*. A.D. 62.[4] The *praenomen* Caius in one mention of Petronius' name in Tacitus is likely to have been an error of manuscript transmission.[5] The name Arbiter, attached to Petronius in the title given by some manuscripts of Petronius, is a most improbable *cognomen* for a Roman of social standing. It was either a nickname coined by the author or his friends, or more likely a grammarian's attempt to associate the author of *Satyricon* with the man whom Tacitus had described as *elegantiae arbiter*.[6] The author may also be identified with the consular T. Petronius who, according to the elder Pliny, when about to die, smashed a very expensive wine dipper to prevent it from passing into Nero's hands and to deprive him of a legacy for his table; and also with a T. Petronius who with whimsical irony reproached Nero the extravagant spendthrift with squalid meanness.[7]

If Tacitus' Petronius was the author of the *Satyricon* the earlier part of A.D. 66 is the latest poossible time for the composition of the work. It will be necessary to argue this point at some length, because a generation ago there was a revival of the old theory that the *Satyricon* belonged to the age of the Antonines or the third century A.D.[8] Neronian dating is supported by internal evidence, particularly in the part of the work known as the *Cena Trimalchionis*, the rich freedman's supper party, where there is a large element of social realism.[9] Some names point to Neronian times. A guest who is a freedman describes himself with comical scorn as the son of a king (57,4); this is probably a reference to the imperial freedman Pallas (d. A.D. 62), who claimed kinship with ancient Arcadian royalty. The allusion would be pointless or incomprehensible later than the reign of Nero.[10] Trimalchio is a keen admirer of a gladiator Petraites (52,3; 71,6); there was a famous gladiator of this name in Campania in Neronian times.[11] Trimalchio murders the lyrics of Menecrates (73,3), a reference to the celebrated vocalist of the same period (Suet. *Nero* 30,2). Another freedman boastfully compares the quality of his own voice in his youth with that of Apelles (64,4); a famous singer called Apelles was strangled by order of Caligula (Suet. *Calig.* 33,1). Similar dating is suggested by references to events and social life. The story told by Trimalchio of the man who was executed by the Emperor for having invented unbreakable glass (51) is associated with Tiberius by both Pliny (*N.H.* 36,195) and Dio (57,21), thus suggesting an early rather than a late imperial dramatic date. In A.D. 65 a Carthaginian persuaded Nero to finance a hunt for Dido's treasure (Tac. *Ann.* 16,1–3). Verses in the *Satyricon* (128,6) allude to buried gold in a dream. The reference is imprecise, but may be of some significance when added to the other evidence for dating.[12] Trimalchio in his pretentiousness wears a golden ring with iron studs (32,3). A ring of pure gold would have been taken at the time as a mark of equestrian status, which he was not allowed to claim. In the period after Hadrian, however, the gold ring was no longer a certain token of equestrian rank.[13] Just as Trimalchio wishes to be depicted on his tomb as wearing five gold rings, he desires with equally dishonest pretension to be described as Trimalchio Maecenatianus, i.e. freedman of Maecenas. By Flavian times fewer ex-slaves of private citizens added to their name that of the family in which they had served even when it was senatorial. In the following century the joke in Petronius would not have been understood.[14]

One of the most important arguments is that concerning *manumissio per mensam*. It is maintained that Trimalchio's slaves crowd round the table expecting manumission (71,1) by a convention that belongs to the third century. But it is impossible to handle a custom of Greek origins for chronological purposes; in any case Trimalchio does not manumit the slaves. The careful research of modern scholars has demonstrated that the social and economic conditions described in the *Satyricon* belong to the first century and to no later period. Large-scale farms worked by slaves in the first century such as those of Trimalchio, were replaced in the second by farms of small tenants (*coloni*). Trimalchio made his money as a Campanian wine-shipper but Campania ceased to be an important trading centre for wine in the next century.[15] Discussions of rhetoric and literature are better suited to the age of Nero than to that of the so-called second sophistic movement of the second century.[16] The theory of a late date may now be regarded as conclusively rebutted, but it has had a good effect in that the social and literary milieu of the *Satyricon* has received a fresh scrutiny.

It is therefore reasonable to postulate a dramatic date of some time about the middle of the first century A.D., but one should not expect complete historical accuracy in a novelistic text. Likewise a certain caution about place may be desirable. Real places such as Croton are the scene of some episodes in the story, but as for the setting of the *Cena Trimalchionis* and the parts of the narrative immediately preceding it, while in strictly naturalistic terms Puteoli (Pozzuoli) is the most likely place, it is perhaps better to propose some imaginary town by the sea on the Bay of Naples.[17]

2. TITLE AND TEXT

The title of the work is generally accepted to have been *Satyricon*, in form a Greek genitive plural with *libri* understood, a convention that corresponds to titles such as *Milesiaka*, the collection of short tales associated with Miletus written by Aristides about 100 B.C., and in the later novelistic tradition to *Poimenikon*, the title of Longus' pastoral romance about Daphnis and Chloe. In Latin there are titles such as Virgil's *Georgicon*.[18] The title *Saturae* has very limited mediaeval attestation and probably arose as a facile gloss on a more difficult Greek title; an original Latin *Saturae* is unlikely to have been corrupted into a more complicated Greek word.[19] *Satyrica* properly means things concerning satyrs, as in the title of a Greek work on the Marsyas story. The work of Petronius has nothing to do with the satyrs of Greek mythology, but the title is appropriate for a tale about lecherous rogues.[20] But *Satyricon* may also have suggested the tradition of satire; John the Lydian, with a knowledge that was admittedly derivative, classed Petronius with Turnus and Juvenal as one who in his virulence violated the law of satire.[21] Menippean titles could be fanciful and obscure, so a hybrid made up of an- ικός suffix and a first half that suggested *satura* is a possible interpretation.[22] Ambiguity of title matches the ambiguity of the shape and contents of the *Satyricon*; it is significant that the author who was placed among the satirists by John the Lydian (or his sources) was viewed by Macrobius as a writer of fictitious narrative like Apuleius.[23] From the title one may expect a tale in the form of a novel that includes ingredients from the Roman tradition of satire.

Encolpius narrates the adventures that befell himself and his boy friend Giton, who were accompanied in the first half of the extant story by Ascyltos, another ne'er-do-well rogue. Encolpius is pursued by the anger of Priapus, who has made him impotent; he is also in constant fear of the police. They pass quickly from a rhetorician's debate to a jealous quarrel, a tussle in the market place, and then to an expiatory orgy conducted by the priestess Quartilla, followed a couple of days later by the dinner party given by the rich freedman Trimalchio. After a further lovers' quarrel at which Giton leaves with Ascyltos, Encolpius meets Eumolpus, an old vagabond poet, in an art gallery. Eumolpus then becomes enamoured of Giton, who had returned to Encolpius. After a brawl in their lodging house and Ascyltos' vain attempt to find the hidden Giton (Ascyltos then drops out of the story) the two lovers accompany Eumolpus on board a ship. When under way they discover that the company includes Encolpius' enemy Lichas and the passionate Tryphaena, from whom Giton had been trying to escape. There is a fight and a reconciliation followed by shipwreck in a storm. Encolpius, Giton and Eumolpus are cast ashore and proceed on foot to Croton, which is said to be a city of legacy hunters. On the journey Eumolpus plans a confidence trick: with Encolpius and Giton as his retainers he is to pass as a rich widower in failing health with property in Africa. Affairs in Croton prosper. Encolpius, after humiliating amatory failures with the glamorous Circe and treatment by an old priestess of Priapus, recovers his lost virility and a legacy-hunting mother makes Eumolpus a present of her daughter's virginity, but as the tricksters fear that their luck may run out Eumolpus makes a will under which his suitably garnished body must be eaten by the beneficiaries.

The remains of the *Satyricon* consist of edited excerpts taken from Books 14, 15 and 16 of the original work. From these long excerpts (L) a further abridgement was made, the so-called *excerpta vulgaria* (O). These were short extracts for teaching purposes, marked by attention to the verse insertions and pieces of moralizing and by an absence of the lubricious. The breaks in the narrative indicated in modern editions by asterisks derive from the manuscript tradition. But one part of the original, the *Cena Trimalchionis* of Book 15, has been transmitted complete without abridgement by a single manuscript, the codex

Traguriensis (H)[25]. Most of the fragments cited by ancient grammarians belong to parts of the *Satyricon* that are no longer extant; these,
together with the references in the text to events outside the surviving
narrative, indicate that it was originally a long tale of adventure.[26]

Reconstruction of the whole of the *Satyricon* is a controversial matter
outside the scope of the present work.[27] There is also wide disagree-
ment on the possible size of the original. It is clear from the *Cena
Trimalchionis* (some sixty pages in the modern edition) that some
episodes were allowed a leisurely expansion and that if the *Cena* was
contained in Book 15 alone the whole work was considerably longer
than the longest of the extant Greek romances, the *Aethiopica* of
Heliodorus. But we do not know if other episodes were treated on a
similar scale. The *Cena* may have been exceptional as a largely self-
contained piece; hence perhaps its separate transmission. In any case
some scholars are sceptical about the reliability of the evidence from
book numbers as a guide to the size of the work.[28] Advocates of a
work of unprecedented size comparable with full length modern
novels would need to have good grounds for assuming that a proved
connoisseur of elegance with a narrative style of spare simplicity, who
seems to have given tacit approval to a disciplined classical poetic
theory, composed a comic tale of inordinate length, the prose
equivalent of a *carmen perpetuum* that moved discursively from episode
to episode.[29] It is nevertheless possible, though unlikely, that Petronius,
the master of subtle irony, composed an enormous rambling tale that
just stopped inconsequently without a final climax or the plot resolved.
Where certainty is not possible it is wiser not to dogmatize. We do not
even know whether Petronius had time to finish the work as he had
intended.

3. PETRONIUS AND THE NOVELISTIC TRADITION

The title *Satyricon,* as already noted, suggests in part at least a work in
the Greek novelistic tradition. Greek novels with titles of a similar
form were love romances, tales of intense emotion presented
rhetorically, in which a virtuous hero and heroine experience a succession of adventures. They undergo various ordeals (separation,
shipwreck, capture by pirates, threats of death and things worse than
death) but remain constant to each other and are finally reunited in
bliss. Most of the extant Greek romances of pathos and rhetoric are
later than the time of Petronius but the tradition goes back to the pre-

Christian era.[30] The *Satyricon* is widely interpreted as a parody of this genre. In place of the upright young man and maiden there is a homosexual couple, Encolpius a cowardly braggart, a thief and trickster, and Giton, effeminate, sharing most of the traits of the Greek heroine (except fidelity), prone to fainting or sobbing with fear, physically weak and lovingly gentle. They are constantly on the run, lurching from one episode of infidelity to another, assailed by the advances of lecherous men (and women); and they too suffer shipwreck. It would indeed be difficult not to read parts of the *Satyricon* as a mockery of the love romance.[31] But some qualification is necessary. Our knowledge of the range of the Greek novel may be defective and the extant romances not entirely representative. Also, as ancient theorists ignore this genre, we have no statements about its *modus operandi*.[32]

While most of the Greek novels concern the deeds of men and women of unquestionable integrity told with unbroken seriousness, in the romance by Achilles Tatius on the adventures of Leucippe and Clitophon not everything is solemn. An assault on the conniving heroine's virginity by the hero is thwarted only by the sudden incursion of the girl's mother (2,23). Clitophon submits to the ardently persuasive advances of a married woman with a cynical sophistry (5,27); like Encolpius, he is something of a coward (e.g. 5,23). In such details Achilles Tatius, without departing fundamentally from the conventions of the genre, seems to view some of them with ironical humour.[33] The widest disparity between Petronius and Achilles Tatius is the consistent baseness and comic roguery of all Petronius' personages; the closest similarity consists in certain formal parallels like the use of first person narrative (as against the normal third person of the Greek novels) and the rhetorical description of a painting that depicts the ravages of love in order to introduce a character who narrates his experiences.[34]

New papyrus discoveries show that the relationship between Petronius and the Greek novel is more complicated than has sometimes been supposed. The *Phoinikika* of Lollianus, a work contemporary with the novel of Achilles Tatius, has a scene of ritual murder and cannibalism (no doubt sham). Expressions occur of a grossness associated with Petronius rather than the Greek novel, and there is a defloration scene apparently similar to that in the Quartilla episode in the *Satyricon*.[35] More important, there are fragments of a Greek tale of adventure and love concerning low characters, including a sexual pervert (*cinaedus*). The language has a degree of vulgarity that seems to vary from speaker to speaker. The narrative proceeds in a mixture of prose and verse. These difficult fragments seem to be part of a comic realistic Greek novel of a kind that some scholars had assumed to have preceded the work of Petronius.[36] Some features of the *Satyricon*, such as Giton's role as pseudo-heroine, must have appeared to the ancient reader as immediate parody of the sentimental Greek romance, but as Greek novelistic narrative had a wide possible range of subject and tone such burlesque should be seen as no more than an incidental, though important, part of Petronius' intention.[37]

The wrath of Priapus that besets Encolpius throughout the extant narrative has suggested to many scholars parody of epic, particularly the *Odyssey*, rather than of the Greek novel, though in the novel too divine wrath, such as that of Aphrodite and Eros in the tales of Xenophon of Ephesus and Chariton, is a source of motivation.[38] The hostility that Priapus shows towards the feckless and cowardly Encolpius, it is argued, contrasts ironically with the wrath of the Olympian deity Poseidon, who pursues the resourceful hero Odysseus through long years of wandering and hardship; thus these points of congruence, together with numerous references to events and persons of the *Odyssey* in the *Satyricon*, suggest that Petronius' satirical intention was primarily epic parody. Though the theory is useful, once again some reservations are necessary. While the anger of Priapus is important in some of the extant part of the *Satyricon* we do not know what part is played in the story as a whole, nor is the fundamental cause of the divine wrath certain.[39] The anger of Priapus does not seem adequate justification for the hypothesis of overall epic parody. Also the epic parody is no more than spasmodic. For example Giton's hiding under the bed evokes the parallel of Odysseus' escape from Polyphemus under the belly of the ram (*Od.* 9,424ff.); but the burlesque has no strategic relevance outside the immediate context. The many references to the *Odyssey* (and *Iliad*) and also some allusions to the *Aeneid* in the prose narrative of the *Satyricon* may be seen as part of the comic story-teller's incidental merriment at the expense of established classics.[40]

Petronius used facets of many literary forms. He introduced two examples of Milesian tales, lubricious short stories associated with Aristides of Miletus (*c.* 100 B.C.) and translated into Latin and adapted by the historian Sisenna (praet. 78 B.C.). One was the Pergamene Boy, which he used as part of the initial presentation of the rascally paederastic poet Eumolpus; the other the Widow of Ephesus, a cynical amorous tale, once again spoken by Eumolpus, which was included in order to assuage anger after the fight on board ship. Eumolpus is a disreputable character, but his stories are little masterpieces of concise narration.[41] Petronius also took an amused glance at folk tales of the sinister and ghoulish, traces of popular superstition of a kind that rears its head from time to time in satire. The grisly tale of a werewolf told by the sombre Niceros is followed by Trimalchio's horror story of witches.[42] It is also possible, though not necessary, to find in the somewhat unreal setting for the swindle in Croton an ironical treatment of the sub-genre of aretalogy, i.e. narrative about wonderful peoples and places.[43]

Mime is not a literary influence on the narrative of the *Satyricon* in the ordinary way, but the characters are made to refer to its gambits. *'Quid ergo,' inquit Eumolpus, 'cessamus mimum componere?'* ('Let's set up a scenario!' says Eumolpus, 117,4), as he unfolds the plan for his great confidence trick. Encolpius' fake suicide with a blade that is like a stage prop is described as *mimicam mortem*.[44] The ham posturing attitudes of Petronius' characters (and perhaps by implication those of his contemporaries) was an object of his amused mockery.[45] As a result the *Satyricon*, though in some respects a hybrid of satire and novelistic narrative, is paradoxically the richest and most variegated example of *satura* as a miscellany.

4. PETRONIUS AND THE MENIPPEAN TRADITION

Whether or not Petronius' title is deemed to have contained a reference to *satura*, the work may be regarded as a part of the 'alternative convention' of satire, i.e. a mixture of prose and verse, which mocked or censured undesirable social behaviour.

i. First person narrative

The status of the narrator poses a problem. In all the examples of satire discussed in previous chapters the author's views are either stated explicitly as in the parabasis of an Old Attic Comedy or else masked by self-effacing irony or by a rhetorical *persona*. Even in the Menippean convention Varro's moralizing, so far as we can judge, is usually formulated openly, and Seneca's attitude to Claudius and his deification is unambiguous. But in Petronius the tale is told by the self-dramatizing wastrel Encolpius, who is both participant in roguery and the narrator who observes the action and expresses general opinions. His indignant disdain at Trimalchio's feast is manifest (see below) and may seem to reflect Petronius' attitude to a vulgar banquet, though elsewhere Encolpius himself is suspect as a parasitical hanger-on.[46] No opinion expressed by any character in the *Satyricon* may be abstracted from its setting and attributed without reservation to the author. It seems that Petronius allows himself the right to grant or withhold his assent to any opinions put into the mouth of his characters.[47] Much may be surmised, but little asserted. Petronius' personal standpoint must remain enigmatic; perhaps he also intended to baffle his contemporaries.

ii. *Social comment and literary theme in the prose parts*

The *Cena Trimalchionis* is a critical description of the pretentious dinner party with indecently lavish fare, and thus belongs unmistakably to the tradition of Roman satire. The reader thinks particularly of the maladroit attempt at high living by Nasidienus in Horace, but Lucilius' brazen Granius is a closer antecedent of the unabashed Trimalchio.[48] The entertainment organized by Trimalchio proceeds with a rumbustious speed and a rich variety of incidents, But Encolpius' comments are consistently condemnatory. He begins with ironical sneers at the singing waiters (31,7), the hors d'oeuvre (32,1), an inept visual pun (41,5) and the banality of the freedmen's conversation (47,1). When Trimalchio offers sympathetic understanding for any guest suffering from constipation or wind, laughter is suppressed by hasty draughts from goblets (47,7). But Encolpius' thoughts become increasingly intolerant (54,1) and Ascyltos (followed by Giton) bursts into uncontrolled laughter, whereupon a fellow guest reviles them for their superciliousness and bad manners (57,1–58,14). Encolpius' ironical admiration of a carver's gladiatorial antics (60,1) soon gives way to violent indignation. Pieces of delicatessen are brought in of which even the memory is offensive to him (65,1). 'I am ashamed to relate what happened next', he comments (70,8), when long-haired boys rub the feet of the guests with perfume. They cannot escape from Trimalchio's foul boasting (*putidissimam iactationem*) even in the bath (73,2), and the final stroke of the nauseating comes with Trimalchio's mock funeral (78,5). At this point the three companions, like Nasidienus' guests in Horace, make a hasty and surreptitious exit.

Literary and archaeological evidence allows a comparison between Trimalchio's feast and the social reality of the age. Seneca tells of a debauched vulgarian who celebrated his own mock funeral every day (12,8) and a freedman with a bad memory who aspired to 'culture' and depended at his pretentious banquets on slave prompters who knew the major authors by heart, Homer, Hesiod and the Greek lyrics poets (27,5–6). Trimalchio's vision of a great funeral monument commemorating his career is reminiscent of the baker Eurysaces' tomb in Rome, an oven in stone with descriptive friezes.[49] Trimalchio's flexible silver skeleton (34,8) has counterparts in such monuments as the cup from Boscoreale.[50] The social discontent in the freedmen's talk reflects the vigorous and sometimes explosive local politics in Campanian coastal towns shown by inscriptions as well as by Tacitus.[51] Allowing for the satirist's exaggeration, the picture of the career of the Asian ex-slave Trimalchio seems to accord with evidence of the first century A.D. concerning the Campanian coast, where some of the wealthiest and the most vulgar traders and businessmen of the age made their home.[52] It is more likely to have been a comic picture of the upstart's unsuccessful attempt to imitate life in Roman high society (even the imperial court) than an ironical slur on Nero and his entourage.[53] Yet a doubt remains. Tacitus records with disgust a vast banquet given by Nero's odious informer Tigellinus (*Ann.* 15,37). Though the emperor's *elegantiae arbiter*, Petronius is unlikely to have helped to organize the monstrous and vulgar spectacle.

The *Cena* may be placed in a wider literary setting than the tradition of Roman satire. It is also indebted to Greek descriptions of feasting and the symposium. In early Hellenistic times an elaborate wedding feast in Macedonia was chronicled with amusement by Hippolochos, and by the first century A.D. the tradition of banqueting and symposiac literature was multifarious.[54] Petronius' *Cena* contains an unmistakable adaptation of one of the archetypal masterpieces of the convention, the *Symposium* of Plato, in the arrival of the uninvited guest at a late stage of the party. There is an extreme contrast between the behaviour of the elegant and urbanely tipsy Alcibiades and the boorish stonemason Habinnas, coarse in his over-eating and drunkenness.[55] In a wider literary framework there may also have been an ironical contrast intended between the civilized conversation on a serious topic by distinguished men in Athens and on the other hand the small talk of a polyglot assemblage of the uneducated in the seamy setting of a Campanian town.

The tastelessness of Trimalchio's banquet is condemned explicitly by Encolpius and his companions. While permitting his characters to strike moral and aesthetic attitudes, Petronius himself for the most part remains aloof. He depicts Encolpius' impotence and Eumolpus' bedroom antics in a tone of amusement, perhaps with an admixture of contempt but not in a spirit of moral condemnation. He was, however, too closely involved in the vice of his circle to be regarded as an Epicurean thinker viewing with composure the turmoil of human passions.[56] Seneca can hardly have approved of him,[57] and Petronius for his part disliked elaborate systems of philosophy and in particular philosophers who preached; in Petronius' last hours there was no place for the moral counsellor.

iii. *The short verse insertions*

Many of the short poems draw on traditional topics of Hellenistic moralizing and of Roman satire. Some allude wryly to reflections on the supremacy of money. Eumolpus laments that there is no money for the inspired artist (83,10) and that the produce of the world is readily available at a price (93,2). But edifying sentiments on materialist values seem incongruous on the lips of a vagabond poet who will soon mount a large-scale swindle. In an earlier passage a world of cash values sees even the Cynic philosopher as venal (14,2), and a reflection on the human lot includes a gibe at philosophers (18,6). Here the comically unedifying contexts (Encolpius' transaction in the market-place and Quartilla's trapping of the three adventurers) suggest that both the action and the accompanying verses are treated with deliberate irony. The conventional picture of ecstatic erotic bliss is immediately shattered when the loved one is filched away into the rival's bed (79,8–9).[58] Two of the most threadbare clichés of rhetorical moralizing, life as a series of dramatic roles (80,9) and the punishment of Tantalus (82,5), are incongruous comments on the comic reversal of Encolpius' fortune in love and his baulked attempt at revenge.[59] Owing to the state of the text it is often impossible fully to evaluate the function of the short verse insertions in their context, but the overall impression from the pieces of ethical content is of a sneer at the gambits of instant moralizing. They are also part of Petronius' civilized comedy.

Other poems are part of the dramatic action. Encolpius prays to Priapus in hexameters, in which according to the accustomed formulae he describes the god, appeals to him, and promises appropriate sacrifice (133,3). His prayer smacks of parody of a poetic theme.[60] Tryphaena in order to pacify the warring sides bursts into pseudo-heroic hexameters which are introduced within the verse itself (108,14): *'quis furor', ex-clamat . . .* ('what madness', quoth she . . .). The form of the verses as well as their high poetic content seems to be intended to raise a laugh at

the convention of the mixture of prose and verse. The dancing perverts
sing in the Sotadean metre verses appropriate to their calling and to the
dramatic situation of Quartilla's orgy (23,3). The drunken Eumolpus
improvises atrocious doggerel on a bald head (109,9–10). Encolpius
kills a gander (136,5), and utters ridiculous hexameters in which he
compares the vanquished geese with Stymphalian birds. Here the sham
heroic verses correspond to the action. Sotadean verses are addressed by
Encolpius to his defective member (132,8). The preposterous
Sotadeans, like the hexameters in the previous example, satirize the
rhetorical posturing that was a characteristic of the first century A.D.

Elegiac couplets condemning a puritanical attitude (132,15) fit
Encolpius' thoughts on his predicament and in their mischievous
reference to the teaching of Epicurus may also be read as the author's
direct address to his readers.[61] In an attempt to show off his grasp of
literary problems Trimalchio essays a comparison between Cicero and
Publilius. Cicero he judges the more eloquent (*disertiorem*) and Publilius
the more morally improving (*honestiorem*). He then recites sixteen iambic trimeters on the immorality of imported luxuries (55,5f.). The lines
are well turned and elegant. Though a plausible pastiche, in all
probability they are not a genuine quotation.[62] Their sentiments on the
lips of Trimalchio are comically hypocritical, and there may also be a
hint that the grammarian's facile comparison between authors is a
fatuous exercise.

iv. Long verse excerpts and passages of criticism

The longer and more elaborate pieces of verse should be read in conjunction with the comments on art, rhetoric and literature that precede
them, and both must be judged in the immediate situation of the story.

On entering the portico (83) Encolpius comments with a superficial
accuracy on works of Hellenistic realistic painters in a way that would
come easily to a man with some pretensions to education.[63] He quickly
turns to the erotic subjects before him and to his own misfortunes. A
little later (88), eager to show himself an intellectual in the presence of
the poet Eumolpus, he asks his opinion on the age of the painting and
on the decline of the arts. In reply Eumolpus does not give information
about the paintings but recites a ready-made general declamation
mainly concerned with the degeneration of intellectual and artistic life.
He then continues with a miscellaneous harangue on modern
wickedness (wine and women) and on men's ignorance of logic and
astronomy. He gives false information about the early classical sculptor

Myron,[64] and includes silly exaggeration, e.g. about Eudoxus. He concludes that in a world of cash values painting has inevitably declined. Then noticing that Encolpius has been gazing on a painting of the capture of Troy, he immediately expounds the work in verse. It is important not to mistake Eumolpus' rambling rhetorical rag-bag for serious objective criticism of art or intellectual values.

Eumolpus recites sixty-five iambic trimeters on the theme of the painting *Troiae halosis* (the capture of Troy). They are a pastiche of part of Virgil's epic narrative in the second book of the *Aeneid*, and tell the tale of the Trojan horse, Laocoon's attack on it, the sea serpents' dreadful killing of Laocoon and his children, and the emergence of the Greek warriors from the horse. The departure point of the recitation purports to be a real picture, but the graphic immediacy of Eumolpus' verses probably belongs to the conventions of the *ecphrasis*, the rhetorical description of a painting of a standard theme.[65] The words are closely dependent on Virgil but there are some marks of Silver Age conventions in exaggerated details of narrative and in pithy maxims at the end of a paragraph.[66] It is possible that Eumolpus' piece suggested to contemporary readers the declamatory format and manner of the tragedies of Seneca rather than those of any other writer of the times, but we should be reluctant to make the assumption with confidence, even though it is unlikely *a priori* that Petronius liked Seneca's verses.[67] There is no parody as such in the *Troiae halosis*. Petronius' comedy is to be found in the contrast between the naturalistic setting and the pretentious preliminaries of the vagabond poet, whose verses in the grand manner, though not ridiculous, are not consistently distinguished.[68] There may also seem to have been a hidden sneer at the glib improvised declamation of one or other distinguished performer of the age, though what seems a likely innuendo to us may have been less certainly so at the time.[69] Eumolpus' performance is greeted by a hail of stones from the bystanders, but this characteristic piece of bathos is not necessarily a critical comment on the quality of the verses.

At the beginning of the extant fragment of the *Satyricon* Encolpius declaims on declamation, giving examples of unreal themes decked out in gaudy meretricious phrases that teachers of rhetoric offer to their young pupils. Such effects of language have enervated the power of oratory (1,1–2,2). These criticisms of declamation correspond to the censure by the best critics of the first century A.D., notably Tacitus in the *Dialogus*.[70] The rest of Encolpius' declamation, however, is a pretentious tirade on the damage done by the recent import of the blowsy Asianic style of rhetoric to Athens. Though possibly relevant to the literary climate of Greece in Hellenistic times, such a view was not applicable to the Greece of the age of Augustus, let alone to Rome.[71] If the opening section is to be taken seriously as contemporary criticism, the later part is more likely to make its effect if it is seen as belonging to the characterization of Encolpius, the purveyor of ready-made opinions. Agamemnon compliments him patronizingly, admits the truth of his comments on rhetorical education, but places the blame on the parents for demanding an unnatural preciosity.

Agamemnon then remarks that, as he does not wish to disparage the *schedium Lucilianae humilitatis* (improvised verses in an unpretentious style associated with Lucilius), which Encolpius presumably had already recited in a chapter just before the point where our text begins, he too will express his views in verse. He declaims eight choliambics on moral integrity followed by fourteen hexameters on suitable authors for reading. The doggerel hexameters have obvious marks of the first century A.D.[72] Agamemnon's improvisation is of poor quality. He is a disreputable figure, a hack professional, about to put his wiles into practice at Trimalchio's feast (48), but his admissions on contemporary declamation should not be dismissed on this account. Petronius may have enjoyed teasing his readers by putting sound views into the mouth of a rogue and of a time-server.[73]

The longest of the verse insertions, the *Bellum Civile*, the poem on the civil war between Pompey and Caesar, is set amid the planning and execution of an elaborately contrived swindle. Eumolpus turns from enunciating his master plan to expounding his views on the poet and the difficulty of writing poetry about the Civil War. In an austere statement he contrasts the facile attempts of tired pleaders with the masterly poetic achievements of Homer, the lyric poets, Virgil and Horace.[74] The writer of a poem about the Civil War will fail unless he is immersed in literature. Historical events are better treated by historians. The unshackled spirit must produce a work of frenzied inspiration, not a report based on the evidence of honest witnesses.

Eumolpus then recites a poem of 295 hexameters:[75] Rome was a city corrupted by imported luxuries, food, clothing, catamite boys (1–60). The three principal figures, the triumvirs, were all destined for a violent end (61–6). Dis, god of the infernal regions, appeals to Fortuna to destroy Rome; Fortuna with the aid of a Fury promises to sacrifice its warriors in vast carnage (67–143). From a pinnacle on the Alps Caesar defends his actions and descends into Italy unperturbed amid unnatural storms (144–208), while Fama brings panic to Rome (209–44). Divine figures are involved, Pax, Fides and Concordia, matched by Death and other horror personifications. Some of the Olympians, Pallas and Mars, range themselves on Caesar's side, Apollo, Diana and others with Pompey (245–70). Discordia rages through Italy and calls on the leaders to make havoc (271–95). By the time Eumolpus has finished they arrive at Croton.

Eumolpus' views in chapter 118 will have seemed old-fashioned classical doctrine in the age of Nero, notably the injunction to control *sententiae*, and the mention of Virgil and Horace as models may have seemed reactionary.[76] Though Lucan is not mentioned specifically as the writer of a poem on the Civil War, the reference would have been unmistakable, the omission of the name of a contemporary being no more than a literary convention. As he renders historical events in verse he is deemed to lack essential marks of a serious poet, imaginative complexities of plot, the world of mythology and the divine machinery that belongs to the epic. Eumolpus in this chapter is not the vehicle for parody. The opinions given to him may safely be attributed to Petronius himself, though the use of the disreputable *persona* affords the author a possible disclaimer.[77]

The poem that follows the preface is not an obvious or crude parody of Lucan's poem but a hastily improvised pastiche. The speech given to Caesar is demonstrably an imitation of speeches in Book 1 of Lucan's epic, but not a parody. Some of the *sententiae* in Petronius' *Bellum Civile* may seem less obtrusive than their counterparts in Lucan and so perhaps a practical demonstration of the criticism in the preface. Others obtrude more obviously, but often in a way that would arise inevitably in Latin poetry of the first century A.D.[78] The spirit of the age appears also in the comparison of Caesar to Hercules and Jupiter, a pastiche of the Silver Age epic convention without overt parody of Lucan. A desire to correct Lucan may be found in the introduction of gods by Petronius, whose unsubtle divine machinery was perhaps a mere sketch to indicate what should be done in an epic. Various unpoetic oddities of expression in Petronius would seem to be the result of the avowedly quasi-improvisatory style and not a deliberately calculated mockery.[79] None the less Petronius may have hinted half seriously that such an improvisation could achieve something in keeping with the tradition of Latin poetry that was out of the reach of Lucan, the most ambitious and mercurial writer of his age.[80]

How much of Lucan's work was known to Petronius when he wrote his own *Bellum Civile* is a question to which there can be no certain answer. Lucan had published three books, presumably the first three, when in A.D. 65 Nero, jealous of his public acclaim, forbade him to publish anything further or to give public recitations.[81] It has been argued that Books 4–6 had also been composed by the time of the ban, for violent hatred of Nero is not noticeable until the powerful Books 7–9, which were probably inspired by a frenzy of hatred.[82] Lucan composed scabrous verses against Nero and his most important friends, joined the Pisonian conspiracy and was forced to commit suicide on 30 April A.D. 65, leaving Book 10 of *de Bello Civili* ending abruptly in the middle of the narrative.[83] It is probable but not certain that Petronius composed his own *Bellum Civile* in the next few months. His theme corresponds approximately to that of Lucan's Book 1. Many of the parallels suggested between the later books of Lucan and the *Bellum Civile* are flimsy, for a common theme may easily give rise to chance resemblances, but there are similarities enough to suggest that Petronius may have had access to the bulk of Lucan through private recitations or an unobtrusively circulated copy.[84] He knew enough of it to realize that it was a poem of consequence that called into question his own standards of Augustan excellence and needed an immediate answer. Lucan's work was tacitly besmirched by a poem based on sounder traditions but put into the mouth of a criminal vagabond. What Lucan had written in inspired but feverish haste, a trickster could rival in a quasi-improvisation composed to pass the time while on the road in the company of two idlers and a porter.

5. ASPECTS OF LITERARY CRAFTSMANSHIP

i. *Characters and narrative*

Encolpius may seem at first sight to be no more than a bundle of shifting attitudes. He is the narrator of a story in which he is a principal participant. He is also from time to time the vehicle of ideas and opinions that need not be attributed to him as an individual. But he is also a character in his own right. His name, an ordinary Greek proper name, may suggest in the context of the story one associated with embraces.[85] He is preoccupied with sex, notably his own impotence, and is often the victim of the initiative of others. By his own account he is quick tempered (94,5). He is also a braggart, intellectually pretentious, eager to impress but superficial in his judgements; and he has a flair for grotesque self-dramatization.[86] Ascyltos' attack on him (9) may be no more than fiery abuse from which little firm fact can be extracted, but it is clear that he has some sort of criminal past. In an outburst of self-pity (81) he depicts himself as an exile, a man on the run, a beggar who escaped the arena, and a murderer. Whether or not it is literally true, as Ascyltos asserts, that Encolpius had been a stabber by night (*nocturne percussor*, 9,9), he is disarmed in the street by a footpad soldier at a time when he is crazed with fury himself and intent on violence (82,3f.). Petronius has chosen a play-acting coward to narrate his comic tale.[87]

The name Ascyltos, by contrast, means 'not pulled about', suggesting something of the 'man who played it cool'. The character himself is utterly depraved and dishonest. He is a bully-boy and a thief, and also somewhat ridiculous in that he excites admiration in the public baths by the sheer size of his phallic equipment (92,9). Giton, whose name implies 'close companion', is described as 'about sixteen years of age, curly-haired, effeminate and handsome' (97,2). In a passage of uncontrolled anger Encolpius describes him as a youngster debauched by every variety of malpractice, but is sentimentally susceptible to his loving gentleness. Giton is constantly faithless, a homosexual lover who is also highly desirable to the opposite sex; hence Tryphaena's importunity. Like Encolpius, he is rhetorical in mundane situations and, if possible, even more stagey in his cheap posturing.[88]

The most powerful of Petronius' female character portrayals is Tryphaena. The proper name was widely spread over the Greek-speaking world, but was probably chosen by Petronius on account of the word's associations with luxurious and wanton living.[89] Tryphaena is described by Eumolpus as the most glamorous of all women, who travels from place to place for the sake of pleasure (101,5); she has embarked on Lichas' ship as an exile. Encolpius, whose mistress she had been, regards her as totally promiscuous. She is regarded by her own maid (if the interpretation is correct) as one to be treated as little better than a whore (113,11). She shows initiative in intervening to stop the fight on board ship; but as an appropriately feminine reaction to Eumolpus' tale of infidelity, the Widow of Ephesus, she hides a blushing cheek on Giton's shoulder (113,1). Quartilla, the hysterical, highly-sexed priestess of Priapus, and the amorous Circe, whose beauty is said to rival masterpieces of art (126,14ff.), though clearly delineated, by comparison with Tryphaena are more stereotyped in their alluring femininity.

Much of the interest in Petronius' presentation of character is centred on Trimalchio. It is not easy to disentangle traits of an individual person from the actions of a type, the vulgar host. The name Trimalchio suggests a Semitic origin, and he states that he came from Asia as a small boy (75,10).[90] The *nouveau riche* freedman with pretensions to learning (39,3) and a leaning to superstition was, as is clear from Seneca, a familiar type in the middle of the first century A.D.[91] Yet although many of Trimalchio's sayings are typical of the ostentatious vulgarian (such as his utterly ignorant comments on *objets d'art* and matters of learning), Petronius shows much skill in presenting a unique individual. Before the guests meet Trimalchio, they hear that they will be dining with an eccentric who has a clock and a trumpeter to tell him how much longer he has to live; they first see him as a bald old man playing an unusual ball-game, surrounded by his slaves including his favourite boy, whom Encolpius describes as uglier than his master. Morbid superstition, particularly a preoccupation with death and its appurtenances, is a constant theme throughout the *Cena*. Late in the proceedings (74) there is a violent quarrel over a slave boy between Trimalchio and his wife Fortunata; yet according to a freedman guest he is completely dependent on her managerial skill and decisions (37,5). He is only prevented from dancing by a whispered admonition from her; Encolpius comments that at one moment Trimalchio was afraid of Fortunata and at the next would revert to his natural bent of acting the fool (52,10f.). Although undoubtedly vulgar, he is always courteous to his guests, tolerant towards Ascyltos and Giton, and kindly towards the glum Niceros (61,2). Though the speech of the slave-owner on the essential humanity of the slave is intended to be seen as humbug, Trimalchio in practice can be considerate, as when he ensures that the slaves who have served at dinner then eat their own meal (74,6). In the later part of the *Cena* much of the portraiture is expressed by Trimalchio's description of himself. He reads out the bombastic wording of the inscription to be carved on his tombstone, the dutiful, brave and loyal self-made man who never listened to a philosopher (71,12), and recounts his life story as the slave boy, who after gratifying the desires of both his master and mistress became chief manager of the house and principal heir, made a very successful career as trader and investor, and then retired to his present affluent ease. But in the end autobiography is engulfed in the noise and confusion of Trimalchio's mock funeral.

In a modern egalitarian age there is some danger of sentimentalizing the character of Trimalchio. Petronius sets out to present him as an object of amused contempt; Encolpius' comments throughout the narrative make this clear, and the reader of the *Cena* may wish that to be the final verdict.[92] But it is possible to argue that Trimalchio has in some way gone beyond his creator's original intentions.[93] He is a complex amalgam of observed behaviour and the imagination of the writer of fiction.

Equally impressive is the portrait of Eumolpus, vagabond, paederast and poet.[94] As with Trimalchio his first appearance is important: 'A white-haired old man in shabby clothes with an intense expression which seemed to offer some promise of greatness' (83,7). He proves to be a lecherous old man (*libidinosus*, 94,5), but he can give a good account of himself in a brawl and he is shrewd enough to organize the escape by sea and to plan the great legacy-hunting swindle at Croton (117,1). He is most conspicuous for his incessant compulsion to declaim ready-made or improvised verses, whether or not the occasion is opportune. After his first speech of polytechnic learning in the art gallery, which he follows with a grandiose poem, he is showered with a volley of stones. Shortly afterwards, unabashed, he is thrown out of the public baths for reciting poetry (90,1; 92,6). After the shipwreck he is dragged ashore, indignant at being interrupted when in the act of writing poetry. Safely ashore, Eumolpus composes a sepulchral epigram and gazes into the distance in search of inspiration (115,20). But this rhetorical *poseur*, a child of his time, is also the mouthpiece for Petronius' serious literary criticisms. He also relates two Milesian tales, one of which at least (the Widow of Ephesus) was an undoubted success for its hearers on board ship.

We also have glimpses of arresting figures who appear only momentarily in the story: the trader with a bald head and warts (15,4) who is depository for the property, the Syrians at the inn who come to rob and then pretend to be asleep (22,3), Bargates, the crippled manager of the lodging house, who is interrupted at his supper by the sound of brawling, and is carried in to deliver a long abusive harangue in a barbarous accent (96,4f.), and Hesus, the seasick passenger who sees the unlucky shaving of the fugitives' heads by moonlight (103,5; 104,5). Petronius' narrative skill is consistently distinguished in the rest of the work as much as in the *Cena*. This is particularly to be noted in situations in which the characters are applauded as figures of fun or derision by the onlookers: Encolpius and Ascyltos tug for possession of a worthless patchwork cloak to the amusement of the traders in the market (14,7); Eumolpus and Ascyltos in their various ways are objects of wonderment in the public baths. Neither example occurs during a main climax of the action but both illustrate the work's unflagging verve and ribaldry.

Another striking aspect of Petronius' accomplishment is the speed at which the characters are whisked from one adventure to another. Encolpius makes a getaway from Agamemnon's prolixity (6,2–3) only to find himself lured into a brothel. On escaping once again from Agamemnon at the end of the *Cena* Encolpius, Ascyltos and Giton rush away in the middle of the night but have a long and painful walk in the darkness over the flints and broken sherds to their lodging house. There they get in only when Trimalchio's courier arrives and breaks down the door (79). Petronius occasionally allows a time of tranquillity in the speedy violence of the action. After the end of the uneasy plotting and the hard fight on the ship, while the vessel is becalmed, the sailors sing, fish and catch birds. The characters are temporarily composed; this gives Eumolpus the opportunity to expatiate on feminine inconstancy and to tell the story of the Widow of Ephesus. By contrast the storm that arises seems all the more violent. At the sight of the abandoned ship fishermen pull out from the shore in small boats hoping for booty, but on discovering that there are survivors who are prepared to defend their belongings they suddenly become eager to help (114,14). The skill of the master of realistic narrative never flags.

ii. Language and style

The style of the parts of the *Satyricon* outside the *Cena Trimalchionis* is akin to the language spoken by the educated of the times. The diction of Encolpius, the narrator and actor, and of Giton, Eumolpus and the others is for the most part pure (though some slang is permitted, e.g. *stabulum* (8,2) 'doss-house', and *conductum* (9,4) 'digs', for lodgings),[95] and the sentence structure is consistently simple and lucid, but it is too orderly and delicately balanced to be a naturalistic reporting of ordinary educated speech. The two Milesian tales, the Pergamene Boy and the Widow of Ephesus, the whole of the narrative on board ship and the exchange of lovers' letters between Circe and Polyaenus, who is Encolpius in disguise (129,4–130,6), are characteristic examples. Even the enhanced emotion of a declamatory passage, such as Encolpius' wistful prose poem (100,1), is strictly controlled.[96] Eumolpus' will that enjoins cannibalism on its legatees, while comically revolting in its contents, has the stylistic elegance appropriate to a formal document.

This discriminating Atticism, which might have been expected from the author of the manifesto on classical principles (ch. 118), makes the *Satyricon* a masterpiece of Latin narrative prose that may be compared in its stylistic accomplishment with the *Commentaries* of Julius Caesar.[97]

The language spoken by Trimalchio and his freedman guests in the *Cena* is fundamentally different. While the language of Encolpius and his friends and of other figures outside the *Cena* includes a sprinkling of vulgarisms, that of the characters in the *Cena* is the *sermo plebeius*, the non-literary speech of the lower classes.[98] Greek words and traces of Greek usage abound, as might be expected in the diction of ex-slaves, but the language of the *Cena* should not be judged primarily as the ungrammatical Latin of a Greek-speaking area; for Greek expressions permeate the rest of the *Satyricon* and were prominent in contemporary Roman usage.[99] That the vulgar speech of the *Cena* is a genuine reproduction of the language of the uneducated is clear from the contemporary evidence of the inscriptions of Pompeii (originally an Oscan settlement)[100] and also from the *glossae*, alphabetical lists of Latin and Greek words, collected after the fall of the Roman empire, that preserve many vulgarisms current also in earlier centuries.[101]

At an early stage of the banquet Encolpius is given a description of Fortunata and her rise to riches in an effective, unliterary language that is rich in metaphor and spiced with Latin and Greek slang, including Graeco-Roman hybrids: *modo modo* (no time ago), *topanta* (his one and only), *lupatria* (old bitch).[102] This is typical of the language spoken by the freedmen throughout the *Cena*. A selection of representative examples will illustrate some of the main characteristics of their language. Forms with gemination and repetition are common as quasi-childish expressions of wonderment or disapproval: *babae babae* (well well!, 37,9), *mixcix* (half and half, 45,5).[103] Diminutives are common; one, *valde audaculum* (bloody brave, 63,5) with the adverb has an intensifying force. There are many morphological anomalies, particularly masculine forms for neuter: *malus fatus* (71,1); also *lacte* for *lac* (38,1), an irregularity found also in Plautus; the quaint superlative *ipsimus(a)* ('himself' or 'herself', i.e. the master or mistress) is used four times by freedmen.

The vocabulary of the freedmen shows a penchant for adjectives ending in *-arius,* e.g. *dipundiarius* (worth only two coppers, 74,15) and *-osus,* e.g. *dignitosus* (a man of standing, 57,10). Though they have an abundance of terms of abuse, such as *vervex* (stupid ram, 57,2) used of Ascyltos, and *cepa cirrata* (curly-headed onion, 58,2) applied to Giton, expressions of approbation are more restricted and are frequently rendered by *bellus* (nice). The few indecencies of vocabulary are comical social gaffes, such as the Greek word in the phrase *frigori laecasin dico* (I says to the cold 'monkeys and nuts', 42,2) or the reflexive hybrid *se apoculare* (bugger off, 62,3). There is much informality in the constructions: ellipses such as *habet unde* (he's got the wherewithal, 45,6),[104] pleonastic negatives, *qui* for interrogative *quis* (58,8, 62,8), *constructio ad sensum*, e.g. *omnium genera avium* (bird of all sorts, 69,8) and the construction of *dico* with an object clause introduced by *quia* (46,4) as is common in the Vulgate and other late Latin texts.[105] Proverbial phrases are noteworthy: in reply to a grumbler Echion says: *Tu si alicubi fueris, dices porcos coctos ambulare* (if you go anywhere else, you'll say that the pigs here walked about ready roasted, 45,4). There is the popular device of identification in place of metaphor: *piper non homo* (he wasn't a man, he was a pepper-pot, 44,7), and plenty of colloquial metaphor: Seleucus expresses his dislike of the cold water: *aqua dentes habet* (the water has got fangs, 42,1).[106]

Nevertheless, Petronius' naturalistic reproduction of common speech, in itself a virtuoso piece of linguistic slumming, seems to have been secondary to his main purpose, which was to create a realistic social and economic sketch of the lives of small-town Campanian freedmen. In the first connected speech of the *Cena* Encolpius' neighbour describes to him Fortunata's rise to riches and Trimalchio's contented affluence.[107] He also points with approbation to a wealthy ex-slave and to an undertaker who went bankrupt with a show of respectability. Encolpius offers the reader an ironical sneer at the information: *tam dulces fabulas* (such fascinating stories, 39,1). When Trimalchio temporarily leaves the banquet small talk flows freely, introduced by the cheerfully drunk and atrociously ungrammatical Dama (41,10–12). He is followed by the morbid Seleucus, who expatiates on the funeral he has attended earlier in the day (*fui hodie in funus*, 'I were at a funeral today', 42,2). The deceased, he suspects, was polished off by the medical profession. It is probably vain to seek for individual linguistic traits in the various freedmen's use and misuse of Latin.[108] They differ from one another not in quirks of language but in the variety of their circumstances and interests.

The freedmen's chatter has functions far beyond a display of linguistic virtuosity. Structurally it forms a placid interlude during the hurried and noisy procedures of the *Cena* while Trimalchio is present. It may perhaps be interpreted as a piece of ironical comedy – the completely negative symposium at which nothing of any cultural significance is said. But the total intention is difficult to assess. To educated Romans the untreated *sermo plebeius* and the banality of the sentiments must have sounded as comical as Trimalchio's linguistic and social *bêtises*. But once again Petronius may have gone beyond the initial purpose of elegant mockery, so that it is perhaps permissible to view with some qualified sympathy the attempts of Echion to ensure his son's betterment through education. Encolpius, it is true, sneers explicitly, and Agamemnon disapproves by implication, but two of Encolpius' companions are shortly to be arraigned by the freedmen for their uncontrolled boorishness. The attitude of Petronius to his characters is, as so often, elusive and baffling.

6. SURVIVAL AND AFTERMATH

Petronius, like Persius, wrote for an *élite*. His audience and reading public would have been a small number of the highly educated and civilized who were capable of appreciating the many facets of his ironical virtuosity and the unfashionable Attic purity of his narrative.[109] As Nero's *elegantiae arbiter* he may well have participated at sessions at court when poetry was improvised and assistance offered in verse composition, but the *Satyricon* is unlikely to have been written primarily as a work for palace entertainment.[110] Nero's intimates in the later years included such men as Vatinius, the deformed buffoon of sinister power; Sporus, the emperor's homosexual bride; and worst of all the loathsome Tigellinus, comrade of the emperor's variegated debauchery, a man of the lowest taste, who out of jealous hatred in the end ensured Petronius' destruction.[111] Few will have had the opportunity to hear or read the *Satyricon*, parts of which were probably written during the last months of Petronius' life; but the literary masterpiece, unlike the valuable *objet d'art* that he smashed in his last hours, was preserved by discriminating readers.

Quintilian and Tacitus are discreetly silent about Petronius' *Satyricon*. Macrobius knew it as a work of entertainment. Marius Mercator and John the Lydian (or his sources) mention Petronius, but in general he was of no great interest to the grammarians.[112] Unlike Juvenal, Petronius was apparently not a highly esteemed author in the later part of the fourth century A.D., when the bulk of his work may have told against a wide circulation. Perhaps it was at about this time that the text was subjected to a savage mutilation even worse than that which bedevilled the tradition of the Greek novels.[113] The two stages of the abridgement of the text have already been mentioned (pp. 182–3). The textual tradition of Petronius is complex and obscure. It will be sufficient here to offer a brief outline. The earliest extant manuscript of Petronius, Codex Bernensis 357, is of late ninth-century date and contains the short excerpts (O); in two Paris manuscripts of the twelfth century the text has deteriorated.[114] The witness of O is much improved by readings in a group of manuscripts of fifteen-century date that derive from a manuscript, now lost, that was discovered by Poggio in 1420.[115] But some learned men in mediaeval times, such as John of Salisbury (c. 1115–80), pupil of Abelard, secretary to Thomas à Becket and bishop of Chartres, knew as much of Petronius' text as we know today.[116] The first printed edition, of the O fragments only, was made in Milan (c. A.D. 1482).

Extant evidence for the longer excerpts (L) comes from sixteenth-century manuscripts such as l, a Leyden manuscript written in the hand of Jos. Scaliger. Two manuscripts only of L had survived into the six-teenth century: the manuscript of Cujas (1522–90), sometimes referred to as the Tolosanus, which was used by Scaliger for his own version (which was an edition rather than a copy),[117] and the vetus Benedic-tinus used by Pierre Pithou (1539–96), which was the basis of his editions of 1577 (p[1]) and 1587 (p[2]) and also the source of all other manuscripts of L. The first edition to use L was that published in 1575 by the Lyons printer de Tournes, known as the *editio Tornesiana* (t). The two old exemplars no longer exist.[118]

The editions of the long fragments (l,p,t) give a very scanty account of the *Cena*. In 1423, three years after his discovery of a manuscript of O, Poggio reported that he had received from Cologne Book 15 of Petronius Arbiter. This was a complete text of the *Cena*, but all trace of this manuscript disappeared until a copy of it (H) was discovered at Trau in Dalmatia c. A.D. 1650. It is certain that Poggio's manuscript from Cologne was of the *Cena* and was cod. Traguriensis or a copy of it, because the Trau manuscript alone has book numbers.[119] The *Cena* was first published in Padua in 1664. But some were not content with the authentic. Nodot published in Paris in 1694 a text and translation, in which lacunae were filled in with fraudulent additions in a barbarous Latin; and in about 1800 the disreputable Spanish revolutionary Marchena was to add an extra scene to the Priapic orgy.[120] With the publication of the *variorum* edition of the whole of the remains of Petronius by P. Burman (Utrecht 1709[1], Amsterdam 1743[2]) the

Satyricon was readily available in a full edition and copiously annotated.

Petronius, who himself played an active part in the decadence of his times, was yet able to view them with a detached and amused contempt. He created the hilarious tale of the adventures of a memorable collection of degenerates, scoundrels and pretentious imposters and in it was also able to vindicate the classical cultural values of former times. Petronius, a relaxed narrator, offers much both for the delight and the enlightenment of his readers. Above all he was a great story-teller and, in the words of Dryden, 'the greatest wit perhaps of all the Romans'.[121]

Notes

NOTES TO CHAPTER 1 (THE GENRE)

1 The only serviceable general handbook on Roman satire is that of U. Knoche, *Die Römische Satire* (Göttingen, 1971³). The thorough rewriting of the second edition was unfortunately terminated by the author's death: the contents and pagination of the chapters on Lucilius to the end are the same as in the second edition and further bibliography has been added by the editor W. Ehlers. Of great value is the introduction to O. Weinreich's translations, *Römische Satiren* (Zürich and Stuttgart, 1962²), vii–civ, perhaps the best single essay on Roman satire. G. Highet, *The Anatomy of Satire* (Princeton, 1962), provides a wide-ranging study of fundamental principles. J.-P. Cèbe, *La caricature et la parodie dans le monde romain antique des origines à Juvénal* (Paris, 1966), is a catalogue of great thoroughness. D. Korzeniewski, *Die Römische Satire*, Wege d. Forschung 238 (Darmstadt, 1970), gathers a number of the most important articles on the subject from 1920. W. S. Anderson has provided useful bibliographies: for 1937–55, *C.W.* 50 (1956), 33–40; for 1955–62, *C.W.* 57 (1964), 293–301, 343–8; for 1962–8, *C.W.* 63 (1970), 181–94, 199, 217–22.

A succinct and reliable history of the period during which all the satirists except Ennius and Juvenal wrote is provided by H. H. Scullard, *From the Gracchi to Nero* (London, 1970³). R. Syme, *The Roman Revolution* (Oxford, 1939) is the fundamental historical study of the times of Horace's satires. The Cambridge Ancient History X, *The Augustan Empire 44 B.C.–A.D. 70* (Cambridge, 1934) and XI, *The Imperial Peace A.D. 70–192* (Cambridge, 1936), though the chapter on Hadrian is undistinguished, are valuable surveys of the Principate. A. Garzetti, transl. J. R. Foster, *From Tiberius to the Antonines* (London, 1974), covers the whole of the relevant imperial period in detail, emperor by emperor.

For the background of social history see J. P. V. D. Balsdon, *Life and Leisure in Ancient Rome* (London, 1969). J. Carcopino, *Daily Life in Ancient Rome* (revised edn, Harmondsworth, 1956) is concerned with life in the early empire; it is entertaining but not wholly reliable. The second part of W. Kroll, *Die Kultur der ciceronischen Zeit* (Leipzig, 1933) is valuable; for the early empire the copious study by L. Friedlaender, transl. J. H. Freese and L. A. Magnus, *Roman Life and Manners*, 4 vols. (London, 1908–13), is unsurpassed in the plenitude of its material but is cumbersome in its arrangement. J. Marquardt–A. Mau, *Das Privatleben der Römer* (Leipzig, 1886) is a work of wide range with a full literary and epigraphical documentation that is conveniently presented for easy reference.

2 Quint. 10,1,93. On the meaning of the words see (against W. Rennie, *C.R.* 36 (1922), 21) G. L. Hendrickson, *C.Ph.* 22 (1927), 60. On Quintilian's judgement see also C. A. Van Rooy, *Studies in Classical Satire and Related Literary Theory* (Leiden, 1965), 117–23.

3 There is an authoritative interpretation of the difficult sentence *alterum illud etiam prius saturae genus, sed non sola carminum varietate mixtum condidit Terentius Varro* (10,1,95) by M. Winterbottom, 'Problems in Quintilian', *B.I.C.S. Supp.* 25 (1970), 191: 'The other well-known type of satire – one that arose even before Lucilius (i.e. the Ennian satire of varied metre) – was exploited by Varro, but now with a variety given not merely by metrical changes (but by an admixture of prose to the verse).' See further D. A. Russell and M. Winterbottom (ed.), *Ancient Literary Criticism* (Oxford, 1972), 380–400.

4 Note Quintilian's censure of Afranius for introducing paederastic episodes into his *togatae* (10,1,100). On Quintilian's treatment of satire see Weinreich viii and on Quintilian in general G. Kennedy, *Quintilian* (New

York, 1969), esp. ch. 5: Quintilian as a critic (101–22).

5 See also Quint. 10,2,22. For Aristotle's broad classification see his *Poetics*, 1447a8 and 16, 1448b24–1449a6, and D. W. Lucas, *Aristotle, Poetics* (Oxford, 1968) on the passages. A. E. Harvey, *C.Q.* 5 (1955), 157–75, examines the subtle distinctions of Hellenistic theory with reference to the 'kinds' of lyric poetry. R. Pfeiffer, *History of Classical Scholarship* (Oxford, 1968), 203–7, traces the Hellenistic beginnings of canons of accepted authors; see also L. E. Rossi, *B.I.C.S.* 18 (1971), 69–94.

6 O. Regenbogen, 'Theophrastos von Eresos', *R.E. Supp.* 7, 1530; G. A. Kennedy, *H.S.C.Ph.* 62 (1957), 93–104; *P. Hibeh* 2,183 and discussion by E. G. Turner. On decorum see also M. Pohlenz, 'τὸ πρέπον', *N.G. Göttingen* (Berlin, 1933), 53.

7 Accius *Didasc.* frg. 13 (Morel) = *Gramm. Rom. Frg.* (Fun.) 27; Leo, *Gesch.* 386–91.

8 Horace discusses generic distinctions and propriety in *A.P.* 73ff.; note esp. 86–8 and 92. See C. O. Brink, *Horace on Poetry* 2 (Cambridge, 1971), on the whole passage. On Roman criticism by kinds, on hierarchy of genres and the notion of decorum associated with it, D'Alton 398–426.

9 In the imagery of his tragedies there are occasional lapses from the high style (e.g. *solvendo non es* (you are bankrupt), *Oed.* 942, where Gronovius' emendation is almost certainly right). Pliny (*Epp.* 6,21,4) describes the dilettante activities of an insignificant writer who wrote in the manner of both Old and New Comedy, distinguishing carefully between the conventions of the one and the other.

10 Mart. 12,94. Contrast his orderly list there with his haphazard list at 3,20 and with that of Statius, *Silv.* 1,3,101–4.

11 See particularly the very important study of the hierarchy of genres in the choice of appropriate vocabulary by B. Axelson, *Unpoetische Wörter* (Lund, 1945).

12 Pers. 1,114–8; Juv. 1,19f. and 51.

13 It is assumed here with Housman, Duff and Knoche (among others) against Clausen and probably the ancient scholiast that 634–7 are a vehement rhetorical question and not an ironical statement. Juvenal uses *operum lex* (7,102) of the historian's literary conventions.

14 Johannes Lydus, *Mag.* 1,41R. This passage obviously derives in part from Hor. *Sat.* 2,1,1f. and Juv. 6,635; see also F. Leo, *Hermes* 24 (1889), 82 (= Leo, *Ausgew. kl. Schr.* I 297f.) and Marx, I xii.

15 Lucilius' level of verbal obscenity may be deduced from 1186M. *futuo*, Hor. *Sat.* 1,2,127: the verb is continuative present: 'While I am actually on the job'; *cunnus*, Hor. *Sat.* 1,2,36 and 70; 1,3,107. Neither word occurs in the later satirists, though both are common in Martial. *Fello* in the obscene sense is not found in any satirist but is common in Martial and the writers of graffiti at Pompeii; see also A. E. Housman, *Hermes* 66 (1931), 408 n. 2 (= *Class. Papers* III 1180 n. 3). *Penis*, which is an obscene word to Cicero (*Fam.* 9,22,2) occurs in Horace only in an epode (12,8); it occurs twice in the violent denunciation of Persius' fourth satire (4,35 and 48) and twice in Juvenal, the witty sneer at 6,337 and the shock tactics of the brutal question at 9,43 (cf. the revolting expression at 2,33). On the avoidance of obscene words see further Cic. *Off.* 1,128f., Quint. 8,3,39, and Kroll 111f.

16 Mart. 5,78, 10,48; Hor. *C.* 1,20 (see Nisbet and Hubbard, *A Commentary on Horace Odes Bk I*, 244ff.); see in general the important study by F. Cairns, *Generic composition in Greek and Roman poetry* (Edinburgh, 1972); note esp. p. 6. On the topic of the invitation to the frugal meal see ch. 7 n. 76.

17 W. H. Auden, in conversation with Richard Crossman on B.B.C. television, 28 Jan. 1973, talked of 'Opera, the last refuge of the high style'. Graham Hough, *An Essay on Criticism* (London, 1966), 84, vindicates the value of a theory of kinds: 'the true and necessary principle that

each literary species offers its own satisfaction, operates on its own level and has its own proper principle.'

18 J. Wight Duff, *Roman Satire* (Cambridge, 1937), 106–14; N. Terzaghi, *Per la storia della satira* (Turin, 1944[2]), 99–154. On problems of dating see B. E. Perry, *Babrius and Phaedrus* (Loeb Classical Library, 1965), intro. lxxix n. 1.

19 Apul. *Apol.* 10. The supremacy of the abusive force of *iambi* is mentioned by Porph. on Hor. *C.* 1,16,22–4. Note Catull. frg 3: *at non effugies meos iambos.*

20 On coarse army songs see e.g. Pliny *N.H.* 19,144; Schanz-Hosius I[4] 21f. On primitive rude verses see also Gell. 15,4,3 and Fraenkel 58; on Octavianus' Fescennines see Macr. *Sat.* 2,4,21. On Ovid's *Ibis* see A. E. Housman, *Journ. Phil.* 35 (1920), esp. 316–18 (= *Class. Papers* III 1040–2).

21 Cicero *Cael.* 6 makes a distinction between *accusatio* and *maledictio* (cf. Austin *a.l.*). To Quintilian (12,9,8) mud-slinging is not the mark of a first-class orator (see Austin on 12,9,9). On the tradition of *invectiva* see R. G. M. Nisbet (ed.), *Cicero in Pis.* (Oxford, 1961), 192–7.

22 E. J. Kenney, *Lucretius, De Rerum Natura Bk 3* (Cambridge, 1971), intro. 17ff., discusses the possible influence of diatribe. C. Murley, *T.A.Ph.A.* 70 (1939), 380–95, provides interesting parallels but his conclusion that Lucretius may have a place in the history of satire is misleading. For Lucretius' place in the poetic tradition of Empedocles see W. Kranz, *Philologus* 96 (1944), 68–107. On didactic poetry see Diomedes *G.L.K.* I,482 and W. Kroll, *R.E., s.v.* 'Lehrgedicht', 12,2,1842–57.

23 F. J. E. Raby, *A history of secular Latin poetry in the Middle Ages* II (1957[2]), 45–54, discusses knowledge of Juvenal in twelfth-century France, but his description of *Speculum Stultorum* as 'a true satire in the Roman sense' (98) is misleading.

24 The thesis of a continuity is developed unconvincingly by C. Witke, *Latin Satire. The Structure of Persuasion* (Leiden, 1970); rev. Rudd, *C.R.* 23

(1973), 42–4. On the reference by Walter of Châtillon see Raby (n. 23 above), 197.

25 The French poet and critic Boileau Despréaux published together with his ninth satire in 1666 a short discourse on satire that was confined to the Lucilian tradition.

26 J. Dryden, 'A Discourse concerning the Original and Progress of Satire', *Of Dramatic Poesy and other critical essays*, ed. G. Watson, vol. II (London, New York, 1962), 71–155.

27 See Rudd 258–73.

28 Diomedes *G.L.K.* I,485 (= *C.G.F.* (Kaibel) 55f.).

29 The author of this article on satire in the standard 11th edn. of the *Enc. Brit.* is Richard Garnett; the definition is rightly retained in the 1973 edn. of *Enc. Brit.*

30 This denial is a passing weakness in Matthew Hodgart's useful general study of the principles and practice of satire, *Satire* (London, 1969), 31; note by contrast his sound formulation of the principles of the classical tradition of formal satire (ch. 5 esp. 132). Hodgart also believes that good satire possesses 'no single fixed style; it works by comparisons and contrasts' (63). This view of the fluid style of satire is in part endorsed by Horace (*Sat.* 1,10,11–15), but the ancient satirist also recognized the limits beyond which he should not proceed.

NOTES TO CHAPTER 2 (ORIGINS)

1 The manuscript tradition of the satirists and grammarians is confused on the point of orthography, but the spelling *satura* is found in such good manuscripts as the Montepessulanus (P) of Juvenal. For a thorough discussion of the orthographical problem see F. Marx (ed.), *C. Lucilii Carminum Reliquiae* (Leipzig, 1904 and 1905), I ixf.; see also Leo's critical note in *C.G.F.* (Kaibel) 55 and G.

A. Gerhard, *Philologus* 75 (1918), 247. See also the discussion by C. A. Van Rooy, *Studies in Classical Satire and Related Literary Theory* (Leiden, 1965), 155ff. (see also index, 223). Van Rooy's book, notwithstanding the reservations expressed in *C.R.* 16 (1966), 72ff., is a very useful contribution to many of the problems discussed in this chapter; see rev. by F. Robertson, *C.Ph.* 61 (1966), 214–16.

2 *adventicia* with *cena* Suet. *Vit.* 13,2, with the noun to be supplied Petr. 90,5; *adventoria* (*cena*) Mart. *Praef.* 12.

3 *Carm. Lat. Epigr.* 1 (Bü); cf. Schanz-Hosius I⁴ 19.

4 Plaut. *Poen.* 6–8; *Am.* 667f.

5 Sen. *N.Q.* 1,5,12 (of purple dye); Pers. 1,71 (of *rus*, the countryside); Cic. *Orat.* 123 (*oratio*).

6 Diomedes I 485 *G.L.K.*

7 Isidore *Orig.* 5,16 and 8,7,7; Fest. 417 L (315 M); the presence of another quotation to illustrate *lex satura* at Festus 416 L (314 M) does not invalidate the point even though this passage of Festus draws on Verrius Flaccus, for it too derives from Varro; see Leo, *Gött. gel. Anz.* (1906), 859 (= *Ausgew. kl. Schr.* I,245). The one independent comment of importance is that of Isidore (20,1,8): *satietas ex uno cibo dici potest, pro eo quod satis est; saturitas autem a satura nomen accepit, quod est vario alimentorum adparatu compositum.* Isidore explicitly makes the distinction between a 'satiety that is caused by one kind of food and taking its name from sufficiency and a repletion that takes its name from *satura*, that is something obtained from a varied provision of things to eat'. To Isidore *satura* contains the notion of the variegated and of a miscellany.

8 Pseudacron on *praef. in serm. lib.* I (= *test.* V d) Marx).

9 See C. O. Brink, 'Horace and Varro', *Entr. Fond. Hardt* 9 (1963), 193.

10 For Varro's discussion of Ennius in *de Poetis* see Gell. 17,21,42f.

11 Wine as the source of the satyrs' hilarity is emphasized by Pseudacron and Isid. *Orig.* 8,7,7.

12 This objection has been made by many scholars, e.g. Knoche 9.

13. Diomedes *G.L.K.* I 490.

14 Arist. *Poet.* 1449a22; cf. 1449a20; also τὸ σατυρικόν Xen. *Symp.* 4,19; for σάτυροι in the sense of 'a satyr play' see Ar. *Thesm.* 157, Hor. *A.P.* 235 and Brink *a.l.* To this may be added Weinreich's point, xxiii, that actors of satyr plays are never called *saturi* in Latin but *ludiones* or *histriones*, noting the gloss *ludio:σατυριστής* (*C. Gl.L.* II 430,2).

15 *lanx* also in Isid. 8,7,7 (= Marx *testimonia* VII) and Pseudacron, loc. cit. (n. 8 above).

16 Plaut. *Aul.* 354f.

17 On offerings to Ceres see Ovid *Fast.* 2,520; Cato *Agr.* 134.

18 Offerings to Pales Ov. *Fast.* 4,743ff., on which see W. Warde Fowler, *The Roman Festivals* (London, 1899), 81 n. 5; first fruits of the kitchen garden to the Lares, Calp. Sic. 2,64f.; bean meal with lard was offered to Carna at the time of the bean harvest (Macr. *Sat.* 1,12,33 and Warde Fowler, 130).

19 *Farcimen* as stuffing or sausage meat, Isid. *Orig.* 20,2,28, as a sausage Gell. 16,7,11.

20 Varro *L.L.* 5,111. On the species mentioned there see the lucid note by J. Collart, *Varron, de Lingua Latina Livre V* (Paris, 1954), *a.l.*

21 Knoche 10.

22 Apic. 2,5,3 for a sausage stuffing (= B. Flower and E. Rosenbaum, *Apicius. The Roman Cookery Book* (London, 1958), recipe 59). Pine kernels and honey in a white sauce served with goose (Apic. 6,5,5 = Fl. & Ros. 231); spelt-grits and pine kernels in a chicken stuffing (6,8,14 = Fl. & Ros. 253).

23 *hordeum* with shoulder of pork (Apicius 7,9,3 = Fl. & Ros. 295). On *polenta* as an item in the simple life Sen. *Epp.* 110,18; see Schol. Juv. 11,20 (*miscellanea*), Pliny *N.H.* 18,72, Prop. 4,8,25 on food for gladiators; barley as food for pigs, Varro, *R.R.* 2,4,6, and as food to fatten stallions, Col. 6,27,8 and K.

D. White, *Roman Farming* (London, 1970), 292.

24 See e.g. Virgil *Georg.* 3,205, Varro *R.R.* 1,31,5, Pliny *N.H.* 18,142.

25 Compare Horace's metaphor *liber nutritus* (*Epp.* 1,20,1–5). As well as referring to literary history *farrago* is self-depreciatory, an attitude sustained by the diminutive *libelli*.

26 E.g. Knoche 10, and Weinreich xi. One may compare the development of the word farce from Latin *farcire,* to stuff, by way of the mediaeval usage of the stuffing for a bird and also of an impromptu amplification of the text of the Mass and of a play (*farsa*) to the modern meaning of a dramatic work intended solely to excite ribald laughter.

27 For *patina* as a cake see Apic. 4,2. It may be noted in passing that Tertullian's list of miscellaneous and anthology works includes the title *Acci Patinam,* but nothing can be safely inferred from it.

28 On the poem of Meleager see Gow and Page, *The Greek Anthology, Hellenistic Epigrams* (Cambridge, 1965), on 4398–407. They refer to *A.P.* 12,44,3 (= 1813 G-P) for another example of λοπάς in the sense of the contents of the platter. Gow-Page, intro. xvi, assign the compilation of the 'Garland' of Meleager to the early part of the 1st C. B.C. Hirzel, *Der Dialog* I 440 n. 4 points to Meleager's knowledge of Latin and of Roman customs in the reference at *A.P.* 12,95,10 to *lanx satura*.

29 On Posidippus' σωρός see Schol. *Il.* 11,101 (a comment of Aristarchus), W. Peek, *R.E. s.v.* 'Poseidippos', 22,1 (1953), 431–9, and H. Lloyd-Jones, *J.R.S.* 83 (1963), 75–99.

30 On σύμμεικτα see αἰτίαι σύμμεικτοι of Democritus (*D.K.V.* II,91,15), αἰτίαι with a diversity of subjects, σύμμικτα συμποτικά of Aristoxenus frg 124 Wehrli. Colourful Greek titles such as are listed by Pliny *N.H. Praef.* 24, e.g. κέρας Ἀμαλθείας, λειμών, should be used with caution as parallels for *satura*. For some at least of these were commonplace books of excerpts from other authors with or

without annotation by the compiler. On the process of compilation see Cic. *Att.* 2,20,6 and Gell. *praef.* 2.

31 For a postulated connection between Demeter and the Σωρός see the argument of Lasserre, *Rh.M.* 102 (1959), 222ff., based on an allegorical interpretation of Theocr. 7,155.

32 The possible influence of the *Soros* on Ennius' *saturae,* as suggested by the author, *Röm. Sat.* 417, is favoured by J. H. Waszink, 'Ennius', *Entr. Fond. Hardt* 17 (1972), 105.

33 On *satura* and *saturae* see W. Kroll, *R.E. s.v.* '*satura*' 2,2 (1921), 192–200.

34 A speech against Tiberius Gracchus by T. Annius Luscus in 133 B.C. (*O.R.F.* 106 = Festus p. 416 L), also C. Laelius Sapiens, *pro se ad populum,* after 145 B.C. (*ib.* p. 119f. = Festus p. 416 L = 314 M). See Marx on Lucil. 48, and Ullman, *C.Ph.* 8 (1913), 177ff.

35 By the *Lex Caecilia Didia* (Cic. *Dom.* 53): see Rotondi, *Leges Publicae P.R.* (Milan, 1912), 335.

36 Amm. Marc. 16,6,3; Lact. 1,21,13 includes no qualifying word: Pescennius Festus (late 2nd C. A.D.) is said to have written *libri historiarum per saturam* (= Marx, *test.* xxix).

37 The relevance to *satura* of E. Lattes' equation of *satir-* and 'speaking' (see Lattes, *Bull. Soc. Ling.* 30 (1930), 82ff.) was first pointed out by P. Meriggi, *Stud. Etrusc.* 11 (1937), 196f. and n. 177 and was amplified by B. Snell, *S.I.F.C.* 17 (1940), 215. On *sátena* = *dictus* see E. Vetter, *Glotta* 28 (1940), 157 and 217.

38 Salutary scepticism on too wide an acceptance of Etruscan loan words in Latin is expressed by O.J.L. Szemerényi, *Hermes* 103 (1975), 300ff.; see also A. D. Momigliano *J.R.S.* 53 (1963), 98. The Etruscan derivation of *satura* is considered as no more than a hypothesis by Walde-Hofmann, *Lateinisches etymologisches Wörterbuch* (1954³), *s.v. satura,* but accepted without discussion by L. R. Palmer, *The Latin Language* (London, 1954), 48.

39 *Ister* is often accepted as one of the

most certain Etruscan loan words in Latin, but Szemerényi, loc. cit. (n. 38), 314–16 considers it to be of Greek origin by way of Etruscan.

40 The phrase *impletas modis saturas* is probably a piece of etymologizing on the basis of *satura* meaning something filled full; compare the other etymologies in this passage: in addition to *histrio* from *ister, fabula* and *argumentum* from *fari* and *arguo*; see Quint. 5,10,9 and B. L. Ullman, *C.Ph.* 9 (1914), 7–8.

41 For the phrase *ad manum* see Liv. 9,19,6: *ad manum domi supplementum esset*; and Pliny *N.H.* 35,97: *ad manum intuenti*; cf. Ov. *Fast.* 3,536. The separation of voice and gesture is confirmed by Cic. *de Or.* 1,254 and *Leg.* 1,11.

42 On *exodia* see G. Duckworth, *The Nature of Roman Comedy* (Princeton, 1952), 6 and F. Skutsch, *R.E. s.v. exodia* 6,2 (1909), 1686–9; on Atellans see Duckworth, 10–13; and for *Atellanicum exodium* see e.g. Suet. *Tib.* 45.

43 On the stages of Livy's account see Leo, *Hermes* 39 (1904), 67ff. and Weinreich, *Hermes* 51 (1916), 392ff.

44 Val. Max. 2,4,4: *paulatim deinde ludicra ars ad saturarum modos perrepsit*. On this passage see Weinreich, loc. cit. (n. 43 above) 404–7.

45 For the first view see e.g. G. Duckworth, op. cit. (n. 42 above) 10. Ullman's advocacy of a dramatic *satura* is fully documented and also moderate: 'The present status of the satura question', *N. Carolina St. Class. Phil.* 17 (1920), 379–401 (= Korzeniewski 1–30). See also J. H. Waszink, *Entr. Fond. Hardt* 17 (1972), 108ff., who refers to H. D. Jocelyn, *The Tragedies of Ennius* (Cambridge, 1969), 13.

46 See Weinreich, loc. cit. (n. 43) 389. It is clear from Cato (frg 77P = Gell. 2,28,6) that such an occurrence as a plague would have been mentioned in the pontifical annals. Livy states (6,1,1–3) that the records for the years after the sack of Rome by the Gauls (387 B.C.) were more reliable. According to Cicero, *de Or.* 2,52, these annals recorded *res*

omnes singulorum annorum; the introduction of dances from Etruria may have been included. On the *annales* see J. E. A. Crake, *C.Ph.* 35 (1940), 375–86, and J. P. V. D. Balsdon, *C.Q.* 3 (1953), 158–64. On sending to Etruria see Liv. 27,37,6 and Tac. *Ann.* 14,21.

47 On Fescennines at a harvest festival, Hor. *Epp.* 2,1,139ff., at a wedding, Cat. 61,120 (and Fordyce, *a.l.*); see also Marx, *Rh.M.* 78 (1929), 398–426.

48 The date 240 B.C. is given by Atticus and, as a result of research *in antiquis commentariis*, by Cicero, *Brut.* 72, who also refers to it at *Tusc.* 1,3 and *Sen.* 50; it seems to have had the confirmation of Varro (Gell. 17,21,42f.; see H. Dahlmann, *Entr. Fond. Hardt* 9 (1963), 13; Accius gave 197 B.C. as the year of Livius' first production, a dating which makes nonsense of Latin literary history and was rightly contradicted by Cic. *Brut.* 72; it has however been revived by H. B. Mattingly, *C.Q.* 7 (1957), 159–63.

49 See Festus 446 L (333 M): *is* (i.e. Livius) *et scribebat fabulas et agebat*; cf. E. Fraenkel, *R.E. Supplbd* 5 (1931) *s.v.* 'Livius', 601.

50 Suet. *Gramm.* 1: *nihil amplius quam Graecos interpretabantur* (i.e. Livius et Ennius); see also Diomedes *G.L.K.* I 489. The transmitted titles of Livius' tragedies are on Greek subjects; the comic title *Gladiolus* (frg 1R³) is based on New Comedy; cf. Menander Ἐγχειρίδιον (136–141 Kö.²) and 128–30 Austin.

51 O. Jahn, *Hermes* 2 (1867), 225–51, believed that the apparent chronological sequence was a schematic construction. His view was amplified by Leo, *Hermes* 24 (1889), 67–84 (= *Ausgew. kl. Schr.* I 283–300), and by G. L. Hendrickson, *A.J.Ph.* 15 (1894), 1–30.

52 Hendrickson, *A.J.Ph.* 19 (1898), 309 argues that the form of Livy's description comes from the same source as the schematic words of the *tractatus Coislinianus,* a Peripatetic treatise of unknown authorship and date, on which see *C.G.F.* (Kaibel), 50–3 and D'Alton 361. On the close parallel between Arist. *Poet.*

1449b7ff. and Livy's words see Hendrickson, *A.J.Ph.* 15 (1894), 7ff. Similarly *in artem paulatim verterat* suggests the way of thought of ὀψὲ ἀπεσεμνύνθη (*Poet.* 1449a20). For another example of an account of the growth and degeneracy of literature (and the other arts) see Vell. Pat. 1,16,3–1,17.

53 On Crates, who visited Rome *c.* 168 B.C., see Pfeiffer, *History of Classical Scholarship* (Oxford, 1968), 235–45; for his writings on comedy, 242. His literary influence is described by Suet. *Gramm.* 2.

54 There was a censorious element in the Hellenistic satyr play e.g. in the *Menedemus* of Lycophron (Athen. 2,55c). On the development of the satyr play in Hellenistic times see Gerhard, *Philologus* 75 (1918), 250–60.

55 Roman theory saw a connection between satyr drama and *Atellana*: Porphyrio on Hor. *A.P.* 221: *satyrica coeperunt scribere ut Pomponius Atalanten* etc.; Diomedes *G.L.K.* I 489, 32–490, 18. See also the Greek term σατυρικαὶ κωμῳδίαι for *Atellana*, Nicolaus of Damascus ap. Athen. 6,261C, and Leo, *Hermes* 49 (1914), 164 n. 1 and 169ff. (= *Ausgew. kl. Schr.* I 252 n. 1 and 257ff.).

56 Dion. Hal. *Ant. Rom.* 7,71,1 also refers to Fabius Pictor. Boyancé, *R.E.A.* 34 (1932), 11–25, sees the origin of a dramatic *satura* in such a dance of satyrs, a view which is refuted by Weinreich xxiii. It is none the less possible that some informal quasi-dramatic pieces were enacted in Rome in early times, but we have no knowledge of their name or nature.

57 On Livy's patriotism see *Praef.* and P. G. Walsh, *Livy* (Cambridge, 1961), 144f.; also Ogilvie, *Commentary on Livy Bks 1–5*, pp. 140ff. and 255.

58 For the feeling of Rome's moral degeneracy see Liv. *Praef.* and P. G. Walsh, op. cit. (n. 57 above) 67f.

59 E.g. Weinreich, *Hermes* 51 (1916), 410 regards Varro as a probable source. For Varro's patriotism see also C. O. Brink, 'Horace and Varro', *Entr. Fond. Hardt* 9 (1963), 182; for his belief in

degeneracy see further his Menippeans *passim*.

60 To Cicero, *Brutus* 60, Varro is *diligentissimus investigator antiquitatis*. Leo, *Hermes* 24 (1889), 79 (= *Ausgew. kl. Schr.* I 295) believed Varro to be the source, but later, *Hermes* 39 (1904), 67, under the influence of Hendrickson, *A.J.Ph.*19 (1898), 288, who argued for Accius as Livy's immediate source and Pergamene writers as the remoter source, modified his opinion and advocated an unknown source earlier than Varro. On Aelius Stilo see *Gramm. Rom. Fragm.* (Fun.), pp. 51–76 and Schanz-Hosius I 232ff.

61 Pomponius, *Satura*: Frassinetti, *Fabularum Atell. Fragmenta* (Turin, 1955), pp. 4of.; frg II is a description of a treacherous and truculent woman. See also Pomponius, *Dotata* (Fras. p. 11). On the meaning of *satura* in play titles see Ullman, *C.Ph.* 9 (1914), 22f. For other unseemly Atellan titles see Pomponius, *Prostibulum* (Fras. pp. 36–8); *Hirnea Pappi* (Fras. p. 14).

62 Naevius *in Satyra* (*frg. poet. Lat.* p. 28 Morel), quoted by Festus 306 L (257 M). For contrasting views of the line see Weinreich xviif. and E. Fraenkel, *R.E. Supplbd.* 6, *s.v.* 'Naevius', 640,46.

63 Older scholars such as Birt saw the influence of dramatic *satura* at Plaut. *Stichus* 683ff. But it may now be assumed on the evidence of Menander's *Dyskolos* that the dances in the *Stichus* were probably from the Greek original. Support for Livy's account is sometimes sought in Horace's description of the development of Roman drama (*Epp.* 2,1,139–60); see Ullman, *T.A.Ph.A.* 48 (1917), 111–32. But for a full analysis of the important differences between the two accounts see Leo, *Hermes* 39 (1904), 67ff. and also Rudd, *Phoenix* 14 (1960), 36–44. Plautus probably also drew on the knowledge of solo performances among Greek Τεχνῖται, see E. Fraenkel, *Elementi Plautini in Plauto* (Florence, 1960), 323, 349 and 439 n.; T. B. L. Webster, *Hellenistic Poetry and Art* (London, 1964), 267ff.

64 F. Muller, *Philologus* 78 (1923),

269ff. On the word *Saturnus* see Walde-Hofmann, (op. cit. n. 38) *s.v.* and for the Etruscan origin of *Saturnus* see K. Latte, *Römische Religionsgeschichte* (Munich, 1960), 137.

65 K. Kerényi, *Studi e materiali di storia delle religioni* 9 (1933), 129–56 (= Korzeniewski 83–111).

66 F. Altheim, *Satura tota nostra est, Epochen der römischen Geschichte* II (Frankfurt, 1935), 245–71; see also Altheim's later study, *Satura, Gesch. d. lat. Sprache* (Frankfurt, 1951), 346–65 (= Korzeniewski 112–36).

67 On the rituals of Ceres see H. Le Bonniec, *Le culte de Cérès à Rome* (Paris, 1958), and on the Horace scholiast see n. 8 above.

NOTES TO CHAPTER 3 (ENNIUS)

1 The standard reference text for all of Ennius' works is that of J. Vahlen, *Ennianae Poesis Reliquiae* (Leipzig, 1928³); *saturae* and *varia* will be found on pp. 204–29. Also useful is the edition by E. H. Warmington, vol. I of *Remains of Old Latin* (Loeb Classical Library, 1956), 382–447. On Ennius' satires in general see particularly the full and judicious discussion by Waszink, *Entr. Fond. Hardt* 17 (1972), 99–137, the chapter by Van Rooy, *Studies in Classical Satire and Related Literary Theory* (Leiden, 1965), 30–49, and U. Knoche, *Die Römische Satire* (Göttingen, 1971³), 11–20.

2 See chapter 1, n. 28.

3 Quint. 10,1,93 and 95.

4 Pacuvius lived until *c.* 130 B.C. (see Schanz-Hosius I⁴, 100).

5 On Rudiae see Strabo 6,3,5; Cic. *de Or.* 3,168; on Ennius and Calabria Hor. C. 4,8,20. On the year of his birth Gell. 17,21,43 (quoting Varro *de poetis*), Cic. *Brut.* 72, Schanz-Hosius I⁴ 87. On the historical background Leo, *Gesch.* 154 and Scullard, *Hist. Rom. World* 753–146

B.C., 124 and 159ff.

6 Serv. on *Aen.* 7,691; Sil. It. 12,393ff.; Suda *s.v.* ''Ἔννιος''; Leo, *Gesch.* 150ff.

7 On the Iapygian and Messapian allies of Rome see Polybius 2,24,11 and Walbank *a.l.*, and Leo, *Gesch.* 155. On Cato's quaestorship see Nepos, *Cato* 1,4 and Scullard 111 n. 4.

8 For Ennius' rank and a fictitious account of his prowess (Sil. It. 12,393ff.) see Leo 151 n. 1; and for a sceptical examination of the tradition concerning Ennius' army career and his meeting Cato see E. Badian, *Entr. Fond. Hardt* 17 (1972), 155–63.

9 Suet. *Gramm.* 1. Cic. *Sen.* 14. Leo, *Gesch.* 157 n. 2. The Aventine was the quarter for craftsmen and merchants (Badian 168).

10 Cic. *Tusc.* 1,3; Scullard 184; on Fulvius Nobilior's *imperium* M.R.R. I, 360 and 366.

11 Cic. *Brut.* 79; on the colonies see Scullard 167ff. However, Cicero's testimony that Nobilior's son was Ennius' benefactor has been discredited by Badian, op. cit. (n. 8) 183–8.

12 *Sat.* 64 V; Hor. *Epp.* 1,19,7.

13 On the date of Ennius' death see Cic. *Brut.* 78 and Scullard 223 n. 2; on the cause Jerome on 1849 = 168 B.C. (Jerome gives 168 B.C. wrongly).

14 Gell. 17,17,1 on Ennius' *tria corda*. On Messapian influences see Leo 153 and F. Skutsch, *R.E. s.v.* 'Ennius' 2589, 68. See also O. Skutsch, *B.I.C.S.* 21 (1974), 75–80.

15 H. Thesleff, *Introduction to the Pythagorean writings of the Hellenistic period* (Åbo, 1961), 97f., who stresses the increasing importance of Sicily.

16 Liv. 27,37,7. Cichorius, *Röm. Stud.* 7.

17 201 B.C. was probably the year of Naevius' death (Cic. *Brut.* 60; E. Fraenkel, *R.E. Supplbd* 6 (1935) *s.v.* 'Naevius', 625. He had been exiled shortly after his release from prison for attacking the Metelli, whose political ally Scipio Africanus was also lampooned (Jerome on 1816 = 201 B.C., Gell. 3,3,15

and 7,8,5). On the circumstances of Naevius' imprisonment see Momigliano, *J.R.S.* 32 (1942), 120ff. and Scullard 254. If Scullard's view is right, the means used by the Scipionic party to silence Naevius were unscrupulous as well as drastic.

18 Cic. *Arch.* 22; *de Or.* 2,276 (on the identity of Nasica see Badian, op. cit. (n. 8 above) 170ff.; Livy 38,56,4).

19 Ps. Aur. Vict. *vir. ill.* 52,3. On the rivalry between the Fulvii and the Scipios see Scullard 141ff. On the poet in the retinue see Cic. *Tusc.* 1,3 and Leo, *Gesch.* 158.

20 Cic. *Ac.* 2,51. Galba was praetor in 187 B.C. (*M.R.R.* I 368); on his political affiliations see Scullard 141 n. 1.

21 *Ann.* 234–51 from Gell. 12,4,1; O. Skutsch, *C.Q.* 13 (1963), 94–6 (= *Studia Enniana* (London, 1968), 92–4) sees here a blend of literary precedent (*G.L.P.* 111) and personal experience. There are autobiographical references in *Ann.* e.g. 377.

22 F. Skutsch, *R.E.* 5,2602,51ff. On the *Annals* see O. Skutsch, *The Annals of Quintus Ennius* (London, 1953) = *Studia Enniana*, 1–17.

23 On the tragedies see Leo, *Gesch.* 187ff. and the edition by H. D. Jocelyn (Cambridge, 1969).

24 For Ennius as disciple of the Muses see Varro, *Men.* 356 (compare Posidippus, *P. Brit. Mus. Inv.* 589,10); for his dream see O. Skutsch, op. cit. (n. 22 above), 9f.

25 On this see O. Skutsch, *C.Q.* 42 (1948), 99 (= *Studia Enniana* 38f.).

26 Cic. *Brut.* 78. The tradition (Gell. 17,21,43) that he wrote the 12th book of the *Annals* when he was sixty-seven years old is rejected by F. Skutsch, *R.E.* 5,2608.

27 It has been argued that *Hedyphagetica* is later than 189 B.C.; see O. Skutsch, *C.Q.* 42 (1948), 99 (= *Studia Enniana*, 38f.).

28 On the founding of Luna see Liv. 41,13,4; Scullard, 167.

29 Porph. on Hor. *Sat.* 1,10,46.

30 Don. on Ter. *Phorm.* 339 (= *Sat.* 14–19V): *e sexto satyrarum Ennii* was conjectured by Stephanus on the basis of *de sexto salis...* of *dett.* The Vatican

manuscript reads *de cen*, which might suggest the beginning of such a title as Laberius' *Centonarius*, but any conjectural restoration is problematical. Vahlen and Leo are sceptical about the inclusion of these lines in Ennius' *Saturae*.

31 E.g. frg. 65. 64 may safely be assigned to Ennius' literary procedure on external evidence (see n. 12 above) and to one of the *saturae* on the grounds that he would have been unlikely to assert in high poetry a necessary connection between drink and poetic composition.

32 See e.g. Cratinus' self-justification in Πυτίνη, 'The Bottle'. There is a full discussion of this fragment by Waszink, op. cit. (n. 1 above) 113–19.

33 In a fragment of dubious attestation (n. 30 above) a parasite exults in his brief and carefree eagerness for food (14–19). The parasite's apologia is found throughout the tradition of Greek comedy and also in Roman adaptation. For the parasite in Epicharmus see 349ff. *C.G.F.* (Kaibel) and Pickard-Cambridge rev. Webster, *Dithyramb, Tragedy and Comedy* (Oxford, 1962²), 273f., in New Comedy Webster, *Studies in Later Greek Comedy* (Manchester, 1970²), 5f. and in Rome, Duckworth, *The Nature of Roman Comedy* (Princeton, 1952), 265ff.

34 *Scen.* 234–41, on which see O. Skutsch, *Rh.M.* 96 (1953), 193–201. There is a similar word play in Philemon *C.A.F.* (Kock) frg. 23. There is artifice in such verbal jingles but nothing in the variegated fragments that is firmly to be associated with the high style. There is likewise variety in the metrical forms used (cf. ch. I, n. 28), for the fable of the lark the so-called *versus quadratus*, trochaic *septenarii*, such as were used in both drama and popular songs; cf. Gell. 2,29,20 and E. Fraenkel, *Hermes* 62 (1927), 357–70 (= *Kl. Beitr.* II 11–24). Other fragments are in hexameters, iambic metres and (59–62) Sotadeans; on 59–62, which cannot be the accentual Saturnian metre, as in Warmington (*R.O.L.* I, 393), see Vahlen ccxi.

35 5. On the *servus currens* see e.g.

Plaut. *Curc.* 28off. and *Men. Dysk.* 81ff.

36 Cic. *N.D.* 2,101; cf. Zeno, *S.V.F.* I 115. Similar words in Ennius' *Euhemerus* describe the man Jupiter gazing up at the sky (*var.* 100). Astronomical passages are common in the tragedies, e.g. *Iph.* 215–8, 242–4.

37 69; see Cic. *N.D.* 1,97.

38 *Mortem ac Vitam, quas contendentes in satura tradit Ennius* (Quint. 9,2,36). M. L. West, *H.S.C.Ph.* 73 (1969), 120, offers as parallel a Sumerian debate between Winter and Spring.

39 The personification of Death alone is found in Eur. *Alc.* 28ff. and Ennius *scen.* 245. Epicharmus' titles include *Land and Sea* (23–32 Kaibel) and *Hope or Wealth* (34–40 Kaibel).

40 Ar. *Nub.* 889–1104 and Dover's commentary. Xen. *Mem.* 2,1,21–34 (= DKV II 313ff.); W. K. C. Guthrie, *A History of Greek Philosophy* III (Cambridge, 1969), 277f.

41 Novius frg 63 Frassinetti (= 63R³) from Nonius 768 L.

42 *Sat.* 65; Hdt. 1,141.

43 *Sat.* 21–58 (Gell. 2,29,3ff.). Vahlen, ccxii, Ribbeck, *Rh.M.* 10 (1856), 290ff., Norden, *Agn. Th.* 379 n. 2.

44 Call. *Iamb.* 4. Contrast also Ennius' simplicity with the satirical reference in Callimachus' fable in *Iamb.* 2 based on Aesop 383 Halm (see *Dieg.*, an ancient commentary on Callimachus, 6,30f.). For Plato see e.g. *Phaedr.* 237B.

45 A. E. Housman, *C.R.* 48 (1934), 50f. (= *Coll. Papers* III, 1232–3); O. Skutsch, *C.Q.* 38 (1944), 85f. (= *Studia Enniana*, 25ff.). See Cic. *Acad.* 2,51 for Ennius' walk with Sulpicius Galba.

46 For a history and a refutation of the view that all the minor poems were included among the *saturae*, see Waszink, op. cit. (n. 1 above) 106f. The miscellaneous poems are grouped together by Vahlen under *varia*; see Warmington, *R.O.L.* I,394ff.

47 That *Scip.* 8 is similar in language to *Sat.* 10f. is not good evidence for assuming that they belong to the same poem. The exact genre of *Scipio* and *Ambracia*,

both of which contain more than one metrical form, is uncertain: F. Skutsch, *R.E.* 5, 2599, 20.

48 Sotades, notorious for his attack on the incestuous marriage of Ptolemy Philadelphus (Athen. 14,621A), wrote in various genres (Suda); Susemihl I 243ff. For the form of Ennius' title see F. Skutsch, *R.E.* 5, 2602, 1.

49 Fragments of Archestratus are preserved by Athenaeus (3,92D; 7,300D; 318F; 320A). The possibly broken quotation by Apuleius, *Apol.* 39 suggests that Ennius adapted freely; see F. Skutsch *R.E.* 5, 2602, 30, and further E. Fraenkel, *Beobachtungen zu Aristophanes* (Rome, 1962), 123ff. on stylization in Ennius' translations. The comment by Apuleius that Ennius' discussion of fish could not be faulted by connoisseurs suggests that the subject was treated neither flippantly nor, as an attack on extravagance, censoriously.

50 On Call. and Ennius' *Annals* see O. Skutsch, op. cit. (n. 25 above) 8ff.; on Callimachus' πολυείδεια (multiplicity of forms) and criticisms of it *Iamb.* 13, where he refers to Ion of Chios as a precedent (*Dieg.* 9,32–8). The artificial style seems to belie the programmatic profession (frg 112,4ff.) of seeking a πεζὸν νομόν (mundane pasturage), and has with justification been called *eine dichterische Umgangssprache* by Page, *Entr. Fond. Hardt* 10 (1964), 249. *Iamb.* 4,13 was an example of disingenuous disclaimer (ἀστεϊσμός) according to Trypho περὶ τρόπων 24, *Rhet. Gr.* 3,206,15 Sp., and *Iamb.* 5 of ἀλληγορία (*Rhet. Gr.* 3,245,6 Sp.).

51 The Greek commentaries of the 1st C. A.D. were no doubt the successors of an older tradition of exegesis: see R. Pfeiffer, *Callimachus* II (Oxford, 1953), xxviii and cii and also Susemihl I 369f. The influence of Callimachus' *Iambi* on Ennius' *saturae* is overestimated by Deubner, *Rh.M.* 96 (1953), 289ff.

52 Gell. 18,5,11. On the whole process of the transmission and *Nachleben* of Ennius see Vahlen's full treatment, xxiv–cxxxi.

53 *saturarum scriptor, cuius sunt electae ex Ennio Lucilio Varrone saturae*: Porph. on Hor. *Epp.* 1,3,1; F. Skutsch, *R.E.* 5,2616,62.

54 See Sen. *Epp.* 58,5 for a characteristically unfavourable judgement; for enthusiasm, Fronto 4,2 (61N); Gell. 13,20,1; cf. 18,9,5; 18,5,11. Vahlen lxxxiiiff.

55 Vahlen lxxxix; W. M. Lindsay, *Nonius Marcellus' Dictionary of Republican Latin,* (Oxford, 1901), 5. On the ancient transmission of archaic Roman poetry see H. D. Jocelyn, *The Tragedies of Ennius,* 54ff.

56 Stylistic uncouthness is a matter of degree: to Ennius Naevius was a crude old-timer (Cic. *Brut.* 76).

NOTES TO CHAPTER 4 (LUCILIUS)

1 In modern times the fragments of Lucilius were first gathered by the Dutch scholar Jan Dousa in the edition published by his son Francis Dousa, *C. Lucilii Satyrarum reliquiae* (Leiden, 1597). Important modern editions: L. Mueller, *C. Lucili Saturarum Reliquiae* (Leipzig, 1872); C. Lachmann, with supplementary material by M. Haupt and J. Vahlen (Berlin, 1876); F. Marx, *C. Lucilii Carminum Reliquiae,* 2 vols. (Leipzig, 1904 and 1905), the standard modern text and commentary (for judgements on Marx see n. 28 below); N. Terzaghi and Italo Mariotti, *C. Lucilii Saturarum Reliquiae* (Florence, 1966³), a plain text; E. H. Warmington, *Remains of Old Latin,* vol. III (Loeb Classical Library, 1938), with English transl.; W. Krenkel, *Lucilius Satiren,* 2 vols. (Berlin, 1970), text, commentary and German translation, a work that is useful for the sheer bulk of information provided: rev. by R. Pierini, *Gnomon* 45 (1973), 550–7 and by Diana C. White, *C.Ph.* 68 (1973), 36–44. There is a plain text of selected fragments in E.

Diehl, *Poetarum Romanorum Veterum Reliquiae* (Berlin, 1935) (Kleine Texte); a text with French translation and short notes by J. Heurgon, *Lucilius* (Paris, n.d.); a book on Lucilius by N. Terzaghi, *Lucilio* (Turin, 1944²), that is in practice a commentary; and a German translation with comments in O. Weinreich, *Die römische Satiren* (Zurich, 1962²).

2 Diomedes *G.L.K.* I 485 (based on earlier tradition); Apul. *Apol.* 10. *Iambus* in Rome was not to be considered an independent genre of consequence; see Quint. 10,1,96.

3 *Sat.* 1,10,46–9: *inventore* refers to Lucilius (see Kiessling-Heinze on line 46) and not to Ennius, as Lejay *a.l.;* 2,1,62–8.

4 St Jerome, *Chron.* gives the date of his birth under year 148 B.C. (in one MS. 147 B.C.); this is impossible as he served in the Numantine war in 134 B.C. (Vell. 2,9,4). Either Jerome's source confused the years 148 and 180, in both of which the consuls had similar names (Haupt's suggestion; see L. Mueller, *C. Lucilii Saturarum Reliquiae,* 289, but also Cichorius 8f.) or assuming that the year of his death given by Jerome as 103 B.C. or 102 B.C. is correct and that his age when he died was not as in Jerome 46 (an impossibly short life span; see Leo, *Gesch.* 406 n. 5) but by an easy corruption of the Roman numeral LXVI (as Cichorius 13f.) we arrive at a birth date 168–7 B.C. which accords better with the known facts of Lucilius' career. On this controversial problem see I. Mariotti, F. Della Corte, W. Krenkel, *Maia* 20 (1968), 254–70; also Krenkel in Temporini (ed.), *Aufstieg und Niedergang d. römischen Welt* I 2 (Berlin, New York, 1972), 1240–59.

5 Juv. 1,20 and Schol. *a.l.;* the words *Auruncae alumnus* suggest place of birth (cf. a similar circumlocution for Horace at 51); at Tac. *Ann.* 1,44 *alumnus* implies born and bred.

6 On the name Lucilius: W. Schulze, *Zur Gesch. lat. Eigennamen* (= *Abh. Gött. gel. Ges., ph-hist. Kl., N.F.* 5,2) (Berlin, 1904), 441f. and 450. The name Lucilius first appears on the Praenestine mirror

(Degr. 1251), but most of its free-born holders are Roman (M. Lucilius *tr. pl.* – Fronto 5,42, p. 83N. – may be of the 2nd *C.* B.C.; see *M.R.R. II 407*); of the Lucilii outside Rome C. Lucilius, magistrate of the Latin colony at Spoletium (Degr. 668), may be assumed to have held Roman franchise *per magistratum* and Lucilius A.f. Macer (Degr. 575) was a *duovir* at Croton, a colony of Roman citizens. On the Roman associations of Gaius see the ancient commentary (*Diegesis*) on Call. *Aet.* 106–7 and Pfeiffer *a.l.*

7 *Stirpis senatoriae* (Vell. 2,29,2). The family relationship given by Porph. on Hor. *Sat.* 2,1,75 (cf. Pseudacron on 2,1,29) is inaccurate; see Marx I, xix and Cichorius 1–7.

8 M'. Lucilius M.f. Pompt, (Münzer *R.E., s.v.* Lucilius 11); the name occurs in the Adramyttium piece of the *S.C. de agro Pergameno* (*I.G.R.R.* 4,262; Greenidge and Clay, Sources² App. II A p. 278) which is probably to be dated 129 B.C. (see *M.R.R.* I 496f.). In a fragment that may be autobiographical (427) Lucilius refers to a brother. The identification of the senator with the brother of the poet (Cichorius 2–5) was opposed by Kappelmacher *R.E.*, 13,2 (1927), 1619,51. On the family tree see also A. B. West, *A.J.Ph.* 49 (1928), 240–52.

9 Marx I xviii.

10 Suessa was one of twelve refractory Latin colonies punished in 204 B.C. (Liv. 29,15) but not so as to diminish their civil rights; see A. N. Sherwin-White, *The Roman Citzenship* (Oxford, 1973²), 104. On the process of acquiring citizenship *per magistratum* see Ascon. *Pis.* 3; Liv. 23,22,5; Sherwin-White 35f. and 111f.; P. A. Brunt, *J.R.S.* 55 (1965), 90 n. 4. Cichorius, 14f., argues that Horace (*Sat.* 2,1,74f.) would not have described himself as *infra Lucili censum* unless Lucilius had been a Roman citizen.

11 Vell. 2,9,4; Cichorius 29ff.; *M.R.R.* I 492.

12 615f. (References to Lucilius are according to the edition of Marx; see n. 1).

Viriathus' victory was presumably that over Q. Fabius Maximus Servilianus in 141 B.C. (see Appian *Hisp.* 67ff. and *Camb. Anc. Hist.* VIII, 316), too early for Lucilius' presence.

13 In similar circumstances Lucilius' enemy Accius won his case: *ad Her.* 1,24; 2,19; R. E. Smith, *C.Q.* 1 (1951), 171, discusses these early cases of defamatory *iniuria*; see further D. Daube, *Atti del Congresso Internazionale di Diritto Romano* (*Verona*) 3 (Milan, 1951), 411ff. esp. 435.

14 Cichorius 23ff. on the basis of 594 and of Horace's personal disclaimer (*Sat.* 1,6,54ff.) argues plausibly that Lucilius owned land near Tarentum, and supports the view by suggesting (*Röm. Stud.* 67ff.) that C. Lucilius Hirrus who had herds in Bruttium (Varro *R.R.* 2,1,2) was a remote heir of Lucilius; on Lucilius Hirrus see also L. R. Taylor, *Voting Districts of the Roman Republic*, 227.

15 Asc. *Pis.* 12: *Lucilii* is the correction of Manutius for *Lucii* or L of the MSS.; see also Polyb. 31, 12–14.

16 On *funus publicum* (or *indictivum*), to which all the citizen body was summoned by town crier, see Varro *L.L.* 5,160 and 7,42.

17 751–6; see Cichorius, 44ff. On Clitomachus' dedication see Cic. *Ac.* 2,102. He was a patriot (Cic. *Tusc.* 3,54) and was unlikely to have visited at least for some years the state that had destroyed his homeland.

18 For the story that Scipio and Laelius helped Terence see Suet. *vit. Ter.* b) 47 Rost.; Ter. *prol. Ad.* 15–21; Cic. *Att.* 7,3,10; Quint. 10,1,99.

19 Plut. *C. Gracch.* 19.

20 On Scipio's education see Plut. *Aem.* 6,4f.; Polyb. 31,22–30; on the so-called *humanitas* of Scipio and his friends, a sympathetic comprehension of all the actions and passions of man, see de Sanctis, *Storia* V 2,1,36 and the sensible and sceptical discussion by Astin, 302–6. He threw deserters to the beasts (Val. Max. 2,7,13) and destroyed Numantia without a specific mandate from the senate; see Appian *Hisp.* 96–8 and

Toynbee, *Hannibal's Legacy* II, 610. On Scipio at Carthage see Walbank, *Hist. Comm. on Polyb.* I intro. p. 19; Scullard, *J.R.S.* 50 (1960), 60.

21 Appian *Hisp.* 84. The company included Marius and Jugurtha. On Scipio at Numantia see de Sanctis, *Storia* IV 3,260ff. See Polyb. 10,45–7 on his own military expertise. On the dating of the Eastern embassy see Astin *C.Ph.* 54 (1959), 221ff. and Scullard, *J.R.S.* 50 (1960), 69 n. 43.

22 Cic. *Rep.* 1, esp. 14ff.; also *Am.* 69; see Schanz-Hosius I 214f. The notion of a wide literary circle seeks to amalgamate the chronologically incompatible: Terence died in 159 B.C. and so could not have belonged to any such hypothetical group. On the elusive movements of Panaetius see Walbank, *J.R.S.* 55 (1965), 1f. For a salutary revaluation of the whole notion of the Scipionic circle see H. Strasburger, *Hermes* 94 (1966), 60–72 and *J.R.S.* 55 (1965), 41, and Astin 302–6.

23 See p. 48.

24 593–6.

25 See (Plut.) *Apopth. Scip. Min.* 15.

26 Hor. *Sat.* 2,1,71–4 and Pseudacron on Hor. *Sat.* 2,1,72.

27 Ennius and Pacuvius were poor men; Caecilius and Terence were of servile origin and Accius' parents were probably born in slavery. Early Roman prose writers by contrast were aristocrats; see de Sanctis, *Storia* IV 2,1,57.

28 This has been achieved pre-eminently by Marx and Cichorius. Note, however, the important review of Marx by A. E. Housman, *C.Q.* 1 (1907), 53–74 and 148–59 (= *Coll. Papers* 2,662–97), who is rightly critical of Marx's unjustifiable tampering with the words as preserved in the citing authority but shows a curmudgeonly attitude towards the reconstruction of a fragmentary author. In this Leo's review is more balanced, *Gött. gel. Anz.* 1906, 837–61 (= *Ausgew. kl. Schr.* I 221–47).

29 On Nonius' method of citation see W. M. Lindsay, *Nonius Marcellus' Dictionary of Republican Latin* (Oxford,

1901), *pass.,* W. Strzelecki, *R.E.* 17,1 (1936), 891,43. On the general reliability of book numbers see H. T. Rowell, *A.J.Ph.* 68 (1947), 28f. and 42f.

30 Marx's theory (Lucilius I lxxxiiiff.) is criticized by Lindsay, *Philologus* 64 (1905), 438ff., also Strzelecki, *R.E.* (n. 29 above), 891,56. Sometimes Marx is compelled to put some fragments from these books in normal order; see W. Krenkel, *Luciliana, Miscellanea Critica* II (Leipzig, 1965), 150f. See also *id. Röm. Sat.* 479–83; and T. Weeple, *H.S.C.Ph.* 70 (1965), 270f. For quotations in reverse sequence at Macr. 6,1,45–9 see H. D. Jocelyn, *C.Q.* 14 (1964), 291. Diana White, *C.Ph.* 68 (1973), 38 n. 3 suggests that Nonius may not have had codices not rolls for most of his texts.

31 Accius, *Didasc.* 13M. For a different view see J. R. C. Martyn, *Mnemosyne Ser.* IV 25 (1972), 157–67.

32 *ludo ac sermonibus nostris* (1039; see Marx *a.l.*). On *sermo* see p. 69 above. *ludus* in classical Latin is not a formal title; it is used of the activity of informal verse making, see *Lustrum* 6 (1961), 246. On *schedium* (1279) see Petr. 4,5, and J. W. D. Ingersoll, *C.Ph.* 7 (1912), 59. For *Deorum Conc.* see Lact. *Inst.* 4,3,12 (cf. the titles of the books of Homer), but Servius on Verg. *Aen.* 10,104, also interested in the subject matter, refers merely to *primo Lucilii*, the grammarian's normal procedure. *Collyra* is a title given to Bk 16 by Porph. on Hor. *C.* 1,22,10, regarding it as a book about a mistress; cf. the Greek parallels given by Marx on 517.

33 Varro *L.L.* 5,17 refers to a collection of twenty-one books, the first line of which is a hexameter (1); see Marx I liiif.

34 Vell. 2,9,3.

35 Hor. *Sat.* 2,1,67. On the censors of 131 B.C., both of whom were political opponents of Scipio, see *M.R.R.* I 500. 676 and 678–9 seem to be a comment on Metellus' notorious speech in favour of compulsory marriage (*O.R.F.* pp. 107f.; Liv. *Per.* 59 and Suet. *Aug.* 89). On Lucilius' attacks on Metellus see E. S. Gruen, *Roman Politics and the Criminal*

Courts, 149–78 B.C. (Cambridge: Mass., 1968), 22 n. 29 and 54. Lupus is mentioned at 784–90; Hor. *Sat.* 2,1,68 and Pseudacron on line 67.

36 1089; Cichorius 208–10.

37 592f.; 595f. On C. Persius see Cic. *Brut.* 99 and O.R.F. 145; for Iunius Congus: Cic. *de Or.* 1,256 and Pliny *N.H.Praef.* 7. Cic. *Fin.* 1,7 (=594) mentions along with Scipio Rutilius Rufus (cos. 105 B.C.), on whom see Cichorius 62, *O.R.F.* pp. 168ff.; he had served under Scipio at Numantia. On Tarentines etc., see Cichorius 23f. J. Christes' study, *Der frühe Lucilius* (Heidelberg, 1971) is mainly (24–140) devoted to the reconstruction and interpretation of the fragments of Bk 26.

38 587 alludes to Pacuvius' famous description of a chariot drawn by winged snakes (*Medus* 397R³; cf. Cic. *Rep.* 3,14); see Cichorius, 130f. 653 is identical with *Chryses* (112R³).

39 Marriage: 678–86 (see Cichorius, 133–42 and n. 35 above); commerce: 667f., probably connected with his rejection of the life of the *publicanus* (671f.); moralizing: e.g. 599f., 609.

40 Cichorius, 181–92, suggests Tuditanus, on whom see *M.R.R.* I 504 and Schanz-Hosius I 196f. His campaign in 129 in Illyria was the subject of an inscription in Saturnians (*Carm. Epigr.* 1859); he wrote the inscription on his own statue (Plin. *N.H.* 3,129) and C. Hostius wrote epic verse on the campaign (frg in *Frg. Poet. Lat.* (Morel) p. 33; Schanz-Hosius I 162).

41 E.g. Hostius frg 3M and n. 40 above; see Cichorius, 183ff. and Warmington, *R.O.L.* III p. 327.

42 He died before the end of the censorship of 126–5 B.C.; see *M.R.R.* I 501 n. 1. Marx (I xxxv–xl) suggests 126 B.C.; Cichorius, 77–83, argues wrongly for 123 B.C.

43 *M.R.R.* I 523f.; Marx I xli–v.

44 *M.R.R.* I 529f.; 1130 is plausibly connected with 210 (see Marx on 1130).

45 On the chronology of the second collection see Cichorius, 86–97.

46 Serv. on Verg. *Aen.* 10,104; see Marx on 3. Lentulus Lupus was cos. 156 B.C., cens. 147 B.C. On his condemnation for peculation see Val. Max. 6,9,10 and *M.R.R.* I 451 n. 2, where it is dated tentatively 154–3 B.C.

47 On Ennius' council see *Ann.* 65V and Ov. *Met.* 14,812ff. As in Ennius (*Ann.* 62f.) many gods are present (19–22). See also M. Mosca, *P.d.P.* 15 (1960), 373–84.

48 On Q. Mucius Scaevola Augur see Münzer, 277f., *M.R.R.* I 523f. On the date of the trial see Cichorius 88 and 238, and on the trial itself see Cic. *de Or.* 2,281 and Gruen, *Roman Politics and the Criminal Courts,* 114–16.

49 Pers. 1,114; Juv. 1,154. Cic. *de Or.* 1,72 talks of *C. Lucilius homo tibi* (i.e. Scaevola) *subiratus.*

50 Albucius was in later years himself convicted on the same charge and exiled (Cic. *Off.* 2,50); Gruen, *T.A.Ph.A.* 95, (1964), 99–110.

51 Cic. *Brut.* 131.

52 On the journey Porph. on Hor. *Sat.* 1,5,1. The mention of the dying ploughman Symmachus, probably a labourer on one of Lucilius' farms (105f., Cichorius 252) does not mean that his illness was the main reason for Lucilius' journey.

53 Journey by sea 125 and 127; Marx's map (p. 51; see on 96) is helpful. On the combat see Marx on 117 and for a less literal view Cichorius 252f. On 119 see R. Kassel, *Rh.M.* 106 (1963), 305.

54 As Cichorius, 260. For the *propempticon* see Menander, *Rhet. Gr.* 3,395–9; see translation in Russell-Winterbottom, *Ancient Literary Criticism* (Oxford, 1972), 580–3; W. Görler, *Hermes* 93 (1965), 342 and for subsequent descriptions of journeys Rudd 281 n. 4.

55 Cichorius 273–7.

56 Some modern reconstructions of Bks 6 and 7 in particular have exceeded what the fragments allow. The end of an anecdote of a social encounter (231f.) does not prove it to have been the prototype of Horace's meeting with a

social climber; see Fraenkel 112f. and 118, and Rudd, *Phoenix* 15 (1961), 90–6.

57 413–5; on uncertainty in the text and the identification see Cichorius, *Röm. Stud.* 77–9, and on the reading *crassi* Münzer 320f. On the elder Cotta's discomfiture see Val. Max. 6,4,2 and *M.R.R.* I 470. For L. Opimius as *cos.* see *M.R.R.* I 520, for his venality and conviction Sall. *Jug.* 16,2–5; 20,1; 40.

58 On Bks 22–5 see Cichorius, 97f.

59 The name Lucilius sometimes suggests personal involvement, e.g. the amatory 774 or the announcement that someone has invited friends 'along with that scoundrel, Lucilius' (*cum improbo illo Lucilio*, 821f.); elsewhere it emphasizes a belief or emotion: ebullient goodwill (688f.), grief at the loss of a family retainer (580) or satisfaction at not being a tax-gatherer (671f.).

60 On the poet as priest and servant of the Muses see 1028 and Kroll 30ff. The rejection of the inspiration of the Muses in Persius' choliambics may have had some basis in Lucilius; see M. Puelma Piwonka, *Lucilius und Kallimachos* 153 and 358–64 with bibliography at 359 n. 2.

61 Cic. *Att.* 13,6,4 and Shackleton Bailey *a.l.* Lucilius mentions the letter as a literary form (341) and uses it in a complaint to a friend (181); cf. Cat. 38.

62 *Sat.* 2,1,30–4. *vita* (34) is way of life βίος; *senis* refers not to Lucilius as an aged man but rather as Horace's illustrious predecessor; cf. Pers. 1,124 on Atistophanes. On *tabella* see Mayor on Juv. 12,27; it is not a distorted picture as is suggested by W. S. Anderson in J. P. Sullivan (ed.), *Crit. Ess. Rom. Lit.: Satire* (London, 1963), 19f.

63 Marx quotes *Anth. Pal.* 5,252; A. Spengel read *Licinius*, the comic poet; see R. G. Kent on Varro, *LL* 6,69.

64 The Hymnis fragments (see n. 125) seem to go beyond the personally uncommitted.

65 273–7; Apul. *Apol.* 10. The interpretation of 273f. is too difficult to allow any certainty about the circumstances. Gentius is an Illyrian name; see

Liv. 44,23,1 and Marx on 273; of the examples listed by Degrassi, three are freedmen and one a slave; both examples of Macedo are freedmen. To judge from their names the boys were like the Carthaginian Philippus, the homosexual boy of Flamininus, on whom see Liv. 39,42,8.

66 Nevertheless, it is perhaps unwise to describe Lucilius as Rome's first subjective love poet, as does G. Lieberg, *Puella Divina* (Amsterdam, 1962), 47; on this see *Gnomon* 35 (1963), 577.

67 Hor. *Sat.* 1,5,82–5 is connected with Lucilius Bk 3 and 1248 e.g. by G. C. Fiske, *Lucilius and Horace* (Madison, 1920), 310f., but see Rudd 55f.

68 *Sat.* 1,4,1–7; 2,1,62–70; also 1,10,3–4. See also Pers. 1.114f. and Schol. *a.l.* On Juvenal's references to Lucilius (1,19f., 154, 165ff.) see W. S. Anderson, *T.A.Ph.A.* 92 (1961), 12 n. 25.

69 Polyb. 6,56; 18,35; 31,25 (see Walbank, *C.Q.* 37 (1943), 73ff.); as commentator on Roman self-interest: 31,10 and Walbank, *J.R.S.* 55 (1965), 5 and 13; cf. Liv. 42,47,9.

70 Liv. 40,44; Scullard 202; *M.R.R.* I 454–6. Appian *Hisp,* 49ff; cf. the career of Sulpicius Galba, who escaped prosecution for rapacity and brutal maladministration in Spain in 150 B.C. (*M.R.R.* I 456f. and Astin 58 n. 3).

71 On Carthage: Polyb. 36,9; see Strasburger, *J.R.S.* 55 (1965), 41 and 47; on Flamininus as protector of Greece see Liv. 33,32; Plut. *Flam.* 10; *Anth. Plan.* 5 (Alcaeus); on the destruction of Corinth Polyb. 39,2, and on L. Mummius its sacker (*M.R.R.* I 465) see Pliny *N.H.* 35, 24.

72 Metellus was probably the enemy of Scipio from no later than 138 B.C.; see Astin 313; on Lentulus Lupus, Astin 92 n. 2, on Brutus Callaicus *id.* 258f. and on Scipio's enemies in general 90–6. Broughton, 'Senate and Senators in the Roman Republic', in Temporini (ed.) I, 1,250–65 (see n. 4 above), in a qualified defence of the prosopographical approach suggests (257) that the acerbity of Scipio's

tongue and that of Lucilius may have lost him important political friends.

73 The unusual fecundity of Metellus' wife (Val. Max. 7,1,1) ensured the ascendancy of the Metelli in the politics of the next decades; see also n. 35 above. For Scipio's unhappy marriage see Appian B.C. 1,20.

74 Vell. 2,4,4.

75 See also Hor. Sat. 2,1,69; Pers. 1,114; on the command against Aristonicus see Cic. Phil. 11,18 and Cichorius, 335–8. Lucilius seems to have been concerned with the political machinery of the voting: L. R. Taylor, Voting Districts of the Roman Republic, 28f., 55f., 99, 248.

76 There is perhaps a reference to the anti-aliens law of 126 B.C. at 1088; see Cichorius 211f., M.R.R. I 508.

77 1312f.; on his prosecution see Cic. Brut. 103 and M.R.R. I 526. On Hostilius Tubulus Cic. Fin. 2,54 and M.R.R. I 475.

78 394ff. Asellus had been accused of extravagance by Scipio as censor and as tribune in 140 B.C. attacked him; Scipio had to make an elaborate defence; see Astin 127 and 175ff. For other examples of Scipio's malicious wit see 1280 (concerning Decius Subulo, the humiliated praetor of 115 B.C., on whom see M.R.R. I 532 and Badian, J.R.S. 46 (1956), 91–6) and Val. Max. 6,4,2.

79 See in general E. Badian, Historia 11 (1962), 197–245 and on the structure of politics based on the family bloc Scullard, B.I.C.S. 2 (1955), 15ff., and foreword to Roman Politics 220–150 (1973²). For an opposing view see Brunt, rev. Earl, Tiberius Gracchus, Gnomon 37 (1965), 189–92.

80 Marx I xlvii and Cichorius 277–81, following L. Mueller, assume that the reference is to Metellus Caprarius cos. 143 B.C. and praetor by 116 B.C.; Cichorius refers to a coarse saying about him by Scipio at Numantia (Cic. de Or. 2,267) that may have been retailed by Lucilius. But the Caecilius mentioned may have been the consul of 115 B.C. who would

have been praetor by 118 B.C. (M.R.R. I 527).

81 M. Licinius Crassus was frequently mentioned by Lucilius: his precociously brilliant oratory (see Cic. Brut. 160) is referred to waggishly during the trial of Mucius Scaevola (86), whose host he is in Bk 6 (240f.); Lucilius once described him as the man who laughed once in his life and gave him the nickname agelastus (mirthless), which he retained (1299f.); yet he desired his friendship (Cic. de Or. 1,72) and in Bk 20 described a party in his honour.

82 See Plut. Quaest. Rom. 83 (= 284 A–C) and Greenidge, A History of Rome 133–104 B.C. (London 1904), 311–14 on this immolation and the politically suspect trial of Vestals also in 114–13 B.C.: M.R.R. I 537 and Gruen, Rh.M. 111 (1968), 59–63.

83 C. Titius ap. Macr. 3,16,14–16 (= O.R.F. 201–3).

84 See Polyb. 31, 29; (Plut.) Apopth. Scip. Min. 8; Astin 27ff., 89 and 121f. Note the comment by Clement Attlee on Stafford Cripps: 'Great man, political goose'.

85 Liv. 39,8ff.; C.I.L. I² 581 (= 511 Degr., where see reff.); Latte, Römische Religionsgeschichte 270–2; Scullard 147f.

86 Polyb. 31,25; see Scullard, A History of the Roman World 753–146 B.C. (London, 1961³), 357 and n. 1. According to the annalist Calpurnius Piso 154 B.C. was the year in which chastity was overthrown (Plin. N.H. 17,244).

87 On the lex Fannia (161 B.C.) see Lucil. 1172, Plin. N.H. 10,139 and Athen. 6,274C. A fragment of Lucillius (1200) is an exhortation (context and tone unknown) to evade the lex Licinia, a measure passed late in the 2nd C.: see Gell. 2,24,7 and Cichorius 267.

88 On Scipio's censorship see Gell. 4,20,1, M.R.R. I 474f., Scullard, J.R.S. 50 (1960), 67f. and Astin 116–20. Probably in the last year of his life Scipio attacked dancing, O.R.F. 133.

89 Cic. Rep. 4,10f.; Aug. Civ. Dei 2,9; on the nota Cic. Clu. 120 and 130 and for

a connection with satire Hor. *Sat.* 1,4,5 and 106; 1,3,24.

90 See e.g. Lucil. 1238–40. *O.R.F.* 56; Polyb. 31,24 *ap.* Athen. 6,274f.; note that the anti-Greek prejudice in Plut. *Cat. mai.* 22 is very similar to that of Plin. *N.H.* 29,14. On Cato's censorship see *M.R.R.* I 374f., on its speeches Scullard 260–5, and on their eclipse in late republican times Cic. *Brut.* 65.

91 On the name see Marx *a.l.*; see Degr. 712 for Cipius. On Gallonius see Pseudacron on Hor. *Sat.* 2,2,47; on Syrophoenix see Friedlaender on Juv. 8,159f.

92 On Troginus see Marx on 1069.

93 Contrast the ironical abuse of 1105, where *animo* and *virtute* are used of the corresponding vices (see Don. on Ter. *Ad.* 176).

94 Warmington, *R.O.L.* III 295 attributes to a satire of Bk 29 Arnobius' reference *Fornicem Lucilianum* (2,6), which he rightly interprets as the title of a poem on the analogy of Arnobius' parallel reference *Marsyam Pomponi;* Pomponius also has the relevant title *Prostibulum* (148R³). The attribution to Bk 29 is conjectural but plausible.

95 1186; 330, 1297.

96 866f., but the interpretation of this couplet is controversial: see Marx *a.l.* and Warmington III 299 n.b.).

97 E.g. 557–64; see, however, Fiske, *Lucilius and Horace,* 230–8.

98 Aristippus: 742, but see Marx *a.l.;* Carneades: 31; Carneades was a popular sensation in Rome, see Plut. *Cat. mai.* 22, Gell. 6,14,8–10, Walbank, *J.R.S.* 55 (1965), 12 n. 83. On Carneades see A. A. Long, *Hellenistic Philosophy* (London, 1974), 94–106. The rhetorical question *ubi nunc Socratici charti* (709) probably makes a general contrast between a theoretical acceptance of philosophy and immorality in personal conduct or politics.

99 On traces of Panaetius in Lucilius see Marx on 738, and on 1326–38 Pohlenz, *Die Stoa* II² (Göttingen, 1955), 134f. On Panaetius in general *see* J. M. Rist, *Stoic Philosophy* (Cambridge, 1969),

173–200; Pohlenz, *Die Stoa* I 191–207, and on his knowledge of Latin, Walbank, *J.R.S.* 55 (1965), 1. Bk 28 (751–70) contains a light-hearted and anecdotal treatment of philosophy (753) and philosophers, particularly Academics (754–6).

100 1225f.: see Porph. on Hor. *Sat.* 1,3,124. On the Stoic use of ἀρχαί and στοιχεῖα see *S.V.F.* 2,299 (= Diog. Laert. 7,134) and of γῆ and πνεῦμα *id.* 2,440, also Marx on 784.

101 Plin. *N.H.* 34,19; Cic. *Arch.* 27. On the *collegium* see E. G. Sihler, *A.J.Ph.* 26 (1905). 1–21; Krenkel, *Röm. Sat.* 249–82 (= Korzeniewski 161–266) has made a wide-ranging and valuable study of all aspects of literary criticism in Lucilius, including a discussion of the *collegium poetarum* (252f. = Korzeniewski 169f.).

102 Hor. *Sat.* 1,10,53; acc. to Porph. *a.l.* Bks 9,10 and particularly 3, but there is nothing in the fragments of Bk 3 to suggest this; according to Plin. *N.H. Praef.* 7 Lucilius was the first Roman to have a critical faculty.

103 Pacuvius was a friend of Laelius (Cic. *Am.* 24) and probably dead by the time Lucilius wrote, so personal animosity is unlikely. The joke about an involuted prologue by Pac. (875) need not carry critical weight, but there is persiflage of his *Chryses* in the same context (see Marx on 876); cf. the dislocation of 212 from Pac. 408R³. Ennius' *Thyestes* is quoted by Lucilius (872f. = *Thy.* 363V). Horace (*Sat.* 1,10,53) uses the word *mutat* of Lucilius' critical attitude towards Accius and Ennius. He proposed, whether seriously or not, a verbal emendation at 1190 (from Enn. *Var.* 14V; see Serv. on *Aen.* 11,601).

104 Lucilius often quoted Homer, e.g. 463, 1244, 1254 and like many ancient writers used him as a comprehensive source of information and of standards and analogies, e.g. 480–3, 538–46. On the text of 347 see Brink, *Horace on Poetry* 1,64 n. 1.

105 386f. See Marx *a.l.*; see also 1133 and 1264f.

106 184–8. The epithet *miraciodes* (childish) occurs again in Dionysus of Halicarnassus to describe Gorgianic figures, e.g. *Isoc.* 12; D'Alton, 47f.

107 Cic. *de Or.* 3,171; see Marx on 84; Quint. 12,10,39; D'Alton 35–9; on Lucilius' ideal orator see 1241 from Cic. *de Or.* 1,72.

108 See Leo, *Gesch.* 417 n. 1, who quotes *C.I.L.* I 199 (117 B.C.).

109 The interpretation of the grammatical fragments is controversial: see in addition to F. Skutsch, *Glotta* 1 (1909), esp. 309 and 310 n. 1 for Lucilius, the bibliography given by Warmington III 117ff. and I. Mariotti, *Studi Luciliani*, Florence 1960, 25–9.

110 Frg. 1100 from Pompeius V 289 *G.L.K.*; 1215–7.

111 Rudd 88ff.

112 The word *archaeotera* (1111) suggests something less specific, probably old Greek classics in general; see Marx *a.l.* and Rudd, *Mnemosyne Ser.* 4, 10 (1957), 319–36; on comedy as a possible part of an apologia see Brink, *Horace on Poetry* 1,157 n. 2.

113 Accius *Pragm.* 23M; other contemporary judgements Cic. *Rep.* 4,10–11, on Naevius, Gell. 3,3,15.

114 Platonius, περὶ διαφορᾶς κωμῳδιῶν 2 *C.G.F.* (Kaibel) I: this section begins with the same three names as in Horace and gives a similar list of wrong-doers; cf. Tzetzes, περὶ κωμῳδίας *C.G.F.* (Kaibel) VI. On the Peripatetic Hellenistic sources of these works see *C.G.F.* (Kaibel) p. 3 and *id. Abh. Gött. gel. Ges.* Ph. Hist. Kl. N.F. 2,4, (1898), esp. 6,8,49.

115 The view attributed to Lucilius' contemporary Panaetius that Old Comedy was an example of urbane humour (*ingenuus iocus*, Cic. *Off.* 1,104) does not suggest an extensive first-hand knowledge; see G. L. Hendrickson, *A.J.Ph.* 21 (1900), 140.

116 There is no modern book which covers the procedures of Old Comedy as

a whole. The following documentation may therefore be of interest. Perjurers mentioned by name: Ar. *Nub.* 398ff.; politicians: Pericles: Cratin. 240K, *id. Dionys.*, P.Oxy. 663; Hyperbolus: Ar. *Nub.* 551–62; Eup. *Maricas* (see Schol. Ar. *Nub.* 551 and Quint. 1,10,18). Comic poets included even such dangerous topics as the mutilation of the Hermae (Phryn. 58K; Plut. *Alc.* 20). Aristophanes advised the expulsion of Sabazios (Cic. *Leg.* 2,37); advocacy of older standards in morals and politics: Ar. *Nub.* 961ff., Eup. *Dem.* 40 (*G.L.P.*) esp. lines 41–4; philosophy: Eup. 361K; Dover on Ar. *Nub.* 230 and 380; literature: *adesp.* 45b (*G.L.P.*); on Eurip. Ar. *Ran. passim*; for criticism by parody see Handley, *B.I.C.S. Supp.* 5 (1957), 22–5; on grammatical theory: Ar. *Nub.* 638 and Starkie *a.l.* There is an excellent general work by K. J. Dover, *Aristophanic Comedy* (London, 1972); see also the study in social history by V. Ehrenberg, *The People of Aristophanes* (Oxford, 1951[2]).

117 Accius, *Pragm.* 24M, may have discussed the parabasis; see Webster, *Hellenistic Poetry and Art*, 291. On the comic poet's address to his audience see e.g. Ar. *Vesp.* 71ff. and Handley on Men. *Dysk.* 1f.

118 Horace on the style of Old Comedy, *Sat.* 1,10,9–17; also Quint. 10,1,65. For sudden shift of level see e.g. Ar. *Ach.* 33 and for a scene of complex tone 729–835.

119 Men. *Theoph.* 1 Kö.; Lucil. 974ff., see Marx on 974.

120 For Thrasonides in the first scene of *Misoumenos* see A1–16 Sandb., supplemented by Turner, *G.R.B.* Monograph 6 (1973), 48–50. For Cnemon as example of the irascible, *Choric.* 32,73 (see Körte (ed.) Menander II p. 51).

121 729–41. This is not a close rendering of Ter. *Eun.* 46–63, the view of Warmington III 239, as is clear both from the incorporation of a complete line (possibly more) from Plaut. *Merc.* (736 = *Merc.* 397), which expresses sentiments inappropriate to the scene of

Ter. and also from the close imitation of Ter. by Horace, *Sat.* 2,3,260–71.

122 At this point Terence's original is Men. *Kolax* (see Ter. *Eun.* 30ff.), and the name Gnatho, found only in Ter. *Eun.* and Men. *Kol.*, would perhaps suggest to contemporary readers a version of this particular story, probably Terence's rather than the theme of the besieging soldier in general.

123 On the possible application of the theme of the boastful soldier to Roman life see J. A. Hanson, in Dudley and Dorey (eds), *Roman Drama* (London, 1965), 57–61. The Spanish armies immediately before Scipio's command were an example from Lucilius' times of failure of commanders and troops.

124 On this poem see Terzaghi, *Lucilio*, 176–80.

125 Hymnis: 888–94, 940f., 1115f., 1193. Hymnis is a stock Greek name for a tart (see Bechtel, *Die attische Frauennamen*, 71) and is the title of plays by Menander, 407–15 Kö. and Caecilius, 65–74R³. Caec. 70 seems to be alluded to in another poem of Lucil. at 663. The indelicate physiological comment, Lucil. 940f. probably belongs to the pimp's auction (891–3): For the assertion of love, 888f., 894. Hymnis is also mentioned in a hexameter poem (1115f.).

126 1193; cf. Liv. 39,6,8.

127 On roisterers in Rome see Polyb. 31,25,3–5.

128 698; Arch. 74D supplemented by P.Oxy. 2313, 1a (= 122W); see in addition to Lobel, *a.l.*, Webster, *Greek Art and Literature 700–530* (London, 1959), 48.

129 699–701; Arch. 67aD (= 128W).

130 Aelian *V.H.* 10,13; on Archilochus as personal poet see B. Snell, transl. Rosenmeyer. *The Discovery of the Mind*, (Oxford, 1953), 46ff.

131 P. Oxy, 2310,14f. (see M. Treu, *Archilochos* (Munich, 1959), 10). On the procedure of Archilochus see Arist, *Rhet.* 1418b21 and K. J. Dover, *Entr. Fond. Hardt* 10 (1964), 183–212.

132 Cic. *Att.* 16,11,2; on traditional poetic elements see D. L. Page, *Entr.*

Fond. Hardt 10, 119–79, and for his structure as well as his sheer genius see (Longinus) *Subl.* 33,5.

133 1041–4; Anacreon 72P (88D); see Bowra, *Greek Lyric Poetry* (Oxford, 1961²), 271f.; A. E. Harvey, *C.Q.* 7 (1957), 211.

134 See his description of the low Artemon, who rose from criminal squalor to effeminate opulence: 43P (54D); see also 79P (87D) and 87P (77D).

135 Hipponax: see A. D. Knox, Herodes, Cercidas etc., in Loeb Theophrastus *Characters* (London, 1953), 62f. and 65; P. Oxy. 2174f. = I–XII D, cf. E. Fraenkel, *C.Q.* 36 (1942), 54ff.

136 Timon, *Corp. Poesis Epicae Graecae Ludibundae* 2 (Wachsmuth) 8–55 (on his works esp. 20–3; for Timon on the Museum see Athen. 22D, on his technique Webster, *Hellenistic Poetry and Art*, 26ff.

137 Geffcken, *N.Jbb.* 27 (1911), 393–411 and 469–93 assembled an amorphous collection of Greek 'satirical' material of dubious relevance for Ennius and Lucilius. This included the *Chreiai* of Machon, scurrilous anecdotes on whores and parasites, on which see A. S. F. Gow, *Machon* (Cambridge, 1965), esp. 12–24, and poems of political and social criticism by the late-3rd-C. writer of *meliambi* Cercidas, on whom see Walbank, *C.Q.* 37 (1943), 11f. and Webster, *Hellenistic Poetry and Art*, 231–3.

138 709; for quotations from Plato see e.g. *Charm.* 154b at 830–3; 751–70 seem to belong to a philosophers' symposium; cf. 821–2, 830–6 (Bk 29).

139 Cic. *Tusc.* 2,62, *Ac.* 2,15, *Q. Fr.* 1,1,23. On the influence of Xenophon in Rome see K. Münscher, *Philologus Supplbd.* 13 (1920), esp. 70–82.

140 The spurious proem to the *Characters* argues for their moralizing purpose.

141 For Panaetius' views on style see P. de Lacy, *A.J.Ph.* 69 (1948), 248f.,; Varro described Lucilius' style as *gracilis* (Gell. 6,14,6; cf. Fronto 113N); cf. Leo, *Gesch.* 230 n. 2.

142 Compare   Fraenkel,   *Elementi*

Plautini in Plauto, 392, for the artistic presentation of conversational language in Plautus.

143 On the Roman aristocratic tradition of *virtus* see T. Frank *C.Q.* 15 (1921), 169–71; D. C. Earl, *The Moral and Political Tradition of Rome* (London, 1967), ch. 1, esp. 34f.; see also *id. Historia* 11 (1962), 482f. Note that unlike some statements of the Roman aristocratic ideal the lines contain no appeal to pre-eminence or to the example of ancestors.

144 Contrast the supple argumentation in the speech on *virtus* at Plaut. *Trin.* 642–51. On the figures of speech in the lines of Lucilius see I. Mariotti, op. cit. (n. 109), 8f. For unfavourable judgements see Marx on 1326.

145 For archaic gnomic poetry see e.g. *praec. rust. et med. (Frg. Poet. Lat.* (Morel) pp. 30ff.). Albinus cannot be identified with certainty; see Cichorius 349–54, Astin 91 n. 9. At 848–50 an Albinus is sneered at.

146 On the gudgeon that is thrown out when a tunny is landed (938) see Cichorius 179–80 and Martyn, *Röm. Sat.* 495.

147 328f.; 659; 765; 897; 1018ff.; see Martyn 498. Acrobats (1298) and a bird-catcher (1319) are subjects of similes of unknown context; the smithy (1165f.) may illustrate a volcano, perhaps Stromboli; see 104, 144f., and Martyn, *A.J.Ph.* 85 (1964), 66–70.

148 On the didactic simile see H. Diller, *Hermes* 67 (1932), 14–42 and W. Kranz, *Philologus* 96 (1944), 79–83.

149 *aigilipes* (113) is a comic use of a Homeric epithet. *Cortinipotens* (276) is formed in mockery of the *-potens* compounds of Ennius and Accius; see I. Mariotti, op. cit. (n. 109), 46–50.

150 On Greek elements in the language of Plautus see Leo, *Gesch.* 140f. and Palmer, *The Latin Language*, 81–4.

151 E.g. *clinopodas lychnosque ut diximus semnos* (15), *mastigias* (669), *cruribus crura diallaxon* (306; cf. 304); in these examples the Greek words are part of a satirical or vulgar presentation.

152 On Lucilius' Greek see I. Mariotti op. cit. (n. 149 above) 50–81, and Leumann–Hofmann–Szantyr, *Lat. Gramm.* II 759–65. Lucilius' *eidola atque atomos* (753) of Epicurus' atoms became in Lucretius *principia* and *primordia*.

153 Rudd, 111–17, discusses Lucilius' practice in relation to Horace's criticism. He also considers Lucilius' versification, 105–7. On prosody in Lucilius see F. Skutsch, *Rh.M.* 48 (1893), 303–7 (=*Kl. Schr.* 69ff.). On metre in Lucilius see further Schanz-Hosius I 158f.; comparative material is assembled by A. Ollfors, 'Studien zum Aufbau des Hexameters Lucans', *Acta reg. soc. scient. et litt. Gothoburgensis Human.* 1 (1967). It is easy to overlook Lucilius' skill in handling dramatic metres in his early books.

154 See Marx I cxxix–x for testimonia on Lucilian scholarship in republican times. On Pompeius Lenaeus see also E. Fraenkel, *Eranos* 53 (1955), 78 and S. Treggiari, *Roman Freedmen during the Late Republic* (Oxford, 1969), 119 and nn. 2 and 3.

155 *de Or.* 1,72; cf. *ib.* 2,25; 3,171; *Fin.* 1,8.

156 *Vit. Pers.* 52ff. Cl.; Juv. 1,19–21, also 1,153f.; Quint. 10,1,93; Tac. *Dial.* 23.

NOTES TO CHAPTER 5 (HORACE)

1 The best modern text of Horace is the Teubner edn, Klingner 1959³; the *O.C.T.* by Wickham and Garrod is of poor quality. The compact commentary by A. Palmer, *The Satires of Horace* (London, 1883), is very valuable; other standard commentaries are: P. Lejay, *Oeuvres d'Horace, Satires* (Paris, 1911), in many respects the best commentary; A. Kiessling–R. Heinze, *Q. Horatius Flaccus, Satiren* (Berlin, 1957⁶), with suppl. material by E. Burck; E. C. Wickham, *Q. Horatii Flacci Opera Omnia*, vol. 2: *The Satires etc.* (Oxford, 1891). For a list of texts of Horace and commen-

taries from the *editio princeps* of *c.* 1470 see Brink, *Horace on Poetry* 2 (Cambridge 1971) 43ff.; the most distinguished are Lambinus (1561) and Bentley (1711). On Lambinus contribution to the text of Horace see E. J. Kenney, *The Classical Text* (Berkeley, Los Angeles and London, 1974), 63–7, and on that of Bentley, *id.* 71–4. The best modern translation is by N. Rudd, *The Satires of Horace and Persius* (Harmondsworth, 1973): The introduction includes translations of some representative fragments of Lucilius. Also useful are the translations by E. C. Wickham *Horace for English readers* (Oxford, 1903) and H. R. Fairclough, *Horace Satires, Epistles and Ars Poetica* (London and Harvard, 1929). A very good general study is that by N. Rudd, *The Satires of Horace* (Cambridge, 1966): see rev. *Hermathena* 107 (1968), 83–6 (Courtney) and *C.R.* 17 (1967), 291–3 (Coffey). E. Fraenkel's magesterial general study, *Horace* (Oxford, 1957), contains an excellent treatment of the satires, particularly those of Bk 1.

2 Suet. *Gramm.* 5. Lucilius' editor, Valerius Cato, wrote a work with the title *Indignatio*, in which he proclaimed that he was free by birth (Suet. *Gramm.* 11): on Valerius Cato see Helm, *R.E.* 2 Reihe 7A (1948), 2348–52.

3 Hor. *Sat.* 1,10,46f.

4 The source of the information is Jerome's catalogue of Varro's works: see Schanz-Hosius I 556 (quoting Ritschl *Opusc.* 3,527, = *Rh.M.* 12 (1857), 152).

5 *R.R.* 3,2,17: *cuius Luciliano charactere sunt libelli.*

6 Treb. in Cic. *Fam.* 12,16,3. For the murder of Trebonius see Cic. *Phil.* 11 and Syme 172.

7 On Caesar's attitude to Catullus see Suet. *Iul.* 73 and to Pitholaus *id.* 75,5. On Pitholaus, perhaps to be identified with Horace's Pitholeon (*Sat.* 1,10,22) see R. G. Lewis, *C.R.* 16 (1966), 271–3 but also S. Treggiari, *Roman Freedmen,* 118 n. 8.

8 On Octavian's verses see Mart. 11,20.

9 See Anderson, *Univ. Calif. Publ. Class. Phil.* 19 (1963), 62ff.

10 The grim tale of late republican unrest and violence is told succinctly by P. A. Brunt, *Social Conflicts in the Roman Republic* (London, 1971), chs. 5 and 6; see also A. W. Lintott, *Violence in Republican Rome* (Oxford, 1968), 175–203. The best account of the events of the years and analysis of Roman society 44–31 B.C. are to be found in Syme's *The Roman Revolution.*

11 The birth date is given by Suetonius, *de poetis* (p. 122 Rost.). His Life of Horace, though amplified by some implausible details, is in the main authentic and reliable. For a detailed modern treatment see ch. 1 of E. Fraenkel, *Horace.*

12 *Sat.* 2,1,34–9.

13 *Sat.* 1,6,86f. with Porphyrion and Pseudacron *a.l.*; Kiessling-Heinze *a.l.*; S. Treggiari, *Roman Freedmen* 108, suggests that Horace's father may have worked as *coactor* in Rome, not Venusia.

14 *Sat.* 1,6,71–84; *Epp.* 2,1,70f. and 2,2,41f. On Orbilius see Suet. *Gramm.* 9.

15. *Epp.* 2,2,43–5. On the educational value of Athens in general and of Cratippus in particular see Cicero's address to his son *Off.* 1,1 (43 B.C.) and the younger Cicero's effusive praise of the philosopher and his followers from Mytilene (*Fam.* 16,21,3–5). Though acclaimed by Cicero (*Off.* 2,8) he was probably of little consequence in the history of philosophy.

16 Plut. *Brut.* 24; *Epp.* 2,2,46–8; Cic. *Brut.* 1,14; Syme 171 and 198. Horace's presence in Asia Minor may reasonably be inferred from *Sat.* 1,7.

17 *Sat.* 1,6,47ff.

18 C. 2,7,9–12.

19 Suet. *vit. Hor.* pp. 110f. Rost.; *Epp.* 2,2,49ff. On the duties of *scriba quaestorius* see Fraenkel, 14f., who refers to A. H. M. Jones, *J.R.S.* 39 (1949), 41.

20 *Sat.* 1,6,54–62. He accompanied Maecenas on an embassy to meet Antonius at Tarentum early in 37 B.C. (*Sat.* 1,5; see p. 74ff.; he may have been present at the battle of Actium: E.

Wistrand, *Horace's ninth Epode* (Göteborg 1958) (= *Opera Selecta* 289–350).

21 *Sat.* 2,6; *Epp.* 1,18,104f. Its position is about nine miles from Tibur (Tivoli). G. Lugli, *La villa d'Orazio nella valle della Licenza* (Rome, 1930).

22 Suet. *vit. Hor.* 113f. Rost.

23 *Epp.* 1,20,23; *Sat.* 2,3,309; Suet. *vit. Hor.* p. 119 Rost.

24 Chronological evidence is given towards the end of the preface to Lejay's commentary on each satire; see also the discussion by E. Burck in the appendix to Kiessling-Heinze (see n. 1 above).

25 *Sat.* 1,4,91ff. looks back to 1,2,26f.

26 On political, zoological and climatic arguments concerning the date and the time of year of Horace's journey see Rudd 280f.

27 Calpurnius Bibulus (86) was governor of Syria from *c.* 34/3 until his death in 33/2 (Appian *B.C.* 4,38; *M.R.R.* II 411f. and 541); *molle atque facetum* (44) is more appropriate as a description of Virgil's *Eclogues* than of his *Georgics*, which were begun *c.* 36 B.C. (Schanz-Hosius) II⁴ 49f.).

28 Probably the curule aedileship; see *M.R.R.* II 415.

29 *Sat.* 2,1,15; 2,5,62. Syme 263–6 and 300ff.

30 *tellure marique* (*Sat.* 2,5,63) corresponds to *terra marique* used of the victory of Actium (*Epod.* 9,27).

31 Fiske, *Lucilius and Horace* 119; Knoche 49; Rudd, *A.J.Ph.* 76 (1955), 165–75.

32 *Sat.* 1,10,48–8; he uses one unobtrusive technical word, *epos* (43). When mentioning poetry Roman poets preferred vague description to specific technicality; see A. L. Wheeler, *C.Ph.* 7 (1912), 454–77.

33 Kiessling-Heinze *a.l.*

34 Wheeler, loc. cit. (n. 32 above) 467f. The view of Hendrickson, *C.Ph.* 6 (1911), 129–43, that *satura* was not used as a generic term until after the publication of Horace's first book will not win credence, for his words can hardly imply an underlying meaning: 'the things I used

to write, to which we have since learned to give the name *satura*'.

35 *Off.* 1,132–5. He desiderates the lack of formal precept on conversation by the rhetorical theorists; cf. *ad. Her.* 3,23. On the elusive informal style of the *sermo* see also Quint. 9,4,19ff.

36 For *nigro* compare *Sat.* 1,4,85 and 100. See Kiessling-Heinze *a.l.*, Fraenkel 6f.

37 *nostrorum sermonum* at *Epp.* 1,4,1 probably refers to satires rather than individual epistles privately circulated; *sermones ... repentis per humum* (*Epp.* 2,1,250f.) is equally applicable to the unpretentious style of his satires and epistles. *sermo* at *Sat.* 2,2,2 and *Epp.* 2,1,4 refers to the contents of the discourse and is not a title; cf. the use of *sermo* at Porph. on Hor. *Sat.* 1,1,108.

38 Fraenkel, 94, argues that the formula of transition is employed with deliberate clumsiness to indicate that digression is a mark of the conversational level of Lucilian *satura*. But while the return gambit, something natural in an unexalted style (e.g. Plin. *Epp.* 3,11,8), is elsewhere handled more neatly by Horace, e.g. *Sat.* 1,6,45, the present example suggests rather the orator's emphatic return after a digression, e.g. Dem. *Cor.* 211, a device discussed by Quint. 9,3,87. When used by Horace so abruptly there is more than a hint of parody. There is also a textual crux at 108, which is fully discussed by Fraenkel, 97–101, and Rudd, 274f. (see rev. of Rudd by Courtney, n. 1 above). But against their choice the best reading is probably that of vet. Bland. accepted by Klingner (see his cautious defence of it *J.R.S.* 48 (1958), 177): *illuc unde abii, redeo, qui nemo, ut avarus,/se probet. qui* thus introduces an indirect question: cf. E. L. Harrison, *Phoenix* 15 (1961), 41–6. As against Fraenkel, *ut avarus* must be a separate phrase; L. P. Wilkinson, *C.R.* 9 (1959), 139 suggests it is equivalent to *ob avaritiam*; see also Wilkinson's account of Housman's interpretation: *nemon, ut avarus, se probat,* 'to think that no one

because of avarice', *Housman Soc. Journal* 1 (1974), 46.

39 Against the views of older scholars such as Palmer and Lejay, who argued for two distinct subjects, discontent and avarice, Fraenkel 92ff. advocates an essential unity of theme and refers to a sermon by Teles, a 3rd C. B.C. reporter of Bion the Borysthenite, in which acquisitiveness (πλεονεξία) is said to be the fundamental cause of discontent (pp. 9–11 Hense) (on Bion and Teles in relation to Horace see p. 92 above). Rudd, 14, argues that a basic love of money (φιλοπλουτία or φιλαργυρία), the theme of the central part, is expanded along with μεμψιμοιρία in the conclusion into the greater vice of πλεονεξία which embraces rivalry as well as greed; he refers to Plat. *Rep.* 1,349B–350C. To the later rhetorical moralist Dio Chrysostom πλεονεξία was the fundamental vice of humanity; see esp. 17,6; his sentimental ideal was the peasantry of Euboea, free from avarice and content with its lot (7,20). H. Herter, *Rh.M.* 94 (1951), 1–42 (= Korzeniewski 320–64) discusses the problem of structure and its bibliography with exhaustive thoroughness.

40 The most significant Greek text on μεμψιμοιρία is a piece of popular moralizing included in the spurious letters of Hippocrates (*Epp.* 17; 9,348ff. Littré; *Epist. Graec.* 298ff. Hercher). Its examples are very similar to those of Horace (see Fraenkel, 93 and E. T. Silk, *Y.Cl.St.* 19 (1966), 233–50). For other occurrences of the same topic cf. Nisbet and Hubbard on Hor. *C.* 1,1,17 and for a representative specimen of the ancient topic of the insatiable demands of greed Sen. *Epp.* 119,9.

41 Fraenkel 96f. sees the contemporary social relevance of the discreet plea to curb avarice; Rudd however judges that 'Horatian satire as a whole implies a conscious rejection of public life' (37).

42 105–8 are a close rendering of Call. *Epigr.* 31 (= *A.P.* 12,102; *H.E.* 1035–40 G.P.).

43 Fraenkel 87 n. 7 refers to Theophr.

Char. 12,2. Horace's 'autobiographical' example has a close literary parallel.

44 The examples are taken from the code of Draco (Plut. *Sol.* 17). Epicurus believed that nature had nothing to do with justice (Sen. *Epp.* 97,15) contrary to the Stoics (see Kiessling-Heinze on 111).

45 Lejay 63–7 is particularly valuable on Lucretian elements, e.g. Horace's tolerance of euphemistic names compared with Lucretius' scorn (4,1153) and stylistic details such as the postponed preposition at 68. Discussions on friendship were in antiquity an accepted department of philosophy.

46 107; Kiessling-Heinze suggest that the obscenity was chosen to emphasize the animal nature of the passion, Lejay, probably nearer the truth, that Horace wished to prevent the tone rising to a grandeur inappropriate for satire. Here perhaps, as in *Sat.* 1,2, Horace also enjoyed coarseness for its own sake.

47 Brink discusses the Callimachean ideal implicit in Horace's attitude, *Horace on Poetry* 1,159.

48 On the theory that comedy is unpoetic see Cic. *Or.* 67 and Brink, *Horace on Poetry*, 1,162f.; also Kroll 48f.

49 Ter. *Ad.* 414–9. The father in *Ad.* is somewhat ridiculous; Horace's father is not, but the literary allusion adds an extra dimension to Horace's story.

50 Brink, *Horace on Poetry*, 1,156–64, has a valuable discussion of the critical background and the flexible inventiveness of the poem; see also Rudd, 88–92.

51 On Sarmentus, Maecenas' freedman, see S. Treggiari, *Roman Freedmen*, 225f. and 271f., where it is rightly argued that the gibe about Sarmentus as a runaway slave should not be taken literally.

52 Whatever the name of the town (see Palmer and Kiessling-Heinze on 87) Horace took the opportunity to allude to a circumlocution in Lucilius (228).

53 The stages are tabulated by Palmer (on line 103) and Kiessling-Heinze (p. 90).

54 The description of the poet's erotic dream (83ff.) suggests an ironical allusion to Lucretius' earnest treatment of the subject (4,1030–6).

55 Ch. 4 n. 53. Porphyrio's testimony (on *Sat.* 1,5,1) to Horace's emulation of Lucilius is supported by such resemblances of theme as 58f. from Lucilius 117f. on which see Fraenkel 107f. Rudd 54ff. is sceptical about Lucilian influences, perhaps unduly so at the contest of the clowns (see *C.R.* 17 (1967), 292), but a reaction against such writers as Fiske, *Lucilius and Horace*, 306–16 is to be welcomed.

56 It is sufficient to refer to Rudd's good-humoured mockery of the portrait of Horace in Lederhosen (60). Contrast his pride in the place of his birth at 2,1,34–9. Fraenkel, 110, eulogizes the description of the landscape at line 26, but *candentibus* may also imply an uncomfortable brightness; note that Horace's first recorded action on arriving is to use an eye-ointment. For Feronia and Anxur see B. Tilly, *G.&R.* 6 (1959), 202f. and accompanying photographs.

57 *Sat.* 1,9 suggests that such disclosures were eagerly sought. On Horace's teasing of the inquisitive reader in *Sat.* 1,5 see Highet, *The Anatomy of Satire*, 201–4.

58 S. Treggiari, *Roman Freedmen*, 232–6 discusses the careers of some sons of freedmen.

59 The simple formula of transition (45) is less obtrusive than that at 1,108 (see n. 38 above), but in later poems Horace was to show greater subtlety (Fraenkel 393).

60 The words also occur in line 6. A similar expression in a poem written some years later (*Epp.* 1,20,20) recollects with pride and without bitterness.

61 On this satire see E. L. Harrison, *C.Ph.* 60 (1965), 111–4 and G. Highet, *A.J.Ph.* 94 (1973), 269–81. Horace's description of travelling without retinue as far as Tarentum, even if comically exaggerated, presupposes an Italy that had been finally cleared of brigands, a task

undertaken in 36 B.C.; see App. *B.C.* 5,132 and Brunt, *Italian Manpower 225 B.C.–A.D. 14* (Oxford, 1971), 291.

62 D. West *Reading Horace* (Edinburgh, 1967), 127, remarks: 'he was just the sort of man who would enjoy watching people working.'

63 Caesar himself in exasperation exclaimed that his cognomen was not Rex (Cass. Dio 44,10,1). For another piece of punning at the court of Brutus, where hearty jesting seems to have been prevalent, see Plut. *Brut.* 34.

64 In the next decade the memory of Julius Caesar was tacitly slighted, Syme 317f. Porphyrio regarded the conclusion of the poem as *urbanissimus iocus*.

65 Fraenkel 121.

66 The elaborate hypothesis of V. Buchheit, *Gymnasium* 75 (1968), 519–55, seems far-fetched. Fraenkel calls the poem 'refined' and a 'little gem' (118–21); Rudd 66f. judges it a failure.

67 The reduplicated perfect *pepedi* (farted) at the end of the line (46) is suitably expressive.

68 Fraenkel 121f. discusses the background of dedicatory poems. For Priapus as the protector of the garden see Leon. Tar. *Anth. Plan.* 236 and 261 (Gow-Page, *Hellenistic Epigrams* 2482–9) and *Priap.* 24. Buchheit, 63–4, has an exemplary treatment of Hor. *Sat.* 1,8 in relation to the earlier tradition. On all aspects of the attributes and functions of Priapus see H. Herter, *De Priapo* (Giessen, 1932), and *R.E. s.v.* 'Priapos' 22,2 (1954) 1914–42; as god of the land, 1927.

69 Horace's importunate man is often referred to as 'the bore' but Rudd's label 'the pest' is perhaps the most helpful succinct designation (74).

70 For the technique of narrative through dialogue see the preface to Henry James, *The Awkward Age.*

71 W. S. Anderson, *A.J.Ph.* 77 (1956), 148–66. Buchheit rightly contrasts Horace's Callimachean attitude with the pest's proffered doggerel. It is also possible to find parody of the beginning of a messenger speech ('I happened to be

. . .'), e.g. Eur. *Or.* 866; for such a parody in comedy see E. W. Handley, *B.I.C.S.* 12 (1965), 42.

72 The restrained critical humour of the *urbanus* (13) is discussed by Quint. 6,3,102ff., who uses a source of Augustan times.

73 The Greek equivalent ὀψιμαθής is used of the man who comes to learning too late and tends to show impudent ostentation (Theophr. *Char.* 27; Cic. *Fam.* 9,20,2).

74 On *molle atque facetum* (playful and whimsical, 44) see Lejay and Kiessling-Heinze *a.l.*). See also L. P. Wilkinson, *The Georgics of Virgil* (Cambridge, 1969), 21 n. (the words have nothing to do with humour).

75 The interpretation of *rudis et Graecis intacti carminis auctor* (66) followed here is that of Palmer, *a.l.* For further discussion see Fraenkel 131 n. 3, Brink, *Horace on Poetry*, 1,165 n. 3, and Rudd, *Phoenix* 14 (1960), 36–44.

76 The eight clumsy lines that precede the opening of the poem in some manuscripts mention Cato by name (see the information in Palmer's critical note *a.l.*). They are spurious but probably near-contemporary; a later interpolator would not have understood the literary climate. On these lines see Fraenkel, *Hermes* 68 (1933), 392–9 (= *Kl. Beitr.* II 199–208), who refers to Horace forgeries mentioned by Suetonius. Hendrickson, *C.Ph.* 11 (1916), 249–69 and 12 (1917), 77–92 regarded them as genuine.

77 See W. S. Anderson loc. cit. (n. 9 above) 63ff. On the literary controversy see also Rudd, *Mnemosyne* Ser. 4,10 (1957), 319–36.

78 On the Greek theoretical basis for Horace's view of the variety of Old Comedy see Brink, *Horace on Poetry*, 1,165 n. 4.

79 On the theophany in the poet's dream and Horace's burlesque see Kenney, *P.C(amb.)Ph.S.* 191 (1965), 45 and n. 2, and on Arbuscula, C. Garton, *C.R.* 14 (1964), 138f.

80 On the problem of the composition of Horace's Book see Rudd, 160; Kroll 228, discusses the careful arrangement of the epodes. On symmetry in the eclogues see O. Skutsch, *H.S.C.Ph.* 73 (1969), 153–69.

81 Detailed correspondences are proposed by C. A. Van Rooy, *Acta Classica* 11 (1968), 38–72.

82 Trebatius is neatly portrayed by Horace (e.g. 7ff.) in terms which accord well with what is known from Cicero's letters to him *Fam.* 7,6–22 and 7,5 (a letter of recommendation on Trebatius' behalf). On Trebatius and Cicero's correspondence with him see D. R. Shackleton Bailey, *Cicero* (London, 1971), 99–104.

83 Horace's use of *mala carmina* is not to be taken seriously as a legal technicality; see Fraenkel, *Gnomon* 1 (1925), 196 (= *Kl. Beitr.* II 410f.). The *Lex Cornelia de iniuriis* from the time of Sulla is sometimes appealed to in discussions of Horace's poem (R. E. Smith, *C.Q.* 1 (1951), 169–79 and Rudd 128). But D. Daube, 'ne quid infamandi fiat': The Roman Law of Defamation', *Atti del Congresso Internaz. di Diritto Romano* (*Verona*) 3 (Milan, 1951), 411–50, shows that Sulla's law dealt only with physical injury (415). He argues (446) that in the middle of the 1st C. B.C. defamation was not yet actionable *iniuria*, but that during the career of Labeo, praetor and jurist (d. *c.* A.D. 10), attempts to make a man 'infamous' by grave insult were liable to court actions. But it seems that there was still an area of uncertainty (see Sen. *Contr.* 10,1); the ancient evidence is not easy to interpret. Horace's frivolity at the expense of the law should be seen against this possibly tangled legal background. A. Ronconi, *Synteleia Vincenzo Arangio-Ruiz* 2 (Naples, 1964), 958–71 explores the confused area of the magical and the abusive in interpreting the ambiguities of Horace's poem. See also M. Marrone, *ib.* 1, 475–85. I am indebted here to Prof. J. A. C. Thomas for bibliographical advice.

84 On *solventur risu tabulae* (86) see Lejay pp. 289ff. and Rudd 130.

85 The notion of fixing a particle of the divine aether to the earth (79) is found in Plato, *Phaed.* 83d. The precept on the proper use of money corresponds to the injunction at Xen. *Oec.* 11,9; apart from contemporary concern for restoring temples the sentiments are un-Roman.

86 260–71 from Ter. *Eun.* 46ff. See ch. 4 n. 121.

87 Plato's *Symposium* contains a piece of rhetoric on a worthless topic (177a). For Plato's *Symp.* in Rome see Quint. 8,4,23 and Fraenkel 136 n. 1.

88 Porph. on *Sat.* 2,4,1.

89 Odysseus' question at 76ff. is not indignant but anxious; line 83 is a proverb: Otto p. 71; G. W. Williams, *C.R.* 9 (1959), 97–100.

90 Diog. Laert. 9,111. Compare Horace's treatment of Penelope with that of Lucilius in a similar tradition (540–6).

91 The judgement of W. Y. Sellar is adequately rebutted by Rudd, 240–2. Sellar's approach is followed by Fraenkel 144f.

92 Fraenkel discusses the poem's prayer formulae, 138–41; on elements of parody at line 20 see also Norden, *Agn. Th.* 146 n. 1. The mock-heroic language 25f. shows that the account of life in Rome is not to be taken without reservation.

93 For a detailed examination of the fable see D. A. West in Woodman and West (ed.), *Quality and Pleasure in Latin Poetry* (Cambridge, 1974), 67–80. On the poem as a whole see Brink, *On Reading a Horatian Satire* (Sydney, 1965).

94 While there may be, as McGann suggests (*C.R.* 6 (1956), 99), a connection between the preceding lines on the mistress and the wantonness of Pausias' subjects, the *tertium* between Pausias' pictures and the drawing on the wall is explicitly naturalistic representation (98ff.).

95 E.g. 47, 66, 70f., 82, 91f., 111.

96 On symposiac literature see ch. 10, 188.

97 The arrangement of poems in the book is discussed by Fraenkel 136ff. and Rudd 160f. An elaborate scheme for the unified structure of Bks 1 and 2 is

postulated by W. Ludwig, *Poetica* 2 (1968), 304–25.

98 Knoche, *Gymnasium* 65 (1958), 151–9, shows the difference between Lucilius' direct presentation of personal experience and Horace's artifice and selectivity. Yet Horace's self-portraiture has been influential; 'Just as the Sabine farm foreshadowed the English country house, so Horace's image of himself foreshadowed and helped to mould the English idea of the gentleman.' (Hodgart, *Satire*, 134).

99 *Sat.* 1,4,91f. refers back to 1,2,26f. Rudd, 132–52, analyses thoroughly the real and fictitious persons in Horace. He identifies Horace's Sallust (1,2,48) with the historian; so too Syme, *Sallust*, 280–4.

100 Rudd 258–73.

101 Anderson in Sullivan (ed.), *Critical Essays on Roman literature, Satire* (London, 1963), 1–37, has a good discussion of the importance for Horace of the irony of *Socraticae chartae* (*A.P.* 310), but Horace would perhaps have been surprised and amused at being labelled 'the Roman Socrates'.

102 See D. A. Russell, *G.&R.* 15 (1968), 130–46, esp. 137–40.

103 On the Diatribe, Hermogenes, *Meth.* 5: Diatribe is more expanded discourse than anecdotes, χρεῖαι, and less direct than narratives concerning a philosopher, ἀπομνημονεύματα (Hirzel, *Der Dialog* I 369 n. 2).

104 For a diatribe by Bion see Diog. Laert. 2,77. διατριβή is used of discourse generally by Plato (*Apol.* 37D; cf. *Gorg.* 484E).

105 For the career of Bion see Diog. Laert. 4,46,58 and D. R. Dudley, *A History of Cynicism*, 62–9; Susemihl I 32–41. On Bion as sophist see Hirzel, *Der Dialog* I 378f.; for novelistic elements in Diogenes' Life, Rohde, *Der griechische Roman* (1960⁴), 268.

106 See O. Hense, *Teletis Reliquiae* (Tübingen, 1909²).

107 Capelle, *R.A.C. s.v.* 'Diatribe', 3, 990–7 esp. 993; Russell, *G.&R.* 15 (1968), 140. On Epictetus see ch. 6, 107f.

and on diatribe elements in the Pauline corpus Marrou, *R.A.C.* 3, 999–1000. But as A. D. Nock points out some elements common to NT and diatribe may be attributed to the spoken language of the day (*Essays on Religion and the Ancient World*, 124f. = *Early Gentile Christianity*, 145f.).

108 Dio Chrys. 32,9f. cf. 34,2; Luc. *Peregr.* 3–6; Quint. 2,4,41; Tac. *Dial.* 26. Roman theorists ignore diatribe as a literary sub-species in its own right.

109 Hirzel, *Der Dialog* I 371f. Bion's personification Poverty is reported by Teles (Hense 6ff.); Diog. Laert. 4,52 mentions parody as a quality of Bion's style.

110 Hippocr. *Ep.* 17 (9,348 Littré = *Epist. Graec.* 298–305 Hercher); cf. n. 39 above and Fraenkel 90–4. The animal analogy in Cynic diatribe is also found in 'The Saying of Simonides' (*P.Hib.* 1,17; 1,26) of *c.* 280–40 B.C. (cf. Powell and Barber, *New Chapters* 2 (1929), 93) and appears in its most grotesque form in the Bodmer Pap. (*Pap. Genev. inv.* 271); see V. Martin and P. Photiades, *Mus.Helv.* 16 (1959), 77–139: 'bulls do not make pastries and fancy cakes nor do they wear diaphanous gowns'.

111 The most important discussion of diatribe elements in Horace is that of N. Terzaghi, *Per la storia della satira* (Messina, 1944²), esp. 47–71; see also Burck in Kiessling-Heinze 390ff., A. Oltramare, *Les Origines de la Diatribe Romaine* (Lausanne, 1926), esp. 54 and 132ff. and C. W. Mendell, *C.Ph.* 15 (1920), 138–57 (= Korzeniewski, 137–160).

112 On the Callimachean poet see F. Wehrli, *Mus.Helv.* 1 (1944), 69–76. W. Wimmel, *Zur Form der horazischen Diatribensatire* (Frankfurt, 1962), contains much of value but is somewhat one-sided; see rev. by Knoche, *Gnomon* 35 (1963), 470–5, and Brink *C.R.* 14 (1964), 161ff.

113 On the expression of a serious subject in a jesting manner see Xen. *Symp.* 1,13, and for Roman formulations Cic. *de Or.* 2,250 and Phaedr. 1 *Prol.* 1–7.

Highet, *The Anatomy of Satire*, 233f. sums up the topic succinctly.

114 Anderson op. cit. (n. 101 above) 12ff. examines the passage of the fourth satire. On the stylistic shaping of Horace's thought see Knoche, *Philologus* 90 (1935), 372–90 and 469–82 (= Korzeniewski 284–319).

115 Rudd 232ff. shows how Horace in *Sat.* 2,5 has many variations of a central metaphor from hunting that arises naturally from the theme of *captatio*. On Horace's imagery in the satires in general see Anderson, *A.J.Ph.* 81 (1960), 225–60.

116 K. D. White, *Roman Farming* (London, 1972), 189, discusses the problems of the owner of the large granary. On the Aufidus see Dr Smith's *Dictionary of Greek and Roman Geography, s.v.*

117 On the rendering of abstract ideas by concrete terms see Bourciez, *Le 'Sermo Cotidianus' dans les Satires d'Horace* (Bordeaux, 1927), 20ff. and A. Cartault, *Étude sur les Satires d'Horace* (Paris, 1899), 219–56. Diminutives are much commoner in Horace's hexameter poems than in the odes; see Axelson, *Unpoetische Wörter*, 40.

118 On hyperbaton in Horace's satires (e.g. 1,5,72; 2,1,60; 2,3,211) see Fordyce on Catullus 66,18 and on ἀπὸ κοινοῦ constructions (e.g. 1,2,123) G. Kiefner, *Die Versparung* (Wiesbaden, 1964), rev. by J. H. Kells *C.R.* 19 (1969), 65–7.

119 *Sat.* 1,2,37ff. from Enn. *Ann.* 465V.

120 N.-O. Nilsson, *Metrische Stildifferenzen in den Satiren des Horaz* (Uppsala, 1952), discusses and tabulates details of Horace's metrical technique with commendable thoroughness; he is also sensitive to the connection of meaning, tone and metre. On *Sat.* 1,4 see Nilsson 172ff.

121 Ter. *Eun.* 49; Hor. *Sat.* 2,3,264; L. P. Wilkinson, *Golden Latin Artistry* (Cambridge, 1963), 95. Wilkinson has many perceptive observations on the metrical technique of Horace's satires.

122 On Davus see Nilsson 193, on the

'golden lines' (2,6,102–4), Wilkinson 216, on the freer technique of the middle section of 1,1 Nilsson 166ff.

123 There is no evidence for the verse epistle in Greek literature: Sykutris, *R.E. Supplbd* 5 (1931) *s.v.* 'Epistolographie', 207f.; Kroll 217ff. But as Lucilius gives *epistula* as an example of a small verse form and Spurius Mummius in the 2nd C. B.C. wrote epistles in verse (Cic. *Att.* 13,6a) the convention may possibly have had some Hellenistic precedent.

124 Porph. on *Epp.* 1,1,1 and on *Sat.* 1,1,1. Horace never refers to his epistles as *saturae*.

125 *Epp.* 1,6 is an impassioned piece of general moralizing and 1,19 a bitter complaint on the reception of the odes but without mention of names. On the continuity of satires and epistles and some differences see Kiessling-Heinze, *Horaz Briefe* (1957⁵), 367–80.

126 On the artistry of *Epp.* 2,1 (the Epistle to Augustus) see particularly Fraenkel 383–99 and Klingner, *Sitz. Bayer. Ak. Phil.-hist. Kl.* 5 (1950), 5–32 (= *Studien* 410–32) and on that of *Epp.* 2,2 (the Epistle to Florus) Brink, *Horace on Poetry* 1, 183–90. On the *Ars Poetica* as a poem see Brink, *Horace on Poetry* 2, 'The Ars Poetica', 445–523.

127 Sen. *Epp.* 86,13 (quoting *Sat.* 1,2,27); Caes. Bass. p. 146 Mazz. (quoting C. 1,8,2). See Brink, *Horace on Poetry* 2,32ff.

128 See n. 76 above. The right reading at 1,6,126: *campum lusumque trigonem* was read by the lost *Blandinius vetustissimus*; the rest of the tradition has *rabiosi tempora signi*. For a valiant but misguided defence of the latter see R. Getty in Henderson (ed.), *Classical and Renaissance studies in honor of B.L. Ullman* (Rome, 1964), I 119–31, and for an explanation of the corruption G. Giangrande, *Mnemosyne* Ser. 4, 20 (1967), 414–18.

129 Brink 36ff.

130 The commentary of Porphyrio is edited by Holder, *Pomponi Porfyrionis Commentum in Horatium Flaccum* (Innsbruck, 1894, repr. 1967); for modern discussion of its status and merits see Brink 39 and Nisbet-Hubbard, *Commentary on Horace Odes Book One* (Oxford, 1970), xlviiff. The Pseudacron Scholia are edited by Keller (Teubner ed. 1904, repr. 1967); notes on the satires are in vol. 2. For an assessment see Nisbet and Hubbard, xlixff.

131 Brink 35. On Mavortius' statement, *legi et ut potui emendavi*, see Brink 30f.

132 For a description of the principal manuscripts and problems of classification see Brink 1–31. He is rightly critical of Klingner's complicated stemmatology, but there is much of value in Klingner's exploration of the transmission, *Hermes* 70 (1935), 249–68 and 361–403 (= *Studien* 455–518). Of fundamental importance is G. Pasquali, *Storia della tradizione e critica del testo* (Florence, 1962²), 374–85.

133 On Horace's satires in mediaeval and later times see G. Highet, *The Classical Tradition* (Oxford, 1949), esp. 84 and 311ff. (with references).

NOTES TO CHAPTER 6 (PERSIUS)

1 The pioneering edition of Persius is that of Isaac Casaubon (Paris, 1605); it was published in an enlarged form by his son Meric together with a *variorum* edition of Juvenal (Leiden, 1695). The most important commentary is still that of O. Jahn (Leipzig, 1843); the most serviceable English commentary is that of Conington–Nettleship (Oxford, 1893³). The fullest modern critical text is that of W. Clausen (Oxford, 1956); the standard reference text (together with Juvenal) is the O.C.T. edited by Clausen (Oxford, 1959), which makes full use of an important MS mentioned only in a note in his edition of 1956. There is a good translation by N. Rudd, *The Satires of Horace and Persius* (Harmondsworth, 1973). The Loeb translation by Ramsay (1918) is in-

accurate and expurgated, that by J. Tate (Oxford, 1930) is in accomplished verse but is often at some distance from the spirit of the original.

2 Suet. *Aug.* 54–6; Cass. Dio 56,27.

3 Tac. *Ann.* 1,72; Syme 486f.

4 Tac. *Ann.* 4,35f. After his rendering of Cremutius' speech Tacitus comments on the futility of totalitarian attempts to suppress human genius; the condemned works of Cremutius Cordus, Cassius Severus and others were circulated publicly after the death of Tiberius (Suet. *Calig.* 16).

5 Tac. *Ann.* 6,29.

6 Phaedr. 3 *Prol.* 38–44; see Schanz-Hosius II⁴ 448 n. 2.

7 On Phaedrus see p. 7.

8 Tacitus (*Hist.* 1,1) attributes the lack of talent to the results of dictatorship; see also 'Longinus', *de Subl.* 44.

9 Aules is an Etruscan form of the Roman *praenomen* Aulus (Schulze, *Gesch. lat. Eigennamen*, 134 n. 6). The gentile name Persius is Etruscan (Schulze 88). Persii are common on inscriptions of Volaterrae. On Persius' name see also the speculation of C. de Simone, *R.F.I.C.* 96 (1968), 419–35. Biographical information is given by an ancient Life, which a number of manuscripts assign to a Commentary by Valerius Probus, a scholar of the 1st C. A.D. The famous Valerius Probus is unlikely to have written a commentary on the work of a contemporary. The Life as we have it contains material by more than one scholar. It is repetitive and badly ordered with traces of later explanatory interpolation, but it may safely be attributed in the main to the scholarship of the late 1st C. or the 2nd C. A.D.; see Rostagni, *Suetonio de Poetis*, 167–76, who gives text and commentary, and Paratore, *Biografia e poetica di Persio* (Florence, 1968), on which see Kenney, *C.R.* 19 (1969), 171–3. The Life is not a compilation of the 4th C. A.D. as has been suggested by R. Scarcia, *R.C.C.M.* 6 (1964), 298–302; contrast the miserable ancient Life of Juvenal. But it is possible that the last sec-

tion (lines 52–60 Cl.), which contains material found also in the Scholia on 1,120f., was composed in late antiquity; see Marx on Lucil. 383. The best critical text of the *Vita* is that of Clausen, ed. Persius (1956), 35–9, and intro. xxvf.; see also his O.C.T. of Persius and Juvenal, 29–34. On some critical details S. Mariotti, *R.F.I.C.* 93 (1965), 185–7.

10 3,27–9; 6,6–9. Wide Etruscan connections are sought by J. Heurgon, *Röm. Sat.* 433–8.

11 There is a discrepancy between the consular dates at the beginning of the Life and the figure XXX at line 51; see also Clausen's *app. crit. a.l.* The Life is referred to throughout this work by the line numbering of Clausen's edn (1956).

12 See Suet. *Gramm.* 23; on his grammar K. Barwick, *Philologus Supplbd.* 15, 2 (1922), 1–272. Schol. Juv. 6,452 says that Quintilian was a pupil of Remmius. On his arrogance and luxury Plin. *N.H.* 14,49–51 and on his experimental verses Mart. 2,86.

13 Quintilian (7,4,40) mentions Verginius with respect; see also Tac. *Ann.* 15,71. On Musonius, a Stoic with commonsense views, see M. P. Charlesworth, *Five Men, Character Studies from the Roman Empire* (Cambridge: Mass., 1936), 31–62; A. C. Van Geytenbeek, transl. B. L. Hijmans, *Musonius Rufus and Greek Diatribe* (Assen, 1962).

14 On Cornutus see A. D. Nock, *R.E. Supplbd.* 5 (1931), *s.v.* 'Kornutos', 995–1005; on his writings see also Schanz-Hosius II⁴ 676–9 and F. Villeneuve, *Essai sur Perse* (Paris, 1918), 54–102; his attested comments on Virgil are gathered by Jahn (ed.), Persius, xvii–xx.

15 Cass. Dio 62,29: according to the Suda he was exiled along with Musonius Rufus.

16 For Caesius Bassus see n. 65 below; Servilius on the occasion of his death in 59 A.D. is assessed by Tac. *Ann.* 14,19; see also Quint. 10,1,102; Syme, *Tacitus* 276 and n. 1, 287–8 and 338; *id. Ten Studies in Tacitus* (Oxford, 1970), 91–109 (=

Hermes 92 (1964), 408–14) esp. 98f. on the political implications of Persius' friendship.

17 *Vit. Pers.* 20–2.

18 *Vit. Pers.* 24f.; Tac. *Ann.* 13,3; see Jahn, xxxvi. Quintilian also reacted against Seneca (10,1,125–31).

19 *Vit. Pers.* 25–9. On Thrasea see Syme, *Tacitus*, 555–62. The word *libertas* is important in Tacitus' discussions of him: *Ann.* 14,12; 14,49; 16,22; it is a key word for Persius also (5,73) but not in a political context. On Thrasea's career and reputation see also Oswyn Murray, *Historia* 14 (1965), 41–61.

20 Tac. *Ann.* 14,12; 48f.; 16,21–35 esp. 22.

21 See *Vit. Pers.* 13–18.

22 Tac. *Ann.* 15,48ff.; 16,18–20. Most of Bk 16 describes the reign of terror. In times hostile to liberal studies (Plin. *Epp.* 3,5,5) only the most harmless literary pursuits kept a man of eminence from harm; see Syme, *H.S.C.Ph.* 73 (1969), 210.

23 *Vit. Pers.* 52–6. This piece of information comes from the part of the Life that may be of late date (see n. 9 above). The text of *Vit. Pers.* 46 is hopelessly corrupt. It is impossible to salvage the name of the *praetexta*. There may also be mention of a volume that described Persius' travels, if Pithou's emendation ὁδοιπορικῶν is accepted; for another emendation see H. Hommel. *Philologus* 99 (1955), 266–76.

24 *Vit. Pers.* 44–9.

25 See p. 110.

26 Nisbet, 'Persius', in Sullivan (ed.), *Critical Essays on Roman Literature: Satire* (London, 1963), 50, argues that in Persius, as in several ancient collections, the second poem is early.

27 On the rhetorical convention of 'ανθυποφορά, or reply to an imaginary objection see Quint. 9,3,87, Schol. Pers. 1,24 and Hendrickson, *C.Ph.* 23 (1928), 102–7, esp. 105 n. 1.

28 See E. G. Turner, *Greek Papyri* (Oxford, 1968), 92 and E. W. Handley, Menander *Dyskolos*, intro. 44–7 and

bibliography listed at 44, esp. J. C. B. Lowe, *B.I.C.S.* 9 (1962), 27–42. There are no names of speakers in the 3rd C. B.C. papyrus of Menander's *Sicyonius*; see edn by R. Kassel (Berlin, 1965), III.

29 On Ennius' dream see O. Skutsch, *The Annals of Quintus Ennius* (London, 1953), 9–11 (= *Studia Enniana* (London, 1968), 7–9); *id. Studia Enniana*, 119–29, esp. 126f.; J. H. Waszink, *Mnemosyne* Ser. 4, 15 (1962), 113–28; *id. WSt* 76 (1963), 84.

30 The epithet *semipaganus* (6) is not found elsewhere. Jahn comments that *pagani* are people who share the same rites; he refers to the Paganalia (Dion. Hal. *Ant. Rom.* 4,15 and Ov. *Fast.* 1,669f.); see also Sherwin-White on Plin. *Epp.* 10,86B. The associations of *semipaganus* like those of *vatum* (8) are Roman. For the poet's *sacra* see Ov. *Pont.* 3,4,67 and 4,8,81; Prop. 2,5,26 and 4,1,61–4.

31 Jahn interprets *suum* as 'foreign'. Persius' ambitious concentration causes difficulties. A mention of his chosen medium, Roman satire, might be expected in the prologue, but *carmen nostrum* (7) is ambiguous: Some see a reference to satire, but others, e.g. Waszink, *WSt* 76 (1963), 84, see it as no more than a metrically necessary substitute for *meum*. Perhaps it also implies 'my own work', i.e. not derived from outside inspiration. *verba nostra* (9) means human speech and not Latin in contrast to Greek.

32 Continuity of theme in *Prol.* and *Sat.* is well argued by R. Reitzenstein, *Hermes* 59 (1924), 1–22.

33 On choliambics see Gerhard, *Philologus* 72 (1913), 484–91.

34 Hendrickson, however, loc. cit. (n. 27 above) interprets the poem as a monologue.

35 The opening line is said to be a quotation from Bk 1 of Lucilius. See Marx on 9; in spite of the Lucretian phraseology of *quantum est in rebus inane* (e.g. 1,330 and 569) it is unwarranted to emend the name to Lucretius, as Hendrickson does op. cit. (n. 27 above)

98ff. D. Henss, *Philologus* 98 (1954), 159 argues that line 2 comes from Lucilius and that 1–2 are a Stoic joke at Lucretius' expense. In the quick exchange of dialogue (1–3) as elsewhere, the punctuation in Clausen's text is a safe guide to the distribution of parts. These lines are also discussed by M. L. West, *C.R.* 11 (1961), 204 (against him Kenney, *P.C(amb.)Ph.S.* 188 (1962), 35 n. 4) and by N. E. Collinge, *C.R.* 17 (1967), 132.

36 5–12. *cachinno* (12) is a verb. The correct interpretation of 11–12 is that of Housman, *C.Q.* 7 (1913), 12ff. (= *Class. Papers* II 845ff.), whose punctuation is accepted with slight change by Clausen; but see also the different interpretation by N. Rudd, *C.R.* 20 (1970), 283.

37 On the effeminate euphony of the Greek proper names in 34 see H. J. Rose, *C.R.* 38 (1924), 63, but see the correction of Rose by Austin on Quint. 12,10,27 (note on p. 175).

38 *sive* (67) means 'even if' (see Clausen ed. 1956 *a.l.*); *in* with acc. occurring three times (67) suggests hostile presentation; cf. the usage at 127.

39 See the discussion of this and other parodies in the poem by Nisbet, loc. cit (n. 26 above), 45ff. Villeneuve, 208–18 analyses the verses of sham high style. It is not to be supposed that Persius advocates a return to the archaic as against the Augustan style.

40 92–102. The interlocutor's judgement that the *Aeneid* is another example of the outmoded is characteristic of a period when there were critics hostile to Virgil; these included Cornutus and Seneca; see Gell. 2,6,1; 12,2,10 and D'Alton 305f. Tate in his translation wrongly assigns 96–8 to Persius himself: see his note p. 62.

41 103–4; cf. 20f. and 87. Degeneracy is also indicated by the mention of proper names and social classes associated with Rome's traditions such as *Titos* (20) and *patricius sanguis* (61); see also 31,73,82.

42 The reference is probably to Roman satire (see Anderson *C.Q.* 8 (1958), 195–7) rather than to the unwelcoming dog of the man of influence. For the latter view see Rudd, loc. cit. (n. 36 above), 285f.

43 The language of prohibition (112) is archaic. On minatory incriptions and on pictures of snakes as guardians of a spot see Jahn on 107–13.

44 i.e. the tradition of Lucilius and Horace, probably not Old Comedy as such.

45 This is the explanation given by the Scholia.

46 The attitude of mockery and laughter is also made explicit at 40f.: *rides ait et nimis uncis/naribus indulges*; compare the description of Horace (116ff.). Korzeniewski 384–433 is on the scale of a full commentary on the first satire. There is much of exegetical interest in the work of Bramble (see n. 84).

47 The Scholia give the information that Macrinus was a scholarly man connected with Servilius and had a fatherly affection for Persius.

48 Housman, loc. cit. (n. 36 above), 15f. (= *Class. Papers* II 848) rightly interprets *fratres ... aenos* (56) as bronze statues of gods mentioned along with those referred to in 57f.

49 The theme is also found in (Plato), *Alcibiades* II. cf. Eur. frg. 327N^2 and Handley on Men. *Dysk.* 447–54.

50 The abandonment of Macrinus for the main topic by the formula: 'you are not one of those who ...' (3f.) is the work of a tiro.

51 Housman, loc. cit. (n. 36 above), 15 (= *Class. Papers* II 848) wrongly questions the use of the epithet *macram* for the baby on the grounds that most babies are plump; he interprets the words as the insatiable hope of the old woman (lines 31–9). On the superstitious rites see E. Fraenkel, *Elementi Plautini in Plauto* 425 (supplementing 187) and Jahn, *a.l.*, who quotes Claud. *Seren.* 89.

52 Housman, loc. cit. (n. 36 above), 16–18 (= *Class. Papers* II 850f.) interpreted the first part of the satire correctly as the poet talking to himself. This solution is followed by Nisbet. Housman's

discussion of the subject matter of 1–62 is splendidly illuminating. Rudd, however, *C.R.* 20 (1970), 286–8 argues that the opening words are spoken by a companion. the opening words of the satire *nempe haec adsidue* mean 'As I thought what I find here is happening continually'; on *nempe* see Hendrickson, *C.Ph.* 23 (1928), 334 and n. 1. If the companion has any substance, he may have been thought of as a fellow disciple in philosophy, certainly not a 'roaring boy'. 5–6 are a reminiscence of Verg. *Ecl.* 2,8.

53 Hendrickson wished to transpose 35–43, placing them after 57, and regarded 88–118 as a passage originally written for this satire but rejected by Persius as unsuitable.

54 Cynthia S. Dessen, *'Iunctura Callidus Acri', Illinois Stud. Lang. Lit.* 59 (1968), 58–68 discusses the relationship between *Alc.* I and Pers. 4; she also has a useful appendix on *Socratikoi Logoi* (97–105). But on Dessen's study in general see reviews by Rudd, *Phoenix* 23 (1969), 411, J. C. Bramble, *C.R.* 21 (1971), 46f. and n. 88 below.

55 Housman's emendation at 36 (see *Hermes* 64 (1931), 406 (= *Class. Papers* II 1178)) is rightly rejected by Clausen. Persius deliberately uses of the effeminate Alcibiades a term that is only applicable to a woman (see Dessen, 69). On 36 see also W. Richter, *WSt.* 78 (1965), 153f.

56 Reckford, *Hermes* 90 (1962), 476–504 identifies the interrupter with Cornutus.

57 It is assumed here that *Camena* (21) implies a contrast with the *Musa* of high poetry; contrast *Musa* (1,68).

58 Housman has shown, loc. cit. (n. 36 above), 18–21 (= *Class. Papers* 2,852f.) that lines 45–51 may be interpreted in precise astrological terms; Persius' model, Hor. *C.* 2,17,15–24 is less exact. Unlike Horace, Persius the Stoic would presumably have accepted astrology.

59 On the interpretation of 60f. and 64–9 see Housman 21ff., whose interpretation of the latter passage is accepted with slight modification by

Nisbet, loc. cit. (n. 26 above), 62. On the use of a delaying *cras* in a proverb see *cras credo, hodie nihil* (Otto 96).

60 For the use of motifs from comedy in satire see pp. 55f. and p. 74 above and for its use by Epictetus see n. 62 below. See also n. 96 below.

61 Anderson, *Philol. Quart.* 39 (1960), 66–81, regards 1–72 as an integral part of the discussion of slavery and freedom on the grounds that spiritual liberty includes freedom from the morally debased poetic language of the day.

62 Epict. *Diss.* 4,1: political advancement (38–40; 149f.); Stoic turned prosecutor, presumably Egnatius Celer (139); the death of Helvidius Priscus (123); Caesar's friend and adviser (43–50); Thrasonides, the braggart soldier from Menander's *Misoumenos* (19–23). Unlike most ancient moralists Epictetus feels pity for the man enslaved by love (147); he is diffident about his own progress (151) and tolerant of the moral weakness of others (177). For a useful analysis of this sermon see D. Nestle, *Eleutheria* I (Tübingen, 1967), 121–8.

63 Epictetus taught in the remoteness of Nicopolis in Epirus under the relative freedom of the time of Trajan.

64 Persius is indebted to Horace (*Sat.* 2,7) as well as to the philosophical tradition; the theme is found in Philo and the early Stoa (see *S.V.F.* III 349–66 and 589–603).

65 On Caesius Bassus see Quint. 10,1,96 and Schanz-Hosius II⁴, 484–6. On the details of the parallel with Horace see H. Beikircher, 'Kommentar zur VI. Satire des A. Persius Flaccus', *WSt. Beiheft* 1 (1969), who discusses problems of interpretation in *Sat.* 6 with a thoroughness that is sometimes misguided; see P. White, *C.Ph.* 67 (1972), 59ff. and E. J. Kenney, *C.R.* 20 (1970), 410.

66 Persius' heir is notional: *meus heres/ quisquis eris* (41f.); the language is like that used of the imaginary objector at *Sat.* 1,44.

67 On Chrysippus' diminishing heap

see Rudd's lucid note to his translation; also *S.V.F.* II 277; Sen. *Ben.* 5,19,9; Beikircher *a.l.*

68 e.g. the difficult *maris expers* (39) 'unmixed with sea-water' (i.e. high-class wine) or 'savourless'; alternatively 'lacking virility'. See the *app. crit.* of Clausen ed. 1956, Beikircher *a.l.* and Rudd's note to his translation *a.l.*; perhaps Persius' ambiguity is intentional.

69 e.g. Petr. 1–5 and also Pers. 1,79 which is a general statement in language similar to the allegedly autobiographical 3,44–7. See, however, Tate, *C.R.* 42 (1928), 63f.; *id. ib.* 43 (1929), 56–9 and G. B. A. Fletcher, *C.R.* 42 (1928), 167f. W. S. Anderson, *Röm. Sat.* 409–16 attributes his remoteness from Roman society, his lack of delineated personality and his abstruse language to a desire to appear a Stoic *sapiens*.

70 Housman, loc. cit. (n. 36 above), 17 (= *Coll. Papers* II 850).

71 *radere* (5,15 and 1,107); *ludo* (5,16) alludes to the urbane approach of Horace (*ludit*, 1,117).

72 Davus: 5,161 and 8; Hor. e.g. *Sat.* 2,7 *pass.* and 1,10,40; the name also occurs in Men. *Eun.* Dama: 5,76 and 79; Hor. e.g. *Sat.* 1,6,38; 2,7,54. Horace's Natta is dirty and dishonest (*Sat.* 1,6,124), Persius' is a debauchee (3,31); his name is chosen presumably for no more than its Horatian sound and without any allusion intended to the disreputable Pinarius Nata who lived in Tiberian times (Tac. *Ann.* 4,34,1).

73 Pers. 1,85 and Jahn *a.l.* On Horace's Pedius Poplicola (*Sat.* 1,10,28) see Fraenkel 133ff. and Kiessling-Heinze *a.l.*; for Pedius Blaesus Tac. *Ann.* 14,18. Persius perhaps enjoyed adding the scandalous modern associations of a name that he might well have used in any case.

74 On Bathyllus Tac. *Ann.* 1,54 and on Masurius Gell. 5,13,5.

75 Schol. on 1,4 states that he was an inept translator of Homer.

76 The facts about the readings of the manuscripts of Persius and of the Scholia at this point will be found in Clausen's

app. crit. to his edn of 1956 on 1,121. According to the Scholia Persius made the change himself, according to the Life (57–60) it was made by Cornutus. But it would seem that *quis non* (121) was necessary to pick up *quis non* (8).

77 Suet. *Calig.* 47.

78 3,20; 3,63; 3,118; 5,100. On Stoicism in Persius see J. M. K. Martin, *G.&R.* 8 (1939), 172–82.

79 Beikircher, op. cit. (n. 65 above), 11f. stresses *inductus aliquatenus in philosophiam est* (*Vit. Pers.* 14f.,81); compare Tac. *Agr.* 4,3 and Dodds' description of 'the Romans with their tidy functionalism and their cheerful obtuseness in all matters of the spirit' (*The Bacchae of Euripides* (1960²) xii). But Persius was probably an exception.

80 1,125. The *O.L.D.* rendering 'ripe' is misleading. The use of the noun *decoctum* and of *decoquo* of a boiled-down concentration of plums and wine at Plin. *N.H.* 23,133 shows the basis of Persius' metaphor.

81 Hor. *A.P.* 47f. For *acer*, used of penetrating criticism, see Hor. *Sat.* 1,10,14; 2,1,1, and also Quint. 8,3,24. The *toga* is a mark of respectability as well as the prosaic; along with *ingenuo* (14–16) it suggests that the style does not drop below a certain level.

82 1,85–91; *Vit. Pers.* 24.

83 *Carm. Einsiedl.* 1 and 2 have many of the qualities that Persius derides. The exact chronology of these poems within the reign of Nero is uncertain, but Calp. Sic. 1, which can be dated early in the reign, though superior, is mannered and stilted. See Momigliano, *C.Q.* 38 (1944), 96–100 (= *Contrib.* 2 (1960), 454–61) and Buecheler, *Rh.M.* 26 (1871), 235–40 esp. 239f. on the question of dating; on *Carm. Einsiedl.* 2, H. Fuchs, *H.S.C.Ph.* 63 (1958), 363–85. See Rudd's intro. to his translation 16f.

84 The works of K. J. Reckford, *Hermes* 90 (1962), 476–504 and C. Dessen (see n. 54 above) concentrate on dominant metaphors. The opposite approach is that of W. Kugler, *Des Persius Wille zu*

sprachlicher Gestaltung in seiner Wirkung auf Ausdruck und Komposition (Würzburg, 1940), who analyses the metaphors and similes as individual entities. The interesting but controversial study by J. C. Bramble, *Persius and the Programmatic Satire: A Study in Form and Imagery* (Cambridge, 1974), is mainly devoted to the imagery and poetry of *Satire* 1. See review by the present writer in *C.R.* (forthcoming).

85 See Schol. on 5,13.

86 22; the reading at 23 is controversial (see Clausen (ed. 1956) *app. crit.*). At 59 and 121 the ears are those of the uncritical or the fool and at 108 of the listener who dislikes satire. The diminutive *auriculae* used in the above examples contains some hint of disapprobation. For Reckford in *Sat.* 1 'diseased ears are a key metaphor', loc. cit. (n. 84 above) 483.

87 At 17f. and 33–5 the quality of the verse and of its delivery are closely connected. The mouth is also associated with popular acclaim; cf. 28, 49 and 87.

88 1,20f.; cf. 87. For Bramble the dominant metaphor of the poem is sexual stimulation, op. cit. (n. 84 above), esp. 41–5 and ch. 4 *passim*. Dessen, op. cit. (n. 54 above) is preoccupied with sexual imagery in Satire 1, but she lacks Bramble's scholarship and literary finesse.

89 At one point imagery of the physiology of sex is telescoped into that of ingestion: the metaphor from the fluid of procreation is applied to the source of literary creation, the bad verse is then described as so frothy and flimsy that it floats on the saliva in the mouth; *delumbe* (spavined, 104) belongs to the previous idea of impotence (103–5), *delumbe* is used literally of something damaged in the hips or hind-quarters, Plin. *N.H.* 10,103. The word recalls *lumbum* (20) and the rest of the mouth metaphor recalls 35.

90 1, 64f.; the metaphor is suggested immediately by Hor. *A.P.* 293.

91 Cic. *de Or.* 2,159 distinguished between the exact *statera* and the less accurate *trutina*. For other examples of the metaphors from measurement see 1,6f., 1,106 and 5,24f.

92 Here Persius may have drawn from personal experience; the cork-oak, which has an outer bark which can be removed at intervals, is a characteristic evergreen of Tuscany. R. Bianchi-Bandinelli, *Tuscany* (London, 1955), pl. 194. For a description Plin. *N.H.* 16,34; the simile of an outer bark is used by Varro, *Men.* 424, in an unknown context. The tree is common nowadays in the Tyrrhenian coastlands and is robbed of its bark every seven years: D. S. Walker, *A Geography of Italy* (London, 1967[2]), 67 and 63.

93 For the lungs (*pulmo*) as a centre of the mind and emotions see R. B. Onians, *The Origins of European Thought about the body, the mind, the soul, the world, time and fate* (Cambridge, 1951), 23–43. *avia* is also the Latin for a plant, possibly a weed such as groundsel. Persius may have intended the ambiguity. I owe this point to Professor Rudd. It is also an extension of *spinas animo . . . evellas* (Hor. *Epp.* 1,14,4f.).

94 Zeno and Chrysippus had used the example of a dog harnessed to a cart to illustrate man in relation to his destiny, *S.V.F.* II 975; see D. Nestle, *R.A.C., s.v.* 'Freiheit', 274.

95 The list is printed as an appendix to the edition of Persius by I. Casaubon (Paris, 1605); it will also be found in the enlarged edition by his son Meric, published together with a *variorum* edn. of Juvenal (Leiden, 1695). D. Henss, *Philologus* 99 (1955), 277–94 (= Korzeniewski 365–83) gives good help on Persius' complex reminiscences of Horace, but only a full commentary can explore adequately the multifarious quality of the reminiscences in context.

96 Pers. 5,161–74 is based on Menander's *Eunuchus*; Terence's adaptation is the immediate source of Hor. *Sat.* 2,3,259ff. The information is given by Schol. Pers. 5,161; see Menander ed. Koerte II p. 66 and Webster, *Studies in Menander* (Manchester, 1960[2]), 67–76, esp. 70.

97 9,3,9. For Persius' usage see ed. Conington-Nettleship[3] on 1,9. It is of course also a contemporary colloquialism, as *meum intellegere* (Petr. 52,3). Persius' metrical usage also is colloquial, e.g. the admission of a monosyllabic ending without special effect; he is master of metrical effect for parody, e.g. the spondaic ending of neoteric preciosity (1,95) and the placing of the caesura after a trochee in the third foot (6,1,5 and 6: Nisbet 66). On Persius' metrical technique see H. Küster, *De A. Persii Flacci elocutione quaestiones* III (Lobau, 1897), 22f. and S. B. Platner, *T.A.Ph.A.* 26 (1895), LVIII.

98 The threat to throw stones at the speaker of something unwelcome derives from Horace (*Sat.* 2,7,116). The explanation of Persius' phrase followed here is that developed by Housman, loc. cit. (n. 36 above), 29f. (= *Class. Papers* II 862–4). The lines were so understood in the Schol., where *exossatus* is equivalent to *elapidatus*. Ov. *Met.* 1,393 refers to stones as *terrae ossa*; this kenning has a Greek counterpart (Choirilos *Trag.* 2N²). See further I. Waern, *ΓΗΣ ΟΣΤΕΑ* The Kenning in Pre-Christian Greek Poetry (Uppsala, 1951).

99 *Vit. Pers.* 44–50; Quint. 10,1,94; Mart. 4,29.

100 *Vit. Pers.* 50.

101 Pers. 2,69 at *S.H.A., Alex. Sev.* 44,9. Note also that at *S.H.A., Pesc. Nig.* 3,11 Severus is made in a letter to allude to Pers. 1,103f.

102 Lact. *inst. div.* 6,2 (quoting 2,29f.); on other citations by Lactantius see Manitius, *Philologus* 47 (1888), 712.

103 Among the more striking imitations are Aus. *Epigr.* 93,3 from 4,39f. and Claudian *Rapt. Pros.* 1,115 from 3,58.

104 Hagendahl, *Latin fathers and the Classics* (Göteborg, 1958), 145, suggests that Jerome had re-read Persius at the time (probably A.D. 393) in order to have a supply of abusive ammunition, e.g. *protensus est aqualiculus* (*adv. Iov.* 2,21 from Pers. 1,57) and the application of mad

Orestes (3,117f.) to Iovinianus (*adv. Iov.* 1,1).

105 *delumbum matronarum salivam* (*Epp.* 22,29,6 (A.D. 384) from Pers. 1,104; Hagendahl, 109f.; for other adaptations see Hagendahl, 255.

106 Hagendahl, *Augustine and the Latin Classics*, 2 vols, (Göteborg, 1967). Augustine quotes Persius 3,66–72 at *Civ. Dei* 2,6.

107 *Sat.* 5,24–5 in *ep.* 132 (= Hagendahl I *test.* 500). See further Hagendahl II, 472–4 for a discussion of citations from Persius.

108 For references to Persius in Porphyrio see the index to Holder's edition; for Donatus and Servius see Mountford and Schultz, *Index rerum et nominum in Scholiis Servii et Aelii Donati Tractatorum*; for Charisius and Diomedes, the index to *G.L.K.* VII,610f., and for Pseudacron the index to Keller's edition.

109 For Priscian's references to Persius see Keil's index and for those of Isidore see Lindsay's index in the *O.C.T.* Martianus Capella 9,908 adapts Pers. *Prol.* 14.

110 On Sabinus' subscript see Clausen, *Hermes* 91 (1963), 252–6. Clausen discusses the place of Sabinus' manuscript in the transmission of the text of Persius in this article, correcting the view expressed in his edition of 1956.

111 Allied to P but not dependent on it is S(angallensis), a 9th-C. *florilegium* which contains a handful of isolated lines of Persius. X was discovered in time to be mentioned by Clausen, 1956 edn, in a note (intro. xiii n. 1); it has an important place in his *O.C.T.* edn of 1959, and may be classed along with another valuable Vatican MS. (V) of late 9th-C. date.

112 On the Scholia see Clausen's 1956 edn, xxiiif. The most recent edn of the ancient Scholia is that of Jahn; a modern edn. making full use of what is now known about the manuscripts is much to be desired.

113 On Persius in mediaeval times see Manitius, *Philologus* 47 (1888), 714–20.

NOTES TO CHAPTER 7
(JUVENAL)

1 The standard text of Juvenal is that of W. V. Clausen, *O.C.T.* (1959). The text by A. E. Housman, *D. Iunii Iuvenalis Saturae* (Cambridge, 1931[2]) is notable for a new depth of critical judgement; for a review of the 2nd edn see U. Knoche, *Gnomon* 9 (1933), 242–54. The edition by U. Knoche, *D. Iunius Iuvenalis Saturae* (Munich, 1950), is more important for the mass of information provided than for its critical acumen; too many innocent lines are bracketed as interpolations. For a brief account of editorial problems in the text of Juvenal see the present writer's new introduction to J. D. Duff's edn of *Fourteen Satires of Juvenal* (Cambridge, 1970), lxxvi–lxxxiii. The standard commentary on the whole of Juvenal is that by L. Friedlaender, *D. Junii Juvenalis Saturarum Lib. V* (Leipzig, 1895); the bulk of Friedlaender's introduction has been translated by J. R. C. Martyn, *Friedlaender's Essays on Juvenal* (London, 1969). The edition by J. E. B. Mayor, *Thirteen Satires of Juvenal*, 2 vols (London, 1886[4] and 1888[4]), is unsurpassed for the width of its learning. The Loeb edn (together with Persius) by G. G. Ramsay (London, 1918) is serviceable but undistinguished.

There is a good translation with useful introduction by P. Green, *Juvenal: The Sixteen Satires* (Harmondsworth, 1967). G. Highet, *Juvenal the Satirist* (Oxford, 1954), makes questionable use of the biographical evidence and has a rather superficial treatment of the individual satires, but his copious annotations show a very firm grasp of problems of interpretation and there is an excellent section on Juvenal's influence on later literatures; some scholars such as W. S. Anderson, after an early unfavourable estimate, *C.Ph.* 50 (1955), 146–8, have come to a more generous overall evaluation: *Proc. Afr. Class. Assoc.* 6 (1963), 45–9. This attitude is shared by the present writer. There is a thoughtful and sober study by A. Serafini, *Studio*

sulla Satira di Giovenale (Florence, 1957). For an excellent general bibliography see Highet 339–46. For the years 1941–61 see *Lustrum* 8 (1963), 161–215 and for more recent work P. Green's translation 299–303 and Coffey, revised introduction to J. D. Duff's edn, lxxxiv–ix.

2 Domitian ordered the suppression of writings that denounced eminent individuals by name (Suet. *Dom.* 8,3); note the disclaimer Mart. I *Praef.* On the general character of the period see Tac. *Hist.* 1,2–3 and *Agr.* esp. I and 44f.

3 Stat. *Silv.* 1,3,103.

4 Schol. Prob. Vall. on Juv. 1,20; Plin. *Epp.* 3,15.

5 On Turnus see Mart. 7,97 and 11,10; also Schol. Prob. Juv. 1,20; the frg is quoted by Schol. Juv. 1,71 (= *Frg. Poet. Lat.* p. 134, Morel); Quint. 10,1,94; for late references see Rut. Nam. 1,603f.; Sid. Apoll. *Carm.* 9,266 and Lyd. *Mag.* 1,41.

6 Plin. *Epp.* 1,13,1; Juv. 1,1–18. Once at a recital of elegiacs a member of the audience heckled. Pliny was shocked (*Epp.* 6,15; see E. Laughton, *C.R.* 21 (1971), 171f.); Juvenal would have been delighted (note the reference to elegies at 1,4).

7 Syme, *Tacitus* 774f.

8 Highet 5 and 235 suggests *c.* A.D. 60, arguing that Bk I, which he dates A.D. 110, was written by a man who was more than forty-five years of age; but *juvenis* (1,25) is not to be interpreted in the strict sense of 'liable to military service' as at Censorinus *de die nat.* 14,2; see Axelson, *Mélanges Marouzeau* (Paris, 1948), 7–17.

9 On the names see Syme, *Tacitus* 775f.

10 *I.L.S.* 2926 (= McCrum-Woodhead no. 156). *trib(unus)* is a supplement to the inscription; it is almost certainly right.

11 On the status of *duumvir quinq.* and *flamen* of the imperial house in a *colonia* see Meiggs, *Roman Ostia* (Oxford, 1960), 174–80, and on equestrian careers, Highet 34f., but note also the caution of Syme, *H.S.C.Ph.* 73 (1969), 208, on the progress from military tribunate to an equestrian appointment.

12 For refs. to Britain see Duff edn xix and n. 48 below. On veterans' stories in general see Epict. *Diss.* 3,16,4.

13 7,24; 7,91 (*facunde Iuvenalis*); 12,18. The poems of Bk 7 would probably have been written A.D. 91–2; see Friedlaender edn, 58. On the dating of Martial Bk 12 see Sherwin-White on Pliny, *Epp.* 3,21,2.

14 Juv. 11,64ff.; on the theme of the literary man's farm see Sherwin-White on Plin. *Epp.* 1,24,1.

15 Printed by Clausen in *O.C.T.* (1959), 179; for the text of other lives see Jahn edn (1851), 386–90.

16 Hor. *Sat.* 1,6,6; Juv. 1,15ff.

17 Juv. 7,90ff. The statement in the Life is presumably derived from 7,82–9.

18 Suet. *Dom.* 10; see *Lustrum* 8 (1963), 167f. Tac. *Agr.* 45 (see Ogilvie and Richmond *a.l.* and on 2,1); Plin. *Epp.* 8,14,7 and Sherwin-White *a.l.* and on 7,33,4.

19 Juv. 7,1–7; see Highet 13f. Those in Rome who suffered exile or death during Hadrian's reign were for the most part consulars; the sophist Favorinus was exiled (if at all) only after gratuitous provocation. For arguments against exile under Trajan or Hadrian see Highet 240f.

20 For interest in Juvenal in late antiquity see p. 145, and for a reconstruction of his life, Highet 4–41.

21 *Anth. Pal.* 9,137 a and b.

22 Pliny on Martial, *Epp.* 3,21, and on Suetonius, *Epp.* 1,24,1 (see Sherwin-White *a.l.*); as a friend of writers also *Epp.* 1,13,6. Juvenal's first Book may have been published later than *Epp.* 1,13 but his talent was probably recognized before. Pliny departed for Bithynia possibly as early as A.D. 109, according to Sherwin-White, 80; but see Crook, *C.R.* 17 (1967), 313f. Pliny is silent about Plutarch, whom he perhaps did not regard as of sufficient social distinction; see C. P. Jones, *Plutarch and Rome* (Oxford, 1971), 61.

23 As Statius' German war, which Juvenal parodies, is that of A.D. 83, strictly speaking Juvenal's dramatic date will be late autumn (4,56–9) of the previous year.

24 Juvenal in his third book (8,120) mentions Marius' depredations as having been committed 'not long ago' (*nuper*), i.e. something vivid in men's memories; see Duff on 15,27.

25 Highet 11f. suggests that Juvenal refers to Tacitus. On the chronology of Tacitus see Syme, *Tacitus,* 117–20, 473, 777 and on the title *Annales,* 253 n. 1.

26 For the date of the comet see Friedlaender edn 8–10 and for the date of the earthquake at Antioch, F. A. Lepper, *Trajan's Parthian War* (Oxford, 1948), esp. 65–9 and the conclusion (83): 13 Dec. A.D. 115.

27 It is possible to see here a reference to Hadrian's foundation of the Athenaeum; the problem of chronology is discussed by Highet 236f.; 15,110 may refer to the same institution.

28 On Trajan's hexagonal harbour see Meiggs, *Roman Ostia,* 58ff., 162–8 and on its date, 488f.

29 Minor chronological arguments are suggested by Anderson, *C.Ph.* 50 (1955), 255–7 (see *Lustrum* 8 (1963), 168), Highet 15f. and Michel, *R.E.L.* 41 (1963), 315–27.

30 See W. Kroll, *R.E. Supplbd* 7 (1940) *s.v.* 'Rhetorik', esp. 1119–24; S. F. Bonner, *Roman Declamation* (Liverpool, 1949); M. L. Clarke, *Rhetoric at Rome* (London, 1953), 85–99.

31 On *color* see Sen. *Contr.* 1,5,9; Juv. 6,280 and 7,155; R. Volkmann, *Die Rhetorik der Griechen und Römer* (Leipzig, 1885²), 113–16; Bonner, op. cit. (n. 30 above) 55ff.

32 Juvenal however (7,166–70) was aware of the differences between declamatory exercises and a real court case.

33 Sen. *Oed.* 1038f.; Tac. *Ann.* 14,8 (cf. ps.-Sen, *Oct.* 369–72). *Prosopopoeia,* the assumption of a role, was a standard procedure of rhetoric (Quint. 3,8,49–54). Tacitus accused some of the opponents of the Caesars of striking a pose (*Agr.* 42,4); cf. his astringent comment on rhetorical mourning *ib.* 29,1.

34 On the historical event, Tac. *Ann.*

13,44 and on Lucan's *controversia* based on it, *vit. Luc. (Vaccae)* 27f. and 65f. Rost.

35 On Lucan as a poet of intense rhetoric see E. Fraenkel, 'Lucan als Mittler des antiken Pathos', *Vortr. d. Bibl. Warburg* 4 (1924), 229–57 (= *Kl. Beitr.* 2,233–266), on details of his use of themes from *declamationes* see Bonner, *A.J.Ph.* 87 (1966), 257–89; see also M. P. O. Morford, *The poet Lucan: studies in rhetorical epic* (Oxford, 1967), esp. ch. 1 and 2.

36 B. Otis, *Ovid as an epic poet* (Cambridge, 1966¹), 340.

37 *indignatio* includes the synthetic indignation of the declaimer as well as a genuine personal anger. On Juvenal's anger see W. S. Anderson, *Y.Cl.S.* 17 (1961), 3–9 (cf. *Lustrum* 8 (1963), 210) and *id.* 'Anger in Juvenal and Seneca', *Univ. Calif. Publ. Class. Phil.* 19,3 (1964), 127–95. Formulae of anger in *Sat.* 1: 30f., 45, 51f., 63f., 77f.

38 Note the word *auditor* 3,322 and 1,1; and *rauci* (1,2). For the recital hall and organized applause see 7,40–7; frequent applause was customary in the rhetorical schools (Quint. 2,2,12).

39 1,19–21; 51; 165ff.

40 On rhetoric in Juvenal see J. De Decker, *Juvenalis Declamans* (Ghent, 1913) and E. J. Kenney, *Latomus* 22 (1963), 704–20.

41 Contrast Persius' choliambics and the prose prefaces of Martial (note particularly the method of work in prefaces to Bks 1 and 2); for a reciter's preface see Plin. *Epp.* 1,13,2 and for a declaimer's 2,3,1.

42 A literary precedent has been sought for the procedure, as in masquerade sequences in Old Comedy: J. G. Griffith, *Proc. Class. Ass.* (1968), 36 and *G.&R.* 16 (1969), 147f., who alludes to the custom of *flagitatio* or public denunciation of a wrong-doer. But perhaps *flagitatio* was too archaic to be relevant for Juvenal. The idea of using writing-tablets at the street corner to record examples of wickedness and absurdity (63f.) is based on Hor. *Sat.* 1,4,65–7.

43 81–6. It is vain to object that

Juvenal does not justify his claim in full to treat the full range of human activities from the beginning of time (Deucalion and Pyrrha are the rhetorician's beginning, Lucian, *Praec. Rhet.* 20). On this problem and on the apologia of the concluding lines see J. G. Griffith, *C.Q.* 19 (1969), 379ff.

44 On theme and structure in *Sat.* 1 as a programme satire, see E. J. Kenney, *P.C(amb.)Ph.S.* 8 (1962), 29–40; J. G. Griffith, *Hermes* 98 (1970), 56–72. In his notes to the chapters on the individual satires Highet has a well-documented discussion of their structure.

45 Apart from the exaggeration of plural abortions, Juvenal's comment on Domitian's hypocrisy (29–33) is well supported by Pliny, *Epp.* 4,11,6.

46 Friedlaender's view (on 36) that Laronia was liable in some way under the *lex Iulia* and that she has nothing to do with the rich widow in Martial (2,32) is convincing.

47 Nero went through a mock marriage with the pathic Sporus (Suet. *Ner.* 28).

48 References to Britain (159–61) seem to have been taken from Tac. *Agr.*: the Orkneys (10), the short nights (12) and particularly a conquest of Ireland (24), where Juvenal the rhetorician exaggerates.

49 Old Rome: *Quirinus* (67), *Quirites* (60, 162f.), *caelum Aventini* (84f.), time of one jail (312–4); unpretentiousness in Italy outside Rome (168–79), safety (190–2), a freehold house and garden (223–31).

50 On the structure see Highet 254 and Anderson, 'Studies in Book I of Juvenal', *Y.Cl.S.* 15 (1957), 55–68.

51 On Domitian's council of advisers (*amici*) see J. Crook, *Consilium Principis* (Cambridge, 1955), Syme, *Tacitus*, 5f. and 636, and J. G. Griffith, *G.&R.* 16 (1969), 134–50.

52 Information on the participants will be found in Crook, op. cit. (n. 51 above) and Highet, 259–61. Veiento and Catullus are compared implicitly in the

anecdote in Plin. *Epp.* 4,22,4, whose opinion of the blind informer has much in common with Juvenal's. On Veiento see also Plin. *Epp.* 9,13,13 and Syme, *Tacitus*, 5f. and on Virro and Acilius Syme, *Ten Studies in Tacitus* (Oxford, 1970), 76f. and 98 n. 4.

53 There is presumably deliberate ambiguity in *vindice nullo* (152): the revolt of Vindex led to the downfall of Nero, to whom Domitian is compared (the bald Nero, 38). For Vindex see also 8,222 and for a pun on his name Suet. *Ner.* 45. Unless *cerdonibus* (153) refers to something not understood in later times (*cerdo*, the cobbler, gives municipal games, Mart. 3,16; 3,59), Juvenal's judgement that Domitian was killed when he became an object of fear to artisans is naïve. His assassins were palace retainers instigated by his wife; see M. P. Charlesworth, *J.R.S.* 27 (1937), 60–2.

54 On Statius' *de Bello Germanico* see Schol. Vall. on Juv. 4,94: the four lines cited mention Crispus, Veiento and Acilius (= *Frg. Poet. Lat.* p. 134 Morel). See also J. G. Griffith, *G.&R.* 16 (1969), 134–50.

55 For a loosely connected prelude see Hor. *Sat.* 1,2; cf. Fraenkel 76f. On Crispinus as a miniature Domitian see W. C. Hembold and E. N. O'Neil, *A.J.Ph.* 77 (1956), 68–73 and W. Heilmann, *Rh.M.* 110 (1967), 362; see also *Lustrum* 8 (1963), 206. G. B. Townend, *J.R.S.* 63 (1973), 153–8 conjectures that Crispinus was let off lightly by Juvenal in *Sat.* 4 because he was one of the men flogged to death ten years later for fornication with the Vestal Virgin Cornelia.

56 Plin. *Epp.* 2,6 (see Sherwin-White on 2,6,2), who prescribes the equality of hospitality and urbanity that Juvenal desiderates; Mart. 3,60; 6,11.

57 The wronged and humiliated husband is present throughout: 136, 184, 232, 270, O 14, 400, 432, 456, 463, 508, 535f., 611, 654. The themes of marriage and the badness of women were traditionally inextricable; see the alternative titles περὶ

γάμου and ψόγος γυναικῶν of Semon. 7 (West); Stob. *Flor.* 4,22,193.

58 The 34 lines found in a single Beneventan manuscript in Oxford after 6,365 (the so-called O lines) and the two after 373 were regarded as genuine by Housman: see his convenient summary, 2nd edn, xxiv, n. 1. Important arguments against genuineness have been advanced by Knoche, *Philologus* 93 (1938), 196–217 and Axelson, ΔΡΑΓΜΑ, M. P. Nilsson, (Lund, 1939), 41–55, but a majority of more recent scholars seems to favour authenticity; see *Lustrum* 8 (1963), 179–84. The position of the larger fragment is not certain. That a section on shams should immediately precede one on genuine eunuchs (366–78) is reasonable (see Courtney, *Mnemosyne* Ser. 4, 15 (1962), 262–6) but the placing of the O lines after 345, as advocated by Griffith, *Hermes* 91 (1963), 104–14, gives a better position for the otherwise intrusive section 352–65; see also Green, *Juvenal*, 157 and G. Luck, *H.S.C.Ph.* 76 (1972), 217–32.

59 Many of the types in *Sat.* 6 can be paralleled from Martial, e.g. the bluestocking who condemns a solecism (11,19) and the user of Greek terms of affection (10,68). For Juvenal's indebtedness to Martial see in general H. L. Wilson, *A.J.Ph.* 19 (1898), 193–209 and G. B. Townend, *J.R.S.* 63 (1973), 148–60.

60 For Juv.'s use of traditional material at 6,523f. see E. K. Borthwick, *Eranos* 64 (1966), 108.

61 The judgement by J. P. V. D. Balsdon, *Roman Women* (London, 1962), 245 on Juvenal's humorous intentions in parts of *Sat.* 6 may mislead.

62 On Semonides' catalogue of bad women 7 (West) see Edmonds, *Elegy and Iambus* II, 217–25; W. Marg, *Der Charakter in der Sprache der frühgriechischen Dichtung*, Kieler Arbeiten 1 (Würzburg, 1938), 6–42; W. J. Verdenius, *Mnemosyne* Ser. 4, 21 (1968), 132–58. On the rhetorical and philosophical approaches to the theme of marriage, e.g. Quint,

3,5,8 and Seneca, *De Matrim.* frg 45–88H, see Highet 264f.

63 Some imprudent approaches to structure in Juv. particularly *Sat.* 6 are criticized by Highet, 93–7, who also discusses various schemes for the poem's contents, 267f. See also Anderson, *C.Ph.* 51 (1956), 73–94, but neither his scheme nor that of Highet carries complete conviction. For Peripatetic strictures on the episodic see e.g. Arist. *Poet* 1451b 33ff. For a useful monumental analogy see Weinreich LXI, who compares the construction of *Sat.* 6 to the succession of scenes on Trajan's column.

64 The interpretation is contrary to that of Highet 111f. and Anderson, *C.Ph.* 57 (1962), 153ff., who see optimism in the introduction. The view of Helmbold and O'Neill, *C.Ph.* 54 (1959), 100–8 that it is an attack on Domitian with oblique criticism of Hadrian is untenable on various grounds; see the criticism discussed in *Lustrum* 8 (1963), 207f.

65 For Martial's direct appeal see e.g. 2,91 and 92, cf. 3,95. Martial's gross flattery of Domitian e.g. 5,3 and 9,28 is matched by that of Statius *Silv.* 1,1. For the laudatory proem in the tradition of Lucan 1,33–66 see Val. Flacc. 1,7–21 (to Vespasian), Plin. *N.H. Praef.* (to Titus) and Stat. *Theb.* 1,16–33 (to Domitian). For the changed attitude after A.D. 96 see Mart. 10,72 and also Plin. *Pan.* 3.

66 On Ponticus see Syme, *Tacitus* 778 as against Highet, 113, 272 and 291. Valerius Ponticus, the legal swindler of Neronian times (Tac. *Ann.* 14,41) could not be cited as an illustrious ancestor.

67 Rubellius Blandus is perhaps a blend of fiction and reality; see Syme, *Tacitus* 576f. and 628; also Highet 273. Tacitus' Rubellius Plautus (*Ann.* 13,19–22; 14,57–9) is relevant in so far as he was probably the brother of Juvenal's figure. The consul Lateranus (8,146–82) has much in common with Plautius Lateranus, who was however executed by Nero in A.D. 65 while still consul designate. Complete accuracy of historical detail should not be expected of

a rhetorical satirist's *exemplum*. On Lateranus see Highet 273 (nn. 4 and 7).

68 Disgust felt at Nero's performance as touring singer was not mere rhetorical hyperbole, but was part of the motive for the revolt of Vindex: see in addition to Juv. 8,221–6 Suet. *Ner.* 41.

69 For the shaping of *Sat.* 8 as a rhetorical *suasoria* see Highet 273; see also S. C. Fredericks, *T.A.Ph.A.* 102 (1971), 111–32.

70 There is gross obscenity at the beginning of the poem; see Jachmann, 'Studien zu Juvenal', *Nachr. Ak. Wiss. Gött. Phil.-Hist. Kl.* 6 (1943), 197–205. 37 derives from *Od.* 16,294 (= 19, 13) and 102 from Verg. *Ecl.* 2,69. Explicit verbal obscenity is at its most drastic at 43f.

71 126–9. Symposiac motifs from love-elegy and epigram are placed deliberately in a base context; clichés on the enjoyment of fleeting pleasures occur at Pers. 5,151–3; on the topic see Nisbet-Hubbard on Hor. *C.* 1,36 (p. 402).

72 There is no reason to suppose that Naevolus and Virro are individuals and not types: for Naevolus in a similar role see Mart. 3,71 and 3,95,13. He applies the name to a mean man at 2,46.

73 See Petr. 61 and Mart. 10,47. It is possible to see 357ff. in more positive philosophical terms. I owe to Mr E. Courtney the suggestion that these lines read almost like a summary of the contents of Cic. *Tusc.*, particularly Bk 5 on the self-sufficiency of *virtus*.

74 On the structural importance of the last lines see E. N. O'Neil, *C.Ph.* 47 (1952), 233f.; on a problem of structure see Highet 277f.

75 The conclusion, *pace* Highet 133, suggests not so much a philosophical pessimism as an older man's natural wish to ration his pleasures. According to Martial the client was so busy indoors in Rome that he had to leave the city to acquire a sun-tan (10,12): for elderly sun-bathers see Plin. *Epp.* 3,1,8 and 3,5,10.

76 On this contrast see Hor. *C.* 1,20 and Fraenkel 216 n. 2. Horace has another version of the same topic at *Epp.* 1,5. The

satirical theme of the ostentatious banquet as found in Lucilius, Horace and possibly Petronius is also relevant literary background. Censorious moralizing on excess is seen as fundamental to the structure of the poem by A. S. McDevitt, *G.&R.* 15 (1968), 173–9. On the conventions of the invitation in Greek and Roman poetry see Williams, 103–31.

77 Cf. the exaggerated lavishness of a sacrificial bull that Juvenal cannot afford (10–14). On the alleged behaviour of the beaver see Mayor on 12,34.

78 Unity of theme may be sought in different aspects of acquisitiveness, Catullus' greedy trading and a technique of legacy-hunting. The poet's sacrifice is described in two parts (1–9; 83–92) interrupted by the narrative of the storm. On the structure see Highet 280.

79 On the *consolatio* in the early empire see W. C. Summers on Sen. *Epp.* 63 (243ff.). To his examples may be added Stat. *Silv.* 3,3 (on which see P. R. C. Weaver, *C.Q.* 15 (1965), 145–154) and Dio Chrys. 28,12f.; see also R. Kassel, *Untersuchungen zur griechischen und römischen Konsolationsliteratur* (Munich, 1958), who analyses rhetorical and philosophical elements, and Ogilvie and Richmond on Tac. *Agr.* 44–6.

80 Moderation: 11–16; philosophy: 19–22, 120–3. An appeal to moderation in grief is part of the *consolatio*, see e.g. Sen. *Marc.* 7,1 and C. C. Grollios, *Seneca's Ad Marciam* (Athens, 1956), 32ff.

81 13,217–22; Highet 140–4, takes the poem's *consolatio* seriously, but Anderson, *C.Ph.* 57 (1962), 150, instancing the portrait of the uncouth Age of Saturn (38–59) and the trite poetical *adynata* (64–70) regards the poem as ironical, a view also held by A. D. Pryor, *B.I.C.S.* 8 (1961), 85; see also the subtle assessment of the poem by L. Edmunds, *Rh. M.* 115 (1972), 59–73. Pliny's reference (*Epp.* 5,16) to crude and tactless *consolatio* suggests that the convention was abused and so open to parody.

82 Such an old republican ideal though morally edifying was of limited relevance

to the agricultural and military circumstances of the early 2nd C. A.D.

83 The attack on the merchant's enterprise is a *locus communis* of ancient rhetoric and poetry; see Nisbet-Hubbard on Hor. *C.* 1,1,16.

84 O'Neil, *C.Ph.* 55 (1960), 251–3 has argued for complete unity of structure, but 256 to the end are recalcitrant; Highet helpfully points to the parallel of Hor. *Sat.* 1,1, in which *avaritia* dominates a more general discussion of human weakness; see also J. P. Stein, *C.Ph.* 65 (1970), 34–6.

85 On the subject matter of this satire see J. Lindsay, *Daily Life in Roman Egypt* (London, 1963), 109–21; for a similar vendetta Plut. *de Isid. et Osir.* 72 (380B); J. Gwyn Griffiths, Plutarch's *de Iside et Osiride,* (Cardiff, 1970), 548f.

86 Juvenal's comments on soldiers apply particularly to the praetorian guards and to some new enactments by Hadrian; see M. Durry, *R.E.L.* 13 (1935), 95–106, B. d'Orgeval, *L'Empereur Hadrien, oeuvre législative et administrative* (Paris, 1950), 87 and 348–51 (on testamentary dispositions), Highet 287. On complaints against the conduct of the army see G. Webster, *The Roman Imperial Army* (London, 1969), 265f.

87 This suggestion by Leo, *Hermes* 44 (1909), 616 is accepted by Housman, 2nd edn, pref. lvii.

88 The view of Ribbeck, *Der echte und der unechte Juvenal* (Berlin, 1865), that the later satires were spurious, is based on a misunderstanding of Juvenal's technical resources.

89 Mart. 6,82; Plin. *Epp.* 9,23,3ff.

90 Pliny finds it necessary to offer an explanation for having recited his own intimate light verse (*Epp.* 5,3,1), elsewhere described as the frivolous expression of immediate personal emotions (*Epp.* 4,14,3).

91 *accusator* (161) implies the public informer; cf. Tac. *Hist.* 2,10 and *Ann.* 2,28. See also 1,33–6 (see Friedlaender on 33); on Baebius Massa (35) see Sherwin-White on Plin. *Epp.* 7,33,4; on the *delator* and

spy see Friedlaender, *Roman Life and Manners* I 220–3 (note particularly among examples given there: Mart. 10,48; Epict. *Diss.* 4,13,5; Ael. Arist. 1 p. 105 Dind.), and Syme, *Tacitus* 326ff.; on the procedure of laying information and of prosecution, Crook, *Law and Life of Rome*, 276ff.

92 On freedom of speech under Trajan see Tac. *Hist.* 1,1, Plin. *Epp.* 3,18,6, and *Pan.* 34f.; also Trai. *ap.* Plin. *Epp.* 10,97. Some *delatores* survived into the reign of Nerva (see Plin. *Epp.* 4,22,4); even if Fabricius Veiento and Aquilius Regulus are not strictly speaking to be included among the delators (see Sherwin-White *a.l.*) an anxious contemporary would not have appreciated a nice distinction. On Regulus and his tainted oratory see also Plin. *Epp.* 4,7,5; 6,2; M. Winterbottom, *J.R.S.* 54 (1964), 90–7 and R. H. Martin, *J.R.S.* 57 (1967), 109–14.

93 It seems that in imperial times political satire could be indicted under the law of treason (*maiestas*); see Tac. *Ann.* 1,72 and Crook op. cit. (n. 91 above), 252f.; also Plin. *Epp.* 10,82,1. For attacks on private individuals see n. 2 above and Tac. *Ann.* 14,50; acc. to Schol. Juv. 1,162 Juvenal would have been liable under a *lex Iulia*, which forbade attacks on the vices of the living; this may refer to the *lex Iulia maiestatis* (*Dig.* 48,4; see also Suet. *Aug.* 55). On the expansion of the law of *maiestas* and our imperfect knowledge of it see A. H. M. Jones, *The Criminal Courts of the Roman Republic and Principate* (Oxford, 1972), 106f.

94 Plin. *Epp.* 9,13,10f.

95 Plin. *Epp.* 9,27 and Syme, *Tacitus* 120.

96 A remote sneer at the system in the manner of Lucan may be detected here and there: e.g. supernumerary gods in the sky (13,46ff.; cf. Stat. *Silv.* 1,1,94–8). But while Juvenal lacks the forthright independence of his contemporary Epictetus, on which see F. Millar, *J.R.S.* 55 (1965), 141–8, he offers no flattery or blandishment. The gibe about a free Rome offering the title of *pater patriae* to

Cicero (8,243f.) belongs to rhetorical unreality in the manner of Lucan.

97 Titinius Capito was imperial secretary (*ab epistulis*) to Domitian, Nerva and Trajan (*I.L.S.* 1448 (= 347 McCrum-Woodhead)): see Syme, *Tacitus* 92f.

98 Martial pledges himself to attack vices but spare individuals, even the humbly placed (*Praef.* 1; 10,33,10). There is no reason to suppose Juvenal's procedure was fundamentally different.

99 For Priscus see 1,49; 8,120; Sherwin-White on Plin. *Epp.* 2,11 but also P. A. Brunt, *Historia* 10 (1961), 200; on the disgrace of Vibius Maximus see *P.Oxy.* 471, Syme, *Historia* 6 (1957), 480–7 and Sherwin-White on Plin. *Epp.* 9,1. Elsewhere Juvenal uses an older example of provincial extortion, that of Cossutianus Capito in A.D. 57 (8,93; see Tac. *Ann.* 14,48).

100 Highet suggests that Juvenal makes oblique attacks on Pliny and his family. Syme, who is in general critical of Highet's discussion of Juvenal's choice of proper names (289–94), allows some possible oblique references (*Tacitus* 777f.; cf. 628 and n. 2). According to Quintilian (9,2,65–9) a declaimer's audience listened attentively for the hidden innuendo.

101 Pliny does not criticize by name living persons of social importance; see Sherwin-White, *Letters of Pliny*, intro. 54ff. Vergilius Romanus recited his Old Comedy in which vices were attacked, but there were fictitious names (*decenter*) acc. to Plin. *Epp.* 6,21. That certain philosophers attacked the vices of named individuals may be inferred from Pliny's laudatory sketch of Euphrates (*Epp.* 1,10,7).

102 See e.g. Sen. *Epp.* 44, Pers. 4, Dio Chrys. 3,4 and Highet 272; see also Mart. 5,17.

103 Note e.g. Sen. *Ira* 2,33,2–4, Syme 420–4 and 490–508, id. *Tacitus* 566–84 (on Galba 575); M. Gelzer, transl. R. Seager, *The Roman Nobility* (Oxford, 1969), 141–61.

104 For Galba see 8,5 and for a possible connection in men's minds with Nerva,

Syme, *Tacitus* 150 and 576f. Pliny talks of nobles who had nothing of worth to show except *imagines* (*Epp.* 5,17,6).

105 Gracchus (2,143–8 and 8,201–10) may have been the grandson of the Gracchus who was *comes* of Lucius Caesar; cf. Groag *R.E.*, *s.v. Sempronius* 58, 2A2, 1427f. For a performing magistrate at Ostia at the end of the 2nd C. A.D. see Cass. Dio 76,8,2 and Meiggs, *Roman Ostia* 423f.

106 E.g. Ch. Wirszubski, *Libertas as a political idea* (Cambridge, 1950), 55. But against Juv. 8,19f. must be set *aequa ibi libertas* (8,177) of the proconsular official surrounded by the lowest company in a dive (see *Lustrum* 8 (1963), 199f.).

107 *Epp.* 4,25. The provincial maladministration testified to by Tac. *Agr.* 6,2 continued; see Plin. *Epp.* 3,4,2: 6,22, and Brunt, *Historia* 10 (1961), 189–227.

108 On the *novus homo* as a rhetorician's *exemplum* see Val. Max. 3,4 and Sen. *Contr.* 2,4,13; for the imperial reality see Tac. *Ann.* 3,53; Strasburger, *R.E.*, *s.v. Novus Homo*, 17 (1936), 1223–8 and J. Vogt, *Homo novus* (Stuttgart, 1926).

109 1,129ff. On Julius Alexander see Furneaux on Tac. *Ann.* 15,28,4; for his probable tenure of the praetorian prefecture see *P. Hib.* 215 and E. G. Turner, *J.R.S.* 44 (1954), 54–64.

110 2, 159–70 (on corrupting the provincials); 15,110ff. (on provincial oratory; cf. J. R. C. Martyn, *Hermes* 92 (1964), 121–3). Compare Tacitus' criticisms of Romanization at *Agr.* 21, and W. Liebeschuetz, *C.Q.* 16 (1966), 126–39.

111 E.g. 1,24–9, 102–9, 129–31; 3,58–125 (note particularly 61–5); 7,14–16.

112 For their rise to political power, Mart. 2,29; Syme, *Tacitus* 510f.

113 Tac. *Ann.* 15,44; cf. Syme, *Tacitus* 530; Mart. 10,65 (a poem of racial contrasts between East and West); the earlier rhetorical tradition is exemplified by Cicero's *pro Flacco*; A. N. Sherwin-White, *Racial Prejudice in Imperial Rome* (Cambridge, 1967).

114 3,12–16; 6,159f.; 14,96–106; cf. Tac. *Hist.* 5,2–5; Sen. *Epp.* 95,47; H. J. Leon, *The Jews of Ancient Rome* (Philadelphia, 1961), 41f., 234f.; E. M. Smallwood, *C.Ph.* 51 (1956), 1–13; Sherwin-White op. cit. (n. 113 above), 98ff.

115 Compare the attitude of Martial, e.g. 10,76; see Green, *Juvenal* 25–35; *id. Essays in Antiquity* (London, 1963), 184.

116 See Plin. *Epp.* 7,29; 6,31, 9–11; 3,14,1 (and Sherwin-White *a.l.*); A. M. Duff, *Freedmen in the Early Roman Empire* (Oxford, 1928), esp. 10ff. and 30f. On inscriptions from Ostia see R. Meiggs, *Roman Ostia* 217–24: these confirm the Semitic origin of many freedmen, but suggest some social responsibility and also friendly relations with the *patronus* (the last point confirms Pliny's picture).

117 E.g. 1,92f.; 6,219f.; 6.475–95; 14,15–22. For the arrogant slave: 3,131 and 5,59–75; for the slave informer: 9,118f.

118 On compassion towards slaves see e.g. Plin. *Epp.* 5,19 and 8,1 and Dill, *Roman Society*, 257f. Such liberality and compassion may not have been representative; see Sherwin-White on Plin. *Epp.* 5,19,1; also Westerman, *R.E. Supplbd* 6,1935, *s.v. Sklaverei*, 1053–4; W. Richter, *Gymnasium* 65 (1958), 196–218; J. Vogt, *Sklaverei und Humanität*, *Historia Einzelschr.* 8 (1965). For examples of enlightened imperial policy see Suet. *Claud.* 25,2, *id. Dom.* 7; *Dig.* 1,6,2 and *S.H.A. Hadr.* 18,7f.

119 Contrast the sneer of Mart. 12,32 with the pity of Juv. 3,200–9; see also 3,257–67. Sometimes the poor man is according to Juvenal's brief the object of envy (10,25f.) or pity (esp. 3, e.g. 282–301). Sometimes pity is combined with contempt as in the self-induced humiliation of the *cliens* in *Sat.* 5 or of the husband in *Sat.* 6.

120 E.g. Mart. 2,66 and Juv. 6,487–96; Mart. 1,96 and Juv. 2; Mart 3,38 and Juv. 3. On the social attitudes of Juvenal and

Martial see R. Marache, *R.C.C.M.* 3 (1961), 30–67.

121 J. D. Duff, comm. intro. xxxvif. warns against using Pliny without reservation; but see Sherwin-White on Plin. *Epp.* 3,1,5; 1,14,4; 7,24,3. On moral integrity in a Cisalpine town see Plin. *Epp.* 1,14,6. See also A. Serafini, *Studio sulla satira di Giovenale* (Florence, 1957), 16, who believes that Juvenal gives a substantially true picture of contemporary Roman morals.

122 Plin. *Epp.* 6,31,4; *S.H.A. Hadr.* 2.7.

123 For educated women in Pliny see e.g. *Epp.* 1,16,6 and 5,16; for the theory see Musonius Rufus 4 (pp. 13–19 Hense), and Van Geytenbeek, op. cit. (ch. 6 n.13 above), 51–77. Pliny's own devoted child-wife who set to music her husband's verses (*Epp.* 4,19; cf. 8,10) is far removed from the arrogant female captain of culture deplored by Juvenal and Martial (see n. 59 above).

124 Quint. 2,4,22–3; see also Sen. *Epp.* 89,22, Plin. *N.H.* 14,137–50.

125 See e.g. Plin. *Epp.* 1,14,9.

126 See Sherwin-White on Plin. *Epp.* 2,20,7, who quotes Juv. 3 and 12,93–130; on *captatio* see the many references in Martial, e.g. 4,56 and 5,39 and the anecdote at Plin. *Epp.* 8,18.

127 On the satirist's need for moral integrity see 4,106; on the qualities of the reputable teacher 7,215–43; cf. Plin. *Epp.* 3,3,4–6.

128 Juvenal's moralizing may be compared with that of his contemporary Plutarch, who dedicated his *de cohibenda ira* to C. Minicius Fundanus (*cos.* A.D. 107); see Syme, *Tacitus* 538. On similarities of technique between Plutarch and satire see D. A. Russell, *G.&R.* 15 (1968), 145 and *id. Plutarch* (London, 1973), 29f. for a vigorous example of moralizing in Plutarch.

129 15,106–9; the poem's sources are wider than the Stoics: see Highet 285.

130 Juv. 13,120–3; Hor. *Epp.* 1,1,14.

131 Stoics: in addition to n.129 above, 13, 184–5 (a compendious *exemplum*); Epicurus: 13,122–3; 14,319. Juvenal

associates rhetoric and philosophy at 15,106–12; Quintilian (10,1,35f.) advocates the value of some philosophical knowledge for the orator. Highet's view, *T.A.Ph.A.* 80 (1949), 254–70, that Juvenal's later satires show a 'conversion' to Epicureanism is thus based on rhetoricians' commonplaces.

132 Pythagorean eccentricity (3,229); hypocritical 'philosophers', *Sat.* 2 (cf. Mart. 9,47). On the Roman prejudice see e.g. Tac. *Agr.* 4,3 (and Ogilvie-Richmond *a.l.*).

133 Quint. 11,1,50. Any technical distinction between 'philosopher' and 'sophist' (Philostr. *Vit. Soph. praef.* 1 and 1,1; cf. Sherwin-White on Plin. *Epp.* 1,10,2) was no doubt blurred in practice.

134 On the career of Favorinus see Philostr. *Vit. Soph.* 1,8; (489) A. Barigazzi, *Favorino di Arelate, Opere* (Florence, 1966), 3–12 (friendship with Plutarch, 5 and n. 5; on his relationship with Hadrian and exile, 6–9). Favorinus' exile is regarded as uncertain by G. Bowersock, *Greek Sophists in the Roman Empire* (Oxford, 1969), 36.

135 Plin. *Epp.* 1,10,2–11; Philostr. *Ap. Ty.* 8,7,11; 5,38. On the social advancement of the sophists, Sherwin-White on Plin. *Epp.* 1,10,8 and on their pretensions, Syme, *Tacitus* 505–12. In the best philosophic tradition Euphrates committed suicide by taking hemlock (Cass. Dio 69,8,3); on the career of Euphrates see P. Grimal, *Latomus* 14 (1955), 370–81.

136 3,116–18; see Tac. *Ann.* 16,30–2 (and Furneaux on ch.32) and Syme, *Tacitus* 553f.

137 On Demetrius the Cynic (*P.I.R.*[2] D 39) see Sen. *Epp.* 20,9; 67,14; but note Tac. *Hist.* 4,40. The dossier in *P.I.R.*[2] is not consistently edifying.

138 The philosopher in Rome who was ready to sing (Lucian *Nigr.* 24f.) will not have been a novelty. For an indictment of the philosophers see Syme, *Tacitus* 552–4; but see also 538; on the expulsion of philosophers from Rome see Sherwin-White on Plin. *Epp.* 3,11,2.

139 On the *exemplum* see Quint. 5,11;
Volkmann, *Die Rhetorik der Griechen und Römer*, 233–9; on the book of historical *exempla* by Valerius Maximus see E. Norden, *Antike Kunstprosa* I (Stuttgart, 1958⁵), 303f.' also G. Bendz, Eine lateinische Exemplabiographie, *ΔΡΑΓΜΑ M. P. Nilsson*, 56–66.

140 E.g. Achilles as docile pupil (7,210); mad Ajax as analogy for behaviour of Tiberius (10,84); Tagus and Pactolus, the gold-bearing rivers (14,299); the gates of Egyptian Thebes and the mouths of the Nile (13,26f.); on geographical lore in Lucan see Heitland's intro. to Haskins' commentary, lxxiv.

141 10,58–107; see Syme, *Tacitus* 255f.

142 B. Lavagnini, *Athenaeum* 25 (1947), 87f. quotes Plut. *praec. rep. ger.* 27,820F and Diog. Laert. 5,77 as parallels for Juv. 10,61–4; see also Dio Chrys. 37,20f. and Lucian *Cat.* 11.

143 Plin. *Pan.* 52; for a modern parallel see the well-known photographs of the destruction of the statue of Stalin in Budapest, 1956.

144 6,115–32. The degrading contrast is emphasized: *rivales divorum* (115); *meretrix Augusta* (118); *tuum, generose Britannice, ventrem* (124; note the high style of the apostrophe and the oblique reference of the possessive adjective). On prostitutes see Herter, *R.A.C. s.v.* Dirne, 3 (1960), 1154–87 esp. 1164f.

145 Both Pliny, *N.H.* 10,172 and Cassius Dio, 60,31,1 testify to Messalina's play-acting as a lecherous prostitute; Tacitus' narrative of Messalina's career is incomplete, but the description of her irresponsible grape-harvest festival and assumption of the role of Maenad (*Ann.* 11,31) suggests that Juvenal's account is at least *ben trovato*. For the details from a *controversia* see Sen. *Contr.* 1,2,1, 7 and 21 (see De Decker, *Juvenalis declamans*, 29 n. 2).

146 8,251f. The size of Germanic tribesmen was remarked on by Juvenal's contemporaries, e.g. Tac. *Germ.* 20; for gruesome rhetorical conceits see e.g. 3,260 (cf. Luc. 9,787f.) and 10,186.

147 Val. Max. 4,4 proem; Juv. 6,167–77; Martial likewise makes comic use of the example of Cornelia (11,104). The white sow is a sardonic reference to Verg. *Aen.* 8,81ff.

148 Aesch. *Supp.* 226; Seneca is particularly fond of this analogy, e.g. *Clem.* 1,26,3; *de Ira* 2,8,3; cf. Sen. *Contr.* 2,1,10. The persistence of some ancient *exempla* is remarkable; see the criticisms at Aug. *Civ. Dei* 1,19.

149 5,149–55; cf. 14,134. The occurrence of an image in a similar style at 6,365, O 15f. may be used as an argument in favour of the genuineness of the O lines; see *Lustrum* 8 (1963), 182f.

150 For the snake simile see Verg. *Aen.* 2,379ff. and for pallor in such a situation *Il.* 3,35. For Caligula's contest see Suet. *Calig.* 20.

151 Cf. *Il.* 9,323f. For a description of the paralytic with an admixture of disgust see Plin. *Epp.* 8,18,9.

152 10,258–71 (265–70 are quoted p. 131). See Verg. *Aen.* 2,501–53 and for the monosyllabic line ending *bos* to express the fall of the animal ib. 5,481; on Priam see also Cic. *Tusc.* 1,85.

153 14,207 is introduced as a *sententia* (205). For characteristic examples of the incisive *sententia* note: *qui Curios simulant et Bacchanalia vivunt* (those who simulate the example of men like Curius but live a life of revelry, 2,3) and the ironical brevity of *mulio consul* (a consul turned driver, 8,148) and of 2,57. On Juvenal's use of *sententiae* see De Decker, *Juvenalis declamans* 154–66.

154 On the problem of the text see *Lustrum* 8 (1963), 175. Juvenal's disclaimers need not be taken too seriously, as the context seems far removed from immediate contemporary relevance.

155 On the rhetorical question and *anaphora* in Juvenal see De Decker, 177–98.

156 4,34–6 (parody invocation). Note also the parody of imperial flattery, e.g. Sen. *Apoc.* 4 in *saecula* (68) and the mockery of the high style's periphrasis of

numbers at lines 16–17. I owe the last two points to Mr E. Courtney.

157 5,46; see Mart. 14,96.

158 On Juvenal's use of the periphrasis for a proper name see Duff on 3,25. *Veneris . . . marito* (7,25); *quantum, Epicure, tibi parvis suffecit in hortis* (14,319). On Lucan's use of the apostrophe see Heitland's intro. to Haskins' ed. lxxf.

159 6,634–7. On the closing part of this satire see M. P. O. Morford, *C.Ph.* 67 (1972), 198. Mythological horrors are also surpassed by the terrible tale from Egypt (15,29).

160 On colloquialisms see Highet 295; for Greek words to describe affectations see e.g. 3,67f. (cf. 11,148); 5,121; 6,195 (explained by the context, 185–99); for the Greek *sententia* see 9,37 (a Homeric parody) and the gnomic Delphic utterance at 11,27. On Juvenal's Hellenisms see also W. S. Anderson, 'Juvenal and Quintilian', *Y.Cl.S.* 17 (1961), 54–7.

161 4,29; cf. 10,138 (this passage sneers at pretensions). On poetic vocabulary created out of metrical necessity see M. Leumann, *Mus. Helv.* 4 (1947), 128f. On archaic forms in Juvenal see Duff on 15,157.

162 On hyperbole in Juvenal see E. L. Harrison, *C.R.* 10 (1960), 99–101.

163 On poetic language in Juvenal see B. Axelson, *Unpoetische Wörter* (Lund, 1945), 142 and Highet 295f. Not all that is claimed as 'poetical' in Juvenal is so: e.g. *arbor* (12,32) in the sense of a ship's mast, is, against Highet and W. Kroll, 264 n. 43, the common usage of the time (see Duff *a.l.*). On Juvenal's metrical technique see G. Eskuche in Friedlaender's edn 57–80; A. Ollfors, *Studien zum Aufbau des Hexameters Lucans* (Göteborg, 1967), who provides valuable material for comparison. Sometimes what is perhaps a calculated device is interpreted as loose versification, as at 1,159 where the monosyllabic ending *nos* seems to express the arrogant condescension of the gaze from above; but see Raven, *Latin Metre* (London, 1965), 102.

164 For Hadrian's verses see *Frg. Poet. Lat.* (Morel), pp. 136f.; on his literary tastes and interests H. Bardon, *Les empereurs et les lettres latines* (Paris, 1940), 425–47. For Fronto's views on Lucan, *Ant.*5 (157N = vol. 2, 104ff. Haines).

165 For Lucian's ignorance of Latin literature, W. Kroll 10, but see J. Bompaire, *Lucien écrivain* (Paris, 1958), 212f. and 507f.

166 Highet 182.

167 Tertullian's knowledge of Juvenal, and Tacitus and the younger Pliny is discussed by T. D. Barnes, *Tertullian* (Oxford, 1971), 199–204; see also the section of Highet's book on the survival of Juvenal's work, which is of the greatest value. A possible exception to the grammarians' silence may be found in the three quotations by the unimportant *Ars* of Phocas (*G.L.K.* V, 414–26), who on Strzelecki's dating, *R.E.* 20, 1(1941)318, is earlier than Donatus.

168 On Servius' knowledge of Juvenal see P. Wessner, *Phil. Woch.* 49 (1929), 296–303 and 328–35. On Ausonius' debt to Juvenal see H. A. Strong, *C.R.* 25 (1911), 15 and Highet 297f., and on that of Prudentius 298. Lactantius, writing early in the 4th C., has only second-hand knowledge, 184.

169 Amm. Marc. 28,4,14; R. Syme, *Ammianus and the Historia Augusta* (Oxford, 1968), 84 and 89–93; see also *id. Hermes* 96 (1968), 494–502 and *J.R.S.* 58 (1968), 217. On Ammianus' pictures of vice in Rome see e.g. 14,6,2 and 25; the platitudinous Symmachus should not be used to correct the portrait.

170 See A. D. E. Cameron, *Hermes* 92 (1964), 363–77, who discusses the question of a Juvenal revival; see also *id. J.R.S.* 54 (1964), 15–28.

171 Highet 301. Macrobius, though knowing his work well, never mentions him by name; note the elaborate periphrasis at *Comm.* 1,92.

172 For St Jerome's citation see H. Hagendahl, *Latin Fathers and the Classics* (Göteborg, 1958), 165 and 181 (Juv. 1,15 is quoted three times). D. Wiesen, *St*

Jerome as a Satirist (New York, 1964), supposes that St Jerome's knowledge of Juvenal was more extensive; but see Hagendahl, *Gnomon* 40 (1968), 582–6.

173 H. Hagendahl, *Augustine and the Latin Classics* II (Göteborg, 1967), 477, who points out that the quotation from Juv: 6,287–95 occurs in a letter written at a time when Augustine was reading pagan authors widely.

174 On the value of Priscian's citations see Knoche, *Handschriftliche Grundlagen des Juvenaltextes, Philologus Supplbd.* 33,1 (1940), 39. Jo. Malalas, *Chron.* 10,341 (*Patr. Graec.* 97,400) is conveniently quoted by Highet 239.

175 For the theory of a double recension see F. Leo, *Hermes* 44 (1909), 600–17; see also Housman 2nd edn, xxxviii–xli and Clausen edn, xiii.

176 See Knoche op. cit. (n. 174), 68. Ch. 1 of this most valuable study gives a general history of the transmission of the text of Juvenal. See also E. Courtney, *B.I.C.S.* 14 (1967), 38–50.

177 On the manuscripts see in addition to the work by Knoche (see n. 174 above), the introductions to the editions by Housman and Clausen. For a brief account of evidence discovered in this century see also M. Coffey, new intro. to Duff's edn of Juvenal (Cambridge, 1970), lxxviii–lxxx. For a taxonomic approach to the manuscripts of Juvenal see J. G. Griffith, *Mus. Helv.* 25 (1968), 101–38.

178 Note Housman's scepticism edn Lucan, xviff.

179 There is an excellent Teubner edition of the ancient Scholia by P. Wessner, *Scholia in Iuvenalem Vetustiora* (Leipzig, 1931); on characteristics of the Scholia see G. Highet 299 and R. Syme, *Ammianus and the Historia Augusta* 86–8. On the ancient Scholia published in 1486 by G. Valla (and included in Wessner's edition) see W. S. Anderson, *Traditio* 21 (1965), 383–424. G. B. Townend, *C.Q.* 22 (1972), 376–87, in an important study on the stratification of the Scholia postulates a not particularly intelligent commentator of the first part of the 2nd

C. A.D., who none the less provided some historically significant notes based on material that was unlikely to have been still available in the later part of the 4th C. A.D. (note esp. 378f.).

180 On Heiric see Manitius, *Gesch. d. lat. lit. des Mittelalters* I, (Munich, 1911), 502.

181 See Clausen edn v and Highet 207f.

182 For renaissance commentaries see Eva M. Sanford, *T.A.Ph.A.* 79 (1948), 92–112 and also her study, *Decimus Junius Juvenalis* in P.O. Kristeller (ed.), *Catalogus Translationum et Commentariorum* I (Washington, 1960), 175–238.

183 On early printed editions of Juvenal see Highet, 317f.

184 Clausen in his edition provides a more accurate reporting of P than any of his predecessors.

185 On basic problems of editorship see prefaces to 1st and 2nd edns by Housman (Cambridge, 1931). For a brief account of modern editorial work and on the vexatious question of interpolated lines see M. Coffey, op. cit. (n. 177 above), lxxvi–lxxxiii; on the latter problem also *id. Lustrum* 8 (1963), 171–9 and E. Courtney *B.I.C.S.* 22 (1975), 147–62.

186 Gell. 3,10,11; see Kroll 280f.

187 Tetradius, the recipient of an epistle by Ausonius, essayed satire (*Epp.* 11); Rutilius Namatianus complimented his friend Lucillus on the excellence of his work in the tradition (*de Red.* 1,603); Rutilius no doubt showed partiality. A. D. E. Cameron, *J.R.S.* 57 (1967), 31–9 offers strong arguments for assigning the date A.D. 417 to Rutilius' work. On a wide range of writers see A. H. Weston, *Latin satirical writing subsequent to Juvenal* (Lancaster, 1915). The piece of elementary comic satire *Testamentum Porcelli* belongs to the 4th C.: W. Kroll, *R.E.* VA, 1020f.; text in Buecheler-Heraeus, *Petronii Saturae* (1958[7]), 346f.

188 The seventy hexameters denouncing the persecution of philosophers by a tyrannical emperor attributed by manuscript tradition to Sulpicia (not the erotic poetess of Flavian times) should not

have been given the title *Satura* by editors. Written at some time around A.D. 400, they belong to the world of fake literary antiques and pastiche exercises. The lines are referred to as *Satura* by Jahn in the preface to his edition, though 11 of the 70 lines are devoted to a pretentious invocation of the Muse. They will be found in the edition of Jahn-Buecheler, and also as poem 39 of *Epigrammata Bobiensia*, which are edited with valuable intro. and *app. crit.* by F. Munari, *Epigrammara Bobiensia* 27 (Rome, 1955), 91f. There is an excellent edition and discussion by H. Fuchs, *Discordia Concors, Festschrift für Edgar Bonjour* (Basle and Stuttgart 1968), 32-47. Fuchs assigns it to a date no earlier than 5th C. and regards *SHA* as a likely influence.

NOTES TO CHAPTER 8 (VARRO)

1 The standard reference text is that included in F. Buecheler and W. Heraeus, *Petronii Saturae* (Berlin and Zürich, 1958[7]); this edn also contains useful indices of proper names, metrical forms and *memorabilia*. Also of value is the edition by A. Riese, *M. Terenti Varronis Saturarum Menippearum Reliquiae* (Leipzig, 1865); this volume includes the fragments of Varro's *Logistorici*, earnest works without any humour, and an *index verborum* to the Menippeans. An important work in progress is the text and commentary by J.-P. Cèbe, *Varron, Satires Ménippées* I: *Aborigines – Andabatae* (Rome, 1972) and II: Ἀνθρωπόπολις – *Bimarcus* (Rome, 1974).

There are useful exegetical studies by J. Vahlen, *Coniectanea in M. Terentii Varronis Saturarum Menippearum Reliquias* (Leipzig, 1858) and by F. Buecheler, *Rh.M.* 14 (1859), 419-52 and 20 (1865), 401-43 (= *Kleine Schriften* I, 169-98 and 534-80). The most important contribution to the

elucidation of Varro's Menippeans is that of E. Norden, 'In Varronis Saturas Menippeas observationes selectae', *Jahrbücher für klassische Philologie, Supplbd.* 18 (1892), 267-358 (= *Kleine Schriften zum klassischen Altertum*, ed. B. Kytzler (Berlin, 1966), 1-87).

There is nothing of consequence to help the English reader except in the translation of Th. Mommsen, *The History of Rome*, vol. 5 (London, 1913), 484-94, whose long note on 492, having started with the warning that these works are 'known to so few and so irksome to study' gives a model *résumé* of the contents of three of them (= *Römische Geschichte* III (Berlin, 1933[14]), 604-11).

O. Weinreich in his *Römische Satiren* 35-50, translates a selection of fragments including all from *Eumenides*.

2 Year of birth: St Jer. on year 1901. His birthplace is attested by Symm. *Epp.* 1,2 and confirmed by his membership of the Quirine tribe (see Cichorius, *Röm. Stud.* 191). On the beauty of Reate see Cic. *Att.* 4,15,5 and *Scaur.* 27 and on the fertility of the district Varr. *R.R.* 1,7,10. B. Tilly, *Varro the Farmer: A Selection from the Res Rusticae* (London, 1973), pl. 1 shows a general view of Reate (Rieti).

3 Whether he was directly descended from the consul is uncertain: Cichorius, *Röm. Stud.* 190 but also Shackleton Bailey on Cic. *Att.* 2,20,1. On the consul of 216 B.C. Liv. 22,34, *M.R.R.* I 247, Scullard 49.

4 As owner of villas Cic. *Fam.* 9,1,2; M. Jaczynowska, *Historia* 11 (1962), 499 and as landowner Varr. *R.R.* esp. 2 *Praef.* 6.

5 Gell. 13,12,6. *M.R.R.* II 484.

6 On the probable date of his quaestorship see Cichorius, *Röm. Stud.* 219f.

7 See the study by Cichorius, *Röm. Stud.* 191-207.

8 The date of his tribunate is quite uncertain; that of his praetorship probably shortly after 76 B.C.: see *M.R.R.* II 473 and 466 and for his naval command against the pirates *R.R.* 2, *Praef.* 6.

9 On *Trikaranos* see p. 153; for the land commission *R.R.* 1,2,10, Plin. *N.H.* 7,176 and for the political circumstances R. Astbury, *C.Q.* 17 (1967), 403–7.

10 On the Spanish campaign T. Rice Holmes, *The Roman Republic* III (Oxford, 1923), 51–77.

11 Suet. *Jul.* 44,2.

12 Varro was very rich indeed: D. Brutus ap. Cic. *Fam.* 11,10,5; Syme, 31. According to the hostile testimony of Cicero (*Phil.* 2,103f.) Marcus Antonius turned Varro's villa into a sex casino (*deversorium libidinum*).

13 The evidence for the life of Varro is set out by H. Dahlmann, *R.E. Supplbd* 6 (1935), art. M. Terentius Varro, (1935), 1173–81.

14 *Catus de lib. educ.* (*Logist.* 19R, from Nonius 155L) describes a boyhood experience of simple clothes and a horse without a saddle.

15 Gell. 16,8,2 and Cic. *Brut.* 205f.; on Stilo see Leo, *Gesch.* 362 and p. 21 above.

16 Cic. *Acad. post.* 1,12; for the probable date see Cichorius, *Röm. Stud.* 225. For Antiochus' place in the history of the Academy see O. Gigon, *Mus. Helv.* 1 (1944), 47–64 and for his influence on Varro Cic. *Fam.* 9,8,1 and Aug. *Civ. Dei* 19,3. According to A. Dihle, *Rh.M.* 108 (1965), 176–9, Varro oversimplified the doctrine of his teacher.

17 F. Della Corte, *Varrone: Il terzo gran lume romano* (Genoa, 1970²) gives a general account of the life and writings of Varro; the best comprehensive treatment is that of Dahlmann, op. cit. (n. 13 above).

18 On Varro's philosophical position see A. A. Long, *Hellenistic Philosophy* (London, 1974), who discusses him in relation to Antiochus (222–9, esp. 225). For Stoic influence on him see Pohlenz, *Die Stoa* I 265–9 and II 136ff. and for Pythagorean Plin. *N.H.* 35,160, Gell. 3,10; Della Casa, *Nigidio Figulo* rev. H. Thesleff *Gnomon* 37 (1965), 44–8; A. D. Nock, *C.R.* 43 (1929), 61 n. 1.

19 His wife Fundania was the daughter of C. Gallus Fundanius, a character in the dialogue *de Re Rustica*; see Cichorius, *Röm. Stud.* 206f. and 240.

20 *Att.* 2,20,1 (see Shackleton Bailey *a.l.*); 2,22,4; 2,25,1; 3,15,3.

21 *Men.* 44. Fragments of the Menippeans are quoted by the numbering of the edition of Buecheler-Heraeus; see n. 1 above. This satire may have had the title *Baiae.*

22 *Fam.* 9,3,1; Rice Holmes, *The Roman Republic* III 277.

23 The protracted stages in which Cicero's resolve overcame his hesitant scruples are found in *Att.* 13,12; 13; 14; 16; 18; 19; 21a; Atticus' hint at Varro's higher standing is reported at 13,19,3 (see Shackleton Bailey, *a.l.*).

24 *Att.* 16,12; cf. 16,11,3.

25 The text printed is that of the Teubner edn by Plasberg (1922).

26 Quint. 10,1,95. The text followed here is the *O.C.T.* by M. Winterbottom, as also his interpretation of the passage, *B.I.C.S. Supp.* 25 (1970), 191. Cicero as speaker in *Ac.* 1,9 comments courteously on the elegance of Varro's verses in almost every metre.

27 Cichorius, *Röm. Stud.* 209. Varro's metaphorical title, in which the world is a mixed drink in a bowl that is stirred by the ladle of warfare, is Hellenistic, e.g. Alexander's cup of international friendship (Plut. *Virt. Alex.* 1,6 (= 329C); cf. Chrysippus' κυκεών, mixed drink (*S.V.F.* II 937). The second half of Varro's title is explicit, περὶ φθορᾶς κόσμου (concerning the destruction of the world).

28 Fighting in N. Africa: Plut. *Pomp.* 11,12; the reference is not to the battle of Thapsus (46 B.C.) as stated by Buecheler, I 545. Varro's resumption of military life: *Men.* 223; Dahlmann, op. cit. (n. 13 above) 1176.

29 Cic. *Man.* 30, Appian *B.C.* 1,119. The same satire may refer to the transfer to Rome of the royal treasure of Nicomedes of Bithynia who died 74 B.C. (197; Cichorius, *Röm. Stud.* 213). For the meaning of the title see Plato *Euthyd.* 272C, which as is argued by P. Lenkeit,

Varro's Menippea 'Gerontodidaskalos' (Cologne, 1966), 87–90, Varro used ironically.

30 On references in the work to Varro's career, Cichorius, *Röm. Stud.* 218ff.

31 Pompey's action is vividly described by Plutarch (*Pomp.* 22). Varro as Pompey's mentor, Gell. 14,7,2.

32 364; Varro's visit is confirmed by the geographer Solinus, 11,6.

33 Appian, *B.C.* 2,9, calls Varro συγγραφεύς and the work βίβλιον. There is no other reference to Τρικάρανος and no fragments are extant; on it see Henriksson, *Griechische Büchertitel* (Helsinki, 1956), 164ff. and Weinreich LXXII. Shackleton Bailey on Cic. *Att.* 2,20,1 contradicts the frequently maintained view that Τρικάρανος was an attack on the Triumvirate.

34 This catalogue derives from information provided by Varro himself: Hendrickson, *C.Ph.* 6 (1911), 334–43; Ritschl, *Rh.M.* 6 (1848), 481–560 (= *Opuscula* vol. 3, 527ff.); note the quotation from it given at Schanz-Hosius I⁴ 556; see also Dahlmann 1181–3.

35 Riese, ed. 38–47, discusses the problems of attributing grammarians' fragments to the Menippeans: some titles are referred to as Menippean or as Cynic; other criteria are περί as second title, works with fragments in prose and verse, proverbial titles. On περί titles see n. 39.

36 See Lindsay, *Nonius Marcellus' Dictionary of Republican Latin* (Oxford, 1901), 100–12 for Nonius' sources; as with his other authors Nonius' quotations of Varro are in rising sequence (see ch. 4 p. 39).

37 Dahlmann 1268 and Knoche 35 are judiciously sceptical about attempts to reconstruct any of the satires.

38 Gell. 2,18,7; 13,31,1; Probus on Verg. *Ecl.* 6,31 (p. 336 T-H). Varro was sometimes referred to by grammarians as *Menippeus* (Charis. *G.L.K.* I 118,8; Diom. 371,26).

39 On double titles in general including those of Varro see ch. 9 n.6 and on Greek background to Varro's περί... titles Henriksson op. cit. (n. 33 above), 26–30.

40 The fragments are collected in Riese's ed. of *Sat. Men.* (see n. 1 above), 247–59); for modern discussion see Dahlmann 1261ff. and Schanz-Hosius I⁴ 560f.

41 A title expressing exasperation in less tolerant terms is ἕως πότε ('how long' sc. 'am I to put up with this?'); cf. Ev. Matt. 17,17. A serious metaphorical title such as κοσμοτορύνη, the ladle of the world (see n. 27 above) may have frivolous associations: θεατροτορύνη, 'the thing that made the theatre stir', was the nickname of a whore (Athen. 4,157A).

42 Naev. *Triphallus*, 96–8R³; Arist. *Triphales* frg 542ff. K. On Triphallus see Herter, *De Priapo* (Giessen, 1932), 175, referring to *Priap.* 83,9; κοσμοτορύνη is ultimately based on e.g. Arist. *Pax* 259ff.

43 Timocles, a writer of Middle Comedy (4th C. B.C.), in his *Orestautocleides* (25K) ridiculed a pathic. Oedipus and Thyestes were by-words for incestuous, or otherwise complicated, family relationships; see the joke in Andoc. *Myst.* 129.

44 Liv. Andr. had the title *Aiax mastigophorus* (15–17R³). Stramineus is sometimes used of straw-filled dummies, Ov. *Fast.* 5,631; cf. *stramenticius* (Petr. 63,8); see Buecheler I 537.

45 Here too there is a dramatic tradition in such titles as Pherecrates' Ψευδηρακλῆς (154K).

46 The proverb is mentioned by Cicero (*Att.* 1,19,2; see Shackleton Bailey *a.l.*) and Gellius (13,29,5), who quotes the Varro title as his source. Lentil soup was the fare at the Cynic symposium described at Athen. 4,156C–F. Cicero discusses εὐκαιρία at *Fin.* 3,45; (see also *S.V.F.* III 630 for the place of εὐκαιρία in virtue).

47 e.g. Archippus' title ἡ ὄνου σκία (the donkey's shadow), i.e. those who quarrel over trifles (Schol. Ar. *Vesp.* 191); Cratinus *Deliades* 24K mentions a

proverb that becomes a Menippean title in Varro, δὶς παῖδες οἱ γέραντες (old men are children twice over).

48 The view of Norden, *obs. sel.* 290–2, well supported by 324B; χωρισμός is used of death by Plato, e.g. *Phaed.* 67D. Hirzel, *Der Dialog* I 449, suggests that the subject was the health of body and soul. The proverb was used by the republican poet Pompilius (Varr. *L.L.* 7,28); its normal application will be found at Symm. *Epp.* 10,1,3 (letter to the elder Theodosius), cf. 1,31,1. On the metre (end of iambic trimeter or trochaic tetrameter) see Otto p. 232 n. 3 and on metrical titles in Varro and in mimes O. Skutsch, *R.C.C.M.* 2 (1960), 197f.

49 Norden, *obs. sel.* 324 quotes Plat. *Rep.* 5,479C with Schol. *a.l.,* Athen. 10,452Cff. and Ar. *Thesm.* 130–43.

50 Gell. 13,11 (cf. 1,22,4f.) = 333–41.

51 The description is that of Buecheler I 562, whose reconstruction along with that of Vahlen, *coniect.* 168–92 is elaborated by Norden, *obs. sel.* 329–46.

52 On similar personifications see Kenney on Lucr. 3,931–77 (p. 212).

53 E.g., 132 is in the tradition of verses describing orgiastic ritual; cf. Eur. *Bacch.* 150 and Pfeiffer on Call. *Iamb.* 3, frg 193,35. Varro's metre is galliambic.

54 122; cf. Cic. *Div.* 2,119, but the interpretation here is conjectural.

55 The criterion of the Academy is suggested by Vahlen, *coniect.* 183. The oppressive emphasis on insanity in this satire should be considered in relation to the Stoic paradox that all men except the sage are mad.

56 The title *Sexagesis* (= *sexagenarius*) is a linguistic oddity; see Walde-Hofmann, *Lat. etym. Wörterb. s.v. sex,* and Buecheler I 554 n.1.

57 Tert. *An.* 55 and Waszink *a.l.* (p. 560) on Stoic *Endymiones* (they associated Endymion in the plural with the moon). Lucian's *Icaromenippus* (15f.), in which Menippus looks down from the moon on the sensational vices in palaces and the even more comical doings in low places, is no guide to Varro.

58 Norden, *obs. sel.* 298–306. Hercules was the hero of the Cynics' moral athleticism (Athen. 13,561D); see also Varro's title *Hercules Socraticus* 211f.) and on moral askesis e.g. Diog. ap. D.L. 6,27, Sen. *Epp.* 88,18.

59 Norden's convincing discussion (*obs. sel.* 278–80) of the *Bimarcus* is followed here, but any reconstruction is of course tentative; see also Vahlen, *coniect.* 128–46. E. Laughton, *C.R.* 6 (1956), 36–8 rightly warns against the uncritical use of the Menippeans for Varro's biography. O. Skutsch, *H.S.C.Ph.* 76 (1972), 170f., proposes an emendation of frg. 45 and its context.

60 See ch. 4 of Lily Ross Taylor's *Party Politics in the age of Caesar* (Berkeley and Los Angeles, 1949).

61 Plut. *Lucull.* 7,5–6.

62 Cicero's portrait in *pro Caelio* is that of a hostile counsel, but clearly Clodia was without moral scruple. Assuming the identification with Catullus' Lesbia to be correct, the promiscuous appetite deplored in *Cat.* 58,5 is reminiscent of Varro 192. The Flora mentioned at 136 is probably Pompey's adored mistress (Plut. *Pomp.* 2), for though the name was commonly used of whores, to a contemporary reader the particular application will have been inevitable.

63 Gell. 2,24,11; Macr. *Sat.* 3,17,11; Greenidge and Clay (revised E. W. Gray), *Sources for Roman History 133–70 B.C.* (Oxford, 1960²), 222.

64 Cicero, drawing on sources of the 2nd C, mentions hunting as an honourable diversion for a man of dignity and breeding: *Off.* 1,104; see also Plut. *soll. an.* 1f. (959A–960B). But note Varro's description (*R.R.* 3,13,2f.) of an artificial game reserve with a masquerade like a circus show and Sallust's tendentious condemnation of hunting (*Cat.* 4,1; cf. Syme. *Sallust* 43ff.).

65 Vahlen, *coniect.* 54–64; Norden, *obs. sel.* 326. That there are female hunters too is suggested by the reference to Atalanta (300; see Buecheler I 577 n. 1) and the

comparison with Thais, but the inference is uncertain.

66 On Varro's religious attitude in his Menippeans see Norden, *Agn. Th.* 94 and 343 n. 1 and Buecheler I 178 and 542f.

67 On the Cynic attitude to Democritus see Z. Stewart, *H.S.C.Ph.* 63 (1958), 184–7, who suggests that the laughing Democritus as contrasted with the 'Stoic' Heraclitus was invented by someone 'within the general circle of Menippus'.

68 Fragments of Varro's Menippeans with Hercules as part of the title: 211–16 (Buecheler I 571); the fragments of Varro's *Prometheus* are 423–36. On the problems of Cynic interpretations of Hercules and Prometheus see R. Höistad, *Cynic Hero and Cynic King* (Uppsala, 1948), esp. 33–7 and 57ff.

69 Z. Stewart, loc. cit (n. 67 above), 185.

70 See the edition by H. Geller, *Varros Menippea 'Parmeno'* (Diss. Cologne, 1966), to which the present discussion owes much.

71 The anecdote is found in Plut. *Qu. Conv.* 5,1,674B (also *de poet. aud.* 18C) and, without the proper name, in Phaedr. 5,5.

72 According to Norden, *obs. sel.* 276 a Roman disputes with a Greek on poetry; less convincing is the suggestion of Geller (67) that the conflict was between the archaic Roman style and neoteric hellenizing influence.

73 On 398 see Brink, *Horace on Poetry* I (Cambridge, 1963), 66f.; id. *Varron, Entr. Fond. Hardt* 9 (1962), 399; H. Dahlmann, *Varros Schrift 'de poematis' und die hellenistisch-römische Poetik* (Mainz, 1953), 112–27.

74 Fragments in *Gramm. Rom. Fragm,* (Fun.) pp. 213ff and 319–23; Dahlmann (see previous note). It is disappointing that the one extant fragment of Varro's treatise *de Compositione Saturarum* is merely a quotation of a line of verse deemed appropriate or inappropriate for satire; see Lindsay's *app. crit.* at Nonius p. 93L.

75 The proverbial title in full is ὄνος λύρας ἀκούων κινεῖ τὰ ὦτα, on hearing the lyre the donkey wags his ears (because he cannot do anything else), Leutsch-Schneidewin, I 291f., II 563.

76 Vahlen, *coniect.* 3,38; Norden, *obs. sel.* 280–4, who quotes Athen. 627A–29D; A. D. Nock, *C.R.* 43 (1929), 60f., E. K. Borthwick, *C.Q.* 16 (1966), 112.

77 Aristoxenus: Fragments and *testimonia* ed. F. Wehrli, *Die Schule des Aristoteles* 2 (1945), esp. Cic. Tusc. 1,19f. On Pythagoreanism in Varro see n. 18 above. G. Wille in his splendidly erudite *Musica Romana* (Amsterdam, 1967), esp. ch. 1, discusses the question how far Roman music was merely an adjunct of social life without notable intrinsic merit. He also discusses Varro's lighthearted apologia for music and his lost work on musical theory (410–20). Some aspects of republican music-making may have been suspect, but worse was to come in early imperial times, the nadir (allowing for satirical presentation) being Petronius' *Cena Trimalchionis* (Wille, 327ff.).

78 The Life in Diogenes Laertius (6,99–101), a debunking compilation, is entertaining but not entirely trustworthy. The best modern study is that by R. Helm, *R.E.* 15, 1 (1931), *s.v.* Menippus, 888–93; see also D. R. Dudley, *A History of Cynicism* (London, 1937), 69–74.

79 *d. mort.* 1, 1–2. All references to Menippus by Lucian must be treated with caution. Lucian has sometimes been used unguardedly as a source for Menippus, notably by Helm in *Lucian und Menipp* (Leipzig, Berlin, 1906); see the sensible remarks by Bompaire, *Lucien écrivain,* 182ff.

80 Lucian *Bis. Acc.* 33; Strab. 759 (16,2,29); Marc. Aur. 6,47.

81 Ath. 14,629E.; D.L. 6,29.

82 For the will of Epicurus see D.L. 10,16f.

83 Ath. 14,664E. On Arcesilaus see E. Zeller, transl. Reichel, *Stoics, Epicureans and Sceptics* (New York, 1962), 529–35.

84 Prob. on Verg. *Ecl.* 6,31; Athen. 1,32E.

85 Luc. *Bis. Acc.* 33; here Lucian himself is being criticized as much as Menippus; see Bompaire, 558f.

86 Varro's verses are listed and classified in Riese's edn pp. 273f. and that of Buecheler-Heraeus 352–3. On Plautine elements in the vocabulary of Varro the Plautine scholar see E. Woytek, 'Sprachliche Studien zur Satura Menippea Varros', *WSt Beih.* 2 (Vienna–Cologne–Graz, 1970), 130f. On the variety of metrical enterprise and licence in Varro, see Vahlen, *coniect.* 65–90; Buecheler I 177f., 549–56; F. Della Corte, *Varrone metricista*, in *Varron, Entr. Fond. Hardt* 9 (1962), 143–72, who emphasizes the maturity of Varro's technique, not least in his hexameters. On the choliambs see also Gerhard, *Phoenix von Kolophon*, 211 and 241.

87 E. Woytek, op cit. (n. 86 above) instances (14) 415f. and 260 as extremes of the careless and the artificial in Varro's prose. The careless *negat nescisse* attested by Nonius (851L = *Men.* 45) has rightly been corrected by O. Skutsch, *H.S.C.Ph.* 76 (1972), 170f. to *negat me scisse*.

88 Hirzel, *Der Dialog* I, 380 n. 1, quoting Cic. *Att.* 12,6,1. Varro as prose writer has his detractors, notably E. Norden, *Die antike Kunstprosa* I, 194ff. and his defenders, esp. H. Dahlmann, op. cit. (n. 13) 1275,23 and 1213,44. On Varro's prose see also E. Laughton, *C.Q.* 10 (1960), 1–28.

89 On the proverbs in the Menippeans see Buecheler-Heraeus ed. 355f. and Norden, *obs. sel.* 286 n. 1, 287 n. 1, 288,290,300; diminutives, e.g. *cultellus* (197), *nigellus* (375); word plays esp. 333–4, see R. Schröter, *Die varronische Etymologie, Entr. Fond. Hardt* 9 (1962), 81–116; some Greek words, as in Lucilius, are used for condemning luxury e.g. 533; on Varro's Greek see Dahlmann, *R.E.,* 1274,53. Kroll 255 points out that Varro's archaisms in *Men.* had no imitators.

90 Schanz-Hosius I 577 assess his literary achievement and Syme 247, his

place in contemporary politics and society. Ancient judgements include Quint. 10,1,95; 12,11,24; Apul.*apol.* 42; Ter. Maur. *de metr.* 2845–8, *G.L.K.* VI,409; Aug. *Civ. Dei* 6,2. In late Renaissance times, a few scholars composed satires that were Menippean in form and spirit, e.g. Lipsius' *Somnium suum*, an attack on inane scholarship, but their practice did not become widespread.

NOTES TO CHAPTER 9 (APOCOLOCYNTOSIS)

1 *Text*: F. Buecheler and W. Heraeus, *Petronii Saturae etc.* (Berlin, 1958[7]), still the standard reference text; O. Rossbach, *L. Annaei Senecae Divi Claudii Apotheosis per saturam quae Apocolocyntosis vulgo dicitur* (Bonn, 1926), a text with full critical apparatus.

Text and Commentaries: C. F. Russo, *L. Annaei Senecae Divi Claudii 'ΑΠΟΚΟΛΟΚΥΝΤΩΣΙΣ'*, (Florence, 1964[4]), a useful Italian commentary with text; O. Weinreich, *Senecas Apocolocyntosis* (Berlin, 1923), an excellent German commentary with translation but without text; F. Buecheler, *Symbola philologorum Bonnensium in honorem F. Ritschelii* (Leipzig, 1864–7), 33–89, a text with a commentary that contains much of value (the commentary is also to be found in Buecheler I 439–507); A. P. Ball, *The Satire of Seneca on the Apotheosis of Claudius* (New York, 1902); W. Schöne, *Seneca, Die Verkürbissung* (Munich, 1957), text, translation and short notes; W. B. Sedgwick, *Petronius, The Cena Trimalchionis* (Oxford, 1950[2]), an expurgated school edition with a few short notes. There is a bibliographical report by M. Coffey, 'Seneca, *Apocolocyntosis*, 1922–1958', *Lustrum* 6 (1961), 239–71, 309–11.

Translations: English: R. Graves, appendix to his novel *Claudius the God* (London, 1934); J. P. Sullivan, 'The deification of Claudius the clod', *Arion* 5 (1966), 378–99; W. H. D. Rouse, (with text) in Loeb edn of *Petronius* (London, 1913, rev. 1930). A more thorough revision of the Loeb edn was made in 1969 by E. H. Warmington. German: O. Weinreich, *Römische Satiren* (Zürich, 1963²), 285–304. French: R. Waltz, *Sénèque, L'Apocoloquintose du divin Claude*, with text (Paris 1934).

2 Tac. *Ann.* 12,69; 13,2 and Furneaux's note *a.l.*; cf. 1,54.

3 ὥσπερ τινὰ ἀπαθανατίσιν. The MSS. of Xiphilinus, the epitomator of Cassius Dio, are divided on the title: ἀποκολοκύντωσις, Lb C p.c.; ἀποκολοκέντωσις, C a.c. V. The nonsensical reading ἀποκολοκέντωσις is note to be used as evidence for the formation of the title or its meaning (see n. 12 below).

4 On the manuscripts and the titles given by them see Russo, op. cit. (n. 1 above), 19–26. The words *per satiram* in the title given by S are clearly a grammarian's gloss. The title *Apocolocyntosis* in the late 15th C. Vat. Lat. 4498 is even later than the manuscript; it was perhaps added by Angelo Mai (see Russo, 24). Some of the later manuscripts have titles such as *Satyra de Claudio Caesare* (Vat. Lat. 2216). A parallel for the disappearance of a Greek title is to be found in the *Halieutica*; see J. A. Richmond, *The Halieutica ascribed to Ovid* (London, 1962), 25.

5 The *Ludus* of Naevius is probably based on a Greek comedy title, Λυδός; see *Lustrum* 6 (1961), 246. On Ausonius' work see Schanz-Hosius IV² 1,31 and 37; and on *Ludus de Antichristo*, M. Manitius, *Geschichte der lat. Lit. des Mittelalters* III, 1052–6.

6 Some titles in Varro are made up of a first title in Greek followed by a second title in Greek consisting of περί followed by an abstract noun or generalization; such second titles are derived from the title of philosophical dialogues, e.g. Aristotle's Εὔδημος ἤ περὶ ψυχῆς. Second titles in comedy are in general true alternatives and not explanations of contents: see the list of titles in *C.A.F.* (Kock). On double titles see Schmid-Stahlin, *Geschichte der griechischen Literatur* I 4,79 n. 6 and R. Cantarella, *Rend. Ist. Lombardo* 93 (1959), 79f; also E. Lobel on P. Oxy. 25,2427 frg 1.

7 On the gourd see *Enc. Brit.*, *s.v.* 'gourd', and on its uses in antiquity Orth, *R.E.* I 11,2,2104–5, *s.v.* 'Kürbis', and F. A. Todd, *C.Q.* 37 (1943), 101–11. On further botanical discussion see J. L. Heller, *Homenaje a Antonio Tovar* (Madrid, 1972), 181–92.

8 Juv. 14,58; *cucurbita* is mentioned not as a symbol of stupidity but as a cupping glass for treating the insane. In a fragment of the Greek comic poet Hermippus (79K) κολοκύντη is used as an illustration of the shape of Pericles' head; nor is there a connection with stupidity at Procopius *Anecd.* 9,37 or Cassius Dio 69,4.

9 On the formation of the abstract noun with the prefix 'απο- and the termination -ωσις see *Lustrum* 6 (1961),│249f.

10 Knoche 63; Russo edn 18f., who refers to a similar view of the 17th-C. scholar Fromond.

11 Schol. Arist. *Plut.* 168; H. Wagenvoort, 'ΑΠΟΚΟΛΟΚΥΝΤΩΣΙΣ', *Mnemosyne* Ser. 3, 1 (1934), 4–27; *ib.* Ser. 4, 11 (1958), 340–2; H. J. Rose, *Handbook of Latin Literature* (1954³), 366.

12 A somewhat similar view is advocated by F. Bornmann, 'Ἀποκολοκύντωσις', *P.d.P.* 5 (1950), 69f. A cumbrous vegetable could easily suggest featureless vacuity. Compare the drawings of C. Philipon, in which the head of Louis Philippe became a pear in four stages of caricature (E. H. Gombrich, *Art and Illusion* (London, 1962²), 291). For a discussion of various hypotheses concerning the title see *Lustrum* 6 (1961), 252–4. H. MacL. Currie, *Rh.M.* 105 (1962), 187f. has since proposed ἀποκολοκένωσις as 'a scatologically humorous title'; but further emendation of a doubtful variant in Dio

is not a firm basis for hypothesis. J. Gy. Szilagyi, *Act. Ant. Ac. Sc. Hung.* 11 (1963), 235–44, takes as Seneca's immediate source of inspiration a punning comment by Nero on Claudius: *morari eum desisse inter homines producta prima syllaba* (Suet. *Ner.* 33) and, while believing that the notion of stupidity underlies the title, argues that ἀποβίωσις (departure from life) not the uncommon ἀποθέωσις is the word parodied. But Nero was not the first to jibe at Claudius' stupidity (see Suet. *Claud.* 38,3).

13 These arguments are used by G. Bagnani, 'Arbiter of Elegance', *Phoenix Supp.* 2 (Toronto, 1954), 27–46, whose theory of a *Ludus* separate from *Apocolocyntosis* is unacceptable; see *Lustrum* 6 (1961), 265.

14 On the death of Narcissus, *Apoc.* 13,2; Tac. *Ann.* 13.1; K. Münscher, *Philologus Supp.* 16 (1922), 49f.

15 Dio 60,35 reports the jibe by Seneca's brother Gallio that Claudius was dragged up to heaven by the executioner's hook.

16 J. M. C. Toynbee, *C.Q.* 36 (1942), 83–93, refuted by A. D. Momigliano, *C.Q.* 38 (1944), 96–100 (= *Secondo Contributo alla Storia di Studi Classici* (Rome, 1960), 454–61).

17 Tac. *Ann.* 12,8; 13,2; Momigliano, art. 'Nero', *Camb. Anc. Hist.* 10 (Cambridge, 1934), 702–17. On Seneca's political and literary career see Miriam T. Griffin in C. D. N. Costa (ed.) *Seneca* (London, 1974), 1–38.

18 M. Pohlenz, *Die Stoa* (Göttingen, 1959²), I 303–27; II 154–6. For a perceptive understanding of inconsistencies in Seneca's career see J. Ferguson in Dudley (ed.). *Neronians and Flavians, Silver Latin* I (London, 1972), 1–23 and for a sympathetic account of his moral philosophy, H. MacL. Currie, *ib.* 24–61.

19 Tac. *Ann.* 13,42 (cf. 12,8); Cassius Dio 60,8; 61,10. Revenge is considered to have been Seneca's chief motive in the psychological study by H. MacL. Currie, *L'Antiquité Classique* 31 (1962), 91–7.

20 Syme, *Tacitus* 590 and 784; see also

id., Colonial Élites, Rome, Spain and the Americas (London, 1958), ch. 1, esp. 18.

21 *Helv.* 6 and 9; *Polyb.* esp. 18.

22 For example strictures such as those of H. J. Rose, *Handbook of Latin Literature* (London, 1954³), 359f. based on the indictments by the informer Suillius in Tac. *Ann.* 13,42 and by Cassius Dio 61,10.

23 On the tradition of invective see R. G. M. Nisbet, *Cicero, in Pisonem* (Oxford, 1961), 192–7.

24 The speech of Augustus is decisive in the debate of the gods (see Weinreich, *Sen. Apoc.* 105). For a judicious appreciation of it see U. Knoche, *Röm.Sat.* 463–70.

25 D. McAlindon, *A.J.Ph.* 77 (1956), 113–32; *id., A.J.Ph.* 78 (1957), 279–86.

26 On Claudius' government see particularly M. P. Charlesworth, 'Gaius and Claudius', *Camb. Anc. Hist.* 10 (Cambridge, 1934), esp. 697–701, and A. D. Momigliano, *Claudius; the Emperor and his Achievement* (Cambridge, 1961²), which contains a chapter on *Apocolocyntosis*; for documents see E. M. Smallwood, *Documents illustrating the Principates of Gaius, Claudius and Nero* (Cambridge, 1967). For a protest against excesses in the rehabilitation of Claudius, e.g. by V. M. Scramuzza, *The Emperor Claudius* (Cambridge, Mass. 1940), see Syme, *Tacitus* 436–8. H. Haffter's chapter on *Apoc.* in *Römische Politik und röm. Politiker* (Heidelberg, 1967), 121–40, places it in the tradition of Roman political lampooning and scurrility.

27 Promises of future military exploits customary in early imperial verse encomia are noticeably absent; see *Lustrum* 6 (1961), 262.

28 The approval of Agrippina for *Apocolocyntosis* is advocated by A. Kurfess, *Ph.W.* 44 (1924), 1308–11 and by F. Giancotti, *P.d.P.* 8 (1953), 53–62. O. Viedebantt, *Rh.M.* 75 (1926), 142–55 and K. Barwick, *Rh.M.* 92 (1944), 159–73, regard the work as part of Seneca's attempt to discredit Agrippina and remove Nero from her influence. The theory of K. Kraft, (*Historia* 15 (1966),

96–122) that it was written in order to discredit Britannicus, the son of Claudius, is over-subtle.

29 This is the view of B. M. Marti, *A.J.Ph.* 73 (1952), 24–36.

30 Russo, op. cit. (n. 1 above), 12 n. 16, quoting *I.L.S.* 233 and *O.G.I.S.* 669. Galba was worshipped in his lifetime, Tac. *Hist.* 1,10.

31 The decree of the senate in A.D. 52 honouring the imperial freedman Pallas is fulsome; the possibility of irony, mentioned by Pliny (*Epp.* 8,6,3) only to be rejected, is accepted by Sherwin-White (on Plin. *Epp.* 7,29,3).

32 Such, however, is the view of J. Wight Duff, *Roman Satire* (Cambridge, 1937), 93, and of Lily Ross Taylor, *The divinity of the Roman Emperor* (Middletown, Connecticut, 1931), 240f. But see A. D. Nock, *Camb. Anc. Hist.* X (1934), 481–503, esp. 501. On ruler worship see also C. J. Classen, *Gymnasium* 70 (1963), 312–38 and for a major study of the early stages in Rome, S. Weinstock, *Divus Julius* (Oxford, 1971); on *Apoc.* 386ff.

33 Verg. *Ecl.* 1,6f.; Hor. *Epp.* 2.1.15ff. Cicero used similar language of Octavian, at *Phil.* 5,43, and of Julius Caesar in *Marc.* See also Weinreich's commentary, 36ff. (on *Apoc.* 4).

34 See Plutarch, *Is. et Os.* 24,360C; Diog. Laert. 9,10,60; Lucan 7,455ff. O. Skutsch, *C.Q.* 14 (1964), 89–91 (= *Studia Enniana*, 109–12) suggests that in the 1st C. A.D. *Romulus in caelo* was a popular joke at the expense of deified Caesars.

35 E.g. *quod mihi in buccam venerit* (1,2,); cf. Cic. *Att.* 1,12,4 and Mart. 12,24,4f.; *suum diem obiit* (1,1) cf. Petr. 61,9, Cic. *Fam.* 4,5,4. For a colloquial construction see e.g. *puto magis intellegi si dixero* (2,2).

36 E.g. 7,1 *ubi mures ferrum rodunt* on which see Weinreich *Apoc.* 74 n. 1 and W. H. Alexander, *C.Ph.* 30 (1935), 350–2. On proverbs in *Apocolocyntosis* see Weinreich *Apoc.* 27 n. 4.

37 Here all scholars must be par-

ticularly indebted to Weinreich's excellent discussion, *Apoc.* 13ff.

38 See Lucian, *Toxaris* 11 and 18, Weinreich, *Apoc.* 22ff.

39 9,2. Tacitus' rewriting of Claudius' speech at Lyons is the obvious example, Tac. *Ann.* 11,24 and *I.L.S.* 212 (= Smallwood, *Documents* (see n. 26 above) 369); see also Tacitus' refusal to adapt (ironically enough) Seneca's last words, *Ann.* 15,63.

40 10,2 and e.g. *Res Gestae Divi Aug.* 3. On Augustus' oratory see Suet. *Aug.* 65; 86f. and H. Malcovati, *Imperatoris Caesaris Augusti Operum Fragmenta* (1962⁴), Proleg. xxviiiff.

41 On the poetic *mise-en-scène* see Arch. Cameron, 'The Form of the Thalysia', *Miscellanea di Studi Alessandrini in memoria Augusto Rostagni* (Turin, 1963), 279–330.

42 3,4–4,1. Golden age terminology occurs also at Calp. Sic. 1,42ff., 4,6ff., *Carm. Einsiedl.* 2,21ff., based on Virgil's fourth eclogue; Seneca's verses are a pastiche, e.g. the lines describing spinning are similar to Cat. 64,311ff. See Momigliano, loc. cit. (n. 16 above), 96ff.

43 A ruler is compared with the sun in the Hymn to Demetr. Poliork. (Ath. 6,253D); Nero is a new Helios to the Greeks (Ditt. *Syll.*³ 814,34f.); cf. *Anth. Pal.* 9,178 and Weinreich, *Apoc.* 44f. The comparison of Nero with Apollo (4,1,21) is deliberate propaganda, cf. Calp. Sic. 4,159 and Cass. Dio 62,20; see *Lustrum* 6 (1961), 262.

44 Weinreich, *Apoc.* 55f. On Vespasian's final joke see D. Fishwick, *C.Q.* 15 (1965), 155–7. One of Seneca's comments at 4,3 is based on biographical fact (Suet. *Claud.* 32).

45 *cluas* (7,2) is archaic (Enn. *scen.* 366V), *altrix* is poetical, cf. *Th.L.L.* 1, 1770,58. Weinreich, *Apoc.* 62,76ff. and 113ff. suggests self-parody. The similarity of manner is more convincing than many of the verbal parallels adduced; see *Lustrum* 2 (1957), 130. G. Binder, *Rh.M.* 117 (1974), 288–317 interprets the scene as epic parody.

46 12,3. Note the ironical emphasis of the repeated *ille*: Claudius took the credit for his generals' success, a success exaggerated by the mention of the Brigantes (12,3,3ff. cf. Tac. *Agr.* 17).

47 p. 57.

48 *Od.* 9.39f. For his learning Suet. *Claud.* 41 and 42; for his Homeric citations 42,1.

49 Verg. *Aen.* 2,274. For Claudius' lameness see Suet. *Claud.* 30 and *Apoc.* 5,2. For another vicious use of Virgilian quotation see 3,2 from Verg. *Georg.* 4,90. At 11,6 Seneca applies Catullus' description of Lesbia's finch in the underworld (3,12) to Claudius; on the distorted context see Russo *a.l.* For other quotations from literary texts see Buecheler-Heraeus, op. cit. (n. 1 above) 360.

50 Thales, Diels-Kranz Vors. A 22 (= Arist. *de anim.* 411a7); see Kirk–Raven, *The Presocratic Philosophers* (Cambridge, 1957), 94, and Guthrie, *History of Greek Philosophy* I (Cambridge, 1962), 65f. The later version occurs in the anonymous *Misanthropos* of the 2nd C. B.C., Diehl, *Anth. Lyr. Graec.*[3] 3, 131–6. Compare the ironical use of the cry of salutation in the Osiris cult at 13,4.

51 On the difficulties in attributing 'Menippean motifs' to Seneca, see *Lustrum* 6 (1961), 266f. Hipponax is brought back from the dead in Call. *Iamb.* 1; Menippus had no monopoly of the νέκυια. Seneca's vigorous and topical subject matter and also his concentration of narrative contrasts with Lucian's eschatological dialogues; note e.g. the lack of climax in *Icaromen.*

52 The comic epic persiflage *The Battle of Frogs and Mice* was composed no earlier than the 1st C. B.C.: see Wackernagel, *Sprachliche Untersuchungen zu Homer* (Göttingen, 1916), 188–99.

53 The reconstruction by B. Snell, *Scenes from Greek Drama* (Cambridge: Mass., 1964), 99–138, of a Hellenistic satyr play *Agen*, which ridiculed the deification of the dead mistress of one of Alexander's generals, shows at least that apotheosis could be an occasion for ribaldry. Lloyd-Jones, however, *Gnomon* 38 (1966), 17 warns against taking *Agen* too seriously as a social document.

54 Furius Camillus Scribonianus wrote an abusive epistle during Claudius' reign demanding his abdication (Suet. *Claud.* 35,2); there had also appeared the anonymous Μωρῶν ἐπανάστασις (the resurrection of the idiots) *ib.* 38, 3.

55 On Cassius Dio's reference see n. 57 below. Suetonius does not mention *Apoc.*, for he passes quickly over the events immediately after Claudius' death (see *Lustrum* 6, (1961), 244); if he used *Apoc.* as a source, it was merely to amplify his main sources. Juv. 6,620ff. may refer obliquely to Seneca's joke about Claudius' ascent to heaven.

56 Quintilian's judgement on Seneca is discussed by Peterson, ed. of Bk 10 (Oxford, 1891), xxiv–viii. See also Austin's edn of Bk 12 (Oxford, 1954), xxiii n. 1.

57 Syme, *Tacitus* 336; cf. 539. Dio's reference to the work (60,35; see p. 166) is unexpected: F. Millar, *A Study of Cassius Dio* (Oxford, 1964), 78f. Gell. (12,2,1) admits that some detractors of Seneca's style judge that he was powerful in his castigation of vices.

58 L. D. Reynolds, *The Mediaeval Tradition of Seneca's Letters* (Oxford, 1965), 82f. and A. D. E. Cameron, *J.R.S.* 57 (1967), 32. Julian in his Συμπόσιον may have been influenced by *Apoc.*; see E. Courtney, *Philologus* 106 (1962), 88 and J. Straub, *Gymnasium* 69 (1962), 310–326.

59 Radbert, *Vit. Walae*, 457 Mab.; see F. Jonas, *Hermes* 6 (1872), 126f. On Radbert see Manitius, *Gesch.* I 401–11 esp. 411. William of Malmesbury, *Gest. Reg. Ang.* 3,269 includes *Apoc.* 4,25 in a poem of his own on the election of Lanfranc to the see of Canterbury. I owe this reference to Mr R. I. Ireland. For another example of Carolingian interest in Seneca see Sangallensis 878 (G), the scrapbook of Walafrid Strabo, abbot of Reichenau (d. 849): L. D. Reynolds, *C.R.* 7 (1957), 5–12.

60 The three principal manuscripts are described by Russo, 19–22. On the later manuscripts see Russo, 22–6, and R. Sabbadini, *R.F.I.C.* 47 (1919), 338–45. There is not as yet an adequate critical assessment of the manuscript tradition of *Apocolocyntosis*.

61 See C. F. Russo, *P.d.P.* 7 (1952), 48–65.

62 For a list of editions see Russo, 34ff.

63 Frobenius was the publisher of the Basle edition. Rhenanus refers to *Apoc.* as *fragmentum nuper in Germania repertum.* Erasmus refers to *Apoc.* as *apotheosis.* The edition of Rhenanus was sent to him in England in 1515 (W. Trillitzsch, *Philologus* 109 (1965), 283); his *Apotheosis of Reuchlin* is a colloquy of 1522. Echoes may also be detected in Erasmus' *Dialogus, Iulius exclusus e coelis* (W. K. Ferguson (ed.), *Erasmi Opuscula*, The Hague, 1933), on Pope Julius II. This work was probably written in 1513–14 in Cambridge and first circulated privately and anonymously; it was first published at Basle in 1516 (Ferguson, 41).

64 The framework of the story of *Apocolocyntosis* but not its literary form was used by Byron in his magnificent *The Vision of Judgement* (1823), a venomous parody of the poet laureate Southey's flaccid official encomium of the recently deceased Hanoverian George III, *A Vision of Judgement* (1821). Byron's masterpiece derides Southey's pretentious and sycophantic doggerel and attacks K. George's personal and political shortcomings. Byron has also recaptured Seneca's tone of nonchalant frivolity.

65 According to Suetonius (*Nero* 39), Nero was unexpectedly tolerant of scurrilities against himself, including an Atellan actor's jibe at the manner of the death of Claudius and Agrippina.

66 Compare e.g. the occupations of the frivolously busy at *Brev. Vit.* 12f. (note particularly his censure of the mime actors for failing to satirize the vices of the age adequately, 12,8) and the description of the drunks and the fast set at Baiae (*Epp.* 51,4 and 12) and of the cult of

gymnastics (15,3–4). To Quintilian (10,1,129) Seneca was a notable castigator of vices (see also n. 56).

NOTES TO CHAPTER 10 (PETRONIUS)

1 The foundation of modern critical scholarship on the text of Petronius is the *editio maior* of F. Buecheler (Berlin, 1862); the 7th edn of the *editio minor*, with revisions by Heraeus and additional notes by P. Bachmann (Berlin, 1958), contains also Varro's Menippeans and Seneca's *Apocolocyntosis*. The standard critical edns are now those of K. Müller, *Petronii Arbitri Satyricon* (Munich, 1961[1]) and *Petronius Satyrica (Schelmengeschichten)*, with German transl. by W. Ehlers (Munich, 1965[2]). Also useful but partly superseded by the work of Müller is the Budé edition by A. Ernout, *Pétrone, Le Satyricon* (Paris, 1950[3]). The only commentary of consequence on the whole *Satyricon* is that of Peter Burman (Utrecht, 1709,[1] Amsterdam, 1743[2]), incorporating notes by N. Heinsius, Jan Dousa and de Salas. There are separate editions with commentary of the *Cena Trimalchionis* by L. Friedlaender (Leipzig, 1906), a standard work, A. Maiuri (Naples, 1945). E. V. Marmorale (Florence, 1961[2]). The edition of the *Cena* with commentary by M. S. Smith (Oxford, 1975) is based on the texts of K. Müller. The best English translation is by J. P. Sullivan (Harmondsworth, 1965). Also of interest is the American translation by W. Arrowsmith, *The Satyricon of Petronius* (Ann Arbor, 1959). The Loeb text and translation by M. Heseltine (1913, rev. 1930) was sometimes inaccurate and generally undistinguished, but the revised Loeb by Warmington (1969) makes full use of the work of Müller. Segebade and Lom-

matzsch, *Lexicon Petronianum* (Leipzig, 1898) is a valuable aid to scholarship. The article by W. Kroll, *R.E. s.v. 'Petron (29)'*, 19,1 (1937), 1201–14, is exemplary.

2 Seneca in an Epistle (77,20) had advocated the need to make a good end to life (*bonam clausulam impone*); cf. his eulogy of the impressive deaths of Cato and Socrates (*Epp.* 13,14). Compare Tacitus' account of Seneca's death (*Ann.* 15,62–3; see Koestermann on 62,2 and 63,1) with that of the equally 'philosophical' death of Thrasea Paetus (16,34). The deaths of Lucan and Mela are described at *Ann.* 15.70 and 16,17.

3 Syme, *Tacitus* 336 n. 5.

4 Petronius Niger is mentioned as cos. on a Herculaneum tablet published by G. Pugliese Carratelli, *P.d.P.* 1 (1946), 381. See K. F. C. Rose, *The Date and Author of the Satyricon* (Leiden, 1971), 50 and n. 2, who suggests *c.* A.D. 61 as the date of his consulship. He was first identified with the author of the *Satyricon* by R. Browning, *C.R.* 4 (1954), 33; this identification is now widely accepted.

5 At *Ann.* 16,17 the name Petronius occurs without *praenomen*, though preceded by *ac* in the Medicean MS.; at 16,18,1 it is preceded by C in the tradition. It has been pointed out e.g. by Rose, op. cit. (n. 4) 49, that T and C are easily confused in Beneventan script. Koestermann reads *ac T. Petronius* in the first passage and deletes the *praenomen* in the second.

6 On the name in the titles of the MSS. see Müller edn 1,1. The holders of the *cognomen* Arbiter who can be identified are slaves and a soldier (Rose, 44f.). Grammarians' citations will be found in Müller's collection of the fragments (185–94).

7 Plin. *N.H.* 37,20; Nero had paid even more for a similar collector's piece; Plut. *de discr. am. et adul.* 19 (*Mor.* 60 D–E).

8 The old view was regarded as dead by Kroll, loc. cit. (n. 1 above) but was revived and amplified by U. E. Paoli, *S.I.F.C.* 14 (1937), 6ff., and presented in a most extended form by E. V. Marmorale, *La questione petroniana* (Bari, 1948). Linguistic and literacy arguments for an Antonine date have been convincingly rejected by R. Browning, *C.R.* 63 (1949), 28f. and Rose, op. cit. (n. 4 above) 9–20. For a report on the controversy see R. Muth, *Anzeig. f. d. Altertumswiss,* 9 (1956), 1–22.

9 The ingenious legal arguments of Bagnani, *Arbiter of Elegance* (Toronto, 1954), 14–24, in favour of a Neronian date (A.D. 58–65) are unconvincing; see Browning, *C.R.* 6 (1956), 45f. and Rose, op. cit. (n. 4 above) 34–7.

10 Tac. *Ann.* 12,53,3. On the relevance for Petronius see K. Latte, *Philologus* 87 (1932), 265 and Momigliano, *C.Q.* 38 (1944), 100 (= *Secondo Contr.*, 461).

11 H. T. Rowell, *T.A.Ph.A.* 89 (1958), 14–24.

12 On unbreakable glass and buried treasure see Rose, op. cit. (n. 4 above) 25; Walsh 244–7. The vulgar Trimalchio invites his guests to break wind at pleasure (47,4–6). This may be an allusion to Claudius' edict in similar terms (Suet. *Claud.* 32,5) but a man like Trimalchio may be assumed to have given such permission even without royal precedent.

13 Also 71,9. The relevance for dating was seen by R. Browning, *C.R.* 63 (1949), 12f.; see also Sherwin-White on Plin. *Epp.* 8,6,4.

14 The significance of Maecenatianus is discussed by P. R. C. Weaver, *J.R.S.* 54 (1964), 117–28, esp. 124.

15 H. C. Schnur, *Latomus* 18 (1959), 790–9. On the wine trade see also Meiggs, *Roman Ostia*, 275f.

16 P. Grimal, *R.E.A.* 53 (1951), 100–6.

17 Rose, *T.A.Ph.A.* 93 (1962), 402–5, argues for Puteoli. Attempts to identify the *Graeca urbs* (81,3) with another town, e.g. Cumae, suggested by Mommsen, and Naples (Friedlaender) are unconvincing (see Stubbe, 25 n. 3). But Walsh, 75f., regards the Greek city as a literary composite and points out that by the 1st C, A.D. Croton, the scene of later adventures, was a ghost town. Ancient writers (see

Servius on *Aen.* 1,159) made a distinction between the imaginative representation of a fictitious place (*topothesia*) and the factual description of a real place (*topographia*).

18 On Greek novel titles see K.-E. Henriksson, *Griechische Büchertitel in der römischen Literatur*, 74–7, and A. Henrichs, *Zeitschr. f. Pap. u. Epigr.* 4 (1969), 205–15, who has published fragments of a new novel by Lollianos entitled *Phoinikika* (on titles, 206); see n. 35 below.

19 Heraeus, the reviser of Buecheler's edition, which was entitled *Saturae*, would have preferred *Satyricon*; see *addenda* (p. 361) to edn 1958[7]. Van Rooy, *Studies in Classical Satire*, 154f. regards *Satyrici* as nom. sing., but *Satyrici* in a manuscript title is to be explained as gen. sing. in agreement with the name of the author. *Satyricon* is the form given in late antiquity by Marius Victorinus.

20 Derkyllos, *Satyrica* : ps–Plut. *de Fluv.* 10,3; *Frg. Gr. Hist.* III A 172 Jac.; see Henriksson, op. cit. (n. 18 above), 75 n. 1.

21 Ioann. Lyd. *mag.* 1,41 (Müller[1], *Testimonia* p. lvi).

22 Kroll 224 n. 46.

23 *Somn. Scip.* 1,2,8 (= Müller, *Test.* p. lv). On the same page Müller quotes the judgement of a Latin Father of the 3rd C. A.D., Marius Mercator, that as a master of pornography Petronius was to be classed with Martial.

24 It is possible that the episode of the peasant in the market-place and that of Quartilla which follows it preceded the debate on rhetoric; see Sullivan 35f. and 45ff. and Walsh 75.

25 According to a mediaeval gloss on Fulgentius (*Myth.* 3,8), 20,7 belongs to Bk 14. The gloss may be an interpolation; see Müller edn 1 on frg VII (p. 186). A subscript to the short excerpts in the Codex Traguriensis describes them as taken from Bks 15 and 16. In a letter dated 1423 Poggio refers to a copy of Bk 15; this is generally identified with the *Cena Trimalchionis* preserved separately in

the Trau manuscript (Traguriensis is Poggio's manuscript or a copy; see A. C. Clarke, *C.R.* 22 (1908), 178f.). According to a Glossary of St Benedict in the British Library MS (Cod. Harl. 2735), ch. 89,1, a part of the work later than the *Cena*, comes from Bk 15. As the *Cena* by itself is considerably longer than the longest book of Apuleius, it is reasonable to assume that, though manuscript evidence for book numbers is usually taken as reliable, the number given by Cod. Harl. is erroneous. Information on this last piece of evidence is given only in Müller, edn 2, 405; on the rest *ib.* 403–12 and edn 1, xxviii-xxxiii. On the transmission as a whole see Müller edn 1, vii-xxxix and edn 2, 381–420.

26 The fragments are to be found in the editions of Beucheler-Heraeus and Müller; note Müller's comment, edn 1, xlvii. Some of the verses may be by Petronius but not part of the *Satyricon*; others are almost certainly spurious. For references to events outside the extant narrative see the edition of Buecheler-Heraeus, 236. In addition to the references to Massilia (Marseilles), where part of the action must have taken place, there is also a mention of girls of Memphis in Egypt (frg XIX), probably participants in the worship of Isis.

27 Problems of reconstruction are discussed by V. Ciaffi, *Struttura del Satyricon* (Turin, 1955), Sullivan, ch. 2, Walsh, ch. 4 and H. Van Thiel, *Petron; Überlieferung und Rekonstruktion* (Leiden, 1971), 25–65.

28 E.g. Walsh 73.

29 Henry Fielding's *Tom Jones* is suggested as a possible analogy for size as well as content by Rose, *Arion* 5 (1966), 293, but the printed book may be a misleading parallel. There are good comments on episodic works in Graham Hough, op. cit. (ch. 1 n. 17 above), 20ff.

30 For scholarly literature on the Greek novel see B. E. Perry, *The Ancient Romances* (Berkeley and Los Angeles, 1967); and the chapter in B. P. Reardon, *Courants Littéraires grecs des 2e et 3e siècles après J.-C.* (Paris, 1971), who discusses

chronology in general, 333–8. On the dating of the earliest of the romances *De Semiramide et Nino* to the 2nd or 1st C. B.C. see Lesky 861.

31 The classic statement of parody of the serious novel in Petronius is that of R. Heinze, *Hermes* 34 (1899), 494–519; also Kroll 223f. and *id.*, loc. cit. (n. 1 above), 1207–10. Heinze's theory is criticized e.g. by Perry, *C.Ph.* 20 (1925), 37. Weinreich lxxviiif. regards Heinze's theory as a literary orthodoxy, but there has since been dissent; see n. 40 below.

32 The genre was regarded as disreputable, certainly in the 2nd C. A.D., for it was deemed possible to discredit an enemy by circulating an erotic novel under his name (Philostr. *Vit. Soph.* 1,22,3).

33 For possible elements of parody in Achilles Tatius see Reardon, op. cit. (n. 30 above), 338 n. 62.

34 The scene introduced by the description of a painting is, however, handled differently by the two: in Achilles Tatius it precedes the introduction of the narrator and protagonist, in Petronius it introduces in Bk 15 the charlatan Eumolpus, who quickly proceeds to retail a dirty anecdote.

35 Fragments of the *Phoinikika* of Lollianus are published by A. Henrichs, *Zeitschr. f. Pap. u. Epigr.* 4 (1969), 205–15. He points to such gems in the scene of cannibalism as the complaint: 'My piece is raw!'; he rightly instances Ach. Tat. 3,15,4 as a relevant example of human sacrifice in pretence. For the defloration he quotes, in addition to Petr. 25, Apul. *Met.* 5,4.

36 P. Parsons. 'A Greek *Satyricon?*', *B.I.C.S.* 18 (1971), 53–68 and pl. VII (*P. Oxy.* 3010). The writing of the papyrus is to be attributed to the 2nd C. A.D. The speech in Sotadeans by the *cinaedus*, compared with the rest, is full of vulgarisms (62f.). Parsons concludes that the work is 'a fragment from a Greek picaresque tradition that Petronius parallels and imitates' (66). See also the formal publication by Parsons in *P.Oxy.* 42 (1974),

3010, 'Narrative about Iolaus' and the ingenious conjecture by E. R. Dodds concerning the plot of the narrative quoted there. The Greek comic romance as forerunner of Petronius had been postulated by B. E. Perry, *C.Ph.* 20 (1925), 33 and *The Ancient Romances* (n. 30 above) 88–95 (Perry minimizes Menippean elements in Petronius).

37 Courtney, *Philologus* 106 (1962), 86–100, assesses parody of the novel in Petronius in relation to the tradition of Menippean satire.

38 Fortune (Τύχη) is important in Achilles Tatius (e.g. 4,9); see Collignon 38. As a study of the literary background to Petronius Collignon's work is of great value.

39 The basic study of the literary and archaeological evidence concerning Priapus is that of H. Herter, *De Priapo* (Giessen, 1932), whose appendix on Petronius (315–7) evaluates the evidence judiciously without exaggerating its importance. There do not seem to be good grounds in the Priapic evidence for the theory in P. Green, *Essays in Antiquity* (London, 1963), 173 and Walsh 77f. that Priapus was angry with Encolpius because of his homosexual affair. Priapus was bisexual.

40 Achilles Tatius also (2,23,3) used the ninth book of the *Odyssey* to illustrate a stratagem of escape. For the *Satyricon* as, in outline, a burlesque of the *Odyssey* see Sullivan, esp. 91–6; more radical approaches are offered e.g. by A. M. Cameron, *Latomus* 29 (1970), 397–425. For references to the *Iliad*, compare Encolpius deprived of Giton (81) with Achilles' lament for the loss of Briseis (1,348); see Walsh 36. Collignon 126–8 examines possible allusions to *Aen.* 1 and 5. It is, however, clear that Petronius' indebtedness to Virgil outside the *Troiae Halosis* is far deeper than parody or comic pastiche.

41 There is a variant in Aelian (frg 69) to the story of the Pergamene Boy (85–7); the Widow of Ephesus (111f.) is also found in Aesop 109 (Halm) and

Phaedr. *App.* 15. Petronius and Phaedrus probably derive independently from Hellenistic sources. For fragments of Sisenna see Petronius, Buecheler-Heraeus (ed.), (1958[7]), 342f., and for the scandalous qualities of Milesian tales see Plut. *Crass.* 32, Ov. *Tr.* 2,413f. As Walsh rightly argues (15ff.), Aristides did not give a narrative link to his stories and therefore is not to be regarded as a direct forerunner of Petronius.

42 Schuster, *WSt* 48 (1930), 149–78, examines in detail Greek and Roman evidence for the werewolf.

43 For the *mendax aretalogus* Juv. 15,16. There is parody of the tall story at *Apoc.* 1 and Lucian *V.H.* 1–4. On aretology e.g. that of Antonius Diogenes (c. A.D. 100) see in general Susemihl I 463–91, R. Reitzenstein, *Hellenistische Wundererzählungen* (Leipzig, 1906), who suggests (30) that Petronius' Croton belongs to such a world (it is also in the tradition of Hor. *Sat.* 2,5) and Aly, *R.E. Supplbd.* 6 (1935), 13 (referring to *P.Oxy.* 1381).

44 94,15 cf. 80,9; 106,1; 19,1, where mime is proverbial for a belly-laugh. The direct literary influence of mime is postulated by K. Preston, *C.Ph.* 10 (1915), 260–9. Sullivan 219–25 is circumspect; he realizes that farcical situations in Petronius are matter from real life as well as a literary model. The Roman mime was a dramatic representation of low life (Diomedes *G.L.K.* I 491,12–19) that was naturalistic (Quint. 4,2,53), without masks (Quint. 6,3,29), allowing naked actresses (Val. Max. 2,10,8), a lack of plot (Cic. *Cael.* 65), an immediate topicality in late republican times (Cic. *Att.* 14,2,1) and a measure of free speech even during the early empire (Mart. 1,4,3–6).

45 The bogus heroism and pathos of the quarrel scene between Encolpius and Ascyltos and the melodramatic intervention by Giton (79,9–80,8) are a characteristic example.

46 Note 10,2 and 6.

47 See P. Veyne, *R.E.L.* 42 (1964), 301–24 especially 308 n. 6.

48 On the *cena* in Roman satire see L. R. Shero, *C.Ph.* 18 (1923), 126–43.

49 Nash, *Pictorial Dictionary of Ancient Rome* II (London, 1968), 329–33; for the inscription 805, 805a Degr., J. M. C. Toynbee, *Death and Burial in the Roman World* (London, 1971), 128 and pl. 34 and 35; on Trimalchio's instructions for a funerary garden, 94f. Eurysaces' tomb is late republican, but the practice will have been imitated outside Rome.

50 Rostovtzeff, *Soc. Econ. Hist. Rom. Emp.* (Oxford, 1957[2]), 56 and pl. VII. Bagnani, *A.J.Ph.* 75 (1954), 16–39, compares Trimalchio's house with the villas of Pompeii and Herculaneum and concludes that it was old fashioned with paintings in the Augustan 'second style' and awkwardly constructed with a small bathroom and a complete lack of contemporary stylishness, thus emphasizing Trimalchio's provincial origin and small-town tastes.

51 Tac. *Ann.* 14,17 records rioting at Pompeii; see Koestermann *a.l.* and inscriptions cited there: *C.I.L.* IV 1293, 1329, 2183. There had been rioting at Puteoli in A.D. 58 (Tac. *Ann.* 13,48).

52 Rostovtzeff 57f.

53 G. Schmeling, *C.Ph.* 65 (1970), 248–51 judges that Trimalchio provided his guests with food obtained on the cheap and served clumsily. J. André, *L'Alimentation et la cuisine à Rome* (Paris, 1961), 226–8 regards Trimalchio's feast as disordered and lacking in food of high quality and therefore a parody of a pontifical banquet. On Trimalchio in relation to Nero's court see Rose, *Date and Author of the Satyricon*, 77–9; he excludes parody of Nero's entourage in the *Satyricon*.

54 Athen. 128A–130D. On the tradition in general see J. Martin, *Symposion* (Paderborn, 1931); id. *R.A.C.* 3, 658–66, *s.v.* 'Deipnonliteratur'; E. W. Handley, ed. Men. *Dysk.* p. 300 and *J.H.S.* 93 (1973), 106ff.

55 The contrast is analysed by Averil Cameron, *C.Q.* 19 (1969), 367–70.

56 G. Highet, *T.A.Ph.A.* 72 (1941), 176–94 interprets the *Satyricon* as implicit

moral condemnation of the actions of the protagonist seen by a writer whose viewpoint was that of an Epicurean who favoured freedom from disturbance. The attempt by O. Raith, *Petronius ein Epikureer* (Nuremberg, 1963), to see Petronius as an original Epicurean thinker has been adequately rebutted by R. Browning, *C.R.* 15 (1965), 67–9.

57 J. P. Sullivan, *T.A.Ph.A.* 99 (1968), 465, sees a gibe at Petronius in Seneca's description of debauchees (*Epp.* 122,4–6). But the words would have fitted other contemporaries as well, particularly the young, whom Seneca mentions explicitly.

58 The image of lovers transferring their breath and so their souls to each other is found at e.g. *Anth. Pal.* 5,78 (attributed to Plato); see the important commentary by H. Stubbe, 170f.

59 See e.g. Hor. *Sat.* 1,1,1ff. and Sen. *Epp.* 80,7.

60 The manuscript reading followed by Buecheler: *deprecatus sum numen versu* (133,2) allows Encolpius to be the self-conscious reciter of the hexameters, but the emendation *aversum* found in Burman is accepted, probably rightly, by Müller.

61 Denunciation of Cato is a commonplace, e.g. Mart. 11,2. Scholars such as Collignon, 54f., and Stubbe, 150–4, who gives a commentary on the lines, take them seriously as representing the author's personal outlook.

62 Marmorale *a.l.* calls the lines 'a piece of Petronian bravura in the style of Publilius'. See also O. Skutsch, *R.E. s.v.* 'Publilius,' 23,2 (1959), 1923f. *Honestior* in the sense of morally improving is appropriate for the passage, but for the meaning 'stylistically elegant' Skutsch refers to *Th.L.L.* VI,2913, 7ff., particularly Quint. 8,3,11. Seneca, however, (*Epp.* 8,8) refers to Publilius as a respectable moralizer.

63 Information on public porticos will be found in Platner-Ashby, *Topographical Dictionary of Rome,* 427 and on art galleries, F. Ebert, *R.E. s.v.* 'Pinacotheca', 20,2 (1950), 1389f. En-

colpius' comments on the realism of Protogenes and Apelles correspond to those in the compilation by Pliny (*N.H.* 35,79,88,102) published later than Petronius but based on a variety of earlier sources including Varro: see Jex-Blake & Sellers, *The Elder Pliny's Chapters on the History of Art* (London, 1896), intro. lxxxii-v. Pliny reflects Varro's erroneously patriotic view that painting developed early in Italy (see Jex-Blake & Sellers on Pliny 35,18).

64 Pliny (34,58) regards Myron's strength as skilful expression of physical movement not *animi sensus*, a view endorsed by modern scholars, e.g. G. M. A. Richter, *Greek Art* (London, 1959), 100f.

65 On literary elements in the rhetorical description of a picture see Stubbe 31 n. 3. Norden's classic note on *Aen.* 6,509ff. shows that even in Virgil Deiphobus' speech has the mark of a *Troiae halosis* as a rhetorical display piece in its own right.

66 For the texture of the Virgilian pastiche in detail see Collignon 133–49 and Stubbe's commentary 40–9.

67 Stubbe 93f. points out that Petronius' metrical technique in the iambics corresponds to that of Seneca's tragedies, but Strzelecki in his redoubtable analysis, *De Senecae trimetro iambico quaestiones selectae* (Cracow, 1938), states that it is impossible to separate the Senecan corpus from the non-Senecan *Octavia* on metrical grounds (2). Seneca's technique is that of his age. The insipid repetitions at the end of lines in *Troiae halosis* (on which see Stubbe, 90f.) are a mark of the author of *Octavia* more than of Seneca. For different views on *Troiae halosis* in relation to Seneca see Walsh, *C.Ph.* 73 (1968), 210 and Sullivan, *T.A.Ph.A.* 99 (1968), 459–67.

68 Stubbe 25.

69 Tacitus (*Ann.* 15,39) states that the rumour that Nero sang a *Troianum excidium* during the fire in Rome in A.D. 64 made him unpopular (Suet. *Nero* 38 and Cass. Dio 62,18 report his performance of *Halosis Ilii* in scenic garb as unquestioned

fact), but he also produced in public a work on Trojan themes in the following year (Cass. Dio 62,29; Schanz-Hosius II⁴, 427f.).

70 Tac. *Dial.* esp. 35; cf. Seneca *Epp.* 114 on the connection between Maecenas' moral degeneracy and that of his style.

71 See Dionysius of Halicarnassus, *de ant. orat., praef.,* translated in Russell and Winterbottom, *Ancient Literary Criticism* (Oxford, 1972), 306.

72 The periphrases of the hexameters at 5,9–12 suggest the Silver Age.

73 Sullivan 159. Nock, *C.R.* 46 (1932), 173, rightly draws attention to bogus elements in Encolpius' declamation but goes too far in seeing the whole of 1–4 as comic parody without any substance. Nock, however, like Sullivan, thinks Petronius had Seneca in mind. Ernout, Budé ed., p. 2 n. 1, is among the scholars who take the whole of Encolpius' speech as a serious contribution to the literary criticism of the 1st C. A.D.

74 Eumolpus' attitude to lyric poetry is at least more enlightened than that of Cicero, as reported by Seneca, *Epp.* 49,5.

75 There are commentaries on Petronius' *Bellum Civile* by Stubbe, 104–51 and Florence T. Baldwin, *The Bellum Civile of Petronius* (New York, 1911).

76 On Petr. 118 as a statement of Petronius' Augustan ideals see D'Alton 304. Note the hostile view of Virgil expressed at Pers. 1,96; in general see Georgii, *Die antike Aeneiskritik,* 560f.

77 Sullivan 159f. is judicious on this problem. Quintilian (10,1,90) is grudging in his praise of Lucan; *sententiis clarissimus* may well refer not to maxims but 'brilliant thoughts' (Winterbottom's rendering). Modern scholars interpret Lucan's intentions as a writer of historical epic with wider understanding. See in addition to ch. 7 n. 35, A. W. Lintott, *C.Q.* 21 (1971), 488–505; O. A. W. Dilke, in Dudley (ed.), *Neronians and Flavians* (London, 1972), 62–82.

78 Petr. 119,45–6: *tristior ille est, / qui vicit, fascesque pudet rapuisse Catoni,* is an example of a serious well-turned *sententia;* cf. Lucan 9,299 and the frequently quoted 1,128. More obvious but none the less effective are *ingeniosa gula est* (their maw is inventive, 33; reproduced by Mart. 13,62,2) and *inops audacia tuta est* (57); cf. similar expressions at Luc. 1,181f.; 8,491ff.

79 Petr. 123 205–8 is an imitation of the hyperbolic Silver Age divine simile, apparently without irony. *vendunt* (35) in the sense of 'make a success of' is unpoetic; sim. *Roma noverca* (166) is not the language of high poetry.

80 Most scholars take *Bellum Civile* not as a light-hearted jest but as a poetic composition in its own right. Sullivan (174) regards it as Lucan's material reworked in a Virgilian manner. Baldwin, accepting the judgement of Heitland that it was 'thrown off half in rivalry, half in imitation of Lucan', describes it as a 'remarkably full and suggestive narrative' (33). Opinions differ on the versification. According to Baldwin, 55–63, and Heitland, xciv–ci, the technique is akin to that of Lucan. Baldwin, however, (57) points to a Virgilian frequency of bucolic diaeresis, and Duckworth, *T.A.Ph.A.* 98 (1967), 106 n., regards the technique as basically Virgilian; see also Stubbe's analysis, 95–103. Repeated words and phrases at the end of the line (Stubbe 90ff.), allowing for the difference of scale, are few compared with those of Lucan: see A. Ollfors, 'Studien zum Aufbau des Hexameters Lucans', *Acta Reg. Soc. Scient. et Litt. Human.* 1 (Göteborg, 1967), 81–109.

81 Tac. *Ann.* 15,49: *ostentare* implies recitation as well as publication (see Koestermann, *a.l.*). Cass. Dio 62,29, in narrating the events of A.D. 65, states that Lucan was debarred from writing because his work was highly esteemed. According to the Vacca Life, 43 Rost., he had published three books of *de Bello Civili.*

82 K. F. C. Rose, *T.A.Ph.A.* 97 (1966), 379–96, esp. 388f.

83 For Lucan's abusive verses and un-balanced behaviour as conspirator see the Suet. Life 15–34 Rost.

84 The argument of K. F. C. Rose, *C.Q.* 12 (1962), 166–8, and *id., Date and Author of the Satyricon*, 65ff., that the end of Petr. *B.C.* (290ff.) deliberately echoes Lucan's ending (10,540ff.) is not convincing, but his conclusion that *Satyricon* 118–24 was written shortly after Lucan's death is reasonable. Yet a pirated copy of later parts of the work may have been available to Petronius.

85 See W. Page and G. E. Benseler, *Wörterbuch der griechischen Eigennamen* (Braunschweig, 1884), on the names Encolpius (p. 332) and Giton (p. 243). For the Encolpius who was a reader of Pliny and for others see Plin. *Epp.* 8, 1 and *P.I.R.*[2] 3, p. 79 (E 58–60). Encolpos is a *puer delicatus* in Martial (1,31 and 5,48), an appropriate choice of name. The adjective ἐγκόλπιος means 'in the bosom'. There seems to be no evidence for the name Ascyltos other than its occurrence in the fiction of the *Satyricon*.

86 For his ham histrionics see e.g. 94,8, 113,9 for his comically exaggerated jealousy of Tryphaena's success with Giton, and 130,2–4 for his melodramatic description of his impotent failure to satisfy Circe. He is at his most comically shameless in his appeal to *ius humanum* when Ascyltos steals his boy-friend (79,9).

87 G. Bagnani, *C.Ph.* 51 (1956), 24–6 and R. A. Pack, *C.Ph.* 55 (1960), 312f. make some good points but are over-confident in their reconstruction of Encolpius' career. It is possible that Encolpius was no more a true murderer than was the Playboy of the Western World who 'killed his Da'.

88 E.g. 94,12 and 102,14. Encolpius' angry judgement (81,5); Giton's prudence (79,3–4), his gentle sensibility (93,4), his infidelity explained in a far-cical situation (91,8), his physical attrac-tiveness (105,7), Tryphaena's prolonged attentions to him (109,2; 113,5). Giton is well assessed by P. George, *Arion* 5

(1966), 336–58: 'Giton not only talks like a declamation, he behaves like one' (341).

89 For the name see F. Bechtel, *Die attischen Frauennamen* (Göttingen, 1902), 40; see also St Paul, *Rom.* 16,12 and Luc. *Dial. mer.* 11. τρυφάω covers a wide range of meanings from 'act daintily' to 'run riot'.

90 It was possibly the Bithynia that Petronius knew well; see Walsh, 113: 'as an ex-governor of Bithynia, Petronius could picture with the mind's eye the infant Trimalchio in his native habitat.'

91 See p. 187.

92 On the *Satyricon* as realistic fiction see E. Auerbach, *Mimesis, The representation of reality in Western literature* (Princeton, 1953), 24ff. G. Bagnani, *Phoenix* 8 (1954), 77–91, regards the portrait of Trimalchio as drawn from real life, and seems to discuss him as a real historical person; cf. the argument of Rose, *Date and Author of the Satyricon*, 80, that the character of Trimalchio was based on Asiaticus, a freedman of Vitellius (Suet. *Vit.* 12,2). But to identify Trimalchio with a historical person neglects the literary and imaginative elements in the portrait. Similarly Petronius may have drawn on some aspects of Iunia Silana (Tac. *Ann.* 11,12; 13,19ff.; 14,12) for his portrait of Tryphaena, but in spite of striking similarities the two should not be equated as by R. Verdière, *Latomus* 15 (1956), 551–8. Equally unconvincing is the view (Rose, *Date and Author* 80f.) that Eumolpus is modelled on Remmius Palaemon, the famous but immoral grammarian.

93 Sullivan, *Petronius* (Harmondsworth, 1965), intro. 17 hints that Trimalchio may have developed beyond his creator's original intention. Compare the contrast made by R. A. Donovan, *The Shaping Vision* (New York, 1966), between Fielding's 'Shamela', that cannot stand except as a parody of Richardson's 'Pamela', and 'Joseph Andrews', a comic masterpiece in its

own right, in which Joseph may have developed beyond the author's original intentions.

94 Eumolpus ('the sweet singer') an appropriate name for a poet, is widely spread in the Graeco-Roman world. A poet Claudius Eumolpus was decreed honours at Delphi, *Fouilles de Delphes* 3,1,118 n. 210; see *P.I.R.*²,2,862.

95 There are a few exceptions, e.g. Encolpius' use of the form *adiuvaturos* (18,3); see Müller's crit. note *a.l.* Such singulars for plural as *quadrata littera* (29,1) and *faba* (136,7) may be viewed as vulgarisms (see Löfstedt, *Syntactica* I (Lund, 1942²), 19) but may also be taken as ordinary collectives, e.g. on *faba* see Kühner-Stegmann I,68. *liberare* in the sense of 'leave' (136,9) is unliterary; see G. Bendz, *Eranos* 39 (1941), 32. M. H. L. W. Nelson, *Actes de premier Congrès de F.I.E.C., Paris 1950* (Paris, 1951), 220–9 warns against judging Petronius by the usage of the 1st C. B.C., e.g. *permittere* with acc. + inf. (Petr. 130,6) is found in the elder Pliny, Suetonius and Tacitus.

96 See Müller's critical note on 100,1 (edn 1 p. 110).

97 E. T. Sage, *T.A.Ph.A.* 46 (1915), 54 remarks that *sermonis puri* (132,15,3) is appropriate to Petronius' work. On the Atticism of Caesar's style see Norden, *Die antike Kunstprosa* I 210f. On the simple style appropriate for narrative (*genus adtenuatum*) see *ad Her.* 4,10,14 and Caplan's analysis, Loeb edn *a.l.*, of the informal style of the example quoted. Norden, *Agn. Th.* 377 n.1, regards this as the style of Sisenna and Petronius.

98 See Löfstedt, *Syntactica* I², e.g. 231f. The standard general works are: V. Väänänen, *Introduction au Latin Vulgaire* (Paris, 1967²) and J. B. Hofmann, *Lateinische Umgangssprache* (Heidelberg, 1951³). There is useful help on *sermo plebeius* in M. S. Smith's edn (See n. 1 above), App. II.

99 A. Ernout, *Aspects du vocabulaire Latin* (Paris, 1954), 81–4 lists all the Greek words in the *Satyricon*. See also A. H. Salonius, 'Die Griechen und das Griechische in Petrons Cena Trimalchionis', *Soc. Scient. Fennica*

Comm. Hum. Litt. 2,1 (Helsinki, 1927).

100 The evidence is studied by V. Väänänen, *Le latin vulgaire des inscriptions pompéiennes* (Berlin, 1966³).

101 W. Heraeus, 'Die Sprache des Petronius und die Glossen', *Kl. Schr.* (Heidelberg, 1937), 52–150: *neniae* in sense of *nugae* (Heraeus 70; see *C.Gl.L.* V, 119, 43); *pullarius* (43,8) emend. Burman for MSS *puellarius* on strength of *pullarius*: παιδεραστής (*C.Gl.L.* II, 392,6), Heraeus 65.

102 The passage (37,2–10) is analysed by L. R. Palmer, *The Latin Lauguage* (London, 1954), 152f.

103 For gemination see Hofmann, *Lateinische Umgangssprache*, 60f.

104 Löfstedt, *Syntactica* II,273; cf. his discussion (254) of *Glyco dedit suas* (Glyco copped his lot, 45,9). Löfstedt has invaluable chapters on ellipse, pleonasm, *constructio ad sensum*.

105 The staple of Petronius' *sermo plebeius* is better studied by the chapter than by the phrase; see Väänänen, op. cit. (n. 98 above), 235–40 and 263–5.

106 On verbal wit in Petronius see Sullivan 225–8 and Housman, *C.R.* 32 (1918), 164 (= *Class. Papers* III 962f.).

107 See P. Veyne, 'Vie de Trimalchion', *Annales, Economies, Sociétés, Civilisations* 16 (1961), 213–47, who rightly emphasizes Trimalchio's contentment as local *princeps libertinorum* (246). See also M. Finley, *The Ancient Economy* (London, 1973), 36 and 50f.

108 The use of language as a means of characterization was discussed in a general way by F. F. Abbott, *C.Ph.* 2 (1907), 43–50. W. Suess, *De eo quem dicunt inesse Trimalchionis cenae sermone vulgari* (Dorpat, 1926), (= *Acta et Commentationes Universitatis Tartuensis B Humaniora* 9) attempts unconvincingly to argue that there were important distinctions in the language of the various freedmen. A. Marbach, *Wortbildung, Wortwahl und Wortbedeutung als Mittel der Charakterzeichnung bei Petron* (diss. Giessen, 1931), provides a useful mass of morphological and lexical data but fails to make good his conclusion (160–6) that characters are differentiated by linguistic

means; see rev. W. Kroll, *Glotta* 22 (1934), 278 and H. Haffter, *Gnomon* 10 (1934), 536–41. In the final analysis, as Kroll observes, loc.cit. (n. 1 above) 1212,4: 'sie reden alle denselben Jargon.'

109 Erich Auerbach, op.cit. (n. 92 above) 30–48, likens the *Satyricon* to the works of Tacitus as products of the highest culture written by men who wrote for a public of a high level of social and literary awareness.

110 On the composition of poetry at court see Tac. *Ann.* 14,16, and for the hypothesis that the *Satyricon* was written to entertain Nero's court, Rose, *Arion* 5 (1966), 293ff. It may be noted that the future emperor Nerva, one of his cultural entourage, was called by Nero 'the Tibullus of the age' (Mart. 8,70,7; 9,26,9f.).

111 Vatinius is described by Tacitus, *Ann.* 15,34 and Sporus by Suetonius, *Ner.* 28. Tigellinus, on the evidence of the dossier of material collected by Mayor on Juv. 1,155, had the qualities of a Beria or a Himmler.

112 On quotations of Petronius in Isidore see W. C. McDermott, C. & M. 23 (1962), 143–7. For references in other grammarians see Collignon, *Pétrone en France* (Paris, 1905), 2f. and W. Kroll, loc.cit. (n. 1 above) 1212, 44–8.

113 Deviations from the manuscript tradition of Achilles Tatius in the fragments in P.Oxy. 1250 (3rd–4th C. A.D.) suggest a deliberate shortening; see Russo, *Rend. Ac. Lincei Ser.* 8, 10 (1955), 397–403. Müller 1st edn, xxxvii, attributes the excerpting of the *Satyricon* to Carolingian times; this is more plausible for the shorter (O) than the longer (L) excerpts.

114 On the date of Bernensis 357 see G. Billanovich, *Aevum* 30 (1956), 336 n. 3, referred to in Müller 2nd edn, 382 n. 2. Some leaves belonging to this manuscript have been stuck into a Leiden MS. On this and on the two Paris manuscripts see Müller, 2nd edn 2, 382f.

115 See Müller 2nd edn 1, 419. Ernout, 3rd edn 1, xxiv–vi gives a table of contents and lacunae in O.

116 On John of Salisbury's knowledge of Petronius see Müller 1st edn, xxi and Janet M. Martin, *H.S.C.Ph.* 73 (1969), 319–21.

117 Müller, 1st edn, xviii; E. T. Sage, 'Scaliger and the text of Petronius', *T.A.Ph.A.* 64 (1933), XLVII. The various articles published by American scholars in the 1930s under the direction of Sage are listed in full by R. Browning, *C.R.* 12 (1962), 219 n. 2.

118 Quotations from Petronius in mediaeval *florilegia* provide a useful subsidiary source of knowledge of the text. There are four copies of a great anthology of Latin literature, including excerpts from Petronius, probably made in France and of dates ranging from the twelfth to the fourteenth centuries; see Ullman, *C.Ph.* 23 (1928), 128–74, esp. 162 and id. *C.Ph.* 25 (1930), 11–21. Other *florilegia* contain the *Bellum Civile*: see Ernout, Budé edn XXXf. It seems that *florilegia* containing passages of Petronius need further investigation; for example no edition has referred to the quotations from Petronius in the 15th C. anthology in the British Library (Egerton 646) described by R. Weiss, *C.R.* 57 (1943), 108–9. New evidence has been published by T. Brandis and W. Ehlers, *Philologus* 118 (1974), 85–112.

119 In the Traguriensis the short excerpts, for which this manuscript is quoted as A, precede the *Cena*. On this manuscript see A. C. Clark, *C.R.* 22 (1908), 178f. and R. Sabbadini, *R.F.I.C.* 48 (1920), 27–39. S. Gaselee published at Cambridge in 1915 a collotype reproduction of the part of H that contains the *Cena*.

120 Nodot published his work with the inscription: 'Nodi solvuntur a Nodot'; its solecisms were denounced by Burman in his preface. On Nodot and Marchena see Rose, *Arion* 5 (1966), 268–8, who gives a text and translation of Marchena's barbarous and obscene interpolation.

121 Dryden, *Of Dramatic Poesy* (ed. G. Watson) vol. 2 (London, 1962), 158.

Index

275

Index

Index of pieces quoted